Best wishes to David !!

A FILTHY WAY TO DIE

COLLECTED MEMORIES OF THE VIETNAM WAR

Thank you for your service !!!

God Bless,

ED LINZ

Also by Ed Linz

Non-fiction

Life Row (1997)

Team Teaching Science (2011)

They Never Threw Anything Away (2021)

Weekly Opinion Columns (1978-present) written under the pen name, *Eyes Right*, and archived at eyesright.us and edlinz.com

Fiction

Hurtling to the Edge (2015)

*In grateful memory of our USNA 1965 classmates
who made the ultimate sacrifice in the Vietnam War*

Richard W. Piatt

Ronald W. Meyer

William M. Grammar

Warren W. Boles

Lynn M. Travis

Edward J. Broms, Jr.

William L. Covington

John C. Lindahl

Gary B. Simkins

*Ask the winds that blow
which leaf on the tree will be next to go....*

About the Title
and Cover Photo

I N 1914 THE AMERICAN POET, Joyce Kilmer, published a slim volume of poems, "Trees and Other Poems." Most people recognize the opening lines of his poem, *Trees*.

> *I think that I shall never see*
> *A poem as lovely as a tree.*

A lesser known Kilmer poem, *Memorial Day,* appears in the same book. Five stanzas glorify soldiers who come to pray at the graves of *the honored dead who kept the faith and fought the fight through flying lead and crimson steel*. Kilmer began this poem with a famous quote, *Dulce et decorum est*, first written in the last century B.C. in an ode by the Roman poet, Horace. This phrase is translated as "It is sweet and fitting." Interestingly, Kilmer did not include the next line of the ode, *pro patria mori*, meaning to die for one's country. Perhaps it was a premonition because Kilmer did just that. After enlisting in the New York National Guard in 1917, he was sent to fight in World War I battles in France where he was killed the following year at age 31 during the Second Battle of The Marne. It is not known if Kilmer's sentimental views prior to the war changed once he experienced the horror of trench warfare where he died.

That same year, a British poet, Wilfred Owen, used the same Latin phrase to title a poem based on his gut-wrenching experiences as a soldier in those same trenches. Although war is anything but poetic, Owen used that poem to graphically describe the true horrors and atrocities of the war around him. One stanza paints the image of a company of desperate, exhausted soldiers crawling with bare and bleeding feet through muddy trenches (*an octopus of sucking clay*) while being gassed by their German opponents. One man is unable to don his gas mask, and the poetic description of his resulting death is difficult to read because of the gruesome detail. Owen stated that his intent was to use stark terms to describe the unimaginable suffering and death in war and the life-long trauma of having watched others so close to him die. He said that he hoped to sway future generations not to encourage their youngsters to seek adventure and heroism with the "old lie" that "it is sweet and fitting to die for one's country." Ironically, Owen was also killed in action just one week prior to the signing of the Armistice and did not live to see his work receive wide acclaim.

Because of their entirely different views about war, several critics have analyzed the two approaches. Most label Kilmer as overly sentimental and side with Owen's view of the ugly realities of war. This categorization may be unfair. Kilmer wrote his piece prior to his own combat in those muddy trenches, while Owen actually penned his poem in the heat of battle, before mailing various versions to his mother back in England. What struck me was one analysis which compared Owen's description of warfare to that of an anonymous German soldier suffering through equally devastating conditions of the battle of Stalingrad 25 years later in World War II. This young man's description of that battle was simply " *A filthy way to die.*"

The sixty stories in this book are an attempt to capture the American experience during the Vietnam War by sharing memories of Marines on the ground, aviators flying missions over both North and South Vietnam, and Navy personnel offshore on ships and on small boats of the "Brown Water Navy" on Vietnamese rivers and canals.

The photo on the cover shows men of the 9th Marines waiting out a North Vietnamese rocket and artillery attack against their outpost at Con Thien in late 1967. Several of the men profiled in this book fought fierce battles in this area. One of our classmates, a Marine, still has vivid memories: *"During one operation near Con Thien, just south of the DMZ, we were fighting there three to four nights. We got mortared terribly every night and took 85 casualties."*

Another Marine classmate remembered, *"We soon got into a significant firefight with North Vietnamese Army regulars from their 324th B Division. They were firing artillery across the Ben Hai River which marked the DMZ. We ended up in three days of a hellacious firefight. The enemy was using a lot of mortars. Our company suffered numerous casualties; our best corporal was killed. We would be taking fire from places you couldn't see, and the Medevac helos were all taking considerable mortar fire every time they tried to come in to pick up wounded or dead Marines."*

While conducting interviews, I came to the realization that no matter the locale, war is inherently barbaric and all-to-often deadly. Weapons of war do not discriminate. They kill not only those directly involved in fighting, but also countless innocent civilians who unwittingly become "collateral damage." In addition, the grief of families who suffered the loss or injury of loved ones is slow to dissipate, if ever. I keep thinking of both the combatants of the Vietnam War and the Vietnamese men, women, and children who died in muddy rice paddies or impenetrable jungles, often with no warning. They were simply in the wrong place at the wrong time as weapons rained down on them.

It was indeed *a filthy way to die.*

Table of Contents

Acronyms and Frequently Used Terms

AAA	Anti-aircraft artillery
AK-47	A Soviet rifle, Automat Klashinikov, used by communist forces
ALPHA Strike	A large air attack by most of the planes in a carrier air wing
AMTRAC	Amphibious Landing Vehicle Tracked, an armored vehicle capable of land and waterborne operations
ARVN	Army of the Republic of Vietnam (South Vietnamese Army)
ATSB	Advanced Tactical Support Base
CEC	Civil Engineering Corps (aka Seabees)
CO	Commanding Officer
CPO	Chief Petty Officer, a senior Navy enlisted man
DIXIE Station	An area of the South China Sea south of the DMZ where aircraft carriers launched strikes against enemy positions in South Vietnam
DMZ	Demilitarized Zone, a 4-6 mile wide strip of land near the 17th parallel separating North and South Vietnam running from Laos to the South China Sea
ELINT	Electronic intelligence
HUEY	The Bell UH-1 Iroquois, a small, multi-purpose helicopter used extensively throughout the war

g's	The force of gravity, 14.7 lb/in^2....used to express pressure felt in an aircraft during a turn or coming out of a dive
KIA	Killed in action
MARKET TIME	U.S. Seaborne and air operations to intercept enemy vessels attempting to supply troops and equipment to communist forces in South Vietnam
MIA	Missing in action
Midshipmen	Naval Academy cadets: 1st year, Plebes; 2nd year, Youngsters; 3rd year, Second Classmen; 4th year, First Class or Firsties
NFO	Naval Flight Officer, an aviator who is not a pilot
ROK	Republic of Korea
SAM	Surface-to-air missile
SAR	Search and Rescue, missions conducted, usually by air, to locate and retrieve our troops in a difficult situation
RPG	Rocket propelled grenade
NVA	North Vietnam Army
POW	Prisoner of War
VC	Viet Cong, National Liberation Front of Vietnam, a communist group organized to fight the South Vietnamese government for control of South Vietnam
XO	Executive Officer, the officer second-in-command.
Yankee Station	An area of the South China Sea north of the DMZ from which aircraft carriers launched strikes primarily against targets in North Vietnam and Laos

Introduction

WHEN 1240 YOUNG MEN STOOD in Tecumseh Court at the U.S. Naval Academy (USNA) on June 28, 1961, to take their oath of office, many had never heard of Vietnam, and most of them could probably not locate the country on a map. Certainly, none of these prospective midshipmen imagined that they might die in a war in Southeast Asia, or even that many would be called to serve in such a distant war. Yet, four years later following graduation and commissioning as Navy or Marine Corps officers, the 801 who graduated (including me) had become well aware not only of Vietnam, but of the ongoing horrors of a war now in full progress. Nine of our USNA class of 1965 died there; several were seriously wounded; many others still suffer physical and psychological problems due to their service in Vietnam.

The intent of this book is to provide an understanding of the horror, brutality, and insanity of war by recounting, in their own words, the memories of those classmates still alive who served our nation in the Vietnam War. Do not be misled if you have heard this period referred to as "The Vietnam Conflict." That is a far too cosmetic descriptor - *it was a war in every sense of the word*: brutal, devastating, and far too often deadly, for the combatants on both sides, and for a far greater number of Vietnamese civilians who were killed or severely injured through no fault of their own, often only because they happened to be in the wrong place at the wrong time. The numbers of fatalities in this war are estimates but remain staggering. On the Vietnamese side, at least two million civilians, over 1.1 million North Vietnamese and Viet Cong soldiers, and approximately 250,000 South Vietnamese troops died. American fatalities were less, but still grim. According to the U.S. National Archives, 58,220 American military combatants perished or remain missing. Some of these American fatalities were as young as 15, and the majority were 21 or younger. Among Americans returning home, there were close to 10,000 amputees. Many participants on both sides in this war have continued to experience various levels of PTSD (Post Traumatic Stress Disorder). Others suffer due to complications from wounds received and life-threatening diseases related to exposure to dangerous tropical infections and chemicals such as Agent Orange. *Like every other war, wounds never fully heal.*

The genesis of this book was an earlier book which I wrote about the Great Depression. For that project I interviewed over 40 Americans during the late 1990's. All were in the later years of their lives, and none lived to see the publication of their stories. In view of the ages of Naval Academy graduates of the class of 1965, it seemed imperative to capture as many of their memories as possible before their stories are forever lost. I interviewed over 60 classmates, many in person, others via computer. Surprisingly, none were reluctant to share memories of their service in Vietnam, and many provided me with photographs, journals, and even daily logs of their war-time activities. All interviews were recorded, and their words are presented exactly as spoken. In order to provide clarity, I have added explanations or descriptions of the equipment, location, acronyms, and background circumstances mentioned by the speaker. Because these reflections are of events a half century past, there may be some inconsistencies or errors in what is presented. I have attempted to correct any that are obvious, but the intent is to present an unvarnished oral history spoken by these men. There were far more members of our class who served in Vietnam than those interviewed for this book. Their stories are undoubtedly equally powerful. My intent was not to relate all experiences, but to present a representative sample of men who were involved to show the terrible consequences of decisions made by political leaders far removed from the actual horror.

I say "men" because in 1965 the Naval Academy was an all-male institution. It was not until 11 years later, in 1976, that women were first admitted. The class of 1965 was also almost exclusively white. Four black midshipmen began studies in the fall of 1961, and three graduated. One has passed away and I was unable to connect with the other two (one rose in rank to become a 4-star Admiral). This lack of minority cadets was not restricted to the Naval Academy; other military academies also did not reflect the actual diversity of the nation. At that time, most young men gained admission to the service academies through slots controlled by senators and congressmen. There was no process in place (nor any apparent desire) to achieve diversity in an incoming service academy class. Prospective candidates typically wrote to a member of Congress requesting a nomination, and then took a Civil Service examination. Many congressmen used the results to make their allotted appointments, but others selected whomever they wanted. At that time there were few rules, other than citizenship, age, character, marital status (had never married), and passing a physical. Few minority youngsters applied, and even fewer gained admission. However, the incoming class at the Naval Academy in that summer of 1961 reflected a diversity of economic backgrounds. Many had sought an appointment simply because their family could not afford to pay typical university costs.

Most interviews contain stories of why and how that individual became interested in attending the Naval Academy. A surprisingly large number told me that they became interested in attending the Academy after having watched episodes of a 1957 television series called *Men of Annapolis* (many are still available online). Others had fathers or grand-fathers (or both) who had attended the Academy and served in previous world wars. A large number had been class Presidents or valedictorians in their high schools. Over two thirds had been varsity athletes. One hundred were Eagle Scouts. A few classmates were enlisted men in the Navy (or other services) and had sea experience. Other than sex and ethnicity, it was an eclectic, talented, highly motivated group.

During the spring of their final year, midshipmen were faced with service selection decisions. Choices were primarily based on class standing (those going into nuclear-powered ship training had a different process). Options were the Marine Corps, surface ships, or flight training, while smaller numbers were directed into Supply Corps or Civil Engineering Corps training. Most who chose surface ships reported directly to their assignments, and if their ship was in the Pacific Fleet, became the first members of the class to participate as young officers in the Vietnam War. Those who became Marines first attended Marine Corps Basic School for six months in Quantico, Virginia; many were hastily assigned as Platoon leaders in Vietnam where they arrived in early 1966. Aviation training was generally 18 months in duration, beginning in Pensacola, Florida, followed by jet or multi-engine schooling which culminated in carrier landing certification before fleet assignments. Hence, most of the aviators interviewed did not begin Vietnam experiences until 1967.

Those of us who were assigned to nuclear submarines had no direct involvement in the Vietnam War. Most of the water surrounding Vietnam (the South China Sea and Gulf of Thailand) is generally too shallow for most submerged submarine operations, so neither the Soviets nor Americans chose to operate nuclear submarines there on a consistent basis. Instead, both Cold War adversaries used their submarines in "cat and mouse" covert operations. Fast attack submarines would attempt to find and follow opponent's submarines, while the role of each side's ballistic missile subs was to avoid detection in order to be able to launch missiles in the event of a nuclear war. Over one quarter of our USNA class served in such submarine assignments.

A few classmates whom I interviewed were aboard ships in the Vietnam theater of operations as midshipmen during summer training cruises. In fact, some were aboard ships off Vietnam at the time of the 1964 Gulf of Tonkin incidents (which will be discussed during interviews in later chapters).

It was not until late summer 1965 that my USNA classmates began to first appear in numbers off the coast of Vietnam. At that time, American public support for the war remained high. A Gallup poll in October 1965 indicated that nearly 2/3 of Americans approved of U.S. involvement in Vietnam. Although many Americans were opposed to war in general, there was considerable sentiment that it was right for the U.S. to be taking action to counter the spread of Communism. Public support began to erode as American casualties rose and televised accounts of the war on evening news programs showed the true horror of this war, both for U.S. troops and for Vietnamese civilians. By late 1967, U.S. forces in Vietnam had reached over 500,000 and support for the war was declining rapidly. When he failed to achieve a significant win in the first presidential primary election in early 1968, President Johnson chose not to seek reelection. Several Democratic contenders for the Presidential nomination were opposed to continuation of our involvement in Vietnam. When Johnson's Vice President, Hubert Humphrey, won the nomination, he promised to halt the bombing campaign in South Vietnam, but his prior role as one of the chief spokesmen for the war caused considerable turmoil. Major riots in opposition to the war began to occur at many universities throughout the United States. Richard Nixon won the 1968 Presidential election by the slimmest of margins in the popular vote. Anger toward Humphrey's role in the war was certainly a factor, along with the presence of a third-party candidate. Nixon began a gradual withdrawal of troops, interspersed with renewed bombing of North Vietnam and other previously protected sanctuaries. But American approval of the war continued to decline, and by mid-1971 had plummeted to 34 %. When the war finally ended in 1975, many of my Naval Academy classmates were still involved; some were an integral part of the final evacuation of our embassy in Saigon and the removal of mines from North Vietnamese waters off Haiphong.

This book is not an attempt to provide a documented, foot-noted history of the Vietnam War. There are many books, articles, and essays providing such information and analysis. Rather, my intent is to relay the memories of a specific group who served there, members of the Naval Academy Class of 1965. These men spent the prime of their youth in a disastrous and contentious period of American history while enduring the highs and lows of a violent, confusing foreign war. They watched comrades, often close friends, fall wounded or dying as their assigned mission often boiled down to kill or be killed.

I am not mentioning military awards or personal recognition received by these men, other than the Purple Heart (received for being wounded or killed in military action against an enemy). I have chosen to do this because there was considerable bravery shown by each Marine and Naval Officer by simply being in harm's way on a daily basis. Most who did receive recognition with medals, such as a Silver Star, were indeed worthy, but many others who were equally deserving of awards received none, usually due to their command being too occupied to submit paperwork and/or simply faulty leadership. This disparity was not unique to the Vietnam War.

In each of the following memoirs, the words spoken to me are shown in italics; comments and explanations which I have added are in regular print. I have not included phonetic marks on English spellings of most

Vietnamese names or places, but I have attempted to use versions reflecting current usage. Much of the history discussed was gathered from a wide spectrum of print and online open sources. Unless otherwise indicated, all photographs are the property of those whom I interviewed or are open source. Any errors or omissions are strictly mine.

The memories recorded in this book include frank discussions of wartime violence, including serious injury and death. That is, unfortunately, the essence of war. *It is truly a filthy way to die.*

Ed Linz
Greenville, Maine, May 2023

Maps

The geography of Vietnam played an important role in the war. As can be seen from the following map, the country is of considerable size, but runs mostly north-south in a sweeping curve. At its narrowest location near the Demilitarized Zone (DMZ) at approximately the 17 parallel, it is only 31 miles wide, but with a coastline of over 2100 miles. The land is mostly hilly and densely forested, much of which in the south is jungle. Tropical forests cover close to 40 % of the land. The Mekong Delta region in the south is a low-level plain varying in height above sea level with tides, but often no more than 10 ft above sea level. This region is crisscrossed by an intricate series of rivers and canals (many dug by the French during their period of control). Although much of North Vietnam can experience cold waves, most of South Vietnam has a tropical climate and is hot throughout the year.

U.S. aircraft carriers operated predominately from "Yankee Station" in the South China Sea roughly near the DMZ and from "Dixie Station" further south closer to Saigon (now Ho Chi Minh City). Air Force B-52 flights originated from bases in Guam and Thailand. The two major trails used by communist forces to bring supplies and troops to the south, were the Ho Chi Minh Trail through Cambodia and Laos. and the Sihanouk Trail through Cambodia.

Throughout the war, the U.S. enjoyed the advantage of essentially unrestricted operations at sea and also in the air, although North Vietnamese Air Force planes posed a threat at times during American attacks near Hanoi. U.S. air operations over North Vietnam faced considerable opposition from surface-to-air missiles and anti-aircraft fire. Because of the challenging terrain, helicopters became a key element to transfer American and South Vietnamese troops while North Vietnamese and Viet Cong forces traveled almost exclusively by land (and small boats in the Delta region).

It is recommended that readers refer to the following maps to locate battle sites discussed in the individual stories which follow.

North and South Vietnam and surrounding nations in Southeast Asia

© 1999 The History Place

Map of Saigon and Mekong Delta region where most U.S. Riverine Forces operated

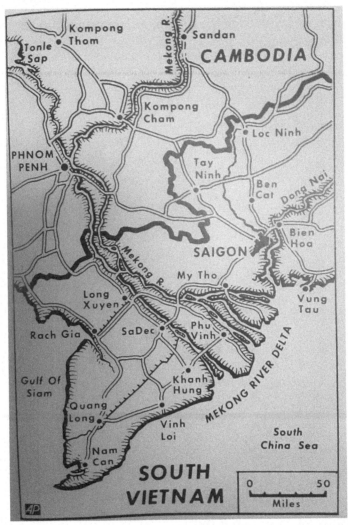

South Vietnam was divided into four **"Corps Tactical Zones"** for the purpose of military operations. In addition, there was an area sur-rounding Saigon called "The Special Capital Zone." These four tactical zones were identified as I-Corps (pronounced "EYE Core"), II-Corps, III-Corps, and IV-Corps. Other than I-Corps, the pronunciation was simply the number, e.g., "Two Corps." These zones had been established beginning in the 1950's by the South Vietnamese government, not only for military operations, but also for the civil administration of the region which was overseen by the ARVN general officer commanding each zone. This dual civil-military responsibility came about due to the necessity of martial law while the country was at war. Once Americans became heavily involved in the war, they continued to use the same geographic nomenclature.

Map of I-Corps region where most U.S. Marine fighting occurred

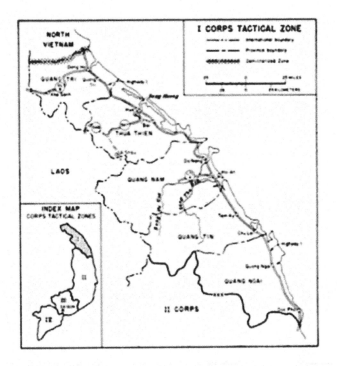

Why the War?

H OW DID THIS WAR HAPPEN? Many asked this question not only during the Vietnam War but in the 50 years since. There was never a threat of an invasion of the U.S. by Vietnam. Nor was there a military attack by the Vietnamese on American soil. Why would the United States become involved in a foreign war nearly halfway around the world while putting its armed forces in harm's way and expending enormous amounts of the country's wealth? Why would a nation, which so celebrates its independence from a colonial power, fight such a long and costly war to deny another nation self-determination? Why would such costly and deadly firepower be unleashed in a manner which essentially guaranteed ghastly numbers of civilian injuries and deaths?

The answers are complicated. Depending on one's political position, there are multiple explanations put forth in countless books, journal articles, and at least two television documentaries within the past ten years, the 2017 Ken Burns and Lynn Novick 10-part PBS film series, and the 2022 Bret Baier five-part special on Fox Nation - both highly recommended but offering significantly different perspectives.

My quick answer is that the United States chose to become involved in a civil war between North and South Vietnam because of hubris, that is, an excessive arrogance of and belief in American military power following the defeat of Japan in 1945. It is easy to understand how American leadership could assume that their nation which was able to defeat Japan, an advanced military opponent on the other side of the Pacific Ocean, while at the same time contributing to the Allied defeat of Germany, would be able to easily crush the militarily insignificant nation of North Vietnam. What could possibly go wrong? The United States had most of the equipment and personnel expertise from WW II and the Korean "Conflict" to project power. There was an industrial base proven to be capable of ramping up production for wartime needs and a large population from which to draw a fighting force. There was, of course, the reality of the early 1950's Korean War stalemate which remained in many minds. But Vietnam presented an opportunity to demonstrate that America was indeed a predominant fighting force in the world. Korea had been an unfortunate aberration; Vietnam would be different.

Of course, there are alternate explanations, and I encourage the reader to search out as many as possible. Most of the chief architects of the war (on both sides) have passed away; some have left rather self-serving memoirs, while others have provided more candid assessments. As a point of reference, keep in mind that there is still disagreement about the root causes of the American Civil War which ended over 150 years ago.

The seeds for the U.S. waging war in Vietnam were sown nearly 100 years earlier when the French began to colonize much of Southeast Asia, often using brutal force. When I visited the war museum in Hanoi in 2016 to view displays showing American POWs in the infamous "Hanoi Hilton" prison, I was surprised to see that there were far more exhibits concerning the torture and inhumanity which the French had used on the Vietnamese during their years of colonial control. It was difficult to look at several of the displays which were shown in graphic detail.

The history of Vietnam is, to say the least, complicated and often controversial, depending on the political lens through which it is viewed. The name, Viet Nam, was first proclaimed in 1804 by the Emperor Gia Long. "Viet" is the name of the people; "Nam" means south. A later emperor renamed the country Dai Nam (Great South). Following his death, "Viet Nam" returned to usage. Throughout most of the early 19th century, Vietnam was a strong united kingdom. The main threat was always China which throughout history made incursions attempting to subjugate Vietnam. But after being routed by the Vietnamese at Dong Da in 1788, the Chinese made no further attempts for the next century.

France's Napoleon III invaded the country in August 1857 by attacking the harbor at Da Nang with 14 ships and 2500 men. (History does seem to repeat itself....this is the same location where U.S. Marines came ashore in 1965!) The French then went south to Saigon, and although facing serious resistance, forced the Vietnamese to sign a peace treaty in 1862 giving the French control of much of the south. It took the French nearly 20 years to control all of Vietnam in what they called "The Indochina Union" consisting of Cochinchina in the south, with four "protectorates" named Annan, Tonkin (central and north Vietnam) and Laos and Cambodia. One French edict even made it illegal to use the word "Vietnam."

Although Vietnam under French rule did make some economic progress, most of its citizens failed to benefit. Rice production showed remarkable gains (mostly due to the construction of canals and irrigation techniques), but nearly all the benefits accrued to French investors and wealthy Vietnamese who were collaborating with the French. Landless peasants who worked the fields and land-owning peasants realized essentially none of the economic gains during this period. Workers on most plantations were forced to labor 15 hours daily and were often paid only in rice. Life for Vietnamese laborers on rubber plantations was particularly brutal; several died each day. Many Vietnamese were placed into forced labor in mines and rubber plantations. Few children were able to attend school, and a vast majority of the population was illiterate. The French controlled nearly all industry, while some Chinese operated small businesses. Taxes to finance French public works projects were especially onerous. France was able to exert this level of control without a large military presence by co-opting local Vietnamese authorities who were despised as traitors by their fellow citizens. The last of the Nguyen emperors, Bao Dai, who benefited from education at the prestigious Lycee Concordorcet in Paris, continued to fully support France in the middle of the 20th century.

The first broad resistance to French rule began as early as 1885, but never seriously threatened colonial control. Early in the 20th century, new nationalist movements began to develop with the goal of creating a free Vietnam. One of the leaders, Pham Boi Chan, actually set up a Vietnamese government in exile in China but was ultimately captured by the French and placed under house arrest. In the late 1920's a new revolutionary group, the Viet Nam Quoc Dan Dang (VNQDD), began a series of terrorist activities but was effectively destroyed by summary executions and prison camps.

Also, in the mid-1920's, another group, led by Nguyen Ai Quoc (who adapted the name Ho Chi Minh) began what ultimately became the Indochinese Communist Party. He had traveled extensively as a seaman and lived in Paris where he joined the local Communist Party. Ho spent several years in the Soviet Union and China before returning to Vietnam in 1930. There, in the north, he organized peasant uprisings which were brutally repressed by the French at the expense of solidifying growing hatred of the colonial rulers.

Shortly after WW II began, Japan signed an agreement with the German-controlled Vichy government in France which allowed the Japanese to station large numbers of troops and to use airfields in Vietnam to stage operations throughout the region. Although the Vichy French were nominally still the administrators of Vietnam, in reality the Japanese were in total control. U.S. policy with respect to Southeast Asia had been shaped by the Tripartite Pact signed in 1940 by Germany, Italy, and Japan. Because American leadership believed at this time that the U.S. would inevitably become involved in the ongoing European war, there was no American desire to intervene in Southeast Asia and cause war on a second front with the Japanese. Hence, what was taking place in Vietnam and its neighbors was not a priority issue for Americans.

Ironically, Japan's attack on Pearl Harbor brought exactly what the U.S. wanted to avoid into reality: a two-front war involving Europe and the Far East. As U.S. forces began to close in on Japan in late 1944, the Japanese worried that the now-liberated France might turn against them in Vietnam. In response, they disarmed French military forces and granted independence to a Vietnamese nationalist government. Still, the Japanese retained actual control in Vietnam until the end of the war.

Meanwhile, Ho Chi Minh had used the war to strengthen the Communist Party in Vietnam which became known as the Viet Minh. During the war he provided useful information about Japanese military actions to the Allies. Immediately following the Japanese surrender, the Viet Minh organized a general uprising and gained control of most of the north. Ho proclaimed a new national government, the Democratic Republic of Vietnam. The French, however, were not going to give up Vietnam without a fight and aided by the British, a fellow colonial power, regained control of the south of Vietnam. The French decided to negotiate with Ho Chi Minh and in early 1946 a tentative agreement was reached to make Vietnam "a free state within the French Union." The U.S. was concentrating on re-building Europe and wanted to maintain strong ties with France so did not intervene or attempt to dissuade the French from regaining colonial control.

This agreement between France and the communists in the north was fatally flawed because each party had different goals. The French wanted to renew colonial rule over all of Vietnam, and the Viet Minh wanted complete independence. Fighting became inevitable and the French opted to use ships to bombard Hanoi in late 1946. Several thousand Vietnamese were killed. The Viet Minh retaliated with battles against French troops in Hanoi. The subsequent warfare over the next eight years became known as the First Indochina War. The French continued to use military force to control most major cities, while the Viet Minh retreated into the jungles to wage guerrilla warfare and gain control over much of the countryside. By 1949 the French decided to unilaterally re-unite the north and south in an entity they called "The Associated State of Vietnam" with the former emperor, Bao Dai, as head of state. This proclamation led to increased attacks by the Viet Minh with several pitched battles taking place mostly in the northern part of Vietnam.

The United States was now closely watching the situation in Vietnam, and as early as 1946, had begun providing financial and military support to the French to fight the communists. President Truman and his civilian and military leadership became strongly influenced by a lengthy analysis of the intent of the communist government in the Soviet Union, written by the American ambassador in Moscow, George Kennan, in late February 1946. This 5000 word secret report, subsequently known as "The Long Telegram," became the intellectual basis for post-war American foreign policy. Kennan had been in the Foreign Service since 1926, spoke fluent Russian, and was well-regarded in Washington. In his cable, Kennan provided a detailed analysis of how and why Soviet communism worked, its goals, and methods. He advocated a plan to counter communism by instituting a policy of "containment," that is, steps which the U.S. must take to deter Soviet "expansionist tendencies." Kennan's advice became the cornerstone for American diplomacy for at least two decades and was the basis for The Truman Doctrine.

Although the immediate effect of this new containment policy was financial and military support for Greece and Turkey, Truman's explanation in a speech to the nation emphasized "the right of all people to determine the form of government under which they live." Truman never mentioned the Soviet Union by name in his speech, but the practical result was that the basic goal of American foreign policy was now to contain communism whenever and wherever it began to flourish. This obviously had serious implications for Vietnam.

Concurrently, the newly established National Security Council (NSC) drafted a document bureaucratically named "NSC 68" which, when signed in 1950, became the blueprint for implementing this containment policy by using all resources to strengthen American capabilities to counter Soviet expansion. This crucial document was drafted primarily by Paul Nitze, who had replaced Kennan as the head of the State Department's Policy Planning Staff. Ironically, 15 years later, each member of the Naval Academy class of 1965 received his diploma and commissioning certificate at graduation from Nitze who was then the current Secretary of the Navy. By this time, the national policies which he was instrumental in developing had become the rationale for the increasing American involvement in Vietnam. Yet, in his remarks to the graduating class on June 9, 1965, Nitze spent most of his speech predicting future military developments and events, such as submarine amphibious vehicles and men being sent to Mars. To his credit, he did emphasize his view that the greatest threat to the U.S. would be the evolution of "Communist China." Nitze's *only* mention of the ongoing war in Vietnam was a passing remark about President Johnson's "firm commitment of U.S. forces to assist South Vietnam." In retrospect, this was a surprising omission. Just two months earlier, on March 8, 1965, a contingent of 3500 Marines had been the first U.S. ground troops to land in Vietnam. Further U.S. involvement ramped up rapidly. Many of those midshipmen to whom Nitze handed their commissions as officers had already received assignments for duty in the Vietnam War. For nine members of that Class of 1965, those orders became a death sentence.

As opposed to the chaotic governmental changes in South Vietnam and the succession of U.S. Presidents during the 1945-1965 time frame, the leadership of the communist north was stable….and focused. Operating side by side with Ho Chi Minh was Vo Nguyen Giap, a former teacher. Also a communist, Giap became a superb military tactician who led the Viet Minh in their guerrilla war against the French. Ho Chi Minh certainly espoused communist principles, but many do not realize that he had lived in the U.S. in Boston and New York while he was traveling the world as a seaman in his younger days. He had apparently developed a deep admiration for America's successful resistance to British colonialism and used much of the American Declaration of Independence as a model for his Vietnam Declaration of Independence which he drafted. When President Woodrow Wilson came to France for the Versailles Peace Conference in 1919, Ho attempted to obtain Wilson's assistance to overthrow French rule of Vietnam. Wilson, apparently, could not be bothered. Who knows what might have happened if Wilson had opted to talk to Ho Chi Minh?

During the Japanese occupation of Vietnam during WW II, Ho Chi Minh again attempted to gain American help and actually cooperated with the U.S. which had parachuted spies from the OSS (Office of Strategic Services - which later became the CIA, Central Intelligence Agency) into Ho's jungle headquarters in Vietnam. Because Ho was judged to be helpful in the American war effort against Japan, the U.S. not only gave the Viet Minh weapons, but also considerable training in the best methods to conduct guerrilla warfare against the Japanese. In return, the communists helped American pilots downed by the Japanese over Vietnam territory. It was certainly a marriage of convenience. Some sources mention that Ho was actually treated for a serious illness in the jungle by an American nurse.

It is still debated today as to whether the U.S. made a mistake in not supporting Ho Chi Minh and the Viet Minh in their subsequent battles to throw the French out of Vietnam. In late 1945, Ho sent at least eight messages to the U.S. through the OSS requesting American support to give Vietnam the same status as the Philippines, but none of these messages were answered. At this point Ho decided to temporarily accept French rule due to fear that the Chinese would step in to swallow Vietnam.

What is certain is that once WW II ended, President Truman's policy toward Vietnam was driven by doing whatever was necessary to counter a communist take-over of the entire country. These concerns were heightened when, in 1950, the USSR and China, both nations ruled by communists, pledged to support Ho Chi Minh and his Viet Minh guerrillas in their fight against the French. In spite of the fact that the Vietnamese Declaration of Independence closely mirrored that of the American version, it was judged by Truman's administration that Ho's version of communism would spread throughout all of Southeast Asia if left unchecked. This belief became known as "The Domino Effect" and was the basis for U.S. policy for the next 30 years. These decisions led the U.S. to spend hundreds of millions of dollars supporting the French in their continuing efforts to control the Vietnamese. In fact, by 1953 the U.S. was sending close to a billion dollars to France to support their ongoing war against the Vietnamese, while also providing considerable covert military assistance to the French.

Even when the French forces were surrounded at the ultimate battle of Dien Bien Phu in northern Vietnam in 1954, the U.S. was still conducting airborne supply drops to the French army. France's position as a Cold War ally trumped the fact that they were brutally subjugating a nation seeking its independence from colonial rule. The total American tab for supporting the French in this "First Indochina War" was over $3 billion.

Shortly after the French forces surrendered to the Viet Minh at Dien Bien Phu in May 1954, France agreed to withdraw from Vietnam. The U.S. saw this as a dangerous vacuum and promptly decided to reinforce military efforts to keep the entire Vietnamese nation from coming under communist control. When peace talks began in Paris, the principal negotiating nations were France, Vietnam, China, and the U.S. Four other countries participated, but on the fringe. An agreement, called The Geneva Accord, was reached two months later in July 1954. There were several compromises. The principal one was that Vietnam would be "temporarily" divided into two regions at the Ben Hai River (which flows east-west just to the south of the 17th parallel). Citizens of both north and south were free to cross into the other side for a period of 300 days. Nationwide elections would be held on July 20, 1956, to determine the ultimate government of the nation. All remaining French forces would be moved south of the demilitarized zone (DMZ) at the 17th parallel and all Viet Minh forces would go north of this line.

Both the United States and the non-communist government in the south (which the French had termed "The Associated State of Vietnam") refused to approve this declaration because both wanted the government in the south to be in total control of all of Vietnam. Eisenhower was now President, but his administration, if anything, had become more wedded to the policy of containment. There was the worry that not only Vietnam, but also Laos and Cambodia, whose borders had been set by the same Geneva Accord, would be at increased risk of falling to communism, further increasing American resolve to protect the non-communist government of South Vietnam.

Few were pleased with the outcome of this conference in Geneva. The Viet Minh under Ho Chi Minh were reluctant signatories; many argue that the only reason they agreed to the separation of Vietnam into north and south was fear that the United States would intervene if they did not sign. The situation created by the Geneva Accords was inherently unstable if only because none of the principal actors had achieved their goals. In the north, a socialist regime was installed, while the south was supposed to have a provisional government until elections could be held. Based on their subsequent actions, it is apparent that leaders in neither the north nor the south had any intention of accepting the provisions of the Accords. The south would certainly never consider a Vietnam-wide election because they were certain that they could not win, probably because the totalitarian regime in the north could produce overwhelming numbers of votes for a communist government for the entire country. Leaders in the north had no intention of recognizing the borders or sovereignty of either Laos or Cambodia and almost immediately went about upgrading the Ho Chi Minh trail system through Laos to supply their supporters in the south with troops and equipment. One can argue that the U.S. ceded ultimate victory to the communists by this latter fact alone. North Vietnam essentially annexed usable war-fighting territory and supply routes, while the U.S. chose not to officially enter these countries with combat troops.

In the south Ngo Dinh Diem had been Prime Minister in the French puppet government under the Emperor, Bao Dai. To American leadership he seemed to be the best bet for stability and was helped by the U.S. to set up a new government with Diem as Prime Minister making him, in reality, the de facto head of the government. The ink on the Geneva Accords had hardly dried before President Eisenhower wrote to Diem promising "support for a non-communist Vietnam."

Diem, a Catholic, who had actually been living at a seminary in the U.S. for several years, had significant internal issues to face. There was considerable opposition from several religious sects and crime syndicates with their own armed gangs. After several pitched battles and political machinations, often aided by the American embassy, Diem ultimately took control. He did this by implementing what many regarded as draconian measures to rid the south of communists by rounding up tens of thousands and executing many. Diem then refused to agree to national elections as dictated by the Geneva Accords. Instead, in late 1955, he orchestrated a questionable election held only in the south in which he defeated Bao Dai to become President of "The Republic of Vietnam." There would certainly now be no talks with representatives from Ho Chi Minh's communist regime in the north.

Diem's youngest brother and advisor, Ngo Dinh Nhu, became his chief "enforcer." He held no official government position, but in reality, controlled the ARVN Special Forces and the secret police. His draconian methods led to the creation of armed, underground groups throughout South Vietnam which opposed Diem and Nhu's dictatorial rule. Many ultimately either joined, or became supporters of, the Viet Cong.

Diem's rise to power was made possible not only by his own ambition and political skill, but also by an American Air Force officer, Edward Lansdale, who was a covert operator for the U.S. Using cash bribes and clever deal-making, he neutralized many of Diem's religious and criminal opponents and made his rise to power possible Many contend that Lansdale was the model for at least two novels about this period of Vietnamese history: *The Quiet American* by Graham Green and *The Ugly American* by Burdick and Lederer. Thanks to ongoing American help, by 1957, Diem felt sufficiently secure to visit the U.S. where he was welcomed by Eisenhower as "the hero" who saved Southeast Asia.

Following the Geneva Accords, over a million refugees from the north crossed the DMZ into the south. Most were Catholics fleeing what they believed to be certain persecution by the communists. Many were not successfully integrated into the fabric of South Vietnam, and the economy became heavily stratified between haves and have nots. Over 80 percent of those in the south lived in small villages and worked the land. Many had only subsistence incomes and had little allegiance to the central government.

Meanwhile in the north, Ho Chi Minh and his communist apparatus used the immediate years following the Geneva Accord to consolidate power. A proletarian dictatorship was established through the brutal elimination of landlords in the countryside. Death estimates vary, but it is likely that at least 50,000 were killed. Members of the Political Bureau of the Vietnamese Workers Party became the ruling elite. By 1960, North Vietnam had become a classic communist state ruled with an iron fist. Ho Chi Minh implemented a political and economic scheme modeled closely on that of Stalin in the Soviet Union, emphasizing a nationalized industry, repression of most intellectuals, and the elimination of the middle class. Catholic priests and nuns were rounded up, jailed, and often tortured. Following other communist models, prison camps were established to "reform through labor." Land reform was high on the communist agenda with landlords taken to trial and often executed. Over a million and a half acres were confiscated and distributed to about four million peasants.

Ho Chi Minh also instructed former Viet Minh supporters (estimated to number 5000-10,000) who had voluntarily remained in the south following the Geneva Accords to begin guerrilla operations against the Diem government in the mid-1950's. These "rebels" had been driven into remote areas of the Mekong Delta until December 1956, when leaders in Hanoi began to encourage a revival of this insurgency. A sporadic assassination campaign began in 1957 with several major incidents involving machine gun killings of civilians in bars and bombings in various locations in and around Saigon. In early 1959 the communists in the north approved a "people's war" in the south and instituted plans to upgrade the historical trail from the north to the south through Laos. It soon became referred to as the "Ho Chi Minh Trail." Many Americans would later lose their lives in actions attempting to counter activity on this trail.

Although the Viet Cong (literally translated as "Vietnamese communist") was officially established on December 20, 1960, members had been politically and militarily active prior to this date. Two U.S. military advisors were killed on July 8, 1959, and two South Vietnamese army units had been attacked in September 1959 by Viet Cong units. Uprisings were also fomented in the Mekong Delta. In September 1960 there were nearly 200 clashes between the Viet Cong and South Vietnamese forces. Much of the agitation in the south was conducted under the cover of "front" organizations, such as "the Saigon-Cholon Peace Committee" and the "Vietnam-Cambodia Buddhists Association." Most of these groups appeared to be leaderless; this apparent anonymity became such accepted gospel that the term "the faceless Viet Cong" was often used by Americans fighting them.

As early as 1960, two command centers for Viet Cong operations had been set up in Tay Ninh province near the Cambodian border. Soon the Viet Cong were proclaiming "liberated zones" in South Vietnam where they, or their indigenous supporters, exerted de facto control. As opposed to the South Vietnamese army, the Viet Cong welcomed women into several of their fighting groups. During this period, the communist government in Hanoi publicly disavowed direct support for the Viet Cong so as not to appear to be violating the Geneva Accord. However, as early as 1961, it was becoming moot whether the South Vietnamese were fighting Viet Cong or regular North Vietnamese (NVA) troops, as soldiers from the north began to move down the Ho Chi Minh trail in large numbers. It is estimated that close to 50,000 NVA troops came south during 1961-63. Hanoi, meanwhile, continued to receive weapons to support this effort from both China and the Soviet Union. By 1966 the Viet Cong and NVA forces had opened yet another significant supply route, called the "Sihanouk Trail" from a Cambodian port through jungles to bases near the Vietnamese border.

As I discussed at the beginning of this section, there are widely divergent opinions concerning the events leading up to American involvement in Vietnam. As an example, there is not even consensus on the origin of the term, Viet Cong. A lengthy discussion of this debate can be found in an article by Brett Reilly in the January 31, 2018 edition of *The Diplomat*.

Once the north became committed to a campaign to take over all of Vietnam, they began to send large numbers of soldiers south on the Ho Chi Minh trail. By 1962 there were estimated to be well over 300,000 communist supporters in "liberation associations" in the south. The Viet Cong used these numbers to not only stage raids and assassinations but also to conduct several major battles against ARVN forces. One such encounter, the Battle of Ap Bac, took place in January 1962 against the South Vietnamese 7th Infantry Division which was aided by American advisors. Although the ARVN had the support of artillery, armored personnel carriers, and 15 U.S. helicopters ferrying troops, the Viet Cong used superior tactics based on information provided by embedded spies in the ARVN forces. During the battle there was considerable acrimony between the U.S. advisors and ARVN commanders, mostly because of a reluctance of ARVN leadership to absorb losses for fear of being relieved by Diem. As a result, the Viet Cong came away with one of their first victories against a numerically superior ARVN force supported by American advisors, helicopters, and sophisticated weapons.

American "advisors" had been in Vietnam as early as 1950. At that time, President Truman established a military assistance advisory group (MAAG) in Saigon to assist the French. He soon sent over a hundred "non-combat" troops to provide further assistance. American planes, maintained by U.S. Air Force personnel, were flown by CIA pilots to aid the French during the early 50's, although the C-119's had French insignia. Two American contractors working for the CIA were killed when their plane was shot down after dropping supplies for the encircled French forces at Dien Bien Phu. American involvement increased again in 1954 when President Eisenhower sent additional personnel to the MAAG to train South Vietnamese army units. The first U.S. Marine, Lt. Col. Victor Croizat, arrived in August 1954 and was assigned to the MAAG. His initial assignment was actually in Hanoi to coordinate the evacuation of the "Passage to Freedom" in which over 800,000

Vietnamese, nearly 500,000 tons of equipment, and 23,000 vehicles in the north were transported by U.S. ships to the south. Over the next several years of the Eisenhower administration, the U.S. increased military involvement in response to heightened fighting in South Vietnam. In November 1961 President Kennedy decided to send additional American military assistance to the Diem government by sending USNS Core (T-AKV-41) with 32 H-21 Shawnee helicopters and 400 U.S. soldiers to Saigon. Less than six months later, there were 12,000 American "military advisors" in Vietnam including pilots, technicians, intelligence, and administrative personnel. As political instability increased in the South Vietnamese government, President Kennedy and his successor, Lyndon Johnson, continued to increase U.S. military support, such that by the end of 1964 the U.S. Military Assistance Command (now led by General William Westmoreland) had grown to over 20,000 personnel.

In April 1961, President Kennedy authorized the first use of airborne-delivered herbicides in Operation Trail Dust. This use of defoliants to eliminate both crops and vegetation thought to be used as cover by the Viet Cong was determined by the U.S. to be effective and was expanded in October 1962 as Operation Ranch Hand. Between 1962 and 1971 over *19 million gallons* of herbicide (mostly Agent Orange) were sprayed by air onto the countrysides of South Vietnam, Cambodia, and Laos. The long-term medical effects of this tactic continue to be felt by both Vietnamese and Americans suffering from Agent Orange related diseases. Many of the men I interviewed for this book are victims today of exposure to these herbicides.

Opposition to Diem's authoritarian rule and his management of the ongoing war generated an unsuccessful coup in 1960. Buddhist leaders throughout South Vietnam were becoming increasingly angry about what had become essentially a Catholic-controlled government. Protests throughout the south increased, followed by massive demonstrations in the Imperial capital of Hue, not far south of the DMZ. On May 8, 1963, government forces and local police led by Diem's brother, Nhu, killed twelve Buddhist monks in skirmishes in Hue to put down the protests. Less than a month later, the world was shocked to see photos of a Buddhist monk setting himself on fire and burning to death on the streets of Saigon. Madame Nhu, the wife of Diem's brother, (often called the "First Lady of South Vietnam" because she lived in the presidential palace) exacerbated the situation by derisively calling the monk immolations "barbecues." Dissatisfaction with Diem's regime increased even further when Nhu ordered police to raid key Buddhist pagodas throughout the south resulting in a death toll in the hundreds. By the 1st of November 1963, Diem had lost the confidence of President Kennedy. A coup had become inevitable.

ARVN Army generals took action. Diem and his brother were ousted and fled from the palace but were found the following day in neighboring Cholon on the west bank of the Saigon River and assassinated. The U.S. had advance knowledge of the coup, and according to many, was closely involved, while publicly proclaiming that America was "neutral." A week later the U.S. recognized the new military-led government. Interestingly, Madame Nhu survived the turmoil and lived the rest of her life in exile in Paris before dying in Rome in 2011.

Predictably a power struggle followed the coup. General Duong Van Minh (a.k.a. "Big Minh" because he was so much larger than most Vietnamese) became President, but within three months he was ousted by another general, Nguyen Khanh. (Ironically, Minh became the 4th and last President of South Vietnam in April 1975, two days before he surrendered to North Vietnamese forces). Khanh named a President, but a junta of generals was actually running South Vietnam. This scenario led to further demonstrations and strikes with almost monthly coup attempts throughout 1965. Finally, Air Marshal Nguyen Cao Ky took control as Prime Minister with General Nguyen Van Thieu as the Head of State. Surprisingly, these two were able to bring a measure of stability to the government, although their methods of control were extreme.

It was in the midst of this chaotic political turmoil that General Westmoreland arrived in Vietnam in 1964 as deputy Commander of the U.S. Military Assistance Command (MACV). He was soon made the Commander of all U.S. forces in Vietnam. Under his direction, American forces were greatly increased from 16,000 troops when he arrived, to 535,000 upon his departure four years later. Westmoreland's strategy (and that of the U.S. government) was to weaken the enemy by attempting to engage them in large battles where they could be killed using superior U.S. artillery and air power. The belief was that if enough enemy were "eliminated," the north would understand that further action in the south was futile, allowing the South Vietnamese government to become sufficiently strong to establish a Korea-model separation of two independent states. Success would be measured by "body count." The U.S. and its allies would now determine success by how many enemy troops were killed compared to U.S. and ARVN losses. This tactic was a catalyst for many of the military actions described later in this book where Americans would engage in a pitched battle for a strategic hill, capture it (often with considerable losses), determine a body count of enemy soldiers, then retreat from the hill the following day. Because there was no land to be acquired as in a traditional war, the plan was to deplete the Viet Cong of the human resources to control areas in the south while also inflicting heavy losses on General Giap's North Vietnamese army. Facing further huge casualties, it was theorized, Ho and Giap would certainly have to choose to withdraw to north of the DMZ.

Predictably, the determination of body count by both U.S. and ARVN forces quickly became a shell game in which numbers were greatly inflated, either due to the enemy dragging dead and wounded with them in retreat or by commanders grossly overcounting to seek favor with their superiors. It has been estimated that at least one-third of all reported enemy dead were actually innocent civilians caught in the midst of a battle. The estimates of official KIA numbers coming from U.S. military actions in the infamous "free fire zones" were especially dubious. When an area was declared a free fire zone, any dead body found there (including innocent civilians) was automatically added to the body count. In his book, *A Rumor of War*, Philip Caputo, a former Marine, described their rule of thumb for counting the dead, "If it's dead and Vietnamese, it's VC." Others point out that there were often large discrepancies between the number of enemy soldiers reported as killed compared to the actual number of weapons found on the same battlefield. In short, the body count numbers being presented to Westmoreland were often false and led to overly optimistic assessments of the effectiveness of the U.S. strategy. Whether or not Westmoreland and his staff were complicit in generating the inflated body count numbers is not known, but what is certain is that the numbers provided by him to Washington did not reflect reality. The overly optimistic reports sent by Westmoreland became painfully obvious to the American public when the Tet offensive initially overwhelmed U.S. and ARVN forces in early 1968. They had obviously not been worn down or discouraged.

In fact, Westmoreland's game plan was proven to be fatally flawed on many accounts, not the least being a total lack of understanding of Giap and the communist mindset whose plan was simple: accept whatever casualties are necessary while inflicting sufficient losses on U.S. forces such that the American public will lose the political will to continue the war, forcing the U.S. to ultimately withdraw. The second major flaw in Westmoreland's game plan was to assume that an effective South Vietnamese government could be created. Based on both historical and more recent history since the end of WW II, the likelihood of a democratically elected nation in Southeast Asia succeeding was highly unlikely - it had never happened. It was also highly presumptuous to assume that the longstanding ethnic and religious rivals in South Vietnam could be easily controlled, especially if there was little attempt at reconciliation. When Diem stacked his government with family and fellow Catholic supporters while concurrently engaging in heavy-handed treatment of everyone else, no amount of American support could prop up his regime.

It can be said that Westmoreland did not have a good hand to play. For international geo-political reasons, there would be no continued commitment by American presidents to use sufficient force to bomb the north into submission, nor would there be an option to take the fight into Cambodia or Laos to a degree that would eliminate the north's option of resupplying its forces in the south. American concerns about drawing China and/or Soviet Union forces into the war, and possibly risking a nuclear exchange, placed such constraints on U.S. military options that when the USNA Class of 1965 joined the war effort beginning in the middle of 1965, they had become pawns in an unwinnable war doomed to failure.

In the following chapters I will be sharing the experiences of many of these young men in various phases of this tragic war.

Phase I, Arrival

T HE FIRST MEMBERS OF THE Naval Academy Class of 1965 to become directly involved in the Vietnam War were those serving on ships operating off the coast. Some arrived within months of graduation in the summer of 1965 after receiving assignments to junior officer roles aboard ships, such as destroyers or cruisers. Much of the operations involved shore bombardment in support of U.S. and South Vietnamese ground forces or support of U.S. aircraft carriers conducting flight operations in the South China Sea.

All graduates who chose to become Marines first attended Marine Basic School at Quantico, Virginia, for six months prior to any subsequent assignment. Many of these new Marine officers received orders to be Platoon Leaders and usually arrived in Vietnam in early 1966. Those who received additional training in tanks or amphibious vehicles reached Vietnam a few months later. Marine aviators required longer training and typically did not see combat until nearly two years later. The standard tour for a Marine on the ground in Vietnam was 13 months. Although it was possible for a Marine to extend his tour in-country, few of our classmates chose to do so.

Naval aviators, both pilots and NFOs, began flight training at Pensacola, Florida, followed by lengthy training in the type of aircraft to which they were assigned. Most aviators joined squadrons assigned to aircraft carriers or fixed wing detachments, which conducted intelligence gathering or surveillance operations. Many began combat duty in early 1967. Carrier deployments to Vietnam varied in length but were typically in the 8-month range.

The following stories are not arranged chronologically but involve action primarily in the early days of U.S. ground force involvement in the war.

Dan Mitchell

Baltimore, Maryland

"Three of us came back alive"

On the first Wednesday of each month, a group of Naval Academy Class of 1965 graduates gathers for lunch at McGarvey's Saloon and Oyster Bar in Annapolis, a few blocks from Gate 1 of the Academy. Since my retirement from teaching in 2011, I have been able to attend many of these enjoyable get-togethers. These lunches provide an opportunity to chat with classmates who have known each other for years. It is also an opportunity to meet others whose careers, both in and out of the military, have been in different directions. I met Dan a few years ago at one of these monthly gatherings. I found out that he had been a Marine and had served in Vietnam. I later interviewed him via computer from his home in Kennett Square, Pennsylvania, where he lives with his wife, Sharon.

I was born in Baltimore and attended high school at Baltimore Polytechnic Institute. I played lacrosse and was sort of recruited to the Academy to play there. I say "sort of" because I was not a star athlete. Not many high schoolers were playing lacrosse at that time, and I was a body. I actually had two appointments to get in because I had enlisted in the Naval Reserve in high school and went through boot camp during summer vacation between my junior and senior years. I never knew which appointment got me in. The reason I wanted to go to a service academy was based on that book and movie, "The Man in the Grey Flannel Suit." I didn't want to be one of those kinds of guys, and the Navy seemed like just the opposite. Once at the Academy, I decided during our second year that I wanted to be a Marine. During later summer training sessions, I found that I liked the Marine approach better than other options. Also, on our senior training cruise I was on USS LONG BEACH (CGN-9), a nuclear-powered cruiser. The Commanding Officer of that ship was so terrible that every midshipman I knew on that cruise opted to go Marine Corps rather than risk ever being assigned anywhere near that officer.

I began Marine training at Quantico, Virginia, in September 1965, and upon completion in February 1966 I was assigned to Charlie Company, 1st Battalion, 9th Marines at Da Nang in Vietnam as a Rifle Platoon Leader. My staff sergeant was superb and had the enlisted rank of E-5; we had three squads, each led by a sergeant. The fire team leaders were corporals. There were 13 enlisted men in a squad. Our platoon had a Navy corpsman; there were other corpsmen assigned to the company. Our battalion had been the first American unit ashore in 1965 and was well-entrenched when I arrived. There was a Marine Corps airbase at Da Nang flying mostly F-4 Phantoms. My first assignment was to use the three platoons of our company to patrol the airbase perimeter, but within 10 days, we were moved to Hill 55, about eight miles southwest of Da Nang. Our whole rifle company was on that hill along with an artillery and an Amtrac unit. Several of my Marine classmates were on that hill with me.

The Marine Corps had adopted the tactics of the British in Malaysia, which was to live among the local population to herd them into strategic enclaves where they could be protected from intimidation by the Viet Cong (VC). As part of this strategy, my platoon was directed to leave Hill 55 and go to a nearby village. We were out there for nearly 3 months by ourselves in this small village. Our job was to secure the village so that they could sleep safely at night and go out to work in their fields during the days without being harassed by the VC. Several other platoons were sent out from Hill 55 to different local villages on this type of mission. We lived in the villages; I actually rented a house from a villager in exchange for C-rations that I gave him. Our hospital corpsman performed a lot of medical work on the children in the village. I thought that what we were doing was very successful and that we were doing good. I don't remember any school there, but they did have a Catholic church. There were four to six village elders whom we worked with. At night I would have our Marines set up a perimeter around the village. There were no attacks on the village while we were there. My experience was that the VC, at that time, were not prone to attacking. They were more involved in guerrilla warfare and would shoot at us from hidden locations whenever we went out on patrol. They also set booby traps with mines and artillery shells to try to take us out as we were walking outside the villages.

While we were out on one of these long patrols in the middle of the summer of 1966, I was walking in the middle of the platoon when everyone suddenly slowed. I went up forward to check on what was going on. Just about the time I got to the front, our lead guy tried to step through a barrier on the road, and a hidden 81-mm mortar round exploded blowing off his leg. I was close enough that I got all kind of crap hitting me from my head to my legs - shrapnel and small rocks and pieces of "stuff." The VC would put these booby traps into narrow spaces, particularly in the hedge rows around rice paddies; we learned that it was stupid to go through any of these openings because they were very likely to be booby-trapped. Our radioman called in a medivac for me and my Marine who had his leg blown off from the knee down. He was a Black guy who had a football scholarship to San Diego State waiting for him upon completing his time in the Marines. A Huey helicopter came to get us and took me and him to the hospital near Da Nang. I was in the hospital two to three weeks, and in a month, I was back with my same unit. The Marine recovered but obviously never played football. I will never forget that.

It was a brutal period there for the Marines. Someone in our unit got hurt just about every day. I went to Vietnam with nine 2nd Lieutenants. Three of us came back alive. Each of us spent close to a month in the hospital and all received Purple Hearts. I can tell you the names of every one of them.

I returned to my platoon in August 1966. We were now living in tents down by the river in the vicinity of Hill 55. There was also action here almost daily, often with NVA whenever we went toward the west. They were operating there in at least a company-sized operation. Most of the weapons being used against us were AK-47's and mortars. These skirmishes would last only about 30 minutes, and then they would disappear into the forest. We would find some bodies, but never were able to take many prisoners.

Dan with some of his troops

In early December 1966 we went back to Okinawa to regroup and re-supply in preparation for a battalion landing from USS IWO JIMA (LPH-2) in the Mekong Delta in January 1967. Some general officer apparently thought that there were enemy forces there, but when we landed, I went into a school building that had the date and time of our landing written on the blackboard! Apparently, the Army under General Westmoreland thought that it would be a good idea to share the details of the landing with the South Vietnamese. Our impression was that as a result everyone in the Delta knew that we were coming. We swept the area for 4-5 days and found absolutely nothing. The whole operation was a nothing-burger, a fiasco. I happened to talk to Westmoreland on the IWO JIMA before we landed, and he seemed to me to not have a clue. I said to him, "General, this thing's going to go on forever. There's no light at the end of the tunnel. It's just a matter of who can last the longest." Westmoreland didn't want to hear this and walked away. In my opinion we were in a war of junior officers - Lieutenants and Captains - where most of the generals didn't know what was really going on.

After this futile landing, they loaded us back on the IWO JIMA and sailed our battalion north to Hue above Da Nang. We were now patrolling along the DMZ for the next several months. During these patrols, we would get shot at all the time. The NVA would drop some fire on us, then withdraw. We were losing four to five guys a week - they were not all killed, most were wounded. My rifle platoon was supposed to have had 40-50 Marines, but by this time we probably never had more than 30 guys. One time when our classmate, Sim Pace, and I were still 2nd Lieutenants, our battalion commander, Lieutenant Colonel Jim Day, assigned us to be company commanders because he didn't have any 1st Lieutenants or Captains to take the job. We had to be the youngest company commanders in the Marines! A Marine company was supposed to have six officers; we had two for 200 enlisted men in the company. I was 23 years old.

Bernard Fall, who wrote the famous 1961 book, "Street Without Joy," about the 1945-1954 French war in Indochina, was with us in an area north of Hue in February 1967 doing research for another book. He had been there for two days and slept in the tent next to me. I saw a booby-trapped artillery shell and told Fall not to go over there in that area, but he ignored me and somehow managed to step on the damn thing. It killed him.

My final job in March 1967 was to visit wounded Marines in hospitals around Vietnam. It was a boondoggle given to us Marines who had been wounded so we wouldn't get killed or wounded again before going home.

My belief is that the VC were a Mafia-like terrorist organization. When I later returned to that village that we had been protecting, we found that the Viet Cong had returned and cut off the heads of each of the elders with whom we had been working. They put the heads on poles in the village as a warning not to cooperate with the Americans.

After I left Vietnam, I had orders to the Naval Academy Prep School in Bainbridge, Maryland, as a Company Officer. I was there from May 1967 to June 1969. I then resigned from the Marines because I knew that I would be receiving another set of orders to return to Vietnam. I didn't want to do that because there was no support for the war, and I didn't care for how it was being run.

Dan went to work for IBM in Philadelphia for the next three years, then did computer work for several companies. In the mid-1970's he partnered with a friend to start a nursery business with a farm in West Virginia. Dan managed sales throughout the northeast from his home in

Pennsylvania. Based on his answers to a few questions I asked about trees in my yard, Dan had certainly become an expert.

Throughout our conversation, Dan expressed strong feelings about U.S. involvement in Vietnam as only someone who faced the horror of war on a daily basis can have. Following his time in Vietnam, Dan became a voracious reader of books and articles examining the French and U.S. role in Southeast Asia leading up to American Marines landing at Da Nang just a year prior to Dan arriving there. He spoke to me at length about how Ho Chi Minh had been repeatedly rebuffed by political leadership in the United States in the 1930's and 1940's when he had requested our assistance to throw off the colonial yoke and allow Vietnam to become an independent nation. As a result of these earlier decisions by American officials, Dan later found himself as a young 2nd Lieutenant in mine-laden fields alongside even younger subordinates being tasked to kill or be killed. During his year in Vietnam, Dan and his Marines had to survive in an environment driven primarily by a stated goal to achieve high body counts to deplete an enemy rarely seen. The odds for survival in Dan's role as a Marine Platoon Leader in 1966 proved to be less than 50 percent. Surviving such a maelstrom etches memories not easily forgotten - or forgiven.

John Lehman

Washington, D.C.

"Just throw him in the river"

I interviewed John via computer from his home in Travelers Rest, South Carolina, where he lives with his wife, Kathy. A classmate told me that John may have a different perspective on Vietnam based on his assignment as a young Lieutenant (junior grade) advising a Vietnamese Navy coastal unit. John spoke with a self-deprecating humor, but occasionally became emotional when recounting memories of several tragic events.

I was born in D.C. in early 1942 while my dad was serving in the Navy during the war. He was in "Security Group" work which may have involved intelligence or spying. During my high school years, we lived in England during his assignment over there. I attended the American School in London for three years; they then advised my dad that he should send me for my senior year to "a boarding school in a very remote area." I am not sure what I had done to earn this recommendation, but I soon found myself at the New Mexico Military Institute in Roswell, New Mexico. Needless to say, this place met the remote criteria. In my senior year I applied for an appointment to the Naval Academy, but didn't get in. I then spent the next year at Pasadena College and was able to obtain an appointment to USNA from a California senator. I hoped to play football at Navy, but on the third day of practice during our plebe year, one of coaches came up to me and said, "Lehman, your only problem is that you are too small, too slow, and have no skills to play football here." That ended my dream of playing for Navy.

Following graduation, I had orders to USS CORRY (DD-817), a destroyer which had been commissioned in 1946. My assignments on

CORRY could best be described as the SLJO type (shitty little jobs officer). My next set of orders was to USS NEWPORT NEWS (CA-148), the last all-gun cruiser in the Navy, as the 5th Division Officer. It was homeported in Norfolk and was the flagship for Commander 2nd Fleet. One day in 1967, as I was standing an in-port watch on the quarterdeck, the XO (Executive Officer) came up to me and said, "John, we're going to Vietnam." I thought that he meant the ship, but he quickly clarified, "No, John, you're going to Vietnam." I had received orders to be an advisor to Coastal Group 14, which I soon learned was located about 15 miles south of Da Nang on the coast of the South China Sea.

Before arriving in Vietnam, I spent several months learning Vietnamese at a language school in Coronado, California. Two of our instructors were young Vietnamese ladies; I gave one of them a ride to work each day. When I asked her how I was doing, she told me what I already suspected, "John, you will never learn Vietnamese."

John at CG-14

When I arrived in April 1967 at Coastal Group 14, I was initially the Assistant Advisor. My boss, the Senior Advisor, was a Lieutenant. Our "base" consisted of two piers in the Cua Dai River (one was later destroyed during a VC mortar attack) and a contingent of South Vietnamese naval personnel with five to ten junks. Two enlisted men (an engineman and a gunner's mate) slept with us essentially in a shack until Navy Seabees showed up to build us a proper hooch. There was an adjacent bunker to dive into whenever the base came under attack, which I soon learned was at least three nights a week. I had two Vietnamese sailors assigned as bodyguards for me whenever I went anywhere outside the base. One was a local Vietnamese while the other was a Cambodian who was all business; I never saw him smile.

We were on the south side of the Cua Dai River which was totally controlled by the VC. Whenever we went over there, we could expect a firefight. Apparently, our bosses in Da Nang felt that we weren't doing enough to take the fight to the VC, so they sent two Swift boats down to "help." I got into the lead boat and as soon as we headed up the river and went near the south side, we came under attack. I grabbed my M-16 and started to fire; my first round went into the water maybe 15 yards out. I emptied all my rounds, but probably hit nothing, or nobody. One sailor on the other Swift boat was hit and killed and two others were seriously wounded. As soon as we got back to the base, we called for a medevac helicopter to take the wounded sailors to Da Nang. Following this experience, the Swift boats returned only to bring us food or to evacuate someone, but never for fighting.

Another time four U.S. PBR's (Patrol Boat, Riverine) showed up "to help." These were small boats built specifically for use in the shallow waters of Vietnam. For their size they had considerable firepower. Unfortunately, the guys running these particular boats were very flippant and thought that they could handle anything. One of my bodyguards went with them on an overnight patrol. I had told them what to expect. They were ambushed by the VC and got shot up real bad. My bodyguard pulled a guy who had been shot from the river. When they came back, the officer-in-charge of the PBR's came to my hooch covered in blood and was crying hysterically. He himself had not been shot, but the blood had come from his men whom he had been holding. The PBR's also never came back "to help."

One of my main roles was to call in air support during enemy action, most of which took place at night. We could also obtain artillery support from a nearby Marine base. There was another Marine detachment in a CAPS unit (Combat Action Platoon) upriver at Hoi An, a decent sized city. There were about 15 Marines and a Navy hospital corpsman in the CAPS; their main job was to protect the bridge across the Cua Dai. Whenever they came under attack, they would send up flares to notify all American forces nearby. Twice we took armed junks up there to help them, and each time the VC withdrew. The third time my Vietnamese counterpart (their CO) refused to go; that night a civilian junk hit a mine along the same path we would have taken. The VC had rigged a U.S. undetonated bomb in the river and exploded it when the junk passed thinking it was us. If we would have gone up there that night, we would have been hit. Not too long later we sadly learned that all the Marines in the CAPS unit had been found shot to death in bed in what was almost certainly some kind of "inside job." We never learned the real story because other Marines would not talk about it.

Occasionally we would have some "Spooky's" fly down from Da Nang to provide fire support. These were small, two-engine cargo planes that had been converted with a lot of guns on just the pilot's side, so he could look out his window and control the shooting. We had received intel that there was a heavy concentration of VC gathering on the far side of the river. The exact wording of the intel was, "It looks like about 45 guys in black pj's are over there." So, I called in fire support and this Spooky plane shows up. I gave the pilot a set of coordinates where we thought the VC were located and, as we watched, he tilted the plane to port and started unleashing an incredible amount of gunfire toward the ground. It sounded exactly like a dragon roaring. As we watched, we suddenly realized that he was taking fire on his starboard side. We immediately radioed the pilot and told him that he was under fire. I always recall him screaming, "Jesus Christ," before he quickly got out of there.

One day a CIA guy shows up at CG-14 and said that he had a plan to kill VC. His grand ploy was to have a Vietnamese sailor go with him to interpret while he would lie hidden on the bottom of a sampan. They would then paddle over near the south shore in the hope of attracting the attention of a "tax collector" (a VC who shakes down locals for money). Then he would suddenly spring up and kill the VC. As far as I know, he never did this, but I did take him upriver with his Vietnamese translator and dropped them off. He had been ashore 3-4 hours when we heard heavy gunfire. The CIA guy came running to our junk, but got shot as he was trying to get in. There was no sign of his translator, so we rushed the wounded CIA man to our base, but he died in the Medevac helo on the way to Da Nang. All night long we could hear on our radios the translator saying, "Where is my Covan?" Then we heard nothing. We assumed that he had been captured or killed.

War creates terrible scenes. One night a young Vietnamese woman somehow ended up in the minefield outside our base and was seriously injured by the explosion. I didn't know if she was VC or what had happened. The Vietnamese Navy guys dragged her inside the perimeter onto the sand and just let her lie there. They weren't interested in helping. She had two severe wounds, one on her upper torso and one on her leg. I called for a Medevac and started to hold her in my arms. I will never forget how she seemed to be staring out at me with pure hatred. But as she began to die, her face distinctly changed away from the hate. She died in my arms.

Another time a U.S. plane on patrol found a small fishing boat in a free-fire zone where anything sighted could be shot. After watching this plane destroy the sampan, we got into one of our junks and found the boat partially submerged with two bodies in it. The older man, probably the father, was dead. I grabbed the young boy who was wounded and in the water. We took him back to the base and put the boy on a Swift boat we called in, but on the way to Da Nang, they radioed us, "We're sorry, but the child is gone." We think he was about 10 years old.

There were other bad scenes. One day I was walking near the perimeter and heard a loud screaming noise from a nearby hooch. I looked in and saw my Vietnamese counterpart interrogating a VC who had been captured. They were waterboarding this fellow, and it was gruesome. I looked away, not sure what I should do. If I reported these guys doing this torture, I knew that I might be either removed from my job or even killed by the Vietnamese on our base. I chose to do nothing, but still have very mixed emotions about my "non-role" in this incident.

It was easy to become oblivious to the insanity. A journalist came down one night to see what we were doing at CG-14. As we were sitting there, we suddenly heard the familiar "zing, zing" sound of bullets passing by. The guy was shaken and looked at me for what to do. I remember casually saying, "Not to worry. He never hits anything." He dove into the bunker and the rest of us just sat there. As I said, it was all insane.

It wasn't all bad during my year there at CG-14. Each month I flew to Da Nang on a Huey and got two nights R&R. I usually spent this time drinking and playing poker. I also had two R&R periods; one was in Hawaii with my fiancée and the other in Thailand. Once at our base we saw a U.S. cruiser offshore, so I jumped into a junk and went out to meet it. They brought me aboard, fed me steak, and gave me enough ice cream to take back to everyone on our base. In general, we ate well because the helos would sometimes bring us American food. I ate often with my Vietnamese counterparts, but I always had to brush the flies off my fork. One day we noticed that our drinking water had a real bad smell. When we investigated, we found a dead rat floating in the water tank. Later I came down with a high fever, but they couldn't send a helo to get me because of bad weather. I remember lying in our hooch and hearing Da Nang on the radio saying, "If his fever doesn't come down, just throw him in the river for a while." Fortunately, I got better.

I left CG-14 in August 1968 and had an assignment doing intelligence work at Fort Meade in Maryland. That helped me to decompress. Kathy and I were married in July 1969, and I resigned from the Navy the following year.

Following his departure from the Navy, John worked as an engineer in the asphalt and concrete business. John emphasized to me that although his year in Vietnam was challenging, he felt that the experience was life changing. He somberly told me that anyone who got to know the Vietnamese loved them as a people. In his opinion, we achieved little. "The idea of going there was wrong, and the way we did it was wrong."

Many books and movies about the Vietnam War have pointed out exactly how many of the young Americans such as John did absolutely "crazy stuff" as a coping mechanism to survive mentally. Several chapters in Tim O'Brien's 1990 book, "The Things They Carried," recount such moments.

Mike Luecke

Macomb, Illinois

"We lost 10 aviators"

Mike is one of the two members of our Naval Academy Class of 1965 who is a member of "The Golden Eagles." This exclusive group was founded in 1956 to honor 100 aviators who pioneered Naval Aviation and provided the leadership for the development of this unique community. The membership has now been expanded to 200, but entrance is by invitation only. Qualifications are still highly restrictive and typically involve being a pioneer in some new aspect of Naval Aviation or having demonstrated outstanding skills as a pilot. I learned from the Golden Eagles website that Mike amassed over 5000 mishap-free flight hours in 70 types of aircraft. He had 1203 fixed wing "traps" (landings) on aircraft carriers, with 400 at night. As a pilot he was qualified not only in fixed-wing aircraft, but also rotary-wing, multi-engine, gliders, and tail draggers. Mike also flew 183 combat missions during the Vietnam War. After viewing the biographies of several other Golden Eagles, it was obvious why Mike was selected to be a member. I interviewed him in person at his home in Gainesville, Virginia, where he lives with his wife, Maggie.

I was born in a small town in Illinois near Springfield. My dad had been a semi-pro baseball player during the Depression and told great stories about his experiences. I went to a Catholic high school in Freeport, Illinois, and played four sports all four years. In track I threw the discus and shot put. I ended up at USNA by accident. I had applied to a few colleges and had some partial scholarships. My dad saw an article in the local paper that our congressman was accepting applications for service academies and suggested that I apply. I did but sort of forgot about it until late May 1961 when I received a bolt-out-of-the-blue telegram that I had received the appointment. The only things I knew about the Naval Academy came from seeing the television show, "Men of Annapolis." I had never been near an ocean. So, I had to make a quick decision. I was the oldest of seven children and realized that I could save my family money by going to Annapolis. I chose to accept the appointment, and five weeks later I was in Tecumseh Court at USNA taking the oath of office.

At the Academy during our aviation training summer, I decided immediately that I wanted to be an aviator. Following graduation, I taught FORTRAN computer programming at USNA during the summer, and then proceeded to Pensacola, Florida, for flight training before getting my wings. Within each community of Naval Aviation there is a hierarchy IN THEIR MINDS where each group thinks it is more important. One of the sayings that went around Pensacola was, "Fighter pilots make movies. Attack pilots make history." I wanted to be a fighter pilot. A flight surgeon told me that I was too tall to fly fighters, the F-4 and the F-8, and wouldn't let me go there. With those choices gone, I received orders to a squadron of A-6 attack planes, VA-196, at Whidbey Island, Washington. I went there with a chip on my shoulder and was determined to be the best A-6 pilot possible. This set of orders turned out to be fortuitous, as I met Maggie at Whidbey. We were married there in the chapel 53 years ago after my first cruise.

Two Navy A-6 Intruders in flight

The Grumman A-6 Intruder had entered service in 1963 as the primary all-weather attack plane. It had two powerful engines giving it high speed and the capability to carry 18,000 lbs of bombs or missiles. It had side-by-side seating with the pilot on the left and the bombardier/navigator on his right who operated the avionics which gave the plane its all-weather strike capabilities.

Our squadron's first deployment was on USS CONSTELLATION (CVA-64), homeported in San Diego. After workups, we sailed to Vietnam in May 1968. Before we left, I received permission from my CO to fly my A-6 back to Chicago to see my mother for Mother's Day. It was regarded as a "training flight." When I was over my home town near Chicago, I put on an unauthorized, and what I regarded as impressive, flight show. If anyone did this now, they would be court-martialed. When I landed, I was met by a JAG officer who read me the riot act and made me call my CO. Fortunately, nothing came of it and the next week I was at sea headed to Yankee Station on Connie [nickname for CONSTELLATION]. We arrived there a month later after doing bombing practice on the way.

There were always at least two carriers on Yankee Station. We started flying combat missions immediately. About half of our missions were over the north, with some others over Laos and Cambodia. They generally try to give new pilots a "milk run" for your first mission to get over your jitters, but I was definitely tense. For most of my flights off Connie, I had the same Bombardier/Navigator sitting next to me; he was a great guy, and we became close friends. I encountered a few SAMs on these flights and saw some of our planes shot down by SAMs or AAA. When this happened, if you saw it and were closest to it, you became the on-scene commander. First, you would report the location and whether there were any enemy forces around the downed pilot. You would then coordinate the Rescue Combat Air Patrol (RESCAP) to suppress enemy fire in that area with A-7's or other aircraft with guns. We always made extensive efforts to try to rescue downed pilots, but we didn't get many back. They were either killed or captured.

**Mike Luecke going to work in his A-6 aboard
USS CONSTELLATION (CVA-64)**

*There was no shortage of planes on CONNIE. We had the only A-6
squadron (12 planes), but there were also two F-4 fighter squadrons,
two A-7 squadrons, an A-3 detachment (tankers), and a helo squadron.
We had some difficult losses. During our two Vietnam deployments my
squadron lost 10 aircraft; three were operational losses, but seven were
shot down with the pilots and bombardier/navigators going down. Of
those 14 aviators, we were able to save only four, so we lost 10. It was
brutal. I always tell my grandchildren that this is why Memorial Day is
personal for me.*

*Most of our targets in North Vietnam were not determined by staff on
the carrier but were based on what came to us from Pearl Harbor or*

Washington. Because we were prohibited from attacking most critical targets in North Vietnam, we were going after truck parks, roads, and bridges. When flying down south, we sometimes supported our troops with suppressing fire. Our A-6's were doing a lot of night flying because of our radar capabilities and moving target indicator. This allowed us to find targets which were moving at night, which automatically were assumed to be bad guys. Most of our flights were under two hours; we would often go in very low to avoid enemy radars. On some flights I did see SAMs in the air but never had one get close. I had a few radar lock-ons but was able to evade. At night we could see the tracers which gave us 1-2 seconds to avoid the AAA. This is one reason I preferred to fly at night. Unfortunately, I did see another one of our planes get shot down.

Mike showed me several of the charts he used with his flight paths for missions over North Vietnam. They were very detailed, but difficult for this non-aviator to understand other than the general direction of each flight. He also introduced me to the phrases "feet wet" and "feet dry" meaning, respectively, that the plane is over water or over land.

There were also some material issues; one caused fire to break out in the engine bay. We lost one aircraft in our squadron due to this problem. We had to stand down and return to the Philippines for three weeks until the Navy came up with a fix for this issue. There were also the usual electronics problems which were frustrating because A-6 capabilities were contingent on working electronics.

Several times I almost ran out of fuel; one situation occurred when I was the on-scene commander for a downed aircraft. I stayed too long but was saved by a tanker the carrier sent out to refuel me. During this cruise we did a few small Alpha strikes with perhaps 12 aircraft, including some F-4's, going together, but these were nothing compared to huge Alpha strikes when the U.S. was bombing the Hanoi area.

My first deployment lasted about 8 months; we got back in February 1969. Maggie and I were married in August before I deployed again in November on USS RANGER (CVA-61), another large-deck carrier, this one out of Alameda, California. We arrived back at Yankee Station in December 1969. There was a bombing pause keeping us from bombing the North for part of this cruise, so we did most of our missions over South Vietnam. We also lost a few planes on this deployment.

In December 1969 I did an 8-day exchange duty with the Air Force 366th Tactical Fighter Wing in Da Nang. The purpose was to familiarize carrier pilots with Forward Air Controller (FAC) operations during our flights in-country. This gave me the opportunity to meet the "Stormies," an elite group of six Air Force crews which performed low altitude reconnaissance missions over Laos. The photographic intelligence these guys gathered was spectacular. Most of their flights were below 2000 ft at speeds over 450 kts. Their work was invaluable in locating camouflaged targets, hidden bypasses on the Ho Chi Minh Trail, and precise locations of enemy air defenses.

While I was in Da Nang, I went out on Swift boat #39 with Ensign Mike Gann and his crew of five. Mike had been doing this for eight months and was a superb seaman. We went south to Coastal Group 14 on the Cua Dai River and met the American advisors there who were assigned to the local Vietnamese Navy forces. There were some Viet Cong bunkers on islands in the river, so we beached the boats and fired mortar rounds into those bunkers. Several previous attempts to dislodge these enemy forces with Vietnamese ground troops had failed while losing ten or so personnel due to mines and booby traps. Mike asked me if I would like a ride in a "skimmer," a small speedboat powered by two 40 hp outboard motors. I foolishly said, "Sure." They threw me a helmet, flak jacket, and an M-16 with 30 clips of ammo. Soon we were flying up the river with a boatswain's mate up forward with an M-60 machine gun. We started up some tributaries of the Cua Dai near Hoi An where the water was only a few feet deep and sometimes only 30 ft wide. We fired some grenades at a partially damaged bunker and then stopped at a refugee camp where they gave us some warm beer. We ran aground at least 3 times, but did return safely for a quick meal before we went upriver to Hoi An. After a brief tour of Army facilities there, we picked up two snipers to set an ambush later in the evening downriver.

As we left, I saw a young Vietnamese man in a sampan who had been shot in the leg and was now dead. A few bystanders were mourning, but most of the crowd seemed indifferent as if they saw these scenes every day. Shortly after we left, we found a few VC crossing the river and took care of them with a torrent of fire. After dark we dropped off the two snipers and then parked our boat to wait for action. Although we heard voices, neither us nor the snipers saw anyone, even with our Starlight scopes. Those two snipers bore no resemblance to any U.S. servicemen I had ever seen. They looked like what I would expect in a prison or a Chicago street gang - very tough-looking hombres. One curious fact I learned was that the local group of Korean troops was having problems convincing U.S. forces that their body count numbers were real, so they started to bring back ears to show what they had done. They no longer had credibility issues.

Back at Da Nang, I next had the opportunity to fly in the back seat of an OV-10 flight performing a Forward Air Control mission. We found several active enemy 23 mm AAA sites and called on strikes from both the Air Force and an A-6 from our carrier. The next morning, I flew as a passenger in an Army helicopter to a Special Forces camp at Nong Son about 30 miles south of Da Nang. Because we had to fly over territory controlled by the VC, we flew only 15 ft above the ground and continuously zig-zagged. I actually became nauseous! While I was out there at the Special Forces camp for two days, I had the opportunity to listen to their frustration with their current mission to "Vietnamize" the war [turn over prosecution of the war to Vietnamese forces]. *After this 8-day interlude, I was back to my own war-flying missions over the same land I had just visited.*

I found Mike's memories of this "visit" to other forces conducting the war to be a perfect explanation of why nations have long sent young men to fight their wars. Most are convinced of their own immortality. Who else would enthusiastically undertake dangerous adventures such as donning a flak jacket and helmet to participate in river warfare in a small boat, or fly airplanes into a wall of flak? Based on interviews with others in our class who were U.S. advisors to these Vietnamese Navy Coastal Groups, I learned that these were incredibly dangerous assignments. One of our classmates was wounded three times in six months during his tour at this same Coastal Group 14 which Mike visited.

While I was talking to Mike, I asked his wife, Maggie, how she coped as a newlywed during Mike's second deployment to Vietnam.

I had met Mike only three days prior to his first deployment on Connie, so our romance had grown only through letters to each other. When he returned and asked me to marry him, I was thrilled. Because my father had flown Navy PBYs throughout WW II, I was very aware of the dangers faced by Naval Aviators based on the stories he had told us. I also knew that Mike's squadron had suffered losses during their deployment, and that he would undoubtedly be going back over there under similar challenges. I suppose, in retrospect, that I was young and naive and assumed that all would be well. While Mike was gone on RANGER, I threw myself into work, and more importantly, embraced my faith. We were able to write each other daily, even though the letters would arrive in bunches at random intervals. Perhaps the worst time for me was the first Christmas we were married when I was home in Illinois visiting relatives. I looked out the window and saw a priest and another man in a dark suit coming to our door. Immediately I started crying thinking that the worst had occurred. It turns out that the priest was a close friend of Mike's and was coming with a mutual friend to visit! Mostly, during his deployment I was happy to be married, and while understanding that he could be shot down, I relied on my faith to keep me steady.

Mike then resumed his thoughts…

While RANGER was beginning our return from Vietnam, I learned that I had been selected for test pilot school. In order to arrive in time for this assignment, I was given permission to fly off RANGER early to reach Patuxent River Air Station in Maryland in June 1970 where this training took place. This turned out to be a very intensive 6-month school with a mixture of classroom and flying. I was able to fly a wide variety of aircraft and became qualified to fly 12 different types of planes. The same flight surgeon who had said that I was too tall to fly in fighter aircraft just happened to be stationed at Pax River at the same time, but he never mentioned anything to me. After these 6 months, my first assignment was to perform acceptance trials on the EA-6B [The Grumman Prowler, a twin-engine mid-wing electronic warfare aircraft]. *I was then selected to come back as an instructor at Test Pilot School teaching out-of-control flight testing. Later on, I was Chief Flight Instructor at Empire Test Pilot School in England flying all types of NATO aircraft. We had Aussies, Egyptians, Israelis, and other pilots from all over the world at this school.*

Following his tour in England, Mike was selected for command of an A-6 squadron in Virginia Beach. On one of his deployments to the Mediterranean there were four members of our class as CO's of squadrons on the same carrier; two later died in aircraft accidents. Peace time flying in the military is also inherently dangerous. Mike went on to a lengthy career in subsequent commands, culminating with his selection for Admiral. I left our interview with an appreciation for our aviator classmates who, after seeing a squadron mate get shot down, could climb into their own plane the next day for missions into the same cauldron.

Jette Browne

Athens, Georgia

"Dooley, forget the #### radio!"

While interviewing other classmates, I mentioned that I would like to talk to someone who had been a Forward Air Controller in Vietnam. Not long afterwards, I received a bolt-out-of-the blue phone call. "This is Jette Brown. I think I can help your project." Jette gave me a brief description of his time in Vietnam; two days later, we were talking via computer from Jacksonville Beach, Florida, where he lives with his wife, Nancy.

I was born in Columbus, Ohio, but my parents soon moved to Athens, Georgia, where I grew up and attended high school. Although my birth name was Joseph Majette Brown, from my earliest days everyone called me Jette. Majette is a family name based on my maternal grandmother. Athens will always be special for me because when I was 10, I met Nancy there in Miss Flossie's ballroom dancing class.

Like a lot of our classmates, I had developed a fascination with the Navy by watching TV shows and movies about ship battles in World War II. Sometimes we would drive up to my mother's family farm in Arnold, Maryland, and I would see midshipmen in Annapolis marching around in uniform. That got me enamored about attending the Academy so that I could be in the Navy. I wasn't sure that my high school had prepared me enough to get into USNA, so I spent a year at Georgia Tech to get a better foundation.

At the Academy, I initially wanted to go Navy Air, but I couldn't get my blood pressure down enough, so I decided to go to the Surface

Navy. Following graduation, after two short training courses, I flew to Yokosuka, Japan, in December 1965 to report to the USS STRAUSS (DDG-16). We went straight to the South China Sea. Our ship had very good air search radars which enabled us to monitor the entire air space around North Vietnam. I was one of the Air Controllers and my job was to help delouse aircraft returning to their carriers from missions over Haiphong Harbor and other targets in North Vietnam. By delousing, I mean that we kept close radar watch to make sure that no MiG's were trying to sneak in behind our guys as they were headed home over the water. We had to pick some aviators out of the water a few times after they had been hit by anti-aircraft fire over the North. Sometimes the pilots would tell me that they had been hit. I remember one cool character calmly saying, "This thing is on fire and I'm not hanging around. If you go out on the bridge wing, you'll see my parachute." So, we went out, and sure enough, he had punched out of his F-8 Crusader and was floating down in his parachute about 2000 yards away from our ship! There was always an Air Force float plane on station up there. They flew out of Da Nang and could fly around in the area for about 6 hours. Their call sign was "Crown" and we would simply vector them to the downed pilots so they could pick them up and take them back to Da Nang. "Red Crown" was our call sign whenever we had the duty for delousing guys coming back to the carrier. That wasn't our own ship call sign; it was used by all ships when they had that duty. The fighter planes up there doing those missions were F-8's and F-4's. We saw a couple dozen pilots picked up; some others crashed into the sea and were not recovered. It was a dangerous time for those guys.

One night I woke up to go on watch at 4 AM and went to get a cup of coffee before taking the watch. As I entered the wardroom, it was full of bloody bodies! They were South Vietnamese Marines who had been on a commando operation off the North Vietnamese coast near Vinh. Their boat had been ambushed and they had multiple casualties. They had managed to find STRAUSS and come alongside for help. First thing I saw when I came in to get that cup of coffee was a trash can with some severed arms in it. I watched as our corpsman did an amputation on a fellow who was lying on our wardroom table. There were several other

Vietnamese waiting to be treated. This was all quite a shock. I didn't stay to find out what, if any, anesthesia, was given. `

Aircraft carriers and some other large ships are equipped to conduct surgeries, but for smaller ships, the wardroom (where the officers eat) can be converted into a makeshift operating room. The wardroom table is lengthy, and above it, there are recessed lights and other equipment which can be used for emergency operations. Even the submarines I served on were so equipped. STRAUSS did not have a physician as-signed, so, as in most ships, medical duties were handled by a senior hospital corpsman who has been certified for independent duty. Jette told me that their corpsman who performed these procedures was a Chief Petty Officer who had never been in such a situation.

I stayed on STRAUSS until April 1967. The detailer told me that I was going to a "great billet" on a squadron staff in Norfolk but when my actual orders came through, I found out that I was going to Naval Gunfire Support School in Dam Neck, Virginia, and then off to Vietnam. This was my first experience learning that naval assignments aren't invitations but are called orders.

My new job was Officer in Charge (OIC) of Sub Unit 1, 1st Naval Air and Gunfire Support Company in Vietnam. I was not a volunteer for this job! The Navy just sent me there. People were volunteering for Swift boat duty, but NO ONE was volunteering for this type of job. I flew into Saigon in October 1967. My "office" was in Tent City B which was near Tan Son Nhut Air Base. By the time I arrived, the tents had been replaced by wooden buildings, but it was still called Tent City. The Marine Lieutenant Colonel who was in charge made me his Ops Officer. My job was to travel all over South Vietnam to visit each of the 24 SPOT teams to be "his eyes and ears." I would fly to each of these places to see what was going on and to talk to their customers. I always joked that my real job doing this was to find out where in Vietnam the cold beer was.

"SPOT teams" refers to spotter teams tasked with coordinating naval fire support from offshore ships to help units on the ground involved in fire fights with Viet Cong or North Vietnamese Army units. The "customers" could be Marines, Army, Allied, or ARVN units. The spotter could be on the ground or in the air observing the ongoing battle and would contact a ship offshore to fire rounds into a designated area. Both the spotter and the ship would remain in communication in order to adjust subsequent rounds to hit closer to the intended target.

*One of the first visits I made was to Nha Trang in III Corps north of Vung Tau. We didn't have our own planes to use on these trips, so I usually had to hitchhike on someone else's plane. One time I got a ride at Ton Son Nhut on a Vietnamese C-47, which was essentially a DC-3. There were no seats on the plane - just an empty fuselage. There were maybe 60-80 Vietnamese with me and everyone had to sit on the floor. There weren't even any straps to hang onto. And, we had chickens in several coops aboard with us! When we got to Nha Trang, we went out to an Army Special Forces unit; afterwards we went over to their club for some drinks. I could not believe it; they had some "round eye" Australian strippers who were pretty good....and **cold** beer! On our flight back, to Saigon the strippers were with us in the same plane. They didn't put on a performance for us, but considering we were in Vietnam, they definitely looked good! I joked that on this flight we had chicks instead of chickens. There were odors because several of the Vietnamese were carrying fresh fish. For the first few months of this job, I did these types of assignments. I did some spotting, but mostly I was flying around for the Colonel.*

The first time I ran into Navy SEALS in Vietnam was in the Rung Sat Special Zone. It was a swamp along the Saigon River which looked like a jungle. The SEALS were operating from a small village called Nha Be. It took me a few days to figure this out, but I learned that the number one specialty of SEALS in Vietnam was assassinations - that's what they did. They would go out at night, infiltrate a village, find the local VC commander, and cut his throat. There was occasionally a destroyer anchored in the river in case the SEALS needed help; my job was to call the destroyer to fire their guns in support, but the SEALS never needed them. Also there were always some young civilian guys from the CIA with the SEALS. They always carried a 9-mm submachine gun called a "Swedish K." The Europeans called it a machine pistol. It was the only gun I carried from that point on in Vietnam as my self-defense weapon. You could jump in and out of a helicopter with it without getting hung up. I only had to fire it in anger once.

The Rung Sat Special Zone was a large area designated by American and South Vietnamese forces. It included a large, forested area covered mostly with swamps and mangrove trees, approximately 25 miles southeast of Saigon along the Long Tau River. Due to its challenging and marshy terrain, the region was a continuous stronghold for the Viet Cong who conducted attacks on shipping headed to and from Saigon. In each year of the war, several merchant ships were sunk by Viet Cong attacks here. In response, the U.S. conducted Operation Ranch Hand to spray defoliant (mostly Agent Orange) on much of the vegetation along the river. Jette told me that he had not seen any defoliation during his time in the area in 1967, but several other classmates reported that by 1969 it was a lifeless wasteland. Jette did not personally observe any throat-cutting, so it may or may not have taken place. However, I have heard several similar accounts about SEAL operations. Today this area is the Can Gio Mangrove Forest which ironically has the nickname "Forest of the Assassins." Supposedly, this name has nothing to do with SEALS or the CIA but is a misinterpretation of one of the original Vietnamese words.

One of my fondest memories of this period came before TET when I had the opportunity to fly into Hue. It was one of the most beautiful places I have ever seen in my life. I was flying on Otters and Beavers which were Army single-engine logistics planes. I also flew a gazillion hours in L-19 Bird Dogs. I was on a job down south in Can Tho in IV Corps when I ran into my USNA roommate, Steve Chubb, at the one-room PX. I was trying to buy a new camera and the clerk was an absolutely beautiful Vietnamese girl. I flew back to Saigon on January 31, and when I called back to Steve to see what had happened there during the TET offensive which had hit the morning after I left, he told me that that beautiful girl was floating dead out in the river. She was still in black VC pajamas and had been leading the bad guys in their attack on Can Tho.

Based on conversations which I had during travels in Vietnam in 2016, it was not unusual during the war for some Vietnamese to "play both sides." I talked to several men who had been working for Americans during the day and became Viet Cong soldiers at night. One of these men explained, "We had to survive. I did what was necessary." Several of my classmates told me that they always suspected that their Vietnamese barbers were Viet Cong. The "PX" is the Post Exchange where service-men can purchase merchandise and services.

My next assignment was in early 1968 up at Da Nang. We flew spotter missions out of the airbases at Monkey Mountain and Marble Mountain but couldn't help anyone because the visibility was less than 1000 yards every day we were there. We were flying over Hue and could hear a lot of the fighting that was going on in the citadel, but we couldn't see any targets. We had all sorts of Navy ships offshore ready to help - even a cruiser - but we couldn't use them to assist anyone because we couldn't see the ground to provide coordinates. I was there for ten days and was working with two Army majors who were intelligence officers. They were crazy. One was a real big guy who had been an offensive lineman for the Los Angeles Rams. His idea of self-defense was to carry around a box of hand grenades. I was glad to get out of there before he killed all of us.

Once I got back to Saigon, I was sent to Phu Bai up in I Corps to coordinate Navy gunfire support for the Army 101st Airborne. I quickly found out that those guys were not at all interested in naval gunfire. In fact, they were just total assholes. The problem was that their commanding officer was a total jerk. He was hated so much that he had to be protected at all times by South Korean Marines. His own troops would even shoot at his helicopter! Fortunately, I got out of there when I heard that there was fighting in a landing zone (LZ) further north in a place called LZ Sally. I bummed a ride on a helicopter to go there and when we arrived the troops below were in the middle of a fire fight with NVA units on the edge of a village. There was a mortar exchange going on and I could actually see the mortar rounds from both sides the entire time they were in flight. I swear it looked like they were exchanging 3-point shots! When we landed, I talked to the company commander on the ground who told me that they could handle the NVA during the day, but that they always slipped away at night. The Air Force had been sending some planes to illuminate during parts of the night, but there were gaps. I told him that we could help by having our ships offshore fire 5-inch/54 illumination shells during those gaps. We started doing that and it worked really well.

I then moved up to an area north of Hue where the Marines had previously occupied a base called Camp Evans. When the 1st Cav moved in, they brought in all their helicopters. The 1st Cav had more helos than all of the Marine Corps. Many of the Army officers were West Point grads and were really sharp guys. They loved naval gunfire support. The only problem was that the Army has the worst food in the world. My Naval Academy roommate's dad, Major General John J. Tolson, was the Commanding Officer of the entire unit. He had me join him for Thanksgiving dinner and basically told everyone how much help Jette Brown could give them. Needless to say, those words opened a lot of doors. I was with the 1st Cav full time from March to October 1968. I had two enlisted Marines working for me and they were great.

Here is how it worked when I was with the Cav. First of all, I was usually in the air at least 6 days. The sun comes up out of the South China Sea and I am airborne in a H-model Huey with the Battalion Commander, the Battalion Operations Officer, an artillery liaison officer, two door gunners, and two pilots. Those Hueys had a whole suite of radios and command/control stuff. What made everyone here love naval gunfire was that our ships could fire at such a rapid rate. Most of our operations were east of Highway One north of Hue. Once an area was selected to become a new landing zone, I would give the ships coordinates to use to direct their gunfire to create a safe landing zone for the Cav's helicopters. It became a carefully timed operation. The ships would light up the tree lines around a rice paddy for five minutes with high-capacity rounds. Then with 30 seconds to go before the infantry got there, we would have the ships fire white phosphorous rounds to make a large plume of white smoke. That was the signal for the Huey Cobras to come in. They would use their rockets to fire into those same tree lines. Then the helos with the infantry would sweep into the rice paddy to offload troops so that they could jump out safely and go into action. One of the two enlisted Marines working for me would usually go with the troops to provide additional naval gunfire support for them if needed. We had this area so pacified by August '68 that my corporal and I could drive a Jeep up Highway One from Hue to Quang Tri without any problems. The only person we saw on this trip was a Seabee driving a road scraper with a M-16 over his shoulder.

I also flew in some UH-13's which were basically like a traffic helicopter. They were called Sioux, like the Indians. It had room for a pilot and one passenger. On May 20, 1968, we got shot down in one of those things. We were looking for a mortar position which was hammering an infantry unit we were supporting. We were low enough that we could see the mortar position but before we could have it taken out, all of a sudden over my radio I heard, "May Day, May Day!" It took me at least a second to realize that it was my own pilot, an Army Warrant Officer named Dooley, who was yelling May Day. Boom! We fell straight down maybe 50 feet into the middle of a Buddhist cemetery we had been flying over. We weren't hurt in the crash, but the NVA was now shooting up the helicopter and we were getting hit by pieces of plexiglass. Dooley had been trained to take the radio in the event the helo was shot down, but I grabbed him and pulled him out while screaming, "Dooley, forget the fuckin' radio, we're going to get fuckin' killed! We crab-crawled through the cemetery maybe 15 yards and found a little ditch that had maybe 2 inches of water in it. It ran perpendicular to the bad guys toward the Delta Company of the 2nd U.S. Cavalry. We crawled along that sucker until we got to the Cav. What I remember most is that I was now so thirsty that I couldn't swallow. I borrowed the company commander's canteen and drained it. But it got even worse! The Army had called the Air Force requesting a supporting air strike by F-4's later that afternoon. Well, the planes had their position off by about 1000 meters. As they came screaming over us, I looked up to see 500-pound bombs heading straight toward us! We burrowed into the sand, and thank God, the bombs fell on the other side of some dunes very close to us. The explosions popped our ears real bad, but we survived. Later that day, some Army resupply helicopters came to bring ammunition. They would be kicking boxes of M-16 ammo out the starboard side of the helicopter and big thermos cans of ice cream out the port side. When this was all done, Dooley and I jumped onto the floor of one of those hovering helos to get the hell out of there. But, we missed having ice cream!

Sometimes I would help Army artillery units by spotting for their rounds supporting troops. I was flying in L-19's above the action, generally below 1500 feet. That plane was remarkable; it needed only 1500 feet of runway. We didn't worry about small arms fire unless we went under

1000 feet. These missions were usually three to four hours and most were over near the Ho Chi Minh Trail in Laos. We would occasionally see some tracer fire but never got hit. On these flights we always tried to avoid bad weather because our plane didn't have radar. We would get coordinates from guys on the ground and relay them to the artillery units.

Cessna L-19 Bird Dog

The "Bird Dog" was a small plane built by Cessna and was used extensively during the Vietnam War for Forward Air Control missions. It was called both an O-1 and a L-19. These planes were mass produced by Cessna based on a similar civilian version, the Cessna 170. It could loiter over an area for up to 5 hours for spotting and assistance in the rescue of downed personnel. Over 3000 of these planes were produced for the military. Because it had excellent visibility in all directions, it was perfect for use above battlefields. These were dangerous missions; during the Vietnam War over 450 Bird Dogs were lost. One of the more famous L-19 incidents occurred after the war when a South Vietnamese Air Force pilot loaded his wife and five children on one to escape the North Vietnamese invasion. He landed it on the carrier USS MIDWAY (CVA-41) which was being used to evacuate U.S. Embassy officials!

Jette explained to me that everyone he worked with used "Universal Transverse Mercator" (UTM) coordinates to define the target. The first two letters indicate alphabet lines on the map and the next set of numbers tell you how many meters east and west of where those letters intersect. For example, BJ100200 meant 100 meters east and 200 meters north of the location on the map where the B and J lines intersected. Everyone had the same maps, so by using UTM it was easy to quickly understand where to shoot.

I really enjoyed that part of my time in Vietnam with the Cavalry. They were professional and very enjoyable to work with. They really appreciated the support that our ships offshore could give them. We were in a war, and I did what I had to do.

As I reflected on Jette's unique experiences, I felt that they provided many lessons about the absurdity of war. There really are few rules when you are placed in harm's way on the other side of the world. Short distances, blind luck, timing - so many "things" are the difference between life and death.

Jette left Vietnam in October of 1968. His next assignment was teaching Naval Gunfire Support at the Naval Amphibious School in Little Creek, Virginia. Later in his career Jette was selected to be an Olmsted Scholar to study at the University of Geneva. After retiring as a Captain in 1992, he worked in the tech industry and later as a financial advisor.

Sim Pace

Teaneck, New Jersey

"Us 2nd Lieutenants weren't worried about what the Generals were worried about"

I interviewed Sim in his home in Northern Virginia. Upon graduation from the Naval Academy in 1965, he had been one of the first in our class to attend Basic School for newly commissioned Marine Corps officers in Quantico, Virginia.

No one in my family had a military background, but my father, who was an electrician, worked building Liberty ships at the Brooklyn Naval Yard during World War II. When I was about 12 or so, my uncle took me to see the Army-Navy football game in Philadelphia. As I watched all those Navy midshipmen march onto to field before the game, I knew right away that I wanted to be like them and go there. I applied during my senior year of high school but couldn't get an appointment from our congressman. So, I went to MaNhuttan College for a year and tried again. This time I received three primary appointments: one each, from a congressman, a senator, and the Vice President. While I was at the Academy, I wanted to become a Naval aviator, but my eyesight was not 20/20, which disqualified me. Instead, I chose to go Marines, because I had always been impressed with the Marine officers stationed at the Academy. I wanted to begin as soon as possible, so I didn't take much leave so I could start Basic right away in July.

The Basic School for Marines was six months long while Sim was there. As requirements for more young Marine officers ramped up due to the increasing American commitment to Vietnam, the course was soon compressed to five months. Upon graduation, these 2nd Lieutenants were assigned to one of nine specialties: infantry, artillery, aviation, tanks, amphibian tractors, engineering, supply, communications, and intelligence.

As soon as I began Basic School, I knew that I wanted to be in infantry. I did well in the school and graduated high enough to get my first choice. As soon as we graduated, I received orders to the 3rd Marine Division, which was in Vietnam. I spent about a month at Camp Pendleton in California, and near the end of February of '66, flew into Da Nang. As soon as I arrived, I was assigned to the 9th Marine Regiment and was made one of the three platoon leaders of Alpha Company of the First Battalion. I had about 45 enlisted Marines in my platoon which were in three about-equal squads. Two men with automatic weapons (machine gunners) and two rocket launcher guys were also assigned to my platoon.

Our first assignment was to guard the outside perimeter of the air base at Da Nang. The section of the perimeter which was ours was maybe 600 yards in length on the southwest corner near the main gate. During the daytime, it was just my platoon, but at night the two other platoons in our company would join us to make sure that there was enough of a force in the event of an attack on the base. We did this for about a month until we were suddenly detached from the battalion to conduct a sweep operation called "Operation Georgia" south of Da Nang. The only action we had on the perimeter happened one night when a pickup crashed through the gate of the base. My Marines fired 40 shots at the truck; in the morning we counted 38 bullet holes. It turns out the occupants of the truck were two very drunk Seabees. Miraculously, neither was hit!

This Operation Georgia thing lasted only a week, but we had a lot of action with the Viet Cong. It was actually a bit of a mess. Two of our guys were killed, but none from my company. One of my classmates, Mike Malone, an amphibious tractor officer, was assigned to take us up a river, the Ai Nghia, in an Amtrac to our new assignment on Hill 55 where we rejoined the First Battalion, already encamped there. We arrived there in April 1966.

"Hill 55" was the terminology used to name sites of various battles, or the location of a central headquarters for a specific American fighting unit (in this case, First Battalion, 9th Marine Regiment, 3rd Marine Division). The number 55 refers to the height of the hill in meters, as marked on the maps in use. Some of these hills became so notorious that they also picked up nicknames, such as "Hamburger Hill." This First Battalion location on Hill 55 was located approximately 10 miles south of Da Nang. The entire region surrounding Da Nang to the north, west and south (the South China Sea is to the east) was essentially a hotbed of enemy territory filled with both indigenous Viet Cong and North Vietnamese Army units which had come south either through the DMZ or via the Ho Chi Minh Trail through Laos. Both U.S. Marines and Army troops and ARVN soldiers suffered considerable casualties in this region throughout the war. When Sim and his battalion of Marines took up their position on Hill 55, it was less than a year after Marines had made the first landing of U.S. forces at Da Nang in May 1965. Most of the region was still under firm control of the Viet Cong.

Our usual assignments were to conduct daily sweeps in the area surrounding Hill 55 which was mostly rice paddies and small villages. These were all small, platoon level operations where we would go out looking for enemy during the daytime, then dig foxholes to sleep in at night. It was not the rainy season, so it wasn't too bad, wetness-wise. Thank goodness that they had given me a 1:25,000 map of the area so that I always had a good idea where we were. That map often saved my life because rice paddies all look alike. We got into a lot of firefights, mostly in the late afternoons. They would fire at us from hiding places, and we would react. It was rare for us to start a fight. We never knew if they were VC or NVA, and we didn't care. They were enemy trying to kill us, and so we were trying to kill them. Every day one or more of my guys would get wounded. If we got into a real bad fight, I could call in mortar or artillery support from Hill 55. Vietnam is not very wide here and we were close enough to the coast so that we could also call in gunfire support from Navy ships offshore, but I never had to do this during these early operations. If we could give our 105-mm artillery guys on Hill 55 a decent location to fire at, we could then walk the following rounds on top of where the enemy was. When we did this, the artillery guys on 55 would fire "10 for effect" which had devastating results for the enemy.

After a few weeks of going out looking for bad guys, I got tired of randomly searching and waiting for someone to shoot at us first. So, I started to develop a new strategy for my platoon. Around two in the morning, I would send out a squad of maybe ten Marines to hide in ambush on one side of a village, then later in the morning, send the others around into the other side of the village to make a commotion and a lot of noise. Sometimes this would scare some of the VC in the village to run the other direction right into the ambush we had set up. This tactic worked pretty well because we would often kill two or three VC.

Sim Pace in Vietnam, 1966

In mid-May 1966, I was patrolling with one of my squads about 2/3 of a mile west of Hill 55 near what we always called "No Name River." I later learned that its name was the Son Yen. We were on the east side of the river, maybe north, not sure because those rivers had numerous twists and turns. We were in the vicinity of a village named Le Son. Other platoons were patrolling nearby when they came under heavy enemy fire. The company commander radioed and said that he was sending me an Amtrac and a tank from Hill 55 for support so we could launch an attack on what seemed to be a large contingent of enemy soldiers. I had my 45-caliber pistol, the only weapon I ever carried; Marine officers had been using that same weapon since World War I. My enlisted Marines were all carrying M-14 rifles. When the tank and Amtrac arrived, I directed the tank to take the lead with its machine gun firing, and I stationed Marines with small arms on each side of it as it advanced. The Amtrac was behind the tank and I was walking to the rear of it so I could be in a position to direct the attack. This battle lasted at least two hours, and we had time to call in some Naval support aircraft. They were firing 20-mm guns and the shell casings were falling all around us....almost like rain. We could see the enemy and were killing a lot of them, but we were taking casualties also. My platoon was now down to just 22 men; just a few months earlier, we had over 50. We were putting our casualties on the Amtrac so that we could continue to move ahead without leaving anyone behind. We ended up with five Marines wounded, some severely, but no dead.

As I was walking forward behind the Amtrac, an enemy soldier suddenly pops up out of a hole no more than five yards to my right. Instinctively, I immediately fired all seven rounds of my 45 into him before he could get off a shot. I was so rattled that I kept pulling the trigger on that 45 after all the bullets were gone. We ended up killing 53 of the enemy, many in hand-to-hand combat. The next day we learned from our intelligence guys that we had run into a NVA company of at least 100 fighters. Just 2000 yards away, one of our other platoons suffered several killed and many wounded in this battle. Thank God that I had that tank and Amtrac to help my guys. I myself was really lucky. That night as I was catching my breath, I found a .30 caliber enemy round in my backpack wedged between two rolls of film. That film saved me from getting shot in the back and probably killed!

An Amtrac similar to the one Sim walked behind

The Amtrac sent by Sim's company commander was an LVTP-5 (landing vehicle tracked personnel). It was basically a large, armored amphibious tractor with several different configurations of weapons. It was originally designed to ferry Marines ashore from ships, but was used extensively by Marines in Vietnam operations because it could be used on land or in water. It was a massive vehicle.

Things calmed down a bit, and we went back to normal daily ops. A few weeks later, on June 13, we were patrolling southwest of Hill 55 - maybe 1000 yards away - sweeping a village named Chau Son looking for VC when we came under heavy fire. I called in mortar support, but one hit too close to us - maybe 10 yards away - and I got hit by shrapnel from friendly fire. I had numerous gashes on my head, but a hospital corpsman who was nearby patched me up pretty quick. In spite of these wounds, I did not miss a patrol.

Less than 10 days later, on June 22, we were patrolling southwest of Cam Van, a village on the other side of the Ai Nghia River about 3000 yards southwest of Hill 55. We had crossed the river on a footbridge. All of a sudden, the VC remotely exploded a mine, a "Bouncing Betty." Two of our Marines were instantly killed, and I was severely wounded. I had wounds on both arms, my left leg, and on my whole left side. I was conscious, but in bad shape due to losing blood. A hospital corpsman patched me up some before I was transported from the scene by a Medevac helicopter to Da Nang and kept overnight. I was then airlifted to the hospital on Clark Air Force Base in the Philippines. I spent two days there and then was moved to the Naval Hospital in Yokosuka, Japan. I remained healing at Yokosuka for two months before being sent back to Vietnam.

The Bouncing Betty mine that injured Sim was, ironically, probably an American mine. Several had been stolen from South Vietnamese army units and were used by the VC to deadly effect. When detonated, either by someone stepping on it, by a trip wire, or by remote control, it is launched into the air to about three feet before detonating to release a deadly pattern of ball bearings or shrapnel. They were first developed by the Germans in 1935 as the "S-mine" and were used extensively in WW II. In addition to the physical carnage, the weapon creates significant psychological effect on troops seeing others being killed or maimed, particularly in the genital area. The Germans manufactured at least 2 million of these devices. The American version used in Vietnam was designated the M16 mine and was simply an updated variant of the German S-mine. The U.S. had other anti-personnel mines, the most common being the M14, called the "Toe Popper." The Viet Cong used their own variant of this mine which is designed to cause serious foot injuries. Land mines were a powerful weapon used by the North Vietnamese and the Viet Cong. They often improvised by putting explosives in used shell casings which were detonated by trip wires. It is estimated that in one year alone, nearly 2/3 of U.S. Marine casualties were the result of land mines and booby traps.

Sim relayed his story of his being wounded with no apparent emotion or anger. He had been out of the Naval Academy for just barely over a year and was twice wounded. Sim had seen a lot of war up close and personal. He was still a 2nd Lieutenant but had received two Purple Hearts and experienced near-death with the bullet which had been miraculously stopped by rolls of film in his backpack. When authorities came to tell his parents of his second set of wounds, his mother initially told them that they had to be mistaken because another group had just come the past week to inform them about his prior wounding. She could not believe that he had been wounded twice.

As soon as I was discharged from the hospital in mid-August 1966, I was sent back to the same Alpha Company. There were now new platoon commanders, so as "an experienced vet," I was now the XO of the company. That lasted for under a week until the Company Commanding Officer received a staff assignment. I became the new CO. Here I was, just a 2nd Lieutenant, 23 years old, and in charge of a company of 200 men, a company of over 100 Vietnamese infantrymen, an Army dog team, tanks, amphibious vehicles, mortars, and artillery. Looking back, it was surreal. A year earlier I could not have imagined being given this much responsibility. My primary job now was to conduct operations which we called "County Fairs." We would surround a village before daylight with two platoons of Marines and then use another platoon to sweep the village using ARVN linguists, a medical team to treat villagers, and the Army dog teams. Frequently, we would capture, or kill, five to six VC who had been identified or had tried to escape. This was all still in that same region south of the river where I had been wounded the second time.

When I asked Sim how he felt about the Vietnamese living in these villages during County Fair operations, he became very animated and emotional.

Us 2nd Lieutenants weren't worried about what the generals were worried about. We weren't concerned about "winning over the hearts and minds" of anyone. What I was worried about was survival, food, ammunition, and security for my Marines. My job was to kill as many enemy as possible, without getting our Marines killed. For me, it was that simple.

I got the impression that Sim did not say this with malice - he was stating the obvious about the ugliness of war: kill or be killed. Seeing so many American youngsters, many still teenagers, die near you, and nearly being killed yourself, does not leave much room for compassion. If you were not totally focused on survival, your chances of leaving Vietnam alive were greatly diminished. During his tour in Vietnam, Marines in his Alpha Company were awarded over 200 Purple Hearts for wounds suffered. Counting replacements, that same company had 100% casualties over a two-month period. No one knows exactly how many Vietnamese casualties, soldiers or civilians, occurred in this same region during Sim's tour in Vietnam. What is certain is that it was brutal for all, and deadly for many.

Sim's battalion was transferred back to Okinawa in October 1966. As he put it, *"That was the end of war for me."* His next assignment was at Camp Pendleton in California where he trained units for upcoming duty in Vietnam. He told me, *"I hated this because I was now practicing war; I had already done war."* While stationed at Pendleton, Sim had the opportunity to learn data processing at an Air Force base in Texas before receiving an assignment in Washington, D.C. He married in May 1968 and resigned from the service in February 1971. Sim received a Master's degree from George Washington University and ultimately became President of Blue Cross/Blue Shield of the National Capital area and Chairman of the local School Board. He also taught for 18 years at Northern Virginia Community College and raised three sons with his wife, Mary.

Tom Dames

Oak Park, Illinois
"We weren't looking for trouble"

Tom and I had several classes to-gether at the Naval Academy, but I had no occasion to see him after our graduation in June 1965. I went into submarines, while he joined the Civil Engineer Corps (CEC). I later learned that he had served in Vietnam. I spoke to him via computer at his home in Atlantic Beach, Florida, where he lives with his wife, Ursula.

I went to Fenwick High School in my hometown of Oak Park, Illinois, not far west of Chicago. It was a very Catholic school run by the Dominican Friars. Another of our classmates, Daven Anderson, was with me in the same high school and was a good friend. I tried out for basketball each year but never made the team. One day in our library, I found a pamphlet about the Naval Academy; the cover showed a midshipman sailing. I immediately thought that this looked like something I wanted to do. Because I was a good student, the school sent my name and credentials to Notre Dame. Our school had a very good reputation and I learned that I had been admitted there without even applying. The problem was that our family was wrestling with how to pay the tuition. Daven was planning to apply to the Academy and encouraged me to do so. I took the Navy physical but failed the eye exam. The hospital corpsman who gave me the exam encouraged me to apply for an eye waiver even though he said "no one ever gets it." By the time I graduated from high school in early June 1961, I had forgotten about the Naval Academy, but on June 23 I received a telegram from USNA with the news that I had received an appointment and that I should be there on June 28. Believe it or not, the telegram also said, "There is no need to reply to this telegram. If you want this appointment, just show up. If you don't show up, never mind." This is a true story! It was not until I picked up my envelope with my name on it at USNA when I arrived that I really believed that I was going to become a midshipman.

At the Academy I found out that I didn't want to be a Marine and was not enamored by the Naval officers who were our Company Officers. My eyes got worse while at the Academy so I started to look at options. Our classmates who had decided to go into the Civil Engineer Corps (CEC) told me that after one year of service we would be sent to one of the top engineering schools in the U.S. This appealed to me, so I applied and was accepted. A dozen guys in our class went directly into the CEC; ultimately, there were 20 members of our class who became CEC officers. After graduation I was assigned to the Naval Base at Great Lakes, Illinois, which was near my hometown. I was the assistant in charge of all Naval construction going on around the Midwest. Following this year, the Navy sent me to Purdue to study Civil Engineering and gave me two years to get a B.A. and M.A. I also took classes to complete all the academic requirements for a Ph.D. I requested another year to complete my Ph.D., but I was told that my services were needed in Vietnam. I was sent to Port Hueneme in Oxnard, California, which was the main Seabee Base, for three months before being sent to Vietnam and assigned to Naval Mobile Construction Battalion (NMCB) 133. Everyone assigned to these battalions is called a Seabee, officer or enlisted.

Many Naval officers, including myself, have been unaware of the distinction between members of the CEC and Seabees. Officers in the Combat Engineer Corps (CEC) are professional engineers whose role is to plan, build, and operate all shore facilities for the U.S. Navy. Most of the current 1500 CEC officers have Master's degrees or above. They authorize contracts and evaluate and approve completed projects. They also administer all public works projects on Navy bases, even to the level of grass mowing. Each officer is trained and "warranted" to be a Contract Officer who has the authority to commit the U.S. to contracts conducted by civilian organizations. These same CEC officers also command Seabee units, which are organized in the same manner as the Marine Corps, namely squads, platoons, companies, battalions, regiments, and brigades (listed from smallest to largest). The original enlisted members of the Seabees during WW II were seasoned craftsmen or heavy equipment operators who volunteered to build things for the Navy. Currently when young men and women enlist in the Navy and want to join the Seabees, they receive extensive training in specialty areas, such as how to maintain and operate bulldozers, make concrete, or construct buildings. Tom proudly told me that morale in the Seabees has always been high and that many Seabees re-enlist.

You need to understand that Seabees are trained both in construction and warfighting. There is some interesting history with the Seabees; they were not your average sailors. The average age of Seabees in WW II was about 40. Apparently, they didn't care much for discipline, but they were all very good at what they did, which was using heavy equipment and building facilities all over the Pacific. These original units were so successful that the Navy kept the concept which continues today.

I had two deployments to Vietnam. The first began in September 1968 when I reported to my battalion which was already at Phu Bai near Hue. I was a Lieutenant in charge of C company. I had a Master Chief Petty Officer as my Company Chief. Each platoon had a Chief Petty Officer in charge, with other Petty Officers in charge of each squad. Our most junior men were not called seamen, but "construction men." When I arrived, conditions at Phu Bai did not involve much fighting. We strengthened the small airport there for heavy combat aircraft by overlaying the runways with pierced steel planking. We also improved the Petroleum, Oil, Lubricants (POL) facilities to protect them from potential incoming fire. All the POL was stored in rubber bladders which made great targets for the enemy. Our first order of business was to build revetments around these POL storage areas. We did this by taking the same pierced steel planks, stacking them vertically, and filling them with sand. We also built these same structures around areas where airplanes were parked. Everything we built we tried to portray as useful not only for our military but also for the people of Vietnam. We hoped that the enemy would recognize this and allow us to build things. We weren't looking for trouble.

While I was there, we mostly built stuff along Highway 1, the main north-south highway in this part of Vietnam. When we did some work west in the jungle areas - usually building firebases - we airlifted small bulldozers and backhoes to do the work. To build these firebases we first dug holes and reinforced them with steel and timber to provide safety for people to hunker down when receiving incoming artillery. Basically, it was not so much a permanent base, but more of a place for troops to come and go on patrols. We always had security provided to us when we were out in the boonies building these firebases. When we were working on roads, the Army or the Marines would sweep these areas for mines before we began our work. When we left a site at night, we would leave much of our equipment unguarded. The only problem we had was some minor pilfering; when we returned the next day, none of our big equipment was booby-trapped or damaged.

When we were in Vietnam after Tet, much of the fighting had been exhausted. When we drove through Hue, for example, the university there was back in operation and things were relatively "normal." Earlier, Hue had been a bloodbath during Tet and the fight to retake it. We did have one SEABEE killed in an unfortunate "friendly fire" situation when he was shot by a South Vietnamese soldier. Writing the letter informing his family of this tragedy was very difficult; I still remember the grief we all felt.

Our Seabee deployments at that time were generally eight to nine months in-country, followed by four months back at Gulfport, Mississippi. We left our heavy equipment in Vietnam so that it could be used by the battalion which rotated in to relieve us. Because I arrived after my battalion had been in Vietnam for several months, my first deployment was only 4 months. I arrived in August and came home in December. While our battalion was back in Gulfport, we would spend some time at Marine bases teaching our new personnel how to fight. We also trained on our heavy equipment at Gulfport. For me, this was not the fun part of being a Seabee.

In May 1969, we deployed to Gia Le which was also in the north part of I Corps, not far from the DMZ. The 101st Army Airborne had taken over this base from the Marines. The Army loved us because we could do things which the Army engineers could not accomplish. For example, we made concrete and asphalt to build hundreds of things in and around this gigantic base. We actually opened a quarry in a nearby mountain and used our powdermen and blasters to open up the mountain. We then used rock crushers to change the big pieces into small pieces. We got the cement in bags from the U.S. The sand came from the beaches, but it had to be washed to remove the salt which will ruin the concrete. For the asphalt, we received 55-gallon drums of pitch which we would heat with rock and put it in a truck to be spread and paved. We had big and little pavers to smooth the asphalt roads we built. The Seabees had a ship designated to take all of our materials from Da Nang to the mouth of the Perfume River where it was offloaded onto trucks to bring it to us wherever we were working.

Our construction battalion also had two Supply Officers, one doctor, one hospital corpsman, a dentist, dental techs, and one chaplain making us a self-contained unit which could be dropped anywhere and go to work immediately. In my opinion the Seabees got more satisfaction out of being in the military than most others because we could always see our results. If we built a runway, it was there for everyone to see. You would be surprised what Seabees could wrangle from the supply system. For a cubic yard of concrete, you could get anything in Vietnam.

Trang Tien Bridge after center span rebuilt by Tom's Seabees

I did have experience during our second deployment to work with a Vietnamese Province Engineer to rebuild the famous Trang Tien Bridge across the Perfume River in Hue. The center span had been heavily damaged by the North Vietnamese during their massive attack on the city during Tet. We "obtained" a large barge and put a crane and pile driver on it to drive three steel pylons into the substrate of the river to hold the new span. Our work took close to three months but when we were finished, the middle part of the bridge could now support a tank. Unfortunately, the other original sections could not, but a steady flow of all other vehicles could now flow from Da Nang north, not only to Hue, but all the way to the DMZ.

Tom spent at least 10 minutes explaining the engineering details of how the Seabees re-built this historic bridge from May to July 1969. The bridge had been originally commissioned in 1886 by Vietnamese royalty. The famous French engineer, Gustave Eiffel, (of Eiffel Tower fame) designed and supervised construction until its completion in 1899. It was twice destroyed in war, first in 1946 and again in 1968. This was a long and elegant metal bridge, built in the Gothic style with six arches. It has long been an important part of the city of Hue and has inspired numerous novelists and poets. Today it is colorfully lit at night and appears to sparkle. Tom's involvement in the bridge reconstruction was far more functional; his goal was to provide a repaired bridge to allow two-way traffic north and south.

When we came back after this deployment, I was preparing for another deployment but was selected to be an aide to the 2-star admiral in charge of all Seabees in the Pacific at Pearl Harbor. When I left there, I was able to finish my Ph.D. at Purdue. The war was over by then.

Tom went on to serve in a variety of CEC assignments throughout the world. Among other accomplishments he supervised building a new base for destroyers in Greece and an air station in Iceland. Ironically, after Tom was selected for Admiral in 1992, he returned to Hawaii in the same position as the 2-star Admiral he had been with 20 years earlier.

Throughout our conversation, Tom spoke with great enthusiasm and obvious pride for the accomplishment of the Seabees both in Vietnam and in other endeavors since. What remains without doubt is that an overseas war cannot be sustained without a military branch which, as Tom frequently said, "builds stuff."

Bob Sullivan

Wallkill, New York

"Not a good way to win the hearts and minds of the Vietnamese"

I did not know Bob during our days at the Naval Academy. Because we began our studies in June 1961 with over 1250 classmates (and ended with 802 in 1965), this was not an unusual situation. Although all midshipmen live in the same building, Bancroft Hall, it is the *largest* college dormitory in the world, housing over 4000. Upon our graduation Bob went into the Marine Corps, while I pursued a career in submarines. It was not until at least 40 years after our commissioning as officers that we met at a monthly luncheon for Class of 1965 members at a restaurant in Annapolis. Since that initial meeting, our families have become close friends. I interviewed Bob at his home in Woodbridge, Virginia, where his wife, Peggy, shared stories with my wife, Sharry, while Bob and I talked about his experiences on Amtracs in Vietnam.

I was born in a small town about 70 miles northwest of New York City. My father was a Registered Nurse at the local state prison. Because I was the oldest of seven children, I knew that my only hope for going to college was to receive a scholarship. As a youngster, I had been fascinated by the TV series, "Men of Annapolis," and decided that I should try to go there. I was fortunate to receive an appointment from Senator Jacob Javits. After graduating from high school, within three days I was a midshipman with a much shorter haircut! Four years later, when it came time for service selection, I chose Marines based on the impression I had gathered of the Marine officers at the Academy. They were very sharp individuals. Upon graduation, I married Peggy and went straight to the Marine Basic School for six months of training. I was then sent to California for training in tanks and amphibian vehicles at Camp Del Mar. I was now the father of a daughter but had to kiss her and Peggy goodbye as they flew back to her home in Pennsylvania while I boarded a flight to Vietnam.

I arrived at Da Nang in March 1966. My orders were to 1st Landing Vehicle Track (LVT) Battalion which was located on the outskirts of Da Nang at the base of Hill 327. There was also an artillery battery at this location which would fire maybe five rounds from their 105 mm howitzers about every hour most nights in H&I operations. These were "Harassment and Interdiction" rounds and were aimed toward pre-determined target areas maybe six miles away. There were not necessarily enemy troops in these locations, but it kept them guessing as to where we might be shooting next. I found that after hearing this BAM, BAM, BAM each night, I could sleep under almost any conditions.

I was the platoon leader of 11 of those mechanical monsters, the amphibian track vehicles. The full name was LVTP-5, where the P stood for Personnel. Everyone called them Amtracs. We used these to resupply infantry units, whether via roads or rivers because Amtracs could go anywhere. We could carry up to 20 combat loaded Marines and drop them off wherever they needed to go. Our biggest challenge was not small arms fire, but land mines the enemy had placed to disable our units. Our Amtracs had 10 fuel tanks underneath, and if these exploded, we could lose that LVT. Fortunately, the detonation would usually damage only the track of the vehicle, but not injure anyone. We would always travel in a column of three to ten Amtracs, so we would leave a damaged one with 2 or 3 other vehicles while we repaired it in the field. We were fortunate to not suffer any personnel casualties on these trips. The other threat was fire from rockets, RPG's, because they could penetrate and explode inside. Again, we were lucky because none of those hit us. I would usually ride in the front vehicle with an open hatch; the crew chief was generally a corporal. We could go seven knots in a river and had a max speed of 30 mph on land. If the Amtrac got stuck, we would tow it out with two of the other LVT's. Because we had to navigate by the light of the moon or compass bearings, we had few nighttime operations. Our general pattern was to go out at least twice a week to resupply Marines in the field. We would get our Amtracs refueled by trucks at a predetermined location on a road in the general vicinity of whatever camp we were near. We could, in an emergency, get refueled using 55-gallon drums, but it was a real pain.

Second Lieutenant Sullivan in Vietnam

For two months, our platoon was attached to infantry conducting operations from Hill 55. While I was there, I met one of the Marine officers whom I had admired at the Academy, Clyde Dean. He had been a Captain while serving at USNA and had since been promoted to Major. He had a superb reputation among both officers and enlisted.

Three Marines were in each LVT: the driver, crew chief, and mechanic. The crew chief tells the driver where to go and the mechanic is invaluable when there is any breakdown. He would also man the machine gun in a firefight. My men became very proficient at changing out tracks whenever they were damaged. As we moved along in a line, we would generally maintain a distance of three to four vehicles between each Amtrac. If trouble with an enemy developed, we would spread out into a fan formation to fight the enemy with our .30 caliber machine guns which were mounted forward in a turret. Sometimes we would move this gun to a better location depending on the situation. There were other Amtrac variants which had a 105-mm howitzer, but none of ours were so configured. Our main role was to move Marines and to resupply them while they were in the field.

Hill 55 was sort of a semi-permanent Marine outpost. We did a few operations with tanks and infantry in nearby rice paddies. Most of the enemy in this area were Viet Cong. One of our occasional assignments was to transport ARVN troops. A humorous thing happened when we were moving some ARVN soldiers in an Amtrac. One soldier was carrying his dinner, a live chicken, tied to his back, but the chicken kept pecking our crew chief. Finally, my corporal reached over and put his thumb under the chicken's beak while placing his fingers on the two breathing holes in the chicken's beak until it expired. When the chicken stopped moving, the ARVN fellow finally realized that his dinner was dead. This created quite a commotion. War is insane.

I had to fire a M-14 rifle on Hill 55 when some rounds were coming in. We were not sure what was going on, but that was the only time I personally had to fire a weapon in Vietnam. I did not spend my entire 13 months in Vietnam because we would periodically rotate back and forth to Okinawa in Japan for repairs and refurbishment of our equipment. After I became trained as an Embarkation Officer, one of my new assignments was to load tanks, jeeps, Amtracs, and motorized equipment from the coast onto ships like LPD's and LSD's for transportation to and from Okinawa. Loading the damaged vehicles was sometimes a problem because they often had to be towed onto LSM's to take them to the larger ships offshore. On the way back from Okinawa in September 1966 we did a landing with the infantry south of Da Nang and encountered resistance. I was told that there were a few hundred KIA's of Viet Cong during this landing, but I was not involved in this fighting.

The vessels which Bob mentions are vessels typically used by the Navy to conduct amphibious operations. A LPD is a "Landing Platform Dock." It can transport up to 800 Marines and all their associated equipment, including Bob's Amtracs and support helicopters. LSD is a "Landing Ship

Dock" and has similar capabilities. The LSM, "Landing Ship Medium," is a much smaller vessel which can be used to ferry tanks and Amtracs from the beach to larger ships offshore.

The amphibious landing Bob mentioned was Operation Deckhouse VI. It was a search and destroy operation conducted from February 16 to March 3, 1967, by the Battalion Landing Force of the 1st Battalion, 4th Marines in Quang Ngai province on the coast of the South China Sea. Bob's platoon of Amtracs was offloaded directly into the sea approximately one half mile offshore and then proceeded to the beach with a contingent of Marine infantry inside each. The Amtrac uses "scoops" on its tracks to "paddle" through water to reach shore. The same mechanism allows the Amtrac to transit rivers, swamps, and lakes. A ramp in front is lowered to allow infantry to exit. During land operations, the Marines would often sit atop the Amtrac rather than inside due to the danger of mines and also due to the high temperatures in Vietnam. The "Deckhouse" concept was to quickly insert a large number of Marines into a hostile area, conduct a sweep of the immediate region to find and eliminate enemy forces, then exit a now-sanitized area. At the conclusion of these combat encounters, the Marines and equipment were re-loaded to the offshore ships which had been waiting for them. As opposed to earlier Deckhouse operations, I have been unable to find official casualty numbers for Marines or enemy forces during Deckhouse VI. A series of these Deckhouse landings and sweeps took place in various South Vietnamese locations from May 1966 through March 1967. It appears that Bob's platoon was involved in the last one.

Life at the remote bases was better than the Marines on patrol who were sleeping in foxholes. We usually slept in canvas tents, but there was no running water. In terms of daily "needs," we would take a leak into "piss tubes" which were casings from a used artillery or tank round embedded at 45 degrees into the ground. For defecation, there were four 55-gallon drums cut in half with a piece of plywood with round holes on top to sit on. Periodically, someone would be tasked to burn these. We would have local Vietnamese come into camp to be barbers and do laundry for us; it was never certain that they were not Viet Cong.

One of the lessons we quickly learned in order to avoid anti-vehicle explosions on the roads was to not use the roads with our Amtracs, but to simply plow through rice paddies. When the rice farmers inevitably complained about the damage, our people would pay them in local currency. It was not a good way to win the hearts and minds of the Vietnamese, but we were not getting killed by land mines.

After Vietnam, I was supposed to go to Iceland, but unbeknownst to me, I had received orders to the Marine Barracks at the Naval Ammunition Depot in Earle, New Jersey. It was shore duty, but keeping track of the young Marines was challenging due to continuing issues of alcoholism and drugs.

I suppose that my honest reaction to what we were doing during my time in Vietnam can best be summarized as "mixed feelings." Knowing what I know now, I do not disavow my role, but I am conflicted about it.

Following his tour in New Jersey, Bob had multiple assignments with the Marines both in the U.S. and overseas, including several in Okinawa. He retired after 25 years of service in the Marine Corps with the rank of Colonel.

Bob Wahlfeld

Paducah, Kentucky
"Rocket Man"

Bob is one of several of my Naval Academy classmates who is battling Parkinson's disease. The seeds for this terrible, debilitating disease afflicting him were undoubtedly sown while he was exposed to the herbicide chemical, Agent Orange, during his service in the Vietnam War. The herbicide was actually a mixture of equal parts of two separate chemical concoctions, both defoliants, which was sprayed relentlessly (some estimate 20 million gallons) by the U.S. on Vietnamese (and Laotian) vegetation over a ten-year period from 1961 to 1971 in an effort to eliminate hiding places for enemy combatants. One of the ingredients, dioxin, has been proven to cause significant health problems, both in those exposed (Americans, Vietnamese, Cambodians, and Laotians), and in some cases, their offspring. Vietnam now claims that over three million of its citizens were affected. In addition to several types of cancer, the Veterans Administration lists numerous other illnesses caused by exposure to Agent Orange, including Parkinson's disease. In retrospect, from the perspective of many American servicemen, the decision to use these chemicals was a devastating example of long-term friendly fire.

Bob, by his own admission, has "good and bad days" due to this disease. His wife, Janine, is very supportive and assists Bob daily. I did our interview in his home in Fredericksburg, Virginia, on what he termed, "a very good day." His voice was weak, but animated, while we enjoyed a lunch which Janine prepared.

Although I was born in Kentucky, I actually grew up in Peoria, Illinois, where my dad returned from service in England following World War

II. For some reason I always wanted to be a sailor, so when I arrived at the Academy, I joined the sailing team and really liked it. My service selection choice was to go naval aviation, but right after graduation, I got sick and ended up being hospitalized at the Naval Academy for three weeks. Once I recovered, my assignment was to teach sailing to the incoming midshipmen. One night I was invited to a reception at the Superintendent's quarters. During some small talk, the Superintendent told me that, instead of going to flight school, I should go surface navy for a while. My orders were changed, and right after I got married in December 1965, I was assigned to the USS LOWRY (DD-770). It was an old WW II destroyer, and we went straight to a deployment in the Mediterranean. My sailing experience served me well, and I quickly qualified as an Officer of the Deck. In fall 1966 I received orders to another destroyer, USS KEPLER (DDE-765), which had been involved in blockade duty during the Cuban Missile Crisis in late 1961. The ship was on its way to Vietnam, and I picked it up in Hawaii.

KEPLER was frequently assigned duty supporting Naval Gunfire Liaison Officers who were stationed ashore. These guys would be up in small airplanes providing support to Army or Marine units on the ground by calling in air or naval gunfire support. They would give us coordinates so we could fire our five-inch guns at enemy locations. I was the Combat Information Officer coordinating this gunfire from KEPLER. Basically, our role was to make life miserable for the VC. We would do this for 3-4 days at a time before moving to a new location.

We were then assigned to participate in Operation Sea Dragon off the coast of North Vietnam. Our main mission up there was to find and destroy small enemy boats attempting to run down the coast to bring supplies, ammunition, and weapons to the communists in the south. We also did a lot of shore bombardment of targets ashore, such as radar installations, bridges, and surface-to-air missile (SAM) sites. On our first Sea Dragon mission we were fired at from the shore, which was sort of a wakeup call. We were often inside 10,000 yards from the beach, and our ship was once hit by the North Vietnamese. Eight of our crew were injured by shrapnel, but no one was killed. One night during an operation we were supposed to fire into an area where there was a suspected "truck park." We would usually fire 100 rounds or so. Because the targets were in the north, we never knew for sure if we actually hit anything meaningful, but the powers to be always put out statistics saying how much we had destroyed. During that deployment we fired over 27,000 rounds and had to replace our gun barrels because they wear out when used that much. We replaced them ourselves. We got re-supplied with food, stores, and ammunition every four days by leaving shore to meet our supply ship, USS SACRAMENTO (AOE-1).

There were several interesting situations up north while we were there. An Air Force plane was shot down south of Dong Hoi and the pilot and his back-seater ejected over the sea, but not too far offshore. We were further out to sea but were tasked to look for them closer to shore. Fortunately, we were able to locate the parachute and then rescue the pilot just 5000 yards off the beach. We fished him out of his parachute, but we never found the other airman. Obviously, we had mixed feelings.

There is always uncertainty at sea, especially at night or in low visibility situations. We had two such situations on KEPLER while I was onboard. The Marines flew A-6 attack aircraft out of Da Nang along with Air Force and Navy aircraft also in the area between 17 and 19 North. We soon learned that there was little, if any, effective coordination between them and us. We could listen to the Air Force airborne command center directing traffic but could not easily communicate with them. One night they were directing Marine aircraft looking for NVN vessels and the A6's apparently spotted us on their radar. They didn't know we were there and didn't know our call sign. Pretty soon we figured out that they were targeting us, so we kept trying to warn them that we were a U.S. ship. Fortunately, at the last minute, they heeded our warning. Apparently, even though they heard us, they thought that the voice they were hearing was some North Vietnamese trying to fake them because our air controller had a strong southern accent that they could not understand!

Our second situation occurred as KEPLER was heading to a port visit in Hong Kong. The direct-path track took us closer to the Chinese island of Hainan in the northern part of the South China Sea. Our radar watch standers reported that an airborne contact was approaching us from the north (as if coming from Hainan). We kept tracking it and went to Battle Stations in order to protect our ship if attacked. The plane strangely was not moving as fast as a fighter or an attack aircraft, so we kept tracking it as it got closer. We had no effective air defense systems on KEPLER and had determined that, if attacked, we would fire whatever we had to deter whatever was coming at us. It kept coming but fired no weapons. As it passed by, we visually saw that it was a 4-engine turboprop plane, undoubtedly one of our own P-3 aircraft. We secured from Battle Stations and proceeded to Hong Kong with a big sigh of relief.

These near-miss friendly fire situations which Bob discussed were not unusual and often did not turn out well. In 1968 three Australian sailors aboard a Royal Australian Navy guided-missile destroyer, HMAS HOBART, were killed while operating at night in the South China Sea just north of the DMZ. HOBART was there with USS BOSTON, USS EDSON, a U.S. Coast Guard cutter, and two U.S. PCF's (Swift boats). Suddenly some unidentified aircraft attacked both Swift boats and destroyed one. The cutter responded immediately and was able to rescue the survivors who claimed that the attackers had been North Vietnamese helicopters - even though none had been reported to be operating remotely close to this area. Soon two jet aircraft appeared and were evaluated as friendly. Much to everyone's surprise and horror, these two planes launched missiles hitting HOBART and BOSTON. The heavy armament on BOSTON prevented any serious damage, but one sailor on HOBART was killed and two others injured. The attacking aircraft came back for another missile launch and both hit the Australian destroyer killing another sailor and wounding six more. It was later determined that the attacking planes were U.S. Air Force F-4 Phantoms thinking that they were firing on the reported North Vietnamese helicopters. It was also thought that the original attack on the PCF's was carried out by USAF pilots. Several instances of friendly fire during the Vietnam War were the result of inadequate training, particularly for situations involving multi-service operations. Of course, one of the most important "fog of war" scenarios, the Gulf of Tonkin incident in August 1964, became the pretext for the U.S. Congressional joint resolution which gave President Johnson authority to conduct military operations in Southeast Asia without a declaration of war.

We continued participation in Operation Sea Dragon until April of '67. We steamed back to Newport, Rhode Island, via the Indian Ocean and the Suez Canal. Basically, we did a round-the-worlder. When we got home, I received a call from my detailer saying that the Navy needed to send someone of my seniority to Vietnam. I said, "Why don't you send someone who hasn't been shot at? I've been to that rodeo." He neglected my plea and began talking about sending me as XO on USS WHITE RIVER (LSMR-536). I knew about this type of ship, a Landing Ship Medium (Rocket), from watching Victory at Sea episodes on TV as a kid. They're "rocket ships" which were used in WW II and in Korea. This particular ship had been taken out of moth balls and recommissioned for use in Vietnam. WHITE RIVER needed both a new Captain (CO) and Executive Officer (XO) at the same time because both had been there together since the re-commissioning. The CO and I were supposed to meet the ship in Vietnam, but because of the Tet offensive in early '68, the ship had sailed back to Japan. So, we met it in Yokosuka right after the USS PUEBLO had been captured by the North Koreans. In fact, that ship had been a member of our flotilla, Landing Ship Flotilla ONE. We were given only 12 hours to do a turnover, so both of us had to learn a lot quickly! The captain had no gunfire support experience, but fortunately I had plenty, and the crew was experienced. The good deal was that I would be "fleeted up" to Lieutenant, which may have made me one of the first Lieutenants in our class.

In addition to three LSMR's, WHITE RIVER and her two sister ships, USS CLARION RIVER (LSMR-409) AND USS ST. FRANCIS RIVER (LSMR-525), the Navy had taken USS CARRONADE (IFS-1), out of mothballs to provide intense close-range seaborne support for forces ashore in Vietnam. CARRONADE (IFS-1), an Inshore Fire Support Ship, was a newer variant of the LSMR. It had similar weapons and capabilities, just a different classification. The original designation, Landing Ship Medium (Rocket), accurately described the missions during WW II in support of amphibious landings in the Pacific. In both Korea and Vietnam, most assignments were to bombard enemy troops and fortifications within range of the shoreline. These four ships fired hundreds of thousands of rockets supporting not only U.S. troops, but also South Vietnamese (ARVN) and Korean (ROK) forces during the Vietnam war. The LSMR had incredible firepower for its size and was feared by both Viet Cong and North Vietnamese units.

USS WHITE RIVER firing rockets

*We had a crew of 140 enlisted men and 8 officers. Living conditions for our crew were terrible. They had to go through the ready room full of ammo and rockets to get to their quarters. The whole purpose of our ship was to launch a **lot** of 5-inch rockets **fast**. We could fire 32 at once, and occasionally fired over a thousand in under a minute. We carried 16,000 solid fuel rockets, but their motors were very unstable. Each had a warhead like a 5-inch gun. The rockets were spin-stabilized by nozzles. They were not that accurate but were better than ones recently used by terrorists. When the rocket motor did not ignite (called a hang fire) that was a big problem because it was stuck in the firing tube. All our guys who had to solve this incredibly dangerous situation had to wear asbestos suits and pray. Almost all received bronze or silver stars for their bravery.*

Our usual tactic was to saturate an area with these rocket projectiles. There were several types of rockets. Some would go 12,000 yards with a small warhead; others were a shorter range, maybe 1500 yards, but with a larger warhead. When we fired these weapons at night, it would light up the sky. The enemy hated our ship and referred to us as "dragon ships." Our firepower was estimated to be equal to that of six destroyers, because in addition to the rocket launchers, we had two 40-mm automatic cannons, one in the bow and one on the stern. There was also a 5-inch/38 gun aft. During my time on the ship, we fired 120,000 rockets. After we had used most of our rockets, we would go into our facility at Cam Ranh Bay to reload.

Because we had essentially no armor for protection, we were supposed to never get closer than 1000 yards from shore, but we often paid no attention to this. We had a shallow draft and could get close to shore whenever needed so that we could pound the enemy. The reason they told us never to go inside 1000 yards was because, if we got hit by a mortar or a B-40 rocket, it could blow up the whole ship like what happened to one LSMR that got hit by a kamikaze at Okinawa in WW II. If we were to take a hit in a critical location, the ship would instantly become a huge explosion taking us all with it.

We were assigned "gun line" duties in all four Vietnamese Corps areas but were often in the south in IV Corps while I was aboard. We had some weapons fired against us down there, but they would have to be crazy to start a fight because, if they did not sink us, they were dead. When we fired our rockets, they would light up the sky for miles around. We would often fire 32 rockets at once, BOOM, BOOM, BOOM! I remember the spotters ashore frequently yelling "Holy, shit!" after we fired these salvos.

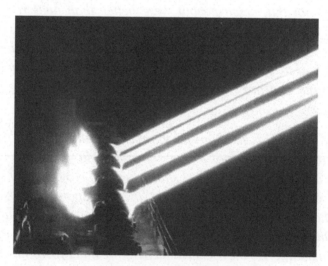

Night rocket fire from a LSMR

We did several ops in the far south of Vietnam around the Ca Mau Peninsula and all the way over to Phu Quoc Island just south of the Cambodian border. We would often work with Swift boats stationed in the region. Most of that area in that peninsula was under Viet Cong

78

control in early 1969. We tried to break that, but don't think that we ever succeeded. What we learned was that if we could get our ship near the VC, they were in big trouble. They sometimes fired at us, but we were never hit. There were splashes in the water near us, but they never scored a direct hit. Our ops near Phu Quoc Island were often with SEAL teams, usually providing diversion for them to get ashore. We actually put our bow right up on the shore to do rocket launching because we could see that it was safe; there were no mangroves on that part of the island to obscure our view. Cambodian patrol boats in this area would generally stay away from us. They were officially neither friend nor foe at that time, but it was believed that the Cambodians had shot down one of our P-3 aircraft. We really had no rules of engagement down there. Our policy was that if they shot at us, we would kill them. Whenever the junks came too close, we would fire shots across their bow to warn them not to get close.

Engineering-wise, WHITE RIVER was fairly reliable, but our Cleveland engines tended to lose cylinder heads. One time we were dead in the water in the middle of the South China Sea but were able finally to get one engine started. We almost always sailed by ourselves, and we were sort of like McHale's navy. At least one of our rocket ships was always in Vietnam during much of the war.

By August 1969, I had had enough and put in my resignation. I got a flight back to San Francisco, and my wife and I bought a VW camper while I did job interviews. I landed a job with Caterpillar and worked for them for the next 35 years until I retired in 2005. We lived in Hong Kong, Manila, Singapore, Indonesia, India, and Switzerland and traveled everywhere. It was a great job.

When Bob discussed his reasons for resigning his commission after four years of service, he remarked that his duty aboard three ships not only kept him nearly continuously at sea in harm's way, but also away from his wife for three years of his first 3 1/2 years of marriage. "And then," he said, "they wanted to send me back to Vietnam again!" Bob certainly had every reason to be weary of war and the long separation from his family. He also had developed a dislike for what he called "a war plan which used heavy weapons in the south."

During the latter part of our conversation, when asked about the personal aspects of fighting a war and killing others, Bob recalled a situation when his destroyer was patrolling along the North Vietnamese coast. All ships and aircraft in the area received new instructions to regard all small boats as enemy combatants presumed to be carrying supplies south. Many small Vietnamese boats were quickly destroyed with untold loss of life. Bob posed the rhetorical question, "Were they military boats or innocent fishermen? We never knew." Also, when firing hundreds of rockets during LSMR operations, it was impossible to be certain who or what those rockets were hitting. As with all previous and subsequent wars, much of what took place in Vietnam was brutal, unfair, and sadly, unavoidable. War blurs moral lines. I cannot help but imagine that Bob recalling such memories 50 years later through the lens of Parkinson's is particularly painful - and ironic.

Frank Peterson
Erie, Pennsylvania
"The Bug-Out Route"

Over the past 20 years I have dined with Frank in Annapolis many times at our USNA Class of 1965 monthly get-togethers. During lunch in early 2022, Frank invited me to his home a few miles away to hear his memories of service as a Marine in Vietnam.

I was born in 1943 while my dad was overseas in the Army. When he got out of the Army, we moved to his hometown of Chicago where he took a job as an internal auditor for a trucking company. I went to Mendel Catholic - it was an all-boys high school run by the Augustinians. Two of my future USNA classmates were also there with me. In high school, I became interested in the military, not sure why. So, I applied to my congressman and got his appointment to the Naval Academy. At Navy, my sport was boxing - mostly at 155 lbs. During my studies I became interested in joining the Marines at graduation. I think this was due to some positive experiences with Marine battalion and company officers while we were there.

After graduation, I went straight to Marine Corps Basic Officer training and was able to be assigned to infantry, my first choice. In December 1965, right after I was married to Kate, I became an infantry platoon leader. I was sent immediately to 3rd Battalion, 4th Marines, and joined them in January 1966 in Okinawa where they were training for duty in Vietnam. I was so naive that I worried that the war would be over before I got there. I was assigned to a rifle company which had three rifle platoons and one weapons platoon which had M-60 machine guns. In March 1966 we arrived near Hue and immediately went to a location near Phu Bai. At that time there was not much action and we lived in tents. When we did local patrols through villages, we would sleep in hooches in the villages or dig foxholes. We always put tablets in the water before we drank it because everything went into those streams. There were a lot of water buffalo wandering around and some met their demise from the young Marines. We spent most of this summer south of Phu Bai.

In late July 1966, the rest of our battalion went north for Operation Hastings up near the DMZ. I was in M (Mike) Company and our job was to remain where we were, providing security. The battalion got hit hard up there and took considerable losses on this operation; two men were awarded the Congressional Medal of Honor during those battles against the North Vietnamese. Pretty soon our company was moved up there to help. We were facing mostly enemy machine gun fire and mortars. We had tanks and artillery support while we were trying to take a ridge on one of those numbered hills, but my platoon began to take losses. One of my Marines who was next to me was shot and killed. I also lost our corpsman while trying to take a hill called 484. The Company Commander had to write the letter home to his family. These were brutal battles. We were throwing grenades, the enemy was throwing grenades, and we eventually had to pull back. The next day we were directed to try again to take the same hill. Another platoon had the lead with us following them. Unfortunately, the fire support from our tanks hit the wrong hill. Our company commander, J.J. Carroll, was killed. A gunny sergeant named Purdy, who had earlier been the first sergeant of my platoon, was seriously wounded. We finally captured this hill, but then we left it the next day. The official line was that the North Vietnamese would grab these hills for observation purposes; I personally believed that they hoped that we would attack so that they could kill more Marines.

Operation Hastings was indeed a brutal battle for three weeks in the summer of 1966. In addition to Frank's Third Marines Division, there were units of the Vietnamese 1st Infantry Division in the fight against the North Vietnamese 324-B Division. In terms of the number of forces, each side had approximately 10,000 men. Well over 100 Marines were killed as the North Vietnamese were crossing the border in a mission to "liberate" Quang Tri Province, south of the DMZ. Thirteen Marines were killed in just one CH-46 helicopter when it was shot down. Several other CH-46's were hit, causing the Marines to refer to the local river area as "Helicopter Valley." In addition to enemy fire, the Marines were handicapped by high elephant grass and unbearable heat and humidity. Numerous stories concerning Operation Hastings can be found online. One of the American commanders, General Walt, described the North Vietnamese as "well-equipped, well-trained, and aggressive to the point of fanaticism."

U.S. Marines attempting to take a hill during Operation Hastings.

One of the most memorable photographs of the Vietnam War was captured by Larry Burrows for *Life* magazine showing wounded U.S. Marine Gunnery Sergeant Jeremiah Purdy on Hill 484 with his head bloody and bandaged while reaching out to assist a fellow wounded Marine. Our Class of 1965 felt a close attachment to Sergeant Purdy because we were exposed to his memorable and inspirational style of training us during the summer 1963 at Dam Neck, Virginia.

We quickly learned the sound of an enemy mortar being fired at us. It makes sort of a "Bloop" sound when it leaves the firing tube. As soon as we heard this, someone would yell, "Mortar!" and we would all jump in a hole - any hole. Because the danger is mostly shrapnel, if we had time, we would pull our flak jacket over our head while we were in the hole. Machine guns had a "rat-a-tat" sound. Their danger was, of course, the bullets. There were many occasions when I had mortar debris land on top of me. The mortar was not a precise weapon, but it could be deadly. Our rifle company had 60 mm mortars to fire back. There was a weapons company in the battalion which had larger 81 mm mortars and also some 105 mm howitzers.

I was with my platoon until January 1967. For my last 45 days, I was assigned as the Liaison Officer to South Vietnamese forces in Quang Tri, south of Dong Ha. This was cushy duty for a few weeks, but suddenly I developed appendicitis and had to have my appendix removed. I was thrown into a jeep bouncing around all the way up to Dong Ha. When I arrived, a Navy medical Captain asked me if I wanted to have him remove it with a local or a general anesthesia. I said local and woke up cold as hell in a fur-lined sleeping bag in an old stone French barracks. I asked the doctor why he had given me an anesthesia choice and he said, "It's probably good that you chose a local because we really don't have a way of bringing you out if something went wrong." There weren't a lot of amenities; I even had to walk down the hall to the head while carrying my IV.

After I recovered from surgery, my 13-month "in-country" time was up, and I received orders to a tank battalion at Camp Pendleton in California. Following this tour, I attended the Navy post-graduate school before getting orders back to Vietnam in 1970. By this time, I was a Captain and was assigned to be a senior advisor to a South Vietnamese army infantry battalion. I was first supposed to go to the Defense Language School to learn Vietnamese, but just before I began, they cancelled the school. Not knowing what to do, I picked up a Vietnamese phrase book. I also had never fired the new M-16 rifle and didn't know how it worked, so I went to Fort Ord's rifle range and learned how to fire it. I flew into Saigon, got flown up to Da Nang, and dumped all my stuff in what was essentially a sandbag compound. I flew a helicopter out to where the South Vietnamese battalion was located. When I hopped off the plane, a Marine captain there greeted me with, "Who the hell are you?" When I told him that I was his replacement, he said, "Good, I'm outta here tomorrow. Good luck." He showed me the "Bug Out Route," which meant where you run if the unit was overrun. Then he left.

Of course, none of the Vietnamese officers spoke any English. We had one interpreter who came up to me and said, "Dai uy," meaning Captain. He wanted to leave, and I said, "Bullshit! You ain't going." Apparently, this was enough for him to stay. I was working with the Battalion Commander who was a Lt Colonel. He was not good and was regarded as dangerous because he could have gotten all of us killed. Fortunately, he was replaced with a senior captain who was good and spoke some English. We didn't have any big action but when we were in the jungles, I killed a huge boa constrictor. We ate it and all I remember is that it was chewy. We also ate some liberated Viet Cong water buffalo; it tasted like gamey beef.

By this time, most of I Corps had been turned over by the U.S. Marines to the U.S. Army, which had begun to work north after Tet in 1968. When Nixon sent people into Laos, our Vietnamese battalion was sent over to some firebases near the border, but never entered Laos. One thing I remember during this phase was all the leeches. I even had one on my balls. The Vietnamese told me to burn it off, so I used my cigar and put the ashes on the spot afterward to heal it. Insects were always a problem. We had to take anti-malarial pills each day, and when I was with Marines on my first tour, I had the responsibility to ensure that each of my men took theirs daily. I had only one of my guys get malaria; I was convinced that he had got it before he came to us.

My tour advising the Vietnamese lasted from April 1970 to April 1971. When I left, it was pretty quiet in terms of fighting. I could drive from our location up to Da Nang in a jeep by myself. I only got to Da Nang a few times. Once I was called up there to "receive some news." I was worried that they were going to tell me something terrible had happened to my wife, Kate, but the news was that my father had passed away. To the government's credit, I was put on a plane and was back in Chicago in two days for my dad's funeral.

My assignment following this tour was to be an instructor at Quantico teaching computer science. During my presentations I would often throw in some Playboy centerfolds to keep everyone awake. I would get fired if I did this today! I taught for three years and then resigned and went into the reserves. I did work for management firms in the DC area for several years. While I was in the Marine reserves, I wore my uniform only once and retired as a Lt Colonel in 1990. It was cushy duty where my initial drills were with a public affairs unit. I then went to law school at Georgetown University and later drilled with a unit of lawyers.

Frank, like many of the Marines I interviewed, saw his role as "kill or be killed." He felt that many of the "body count" reports were "bullshit." He frequently told me how proud he was of the young Marines who operated with him: "When your unit operates in the manner you taught them, you're very proud."

John Quisenberry

Jackson, Mississippi

"Well, this is going to make a great story"

When a classmate mentioned to me that "Quis" was one of our aviators who had the bad fortune to have to eject from his aircraft, but the good fortune to have survived, I called to hear his story. I interviewed him via computer from his home in Los Angeles where he lives with his wife, Kathleen.

I was born in Jackson, Mississippi, where my dad was an independent oil lease broker. My mom was a newspaper editor. In high school, I played football for three years and ran some track. I applied to the Air Force Academy but received an appointment to Navy from Senator Stennis. I was initially interested in submarines, but everything changed during our introduction to aviation at Pensacola in the summer between our second and third years at the Academy. I became very enthusiastic about flying and chose that route when service selection arrived. I did well at flight school and got my first choice, to fly jets. I also wanted to be in a single-seat fighter, the Vought F-8 Crusader, and be stationed on the west coast. I was rather naive because my thinking was that I needed to get to Vietnam as soon as possible before the war ended so that I could get aerial action against some MiGs. After training in the F-8 Replacement Air Group (RAG) squadron, I joined squadron, VF-124, which was about to deploy to Vietnam from San Diego on USS BON HOMME RICHARD, (CVA-31), an old WW II carrier with an angled flight deck.

We arrived off the coast of North Vietnam at Yankee Station in late 1967. The U.S. was again bombing North Vietnam, but there were still restrictions on various targets in the Hanoi and Haiphong area. We were flying nearly every day; I did 30 traps in one month. [A trap is a landing - so called because the incoming aircraft lands by catching a wire on the deck of the carrier with a tail hook on the plane.] *The only problem with flying F-8's was trying to land them on a carrier at night. It is very challenging because it is difficult to position yourself properly as you approach the ship, especially on that angled deck on the old Essex class carriers. I never made a night landing that was not terrifying. We did a lot of airborne refueling near the ship; I would generally "tank"* [get fuel] *at least once a flight from one of our airborne tankers. I nearly ran out of fuel three or four times due to problems trying to coordinate the "plug in" to the tanker.*

When the Tet Offensive began in early February 1968, our focus shifted away from flights over North Vietnam to missions around Hue in support of our ground forces who were fighting there. Although our planes were fighters, everyone was now required to carry bombs to support the ground operations. Our vision of these targets was limited by trees and ridges, even when we were very low. We had to rely on Air Force and Army FACs (Forward Air Controllers) to tell us where to drop weapons or fire our guns. We did numerous missions around Da Nang, Hue, and Khe Sanh during this period.

Later, on a mission over the North near Vinh, while we were escorting some A-4 Skyhawks on a bombing mission, two MiG-21's suddenly appeared overhead. One of our F-8's fired a Sidewinder missile which hit the MiG and downed it. I took off after the other MiG, but he pulled up toward the sun where I could no longer see him. As I climbed in chase, I began to lose air speed and was concerned about stalling or having that MiG suddenly show up behind me. So, I dropped my nose and saw the first MiG pilot now in his parachute heading to the ground. Just them I saw the other MiG pass directly over us heading north. He was not in a position to shoot. We never saw him again; I assume that he hightailed it back to his base.

On another mission over the North, I heard an explosion, and my engine began to come apart. I still had control of the plane and tried to head out from land over the South China Sea. I had no desire to eject over North Vietnam where I would almost certainly become a P.O.W. or be killed as soon as I landed. My wingman was with me all the way and as soon as I was over water I attempted to eject. My exact thoughts were, "Well, this is going to make a great story." I pulled the face curtain to initiate the ejection process, but nothing happened! I didn't have time to even yell, "Oh, Shit!" because in about two seconds the black powder under my seat ignited, giving me what can best be described as a hard kick in the ass. I had ejected at about 4000-5000 ft and suddenly I was in the air clear of my plane, but tumbling. I didn't notice getting hit by a wall of air as I was ejected, but I did receive a nasty bruise on the side of my neck from something during the ejection. Soon a small chute opened, and then the main chute popped open. My wingman watched the entire process and stayed close to where I landed in the ocean. Before I hit the water, I followed procedures and released my raft. As soon as I entered the water, I was able to get clear of the parachute and began to paddle away. I wasn't in the water long before a helicopter showed up to get me. They dropped a collar for me to grab and then pulled me up into the helo. As soon as I got in, the crew chief shook my hand and said, "See all those sharks down there circling your raft?"

We were never able to determine what caused my engine to disintegrate. I may have been hit by AAA or the engine may have thrown a blade and destroyed itself. I wanted to fly the next day, but my skipper sent me back to Subic Bay on someone else's plane. I then was told to catch a flight up to Atsugi, Japan, to pick up a replacement F-8 to fly back to the carrier. As I flew that plane back to BON HOMME RICHARD - it was a night flight - I found myself thinking all the time that the engine was making funny sounds. It wasn't, of course; it was all in my mind. I suppose that the eject scene had more of an effect on me than I had realized. Still, I was back flying missions the day after I returned to the carrier.

We were occasionally tasked to do SAR (Search and Rescue) mission for pilots shot down over the North. I did this about a half dozen times. One time I saw a downed Air Force pilot who was in a rice paddy and trying to get to a row of trees. I got as low as I could and began firing 20 mm cannon to suppress anyone who might try to come capture him. After I ran out of ammunition, I continued to fly low and fast to discourage enemy from going after him. I was beginning to run low on fuel and had to leave. Two helicopters came to try to rescue that pilot, but both were shot down. Those SAR helos had possibly the most dangerous missions of the war. I don't think that the pilot on the ground was rescued, but I'm not certain.

On another mission over the North, I watched an A-4 get shot down. I think that it was hit by a SAM, because as I looked over my left wing, it just disintegrated into silver sparklets at 400 kts and disappeared out of sight. When I got back to the ship, I learned that the pilot was due to rotate soon. I thought about that for several days.

Whenever our battle group at Yankee Station conducted an "Alpha" strike, we would be escorting a large group of attack aircraft with targets in the Hanoi and Haiphong region. We would generally be at 20,000 ft looking for any MiGs which might decide to come in for an attack. We were high enough to not have to worry about small arms fire, but higher up we had to contend with surface-to-air missiles, higher-powered AAA, and MiGs. I never saw any MiGs during those strikes.

An Alpha strike was a Navy term used to denote a large air attack by essentially a "deck load" of aircraft, often half the air wing aboard the carrier. During these high-value target operations, the carrier would steam into the wind and remain at General Quarters to recover any aircraft returning with battle damage. Almost always, an Alpha strike was conducted against a target designated by officials in Washington, and it required approval by the Joint Chiefs of Staff.

During normal flight operations, a carrier on Yankee Station would launch and recover aircraft every 90 minutes and do perhaps nine cycles daily over a 12-13 hr period. Then another carrier at Yankee Station would commence flight operations. A carrier would conduct flight operations for 30-35 days, then go "off line" for 6-8 days of R&R and repairs (usually at Subic Bay in the Philippines) before returning to Yankee Station.

A typical deployment of a carrier to Vietnam would last about eight to nine months, including transit time. There were instances of major air operations involving multiple carriers and even U.S. Air Force assets. In order to minimize losses, most missions involved less than two minutes over a given target area, sometimes followed by another attack 15 minutes later. These were grueling, dangerous missions and not everyone returned.

SAMs were a genuine threat to U.S. aircraft conducting missions over North Vietnam. Close to 200 U.S. planes were shot down by SAMs during the war, even though these missiles were mostly 1950s-era Soviet systems. The SA-2 SAM missile was indeed a formidable weapon. They were mobile and were located in well-camouflaged sites. After launch, the missile would accelerate to Mach 3.5 with a maximum range of 25 miles. It could kill targets with its blast-fragmentation warhead at altitudes up to 60,000 ft. There were also hundreds of radar-controlled antiaircraft artillery throughout the North.

By 1968 the North Vietnamese had 8000 AAA weapons, over 350 radar sites, and close to 300 SAM sites. John told me that on some of his missions at night he saw red tracer rounds so thick in the air that they looked like fire hoses. More sobering, he said, "We knew that for every tracer round you saw, there were 6 to 10 actual bullets flying in the air near those firehoses." Most pilots agreed that the most effective Vietnamese air defense was not the weapons being fired, but the bad weather which kept American pilots on their carriers.

On my second cruise on BON HOMME RICHARD, the U.S. was in a bombing halt and did not have nearly as much action. I had this brilliant idea that if I talked young pilots into letting me swap their night missions for my daytime ones, I could become really good at night landings. Usually, my offer was readily accepted. I had been doing this for a while when my Executive Officer came to me and said that he knew what I was up to. He told me that there are two types of F-8 pilots: those who think they can be great by doing extra day landings, and those who think they can improve by doing extra night landings. He then said, "Quisenberry, you're the only dumb ass I have met in that second group." That advice ended my brilliant idea.

John left the Navy in late 1971 and went directly to Europe to ski. He spent summers flying crop dusting jobs in Mississippi while using the winters to study in Germany (and doing a lot more skiing). He then went to law school, and eventually started his own firm in Los Angeles, ultimately increasing in size to 80 employees. He closed the firm in 2009, but still does occasional legal work.

I am not sure how one willingly hops into the cockpit of a fighter plane - any plane - after having to eject. But my experience in getting to know many aviators is that most love to fly so much that it takes priority over much else in life, sometimes including marriage. The only other occupation which I have seen which comes close to this type of almost narcotic behavior is football coaching. Once these thrills are in your blood, they begin to define you. For our Vietnam-era aviators, the thrill of flying combat missions trumped the constant threat of SAM's, engine failures, and landing the F-8.

Cary Van Haaren

Bay City, Michigan
"You guys are doing great"

My goal in talking to Cary was to learn some of the logistics issues associated with the Vietnam War. I interviewed him via computer from his home in Southport, NC.

My father had been a Seabee in the Navy. My hometown, Bay City, Michigan, was a port on the lower end of Saginaw Bay on Lake Huron. Navy ships were being built in the shipyard there, so I had had an early interest in the Navy. Although I was a second alternate for an appointment to the Academy from our congressman, the other two in front of me withdrew or something, because I ended up with the appointment. When service selection time came at Navy, I picked Supply Corps because I was color blind, which disqualified me from being a line officer. Apparently, I had been color blind since childhood, but it was somehow missed on my entrance physical. My interest in the Supply Corps originated during one of our summer training cruises when I was assigned to an AF in WestPac on our first class cruise. I was able to be in the Supply Department for the entire cruise and really enjoyed it.

Cary mentioned that his dad was a Seabee. Unbeknownst to many, Seabees also have a combat role. There is a fascinating 1944 war film, "The Fighting Seabees," starring John Wayne, which highlights this combat mission. The "AF" which Cary discussed was a refrigerated stores ship which carried fresh and frozen food for transfer to deployed ships, both in port and at sea. In the latter case, a ship pulls alongside the AF while both are moving through the ocean and goods are sent from the AF to the receiving ship via temporary lines attached to each ship.

This is called "underway replenishment." These AFs are no longer operated by the Navy, but by the Military Sealift Command. There were also AFSs - a Combat Stores Ship which carries a combination of refrigerated food, fresh and dry stores, repair parts and other consumables, such as toilet paper. WestPac refers to the Western Pacific which is, as far as most American sailors are concerned, basically the Pacific Ocean west of Pearl Harbor, Hawaii.

After I attended Supply Corps School for six months in Athens, Georgia, my first sea assignment came in early 1966 on USS JAMESTOWN (AGTR-3). It was previously the J. HOWLAND GARDNER, a WW II Liberty ship, and had been built in two months near the end of the war. The Navy pulled five of these Liberty ships out of mothballs and converted them into spy ships for use in Vietnam. The TR designation stood for Technical Research, supposedly to help disguise the spy mission. It was essentially a signals and intelligence collection ship. Most of the crew were communications technicians.

When JAMESTOWN left its homeport in Norfolk, I assumed that I would meet it in San Diego. Bad assumption! After it had been fitted out for intelligence gathering, it sailed from Norfolk around the Cape and straight to WestPac. After several plane flights across the Pacific, I arrived aboard by being transferred across water on a high-line from an AF to JAMESTOWN when it was on station in the Gulf of Thailand near the Cambodian border.

The "high-line" which Cary mentions is a method of transfer between two ships at sea. It is hazardous even in calm waters but has the potential to be extremely dangerous in rough seas. The procedure is used to move materials or personnel from one ship to another via a wire strung between the two ships with both moving on the same course (direction) and same speed (often about 10-12 knots). The distance between the ships varies from 50 to 100 feet, which is very close for two large vessels at sea. Complicating matters is a "Venturi effect" - a Physics phenomenon created by the seawater speeding up as it passes between the two ships causing the ships to be drawn closer to each other. A line (rope) is tossed (or shot) from one ship to another to allow a larger line, or metal wire to be secured on each ship. Then material can be passed back and forth via a pulley system. Personnel can be transferred in a basket chair in a similar manner. If the ships come closer during the transfer, the person in the basket can get soaked if dunked in the water. Of course, there is also the constant danger of the line parting which creates an extremely dangerous situation if a person is being transferred. Supply ships carrying food, provisions, repair parts, and fuel become very adept at such transfers. Most of these ships have designated members of the crew to be at critical stations for these operations. One officer to whom I have spoken described these maneuvers as some of the most tense watches he had as Officer-of-the-Deck (the officer "driving" the ship). He always insisted on having the same helmsman (enlisted man who controls the direction of the ship via the rudder) due to his skill and reliability. I have met no one who looks forward to being transferred ship-to-ship via high-line.

Because the Viet Cong had a communications station onshore in Cambodia, the U.S. wanted to monitor its activities 24/7. To do this, we rotated on station with USS OXFORD (AGTR-1). When it was our turn, we would usually anchor in international water at least 12 miles off the coast of Cambodia to be as close as possible to that comm station. About once a month we would get underway and transit a short distance to the U.S. base on a Vietnamese island, Phu Quoc, to drop off reports and intelligence tapes to be sent to Fort Meade. While we were there, we would also pick up mail and get some new movies. If we needed relatively small repair work, a tender was there to assist. Most of our resupply came from an AF which would come to the Gulf of Thailand about once a month. As I said, either us or OXFORD would be on station all the time. That allowed JAMESTOWN to go occasionally to liberty ports, such as Hong Kong, or a logistics base such as Subic Bay in the Philippines. Out of our crew of 300, I had 33 men working for me running the messes (food service) and ship's store and managing our logistics. I was also the Disbursing Officer responsible for paying the crew. I had a large amount of cash, at least $250,000, which I would get from Subic Bay for paydays. Our top speed was 11 knots, so it took quite some time to transit to these other ports. The ship was really an old bucket of bolts which kept breaking down, but the good news was that we never came under enemy fire. There were three places on the ship where none of us who did not possess the appropriate security clearances could go.

I never really asked details about what was going on in there and was never told. During my entire time on JAMESTOWN, the only feedback I heard on what we were doing was an occasional message from Fort Meade saying, "You guys are doing great." I assume that those in our crew doing the intelligence collection received more detail!

USS JAMESTOWN (AGTR-3) off Phu Quoc island

I was aboard JAMESTOWN for 13 months and detached while we were getting repairs in Yokosuka, Japan. I had chosen to go to this ship because I thought that I would be living in San Diego, at least part of the time. I never saw that city until I had an assignment there 12 years later. My next set of orders after JAMESTOWN was to the office of the Supervisor of Shipbuilding at Defoe Shipbuilding Company where I would be the Contract and Materials officer in Bay City, Michigan. When I had left to attend the Academy, I never dreamed that I would end up with an assignment in my hometown in Michigan!

Cary continued his naval career in the Supply Corps in a series of assignments both ashore and at sea until his retirement in 1986. His experience on JAMESTOWN illustrates the clandestine aspects of the Vietnam War of which most Americans were totally unaware. Only recently were materials declassified for the public concerning the operations of these intelligence gathering ships during the Vietnam War. There is little unclassified information available to evaluate how effective the intelligence gathered by these ships on Viet Cong/North Vietnamese activities was in terms of saving American lives or gaining an operational advantage for U.S. forces. It is also interesting that neither the Cambodians nor the Viet Cong attempted to attack these essentially unguarded ships. There were always U.S. Swift boats operating out of Phu Quoc Island which could have come to the rescue, but it certainly appears that JAMESTOWN and OXFORD would have been easy targets for destruction or capture. With their vast array of antennae and communications gear readily visible, there was no doubt of their mission. Because of her age and the availability of other intelligence assets, JAMESTOWN was decommissioned in late 1969 and scrapped in 1970.

It is also important to understand the massive logistics chain necessary to support armed forces deployed in a foreign land. Although many of the post-Vietnam "military entanglements" in which the U.S. has become involved have been based on political decisions, the prosecution of these wars in distant locations is made possible by the logistics capabilities refined during the Vietnam War. Lengthy foreign wars are not possible without ships such as the AF's and AFS's carrying food and supplies to the ships and shore bases engaged in the fighting.

Ron Wecht

Bishop, California

"Boom !! Wham !!"

Several of Ron's Marine friends insisted that I talk to him about his experiences both as an infantry officer and as an aviator. I did not know Ron at the Naval Academy, nor in our subsequent years in the service. I talked to Ron twice via computer from his home in Orinda, California, where he lives with his wife, Sue.

I was born in California in a small town on the east side of the Sierras, not far from the Nevada border. During high school, I watched several episodes of the television series, "Men of Annapolis," and wanted to go there. I applied for an appointment with a California congressman and received it after taking an exam. During our plebe year at Navy, I decided that I wanted to be a Marine because the Marine Corps officers I observed at the Academy were very sharp in comparison to many of the Naval officers. The Marines led by example. After graduation, I took some leave and began Marine Basic School at Quantico, Virginia. My vision had dropped below 20/20, so I wasn't eligible for aviation. My next choice was infantry and I got it. I received orders saying, "Marine Ground Forces, Western Pacific." That translates as Vietnam. I was assigned to the 9th Marine Regiment based at Da Nang, and upon arrival, rode in a truck to 2nd Battalion, 9th Marines, in Cam Ne where I became a platoon leader in F (Fox) Company. The Company Commander told me to shadow one of the other platoon leaders for a week or so to learn my job.

This small village, Cam Ne, became famous in 1965 when Marines were conducting sweeps of areas south of Da Nang which had been Viet Cong strongholds. After receiving enemy fire from inside Cam Ne, Marines carried out orders from their superiors to burn all huts and deport all civilians to refugee camps. The entire operation was filmed by a CBS News television crew and became a flash point back in the U.S. when it was shown on the evening news. The image which stuck with many Americans was that of a Marine lighting a hut on fire with his Zippo cigarette lighter. Much of the background surrounding Marine actions in this village had not been made known to the public. A Viet Cong mortar attack on the U.S. air base at Da Nang in early July 1965 had destroyed several aircraft. In response, Marines received orders to increase patrols south of the base where the suspected attack had originated. When Marines came under fire from one of the hamlets in Cam Ne village, they moved in and found considerable VC weapons, as well as trenches and tunnels. Following standing guidance, the Marines, still under sporadic fire, destroyed all huts and trenches. The CBS crew filmed the entire operation, including scenes of older men and women unsuccessfully pleading with the Marines to spare their huts. Four Marines were wounded in the action. Many of the Marines felt that the CBS report was distorted by failing to include their perspective. When Ron arrived in Cam Ne a year later, the Marines were well aware of this history and had an uneasy relationship with any members of the press.

My company had three rifle platoons and a weapons platoon. I was assigned to one of the rifle platoons which nominally had 42 Marines, but usually far less due to casualties. The Company Commander had a tent and the rest of us lived in foxholes with our ponchos over us when it rained. When I arrived, other than the Company Commander, there were only three officers in the company. We stayed near Cam Ne for a few weeks, then went on an operation to the southwest near Hoi An. There were frequent firefights, and we lost several men. We had a Forward Air Controller working with our company who could call in air support from Marine aviators out of Chu Lai flying F-8's. We never had support from the carriers off the coast while I was there.

The big problem when I arrived was "the Buddhist Uprising." This came about because many of the Buddhists were essentially in a civil war with the Catholic leaders in Saigon. Corruption was a way of life in Vietnamese politics and Thieu and Ky, the two leaders who were running South Vietnam, were Christians. The I Corps region of Vietnam (in the north near the DMZ), which was where we were, was heavily Buddhist, including most of the ARVN troops there. Early in my time in-country when I was still shadowing one of the Platoon Commanders, our company was ordered to go to this bridge on Highway 1 to place a truck on the bridge to block traffic. We had received intelligence that a battalion of dissident ARVN troops was headed north to join the ongoing Buddhist revolution in Da Nang. The plan was to do whatever was necessary to prevent these dissident ARVN forces from reaching an ongoing battle in Da Nang between the two South Vietnamese groups. Soon a convoy of ARVN trucks arrived from the south and found the bridge blocked by our truck. Our Company Commander, a Marine Captain, began negotiating with a senior ARVN officer who had brought up artillery which was now aimed at our truck (and the Captain). There were perhaps 1000 ARVN soldiers facing our platoon, but their troops were strung out all along the road leading to the bridge. The standoff lasted about four hours with both sides continuously talking to higher-ups. Finally, the ARVN decided to turn around and head back south. The entire incident ended up in Time magazine. It was during this incident that at least 700 American mines, "Bouncing Betty's," were stolen by the VC from the ARVN compound while they were gone. Every one of those mines came back to haunt Marines, including me.

The Buddhist Uprising, sometimes called The Crisis in Central Vietnam, took place from March 26 to June 8, 1966, and resulted in close to 150 killed and over 700 wounded (including 23 Americans). In addition to the religious factor, one of the major contributing issues was a power struggle between General The, the ARVN commander in I Corps, and Ky in Saigon. Further information on this conflict can be found online. One of the unintended consequences was that hundreds of American Marines were wounded or killed by the stolen mines left unguarded when the supporters in the ARVN marched north to the bridge where Ron happened to be.

A few weeks later we were on patrol and had just crossed a railroad when I heard a sudden BOOM to my rear. I had been near the front of my platoon when I heard the explosion. My platoon sergeant had been hit by a mine with his foot separated from his leg. His foot was still in his boot a yard or so away from his body. Another Marine had been hit in the jugular. As we tried to clear an area for a medevac helicopter, another mine went off. I found myself with my hand in the Marine's neck wound trying to stop the bleeding while our two corpsmen were desperately working on other wounded. We ended up with three killed and eight wounded. I had also been wounded by one of the explosions which had killed the three Marines near me. The mines were the U.S. ones which had been stolen by the VC from the South Vietnamese while they had left their barracks to drive north. We weren't actually in a minefield; these were just individual mines which had been randomly placed to kill Marines on patrol. I had been hit in the chest by a piece of shrapnel. I was lucky; our corpsman patched me up and sent me back to duty. Later that day I was sent to Da Nang via a medevac; they gave me some pain killers while they fished some metal out of my chest. I thought at the time that everything had been taken out, but just recently learned that I still have a piece in my left side 50 years later. The medical unit at Da Nang was in a tropical hut and looked like what was seen in the TV series, MASH My platoon was pretty much depleted when I got back because they had got hit by more mines while I was gone.

We next learned there was now a major battle going on in Da Nang between Buddhists and loyal ARVN units. Our company was assigned to do a night truck ride to a location east of Da Nang to provide security for a compound that was being built. In the morning, all of a sudden, a South Vietnamese Air Force plane dove in strafing us. Initially, no one was hurt, but soon more planes came in for additional strafing attacks which did injure some of our men. Still, we received orders not to fire back. Many years later I learned that there was an ammo dump across the street from where we were, and a Vietnamese officer was threatening to blow it up if we intervened. If that dump would have gone up, it would have taken out all of us and half of Da Nang. That's why we were ordered not to shoot at those planes, because the Vietnamese guy would have probably blown up that ammo dump. At the time, we had no idea of what was going on. It was a strange, and perplexing, war.

The next morning, we were ordered to sweep south to clear an area toward Hill 55 where there was a major Marine encampment. Due to casualties, I was now the senior platoon leader. My platoon was in the middle of three platoons as we crossed a stream. I again heard the loud unmistakable boom of a mine, followed shortly by another boom which killed our company commander. We were also taking fire, and I was now in charge of the company. I called in air support which helped silence the opposition. Strangely, as we were in the middle of this fight, all I could think of was how those pilots would be drinking beer that night in the Officer's Club in Da Nang while I would be in a foxhole trying to stay alive. It turned out that we had to set up for the night in a cemetery where we slept on the ground instead of digging the usual holes. The next day I took the company back to Hill 55. I was so new and so inexperienced that I was probably the least qualified company commander in Vietnam at the time.

The young Company Commander Wecht

The second time I was wounded happened when we were on patrol not far from the Battalion Headquarters. I was now the Company Commander in a Captain's position, still being a 2nd Lieutenant. We had lost a lot of people; out of 150 we started with, we now had 72. For some reason, I was carrying a rifle, instead of my usual pistol. All of a sudden, WHAM! A bullet had hit my rifle sending bits and pieces of wood and metal into my left arm. The shot had come from somewhere along a nearby river. I was the only one shot that entire day. I was medevaced out for treatment but was soon back with the company.

In early October 1966, we were now near the DMZ in the vicinity of the "Rockpile." It was simply a strange looking, tall outcropping of rock. We were sleeping in foxholes, and on our frequent patrols we would often encounter North Vietnamese troops who had come down across the DMZ. By now most of the villages had been evacuated. It was a total war zone. We had some tanks for support, but they proved not to be very useful because they had been dug in for defensive purposes. None of these firefights was significant. We stayed in the vicinity of the Rockpile for 3-4 weeks, then went on a battalion-level sweep through dense jungles toward Khe Sanh to the southwest. We were the first large Marine unit to go into the Khe Sanh valley. There was no base out there at the time. We became involved in a very serious firefight in which we lost my platoon sergeant. We were doing a hike up a hill at night, and we soon learned that there was a contingent of NVA between our company and the rest of the battalion. We had to carry our deceased Marine though heavy triple-canopy jungle for three days. The trees were 60-80 ft high; in clearings there was elephant grass 8-10 ft high on the ground. The elephant grass had sharp edges and caused a lot of cuts on our arms and legs. Insects were just a way of life in the jungle. Also, everyone had leech bites from wading through water. At night we would establish a defensive perimeter with some of the machine guns which were in our weapons platoon. The machine gun weighed about 21 lbs and the tripod weighed about 30 lbs. Two other Marines carried the machine gun ammo. Those young Marines were tough kids.

We encountered little resistance until we were in the upper reaches of the Khe Sanh valley where we encountered a lot of NVA troops. The replacement for my platoon sergeant was a Lance Corporal who had been busted in rank several times. He turned out to be a great guy. As we were talking, we both remarked that the forthcoming U.S. plan to establish a Marine base at Khe Sanh was going to be a lousy idea because it reminded both of us of the French disaster at Dien Bien Phu. Little did we know that our concerns were going to become reality the following year.

Our next assignment was to guard a bridge on Rt. 9, but I came down with fever and chills. I was again medevaced, this time initially to an area near Dong Ha. I was lying on a cot with medics trying to cool me down by spraying water and alcohol over me when I suddenly heard, "Martha Raye is here." I was buck naked when she appeared. She immediately came over to me and said, "Hi, Marine, how ya doing?" She was very personable and, because she had earlier been a nurse, was very interested in visiting those who had been wounded. I finally recovered in the hospital in Da Nang before being sent to join my company at Phu Bai which was just south of Hue. Here we were sleeping in huts - fine living! For a brief time, I was Embarkation Officer supervising the loading of trucks on boats taking equipment back to Okinawa. After this I was back with my company doing local patrols along Route 1. In January 1967, we were worried about the VC using Tet to begin an offensive, but that didn't happen until the following year.

Martha Raye was an actress and singer who frequently joined tours of entertainers to put on shows in Vietnam for U.S. troops. She was in her early 50's when she visited Ron, and, by her own admission, had never been a "pin-up" on lockers. But she was beloved by the troops because of her great style of slapstick comedy, often making fun of herself. Because her mouth appeared to be over-sized, her professional nick-name was "The Big Mouth," which she used to great comic length. Raye appeared in numerous films and several Broadway plays and received numerous awards for her overseas tours performing for troops in WW II, Korea, and Vietnam. She was made an honorary Colonel in the Marines and received special consideration to be interned at Arlington National Cemetery, but insisted on being buried in the Main Post Cemetery at Fort Bragg, North Carolina, to be near her beloved Army Special Forces.

I was now back to being a platoon leader. It was March 1967. We were doing patrols north of Hue in an area where all the civilians had been evacuated. We lost one guy during a couple of scrapes. One of the worst nights we had involved escorting a new battalion commander to replace one who had been killed in an ongoing battle up near the DMZ. The Marines were on a hill and had been under heavy fire from the NVA. We had been dropped off near a Marine fire base but had a night hike ahead. After crossing a bridge over the Cam Lo River, we saw a trail, but decided that it would be too risky. Instead, we hiked straight up the hill through mud and vegetation toward our objective. We were communicating with the battalion so they would not shoot us in the dark. Finally, we found our Marines dug in deep after having been in a major battle. We formed a perimeter around their perimeter to give them a break and dug in deep ourselves. In the morning we decided to directly assault the area where the enemy fire had been coming from but when we got to the top, the NVA were gone. There were several bodies lying there, both NVA and our Marines. It was very spooky. We spent the next day picking up bodies and placing them in body bags to be taken back on tanks.

I left Vietnam in April 1967 with orders to the Marine Barracks in Washington. I was only there one year because I took another eye exam and passed it and applied for flight school. They needed pilots fast and within a year I was flying jets. By August 1970, I was an A-4 pilot on my way back to Vietnam. When I arrived in Japan, I was told that half of us were going to Vietnam and half staying at the air base in Iwakuni, Japan. I was in the Japan half and didn't see any aviation action in Vietnam. After this tour, I received orders to a staff officer job in El Toro, California. I had no desire to be a staff officer and resigned to attend law school. I married Sue just before I got out, and ultimately became a personal injury attorney for a firm in San Francisco.

Although Ron spoke in a matter-of-fact tone when discussing his own wounds and the deaths and terrible maiming of so many Marines around him, make no mistake, he was bitter about U.S. political leadership which had sent so many young men to their deaths in Vietnam. He quoted Medal of Honor recipient and Marine General David Shoup who had been the Commandant of the Marine Corps. In retirement, Shoup became a vocal critic of U.S. involvement in Vietnam, saying publicly that the war was "not worth the life or limb of a single American." What is not debatable is that there were more Marine casualties in the rectangular area south of Da Nang to the Cua Dai River and west to Hoi An than in any other area of Vietnam. The book, *Lullaby for Lieutenants*, by Franklin Cox, captures some of the chaotic experiences of Marines in this region during Ron's time in-country. Receiving so many injuries and deaths due to explosions from mines stolen from Allied forces had to increase the angst during every patrol. I have no idea how those young Marines continued to walk forward knowing that their next step might be their last.

Bill Frigge

Vincennes, Indiana

"If it blew, we would go with it"

I drove down to Fredericksburg, Virginia, to meet up with Bill at a location about halfway between our homes. Bill lives with his wife, Caren, on the shore of the Chesapeake Bay in Hallieford, Virginia. Ironically, as a former Navigator on two submarines, I had a few issues finding our rendezvous location, but Bill vectored me via phone.

My dad worked for DuPont in the construction end of the business, so we moved around quite a bit, including stops in Washington, Georgia, Virginia, and Indiana. When I was six years old, my parents took me to New York City where I saw the Atlantic Ocean for the first time from the top of the Empire State Building. I still recall being fascinated by a steamer, hull-down, heading out to sea creating a huge V in the ocean behind it - that is my first memory of wanting to go to sea. Later, in the 6th grade, I had a job delivering newspapers and won a trip to D.C. and Annapolis. When I saw those midshipmen marching around in their uniforms and the sailing boats there, I had a new goal: go to the Naval Academy. Unfortunately, I did not do well on the SATs and went to Vincennes University for a year to get better at math. My uncle used to play poker with the editor of the local newspaper, and our local Congressman apparently owed this editor a big favor. Not long later I received the Congressman's principal appointment to the Naval Academy. I was that favor!

At the Academy I spent a lot of time in the sailing squadron. My favorite boat was a 44 ft yawl named Restless, which we raced frequently. I had always wanted to be in the Surface Navy, and when service selection came, I picked a destroyer as far away from Annapolis as possible. It was the USS RUPERTUS (DD-851) homeported in Yokosuka, Japan. All of our ships there in DESRON 3 were in excellent condition because the Japanese workers who were supposed to get off work at 4 PM would always stay until 8 if we gave them food to take home to their families. Even though I was just a junior Ensign, the new captain who had just arrived put me in training to be the Navigator.

RUPERTUS was in the South China Sea doing plane guarding operations for the carriers USS RANGER (CV-61) and USS INDEPENDENCE (CV-62). We also were providing a lot of gunfire support both off the coast and up some of the larger rivers. I recall us going six to eight miles up the Mekong River. We did so much firing with our 5"/38 guns that we had to go to the shipyard in Subic Bay in the Philippines to have the barrels replaced. Those guns had a range of nearly nine miles, but our best accuracy was at six miles or less. While we were on gunfire support duty, we would get a call from the Marines asking for help. The captain would then have us maneuver the ship near the shore, often as close as two miles. These requests were usually at night so we would first fire a star shell to illuminate the target area so that the Marine spotter could see where our shells were landing. Their feedback allowed us to home in on the target. We would then fire 200-300 shells at six rounds per minute with, as you can imagine, considerable effect. RUPERTUS never ran out of ammunition or supplies because of what we called "the conveyor belt." This consisted of an oiler, an ammo ship, and a food ship which were running continuously up and down the coast to re-supply ships like ours. Almost all of our gun fire was at night, because at that time in the war, most of the enemy were Viet Cong who tended to farm during the day and fight at night.

Although we were in the South China Sea during typhoon season, we never hit a bad one. As Navigator I did have some other bad weather moments. On one transit to a liberty port in Kaohsiung, Taiwan, the sky was covered with clouds for two days making it impossible to see the sun or the stars to get a fix to determine where we were. This was worrisome because another destroyer, USS FRANK KNOX (DDR-742), had run aground on Pratas Reef in this same area. We were in trouble. Fortunately, daytime came and our radar got a return blip from some mountain tops on Taiwan. I say "fortunately" because if it was at night, I probably would have assumed that the radar blips were coming from the shore instead of the mountains 20 miles inland. We would have driven the ship right into the beach! We did have some other challenging transits. One time we were in the tail end of a typhoon and were taking "green water" over the bow onto the bridge window. We even had a fish hit right in front of my face on the bridge window!

The term "green water" means that this portion of the ship was actually under water temporarily. Smaller ships such as destroyers often have "white water" (sea spray) hit the bridge windows, but a green water event can be scary – and dangerous. This situation occurs as the bow of the ship rises up and down as the ship plows through heavy seas.

The grounding of FRANK KNOX on Pratas Reef 200 miles southeast of Hong Kong was seared in the minds of Navigators and Captains transiting the South China Sea. It had occurred at night in July 1965 as the ship was steaming at 16 kts. The force of the collision drove Knox so hard on the reef that it took multiple salvage ships nearly 6 weeks to free it. The reef was on the chart, but a serious navigation error led to the grounding. While grounded, the ship was battered by a typhoon leading to the evacuation of the ship's crew by helicopter. KNOX was towed to the Naval Shipyard in Yokosuka, Japan, for repairs and was ultimately returned to service.

It was about a four-day run for us to get from Yokosuka to Yankee Station. We did this five or six times. During my first 11 months we would stay on station for 6-8 weeks and then come back to Yokosuka for a few weeks. RUPERTUS then headed back to San Diego for an overhaul. We had a funny incident on the way back. We made a stop at Midway Island to refuel. Our Commodore was aboard and advised our Captain not to allow the sailors to go ashore because he had seen some bad incidents resulting from crews getting very drunk, very quickly at the Enlisted Club there. So, we sent only one crew member, the mail clerk, to pick up mail for us. As you can imagine, this was not a popular decision for our crew. I happened to have the Quarterdeck Watch as the mail clerk came back to the ship. He was wobbling somewhat and had several very, very, full mail bags. As we began to head back out the channel, the Commodore's phone starts ringing on the bridge like crazy and he is yelling at me,

"Get the Captain to my cabin!" It turns out that the mail clerk had picked up a live gooney bird on the island and someone let it loose in the Commodore's cabin while he had been on the bridge. The bird had shit all over the Commodore's cabin. Our crew had BIG smiles on their faces the remainder of the way back to San Diego!

Upon completion of the overhaul in May 1967 we headed straight back to Vietnam. This is when we were involved in the USS FORRESTAL (CVA-59) fire. We were plane guarding for FORRESTAL on July 29, 1967, and I was the Officer of the Deck (OOD). I would always give my JOOD (Junior Officer of the Deck) the conn during these operations and I would station myself on the bridge wing with binoculars so that I could closely observe the carrier catapult during flight operations. If something bad happened and the plane did not become airborne and went into the sea as it was being catapulted, I had to be prepared to respond instantly. Around 10:30 in the morning, I suddenly saw a streak of smoke go across the flight deck and then a ball of fire under an A-4. We immediately went to general quarters, and quickly learned that the CO of the carrier wanted us to make an approach close to him to help fight the large fire which was now raging as he turned the carrier into the wind to try to keep the fire confined to the after part of the ship. Sailors were jumping off the stern of the ship into the sea to avoid being burned. We launched our whale boat and picked up at least six men out of the water. The entire stern of the carrier was now on fire. To make matters worse, some bombs went off on the flight deck punching a hole in the deck allowing burning fuel to pour below into some berthing areas.

**RUPERTUS alongside assisting FORRESTAL
during fire July 29, 1967**

In this photo, RUPERTUS is shown on the forward port side of FORRESTAL. Bill told me that for the majority of the time they were fighting the fire, RUPERTUS was stationed near the port aft end of FORRESTAL in the smoke in order to direct water from their hoses onto the major danger, the port ammunition magazine.

The carrier was now doing 25 kts into the wind. Because the fire was raging close to the after magazines, the FORRESTAL skipper asked us to come alongside as close as possible to aim our fire hoses at this ammo and oxygen storage magazine. If it went up, the carrier would undoubtedly go down with everyone aboard. Of course, as close as we were to the carrier, we probably also would have been seriously damaged. As you can imagine, trying to keep our ship that close in the heavy smoke - we were only maybe 25 ft away - was extremely difficult due to the Venturi Effect. Our skipper now had the conn and did a magnificent job keeping us close, but safe. To make matters worse, the carrier crew started pushing burning planes off the deck in front of us causing us to have to dodge these flaming hazards! One of my jobs was Damage Control Assistant, and once we began fighting the fire, me and a hose team took a 2 1/2-inch hose to the forecastle to try to direct water onto that magazine area of the carrier. It was already so hot that when the first stream of water from our hose hit that magazine, it instantly turned to steam. Due to the wind and the ship speed, the water from our hose was being blown aft creating sort of a relative motion problem as we tried to direct the water onto the magazine, I was wetting my pants knowing that if that magazine blew, we would go with it.

USS GEORGE K. MacKENZIE (DD-836) was on the starboard side of FORRESTAL doing the same thing as us trying to hose down the other large ammo magazine on that side. The carrier crew was also frequently having to roll bombs off the side of the ship to keep them from exploding but fortunately, they were hitting the water between us and the carrier. It seemed to me that we were fighting the fire all day, but by mid-afternoon the fires were somewhat under control. Unfortunately, there were numerous deaths and injuries among the carrier crew. MacKENZIE was assigned to escort FORRESTAL back to Subic Bay for what were obviously major repairs.

A "magazine" is a special storage area on a ship where high explosives and other dangerous materials are stored. If either of these aft magazines were to have exploded during the FORRESTAL fire, the carrier and its crew of 5000 men would have been in significant danger of being lost because these magazines were located below water level and would have flooded instantly. As mentioned earlier when discussing "high lines," the Venturi Effect occurs when any fluid flows through a narrow opening. The fluid speeds up and concurrently creates a force pulling the sides together. If the sides are fixed objects, this force is not noticeable. However, if the sides are two moving ships, there is a definite tendency to be pulled together. Warships which do frequent underway replenishments from other ships become experienced in countering this effect.

For those unfamiliar with how a ship at sea is "driven" on a daily basis, the Officer of the Deck (OOD) is "the Captain on the bridge" when the Commanding Officer is not present. He is responsible for keeping the Captain informed of all major happenings. He is often assisted by a Junior Officer of the Deck (JOOD) who is in training. One of these two individuals has "the conn" which means that person has control of the speed and direction of the ship. If the Captain comes to the bridge and gives a direct order to the helmsman (who is steering), the Quartermaster of the Watch will loudly announce, "The Captain has the conn." This change of responsibility is entered in the ship's log. It is a rather long story, but as a junior officer on my first submarine, my own naval career was saved due to such an entry just before our submarine hit bottom off the coast of San Diego in 1968.

The fire on FORRESTAL was indeed a major tragedy. The events are well-chronicled online with scores of photos and a timeline of events. It began when a Sparrow missile on a F-4 Phantom fighter aircraft on the deck ignited due to an electrical malfunction. It then flew into an external fuel tank on a nearby A-4 Skyhawk (which had been flown by the future POW and U.S. Senator, John McCain). Jet fuel was ignited, quickly ran across the flight deck, and started other fires and explosions. In the ensuing conflagration, 134 sailors perished and over 150 others were injured. The ship was severely damaged but was able to return for repairs costing over $70 million (not counting the numerous aircraft and equipment which were lost).

After the FORRESTAL fire, we began participation in Operation SEA DRAGON in late 1967. This was prior to the Viet Cong Tet offensive in early 1968. Intelligence noticed that the North Vietnamese had installed 130 mm artillery about every 6 miles along the coast. These guns had a range about 9 miles which was 3 miles more than the accurate fire of our shipboard 5"/38 guns. We also observed that the North Vietnamese were now sending barges down the coast to provide supplies to the Viet Cong below the DMZ. On our first attempt to sink those barges, as we approached the targets, we had splashes all around us from those shore guns. Thank God that they did not have very good fire control radar, or we would have been hit. These barges (which we called "wiblics" for waterborne logistics craft) would generally cling to the shore and run south, mostly at night. Our mission was to find them and then sink them with our guns. They were carrying food and ammunition for the Viet Cong and usually had a crew of four. Our ship took out a lot of these wiblics with direct fire and observed many secondary explosions when they were hit. We did not attempt to pick up survivors because the wiblics were hugging the coast and we would have been sitting ducks for the artillery if we went in there.

Operation SEA DRAGON had begun in October 1966 to curtail enemy supplies and personnel going south from North Vietnam. When Bill's ship became involved, U.S. destroyers were ranging as far north as the 20th parallel, roughly 230 miles north of the DMZ. In addition to seeking out wibliks, Navy ships were targeting shore radar installations, bridges, and surface-to-air missile sites within range from sea. As with all wartime operations, SEA DRAGON was not without risk. Approximately 30 U.S. ships were damaged by Vietnamese shore artillery with 5 American sailors killed and 26 wounded. Although they had near misses, RUPERTUS suffered no casualties.

I left our ship when it returned to our new home port of Long Beach, California, and spent the next six months in Destroyer School in Newport, Rhode Island, where I met my future wife. We were married in December 1968, and I went as Chief Engineer on another destroyer, USS JOHN W. THOMASON (DD-760). This was an old ship which I described as "a floating junk pile." While we were in Subic, I "borrowed" a lot of parts the night before we left from a similar ship which had been literally cut in half by an Australian carrier. This ship had six 5-inch/38's which the Marines ashore loved when we used them against enemy forces they were fighting. Our ship was also supporting troops in the Mekong Delta; we were often so close to shore that we could almost jump onto the sand. When we anchored in the river near Saigon, we dropped grenades over the side at random intervals each night to deter any sappers who might be in the water. We never saw any bodies come up. On some of our missions the Marines would give us a body count the next day. Sometimes they told us that we had a body count of 150-200 dead. I have no idea if these numbers were accurate, but when you fire six guns at the same time, there was probably a lot of damage being done.

Following this third deployment to Vietnam, Bill was sent to the Naval Postgraduate School with follow-on assignments on ships deployed to the Mediterranean, the Indian Ocean, and the Black Sea. He also had shore assignments in Korea and several locations on the East Coast. Bill made two Mediterranean deployments as Commanding Officer of USS TRUETT (FF-1095). He retired in 1991 as a Captain and spent the next 10 years as a civilian contractor running computer war games.

Bill's experiences on surface ships illustrate that the dangers faced at sea in a wartime environment were sometimes no less than those encountered fighting in-country. The sailors burned to death in their berthing area on FORRESTAL were just as indiscriminately killed as those Vietnamese civilians blown apart in their rice paddies by B-52 bombs, or the Marines who happened to step on a mine, or the aviators whose planes were shot out of the sky by anti-aircraft weapons, or the North Vietnamese in wiblics shot by the guns on Bill's destroyers. Civil War General William Sherman captured it well, "War is cruelty, and you cannot refine it." As the title of this book suggests, war is indeed a filthy way to die.

Tom Craig

Las Vegas, New Mexico

"It was kinda hard to sleep"

I roomed with Tom during our first class (senior) year at Annapolis. Having watched countless western movies growing up, I always saw Tom as a genuine cowboy in his native New Mexico prior to his days as a midshipman. He was a tough guy, but friendly and likable. When Tom decided to go into the Marines. following graduation, we lost touch as our professional lives diverged. Sixteen years later he gave me a surprise phone call allowing us to catch up on events in our lives. After his retirement from the Marine Corps, Tom and his wife, Blaine, spent many years traveling around the U.S. in their truck and fifth wheel trailer. They now live in San Antonio, Texas, where I interviewed him via telephone.

I was raised on a ranch in New Mexico outside a small town named Las Vegas. Our family raised sheep and cattle and never had a lot of money. I attended Wagon Mound High School and played basketball and baseball. We didn't have much money to send me to school, but I was able to attend Colorado State University for a year to study Engineering. While I was there, I applied to my congressman for an appointment to either the Naval Academy or the Air Force Academy. It ended up with me getting an appointment to Annapolis.

While at USNA, I decided that I would like to be a Marine aviator. After our graduation, I went to Marine Corps Basic School at Quantico, Virginia, but there were no flight slots available, resulting in me getting a direct ticket to Vietnam. In March 1966 I arrived at Da Nang where I was placed in charge of a security platoon for six months. Not much happened during that assignment. I was then assigned to an Infantry platoon as 3rd Platoon Commander, B Company, 1st Battalion, 4th

Marine Regiment. In October 1966 I joined my platoon at Dong Ha near the DMZ. We were going on daily company-sized patrols, usually eight to ten kilometers in length, looking for any enemy movement. The terrain was mostly flat coastal plains with shrubs and trees. We did a lot of work patrolling along Route 1 and would occasionally have some potshots taken at us. Our patrols went south to Hue and then spent 3 weeks west of Phu Bai. We would dig fox holes for protection at night. Our perimeter did get probed frequently by enemy patrols, but there were no big firefights.

In late November 1966 we were embarked on LPH's [Landing Ship Helicopter, an amphibious warfare ship designed primarily to launch and recover helicopters] *to send us back to Okinawa where we did some practice landings using live ammo in preparation for a landing in Vietnam. We then were transported back to Vietnam on the Iwo Jima (LPH-2) and landed near Duc Pho at the southern tip of I Corps. There was some opposition on the beach, but once we were past the initial resistance, we did a lot of walking in the semi-jungle terrain on hills. We soon got into a firefight with Viet Cong forces and suffered some casualties. Throughout all of this we didn't have good intelligence support and were basically just wandering around looking for trouble. In a week or so we got back on Iwo Jima and sailed to the Philippines. Here they put us on USS PRINCETON (LPH-5) and we went back to Vietnam. We were transported to shore via helicopters and put down just south of the DMZ near Gio Linh.*

Secretary of Defense McNamara had ordered that the U.S. should create a barren strip of land just south of the DMZ from Gio Linh near the ocean west to Con Thien. However, it was not exactly barren. We soon got into a significant firefight with North Vietnamese Army regulars from their 324th B Division. They were firing artillery across the Ben Hai River which marked the DMZ. We ended up in three days of a hellacious firefight. I was now XO of the Company and had our radioman with me. The enemy was using a lot of mortars. Our company suffered numerous casualties; our best corporal was killed. We would be taking fire from places you couldn't see, and the Medevac helos were all taking considerable mortar fire every time they tried to come in to pick up wounded or dead Marines. My radioman and I were sharing a foxhole and took turns trying to nod off. It was kinda hard to sleep. One night

I was so tired I fell asleep at the top of a bunker and had to be pulled into the bunker when mortar rounds started to come in. The whole time we were near Gio Linh we were taking fire. From my point of view, our tactics up there were all messed up and resulted in a lot of unnecessary deaths and injuries.

We were now reassigned back to the 4th Marines at Dong Ha and took over perimeter duty. We conducted aggressive patrols and found a lot more activity than when we were initially there. Most of our patrols were about seven to eight hours in length during daytime. For my last five days in Dong Ha, they assigned me to do paperwork. I took a C-130 flight to Da Nang and then flew on a chartered flight back to California where I met up with my wife, Blaine, in San Francisco. I had orders to go to the Naval Academy as a Company Officer but received a telegram to report immediately to Camp Pendleton in southern California with the 5th Marine Division. There I had several interesting temporary assignments, including six months in England doing arms control work.

I still wanted to be a Marine pilot and finally was selected to receive flight training, but at an Air Force base in Valdosta, Georgia. I ended up flying the EA-6A Electronics Warfare plane and deployed to Japan in 1973. There I also flew the F-4 Phantom configured with a camera to gather intelligence on North Korea.

Tom continued his career in Marine aviation with assignments on U.S. east and west coast bases until his retirement in 1985. He loved flying, but expressed disappointment that he did not receive his wings until far later in his career. Tom was bitter in his disappointment in how Marines were directed to fight the war in Vietnam. His exact words were, "When the White House calls the shots, you don't have a chance."

Matt D'Amico

Brooklyn, New York
"You often had trouble breathing"

Matt had several classes with me at the Naval Academy, but I had not seen him since graduation. I was looking forward to our conversation because I had heard of Matt's interesting experiences in the Mekong Delta. We talked via computer from his home in Shelton, Connecticut, where he lives with his wife, Terry.

I was born on June 7, 1944, and I am pretty sure that I am the youngest graduating member of our class. Both of my parents were immigrants. My mother came here from Sicily in 1930 and was a seamstress in a sweat shop in Brooklyn; my father was born in a small village outside Naples. He served in the Italian Navy in WW I and later came to the U.S. through Ellis Island. He was a mechanic, but had a stroke when I was a teen, so Mom became our only source of income. I attended a Christian Brothers high school in Brooklyn. One of my classmates was the politician, Rudy Giuliani. I ended up at the Naval Academy strictly by accident. I had good grades, but we had no money for my college education, so I applied to the Academy. I did not receive my congressman's appointment but was the first alternate. Not certain that I would gain entry, I still took the entrance physical but failed it because they did not like my urine; it had too much protein. I then assumed that I was no longer a candidate, but just before Memorial Day in 1961 I received a telegram telling me to come to the Academy for a physical. I got up at midnight, took a bus to the Port Authority, took a bus to Baltimore arriving at 5 AM, got another bus to Annapolis, found the medical guys, was told to pee in a bottle. That was it. I was then told to go home and took the same series of busses back to my home in Brooklyn. A few weeks later, just before

Induction Day, I received another telegram telling me that I was in. I guess they now liked my pee.

When service selection came around during our last year at the Academy, I chose to go surface and received orders to USS STICKELL (DD-888), a destroyer out of Newport, Rhode Island. The Navy first sent me to various schools to be the ASW (anti-submarine warfare) officer but there was already one on STICKELL, so I didn't get that job until the spring of 1966. Our ship left Newport in January 1966 to go to the Pacific to relieve some of the pressure on the West Coast destroyers which had been doing continuous Vietnam duty. In Hawaii they installed additional air conditioning units on the ship before we went to Yankee Station. Almost all our time there was doing plane guarding for the carriers, primarily USS RANGER (CV-61). We had gone to the Pacific via the Panama Canal but returned to Newport the other way via the Suez Canal and the Mediterranean. As a youngster who had never left Brooklyn, I now had seen the world. Shortly after we arrived back at Newport in September 1966, I received orders to USS CHARLES F. ADAMS (DDG-2). Again, I was the ASW Officer and did a deployment to the Mediterranean on that ship in 1967.

I ended up back in Vietnam almost by accident. I was due for orders so I filled out my "dream sheet" of jobs I would like to have. I put down all the good ones, like assignments with NROTC units at various universities. My last choice was OIC of a PCF, a.k.a., a Swift boat. You can guess what I got: orders to Swift boat school. I called the detailer and asked why I was going to Swift boats. His predictable response was, "Well, you had it on your dream sheet."

The detailer is an officer in the Bureau of Naval Personnel who makes assignments for officers. It is a generally thankless job because the assignments are not made to make you happy, but to fill the needs of the Navy. A PCF is a "Patrol Craft Fast," commonly called a Swift boat. The typical crew on a Swift boat was six. The skipper, an officer, did not carry the title of "Captain," but was officially termed the officer-in-charge (OIC). There were usually five enlisted men: a boatswain's mate, a radio operator, an engineman, and two men who operated guns. The boats were 50 ft long, had a shallow draft, and were made of aluminum. Weapons consisted of twin .50 caliber machine guns in a turret above the pilot house, and a combination machine gun/grenade launcher aft. The boats were powered by twin 480-horsepower diesel engines, were fast (over 25 kts), and highly maneuverable

I went through Swift boat school in Coronado, California, for a few months along with my crew. In June 1968 we flew together to Cam Ranh Bay in Vietnam. I didn't know at this time, but my crew and I were to stay together mostly for the whole year in-country. When I arrived, essentially all of the OIC's were senior Lieutenant jg's or junior Lieutenants, like me, but later they started to send young officers straight out of Officer Candidate School who had zero sea experience. We arrived in Vietnam as a group of five or six Swift boat crews all coming out of training at the same time. They gave us bunks in a Quonset hut and the next morning we received our assignments. Mine was down south in Coastal Division 13. To get there we flew to the airfield at Vung Tau on the South China Sea, southeast of Saigon, and were taken by truck to a small village not far away called Cat Lo where the South Vietnamese Navy had a base. It was strategically located with easy access to the South China Sea, the river approaches to Saigon, and the Mekong Delta. The base was reasonably secure but did come under mortar attack at least once while I was there. I remember that we could not drink the water because it was contaminated with diesel fuel, and we also were instructed to take 1-2 malaria pills each day. What I remember for certain is that we did not have air conditioning in our Quonset huts.

When we arrived at Cat Lo, we had more crew than boats, so we shared a PCF with another crew. We would take turns going on deployments, 24 hrs on and 24 off, patrolling in the waters around Vung Tau. Nothing much happened on these initial missions. We were then ordered to deploy south to the Ca Mau Peninsula at the southern end of the Delta. There we had 8 crews for 4 boats and operated from a nest tied up next to a LST [Landing Ship Tank…a large amphibious ship which had quarters for the crews]. *We would patrol for 24 hours, then rest on the LST for the next 24 hours while the other crew took out our boat. Almost all our meals on the Swift boats were cold cuts or C-rations. These were 4-week deployments doing Operation Market Time missions looking for small enemy boats bringing supplies and personnel to the Viet Cong in the Delta. At this time, we weren't allowed to go up any of the rivers which we called "Indian Country." The Cua Bo De River was notorious;*

one of our classmates, Mike Brown, became famous for transiting this river from the Gulf of Thailand to the South China Sea - and surviving. Following this, Admiral Zumwalt instituted Operation SEALORDS with the belief that the U.S. Navy should be able to contest these previously untouched rivers and lakes. The PBRs [Patrol Boat Riverine], a different type of small patrol boat, would do the northern part of the rivers near Cambodia and we now patrolled the southern sections. We would spend two to three days on these patrols. For example, we would leave Cat Lo on a Monday morning and return late on Wednesday. It was about a four hour transit to get south to the rivers. During the southwest monsoon season, it was not pleasant battling the seas on the way home. We would cruise upriver at 10 kts to conserve fuel and then drift downriver inspecting every boat we encountered. Once we started patrolling in the rivers, that's all we were doing.

Swift boat operating at speed

One of our jobs on the rivers occasionally was to provide gunfire support for our forces engaged with the enemy in the Delta. During these operations we would often use our mortar to attack an enemy position inland. We often received spotting information from OV-10's or Sea Wolf helicopters. You would be surprised how accurate we could fire from the rivers where there was little wave motion.

We were involved in at least eight firefights on my boat, PCF-37. Whenever we went up the rivers, we would often experience casualties. In October 1968 my boat began ops in the canals of the Delta. We would never go into the small rivers and canals by ourselves. Generally, we would take two to three boats and be covered by attack helicopters because it was totally Charlie territory [slang for Viet Cong]. *Because our boats were noisy, the Viet Cong could always hear us coming. Our best defense was our speed, which was difficult to use effectively in the narrow canals. When they opened fire on us, we would return fire with our machine guns. We really could not know how many enemy we may have killed; sometimes the Army might find some bodies a day or two later. Once in a while we would find some enemy body parts floating in one of those small rivers.*

A typical canal in the Mekong Delta

As you can see from the preceding photo, taking a Swift Boat up such a narrow canal with dense vegetation on each side was exceptionally dangerous. Matt discussed the problems of turning around a PCF in these narrow waterways. He had to pull the boat into the bank and reverse the engines to be able to head back the other direction. The depths of these waterways varied with the seasons and his boat would often scrape bottom. The dense vegetation provided superb cover for an enemy ambush. Ironically, a major tourist attraction now in Vietnam is kayaking these same canals and rivers. Times certainly change!

Fortunately, we were never hit by the numerous VC rockets fired at us. Other boats did have casualties. One of our PCFs was conducting psychological operations playing tapes encouraging the VC to surrender and was hit by a rocket. The crew member who was killed was the best friend of one of my crew who took it real bad and never really recovered. After the war he became homeless in Detroit fighting PTSD [post-traumatic stress disorder]. After the war I stayed in touch with him and looked him up in 2000. He was still in a bad way and was living in a log cabin in the woods. Some people come back with physical injuries; others come back injured mentally.

After my year on Swift boats, I had an anti-submarine training job on Point Loma in San Diego. I married in June 1969 after having met my future wife years earlier in a candy store. It must have been a "sweet" moment because we are still married!

Matt resigned from the Navy in July 1971 and worked in marketing for Mobil Oil Corporation for over 30 years. During our conversation he commented about the inherent beauty of Vietnam, particularly when viewed from the rivers. Of course, during the war, those same rivers could be deadly due to ambushes from the surrounding jungle. Matt described how the adrenaline kicked in during those ambushes, "When some of these were over, you often had trouble breathing."

Mike Malone

Los Angeles, California

"A corn field…in Vietnam! "

I knew about the use of tanks in previous wars; they are still involved in the ongoing war in Ukraine. But my knowledge of Amtracs was considerably less. Earlier I had talked to another Marine Amtrac officer, Bob Sullivan, who suggested that I obtain the thoughts of his friend, Mike Malone, another of our classmates. I interviewed Mike by computer from his home in San Rafael, California, where he lives with his wife, Katie. They had just returned from an extended cruise in northern Europe. Some of their Polish guides told Mike of their harrowing experiences under the rule of the Soviet Union, and added that when the Russians left, they took everything that they could carry with them. Mike contrasted this with how the United States did the opposite in Vietnam, by leaving considerable equipment behind for use by the South Vietnamese military. Mike began our discussion of his experiences in Vietnam by telling me about his life prior to the Naval Academy.

I was born in the southwest part of Los Angeles in April 1943. My father was a warehouseman for a grocery chain; my mother did some bookkeeping for a few small businesses. I attended George Washington High School where I was something of a nerd. I played on a lot of local sports teams, but not on high school teams. I became interested in the Naval Academy because my uncle was career Navy. He enlisted in January 1942 and ended up retiring as a Commander in Navy Air. While I was in high school, FDR's son, Jimmy Roosevelt, was our congressman. My uncle was Commander of the American Legion in California and put a word in for me with Roosevelt. I had skipped a year of school and was Roosevelt's first alternate for an appointment in 1960, but didn't get in. So, I joined the NROTC program at the University of Southern California and received the primary appointment to Navy the following year.

At the Academy, on our "youngster" cruise (takes place in the summer between a midshipman's first and second years), *I was stationed on an aircraft carrier and was assigned to the engineering department. I rarely saw daylight. It was hot and sweaty. Basically, I didn't like it. In contrast, during our training with the Marines the following summer I really enjoyed the experience. During our first class cruise* (between junior and senior years), *I was assigned to USS VALLEY FORGE (LPH-8), which had a Marine Corps detachment aboard. I was allowed to work with the Marines and loved it. So, I chose to go Marine Corps and following graduation went directly to Basic School in Quantico, Virginia. There we had three choices: Armor, Artillery, or Infantry. My first choice was Armor and I got it. I wanted to go into tanks and was sent to Camp Pendleton in California for Armor School which was three months long. On our first day we went into an auditorium for a presentation. The officer giving the talk began motioning his arms and saying, "Everyone on this side, you're going tanks. Everyone over there on the other side, you're going amphibs." I was on the amphib side. That's how I ended up in Amtracs!*

I learned Amtracs in Track Vehicle School before heading to Vietnam. There were three battalions of Amtracs, two in Vietnam and one at Camp Lejuene in North Carolina. I was assigned to the First Amtrac Battalion, which is part of the Third Marine Division, in Vietnam. In mid-March 1966 I flew into Da Nang. My battalion was located on a hill just south of Da Nang. I was a platoon commander in charge of ten Amtracs. Usually, we would go out in sections of three or four. I rode in the rear one which is designated as the Command Amtrac which allowed me to see ahead and communicate with the others ahead on radio.

Marine Corps Amtracs (LVTP-5) used in Vietnam were large rectangular-shaped amphibious tractors which moved on tracks essentially in the same manner as a tank. These vehicles were originally designed to carry troops ashore from ships during an amphibious assault. In Vietnam, instead of landing operations, they performed a wide variety of other missions, such as armored personnel carriers. They could move freely in most Vietnamese rivers and were used in a variety of missions. Each

Amtrac weighed about 35 tons. It was powered by an 810-HP engine which gave it a land speed of nearly 30 mph; in water it was considerably slower, usually about 7 mph. Most had a .30 caliber machine gun on top; some had a 105 mm howitzer instead. A few were even fitted with a bulldozer blade on the front to clear mines. Each Marine Amtrac battalion had 120 of the LVTP-5s and each platoon, such as Mike's, had about 10. One significant problem was that the fuel was stored in the belly, which was the least protected part of the vehicle, making them very vulnerable to mines. Another vexing problem was that the Amtrac had not been designed for use in rough terrain, such as inland in Vietnam. This shortcoming led to endless maintenance issues.

We could carry 20 Marines in one Amtrac if they were jammed in, but most everyone rode on top of the vehicle. If you were inside when you hit a mine, you were probably dead. We did hit a mine once, but were lucky because it exploded on the track, not under the belly. Two of my goals in Vietnam were to never lose a Marine while on an Amtrac and to never have to write a letter home to relatives telling them that they had lost a loved one. Fortunately, I was lucky and never had to face such issues.

The Amtracs could go through wet rice paddies, but generally we favored dry ones. Obviously, we damaged farmland as we traveled on land. I know that there was some military unit which compensated a few farmers for damage caused by Americans, but this is not something we were ever involved in. One time we came upon a corn field....in Vietnam! Our policy was always to have each Amtrac follow the one in front of it to minimize hitting mines, so we didn't tear up that farmer's corn patch too bad. If the lead unit didn't hit anything, we figured that it would be safe for all of us.

We never knew what type of assignment would be next. We had been near Hoi An with a tank battalion, but were ordered to go up to the Marble Mountain area outside Da Nang to protect a village where the Chief had been supposedly marked for assassination by the Viet Cong. We stayed there for a week or so, but there was no attack. Shortly after that we were assigned to Hill 55 south of Da Nang. This was a major Marine encampment with the First Battalion, 9th Marines. We were responsible for the security of a bridge which all the Marine infantry crossed when going on sweeps. We would resupply troops with food, ammo, and other supplies while they were out on those patrols. The bridge we were protecting received a lot of sniper fire but never a direct attack. The infantry we were working with had taken so many casualties from mines that their nickname was "The Walking Dead."

There is a story of how they got that name. Shortly after I had arrived in Vietnam, on Easter Sunday,1966, I was sitting on a hill when we were surprised to see some South Vietnamese planes intentionally strafing South Vietnamese Army units. Apparently, the Vietnamese Army and Air Force were at odds. I learned that there seemed to be a lot of internal politics affecting various units of the Vietnamese forces. Another time we were involved in a Vietnamese dispute where a bridge on Highway 1 near Da Nang was seized by a dissident ARVN unit which was threatening to blow up the bridge. We "swam" our Amtracs down the river to support our Marine unit which had orders to take back the bridge. At the last moment, as our forces were ready to attack, the South Vietnamese gave up the bridge. It turned out that this ARVN group had abandoned their fort to come there. While they were gone, the Viet Cong came in and stripped the fort of everything, including thousands of Bouncing Betty mines. These same mines came back to haunt the 9th Marines with countless casualties. This is how they became known as the Walking Dead.

We were also sent to a hill west near the Laotian border for a month before being sent south near the Song Thu Bonh - Song means River in Vietnamese. The river was about 40 meters wide and not that deep. Our Amtracs could cross this easily; on this crossing we were expecting resistance and kept the troops inside in case of enemy fire. But there was no resistance on the other side and the crossing went well. Unfortunately, we threw a track on one of our Amtracs while in the river causing us to be stuck there for three days. I set up my platoon in a perimeter on the shore, but no one attacked us. On the third day, two U.S. F-8's flew over strafing and dropping napalm just downriver from us. Apparently, there was a VC group massing in the area to attack us. A retriever (an Amtrac configured to act as a "tow truck") *from our company came to get us out of the river and we moved on.*

We were pulled out of Hoi An on a very rainy Christmas Day in 1966 to head back to Okinawa, Japan, for refitting of our Amtracs. Our equipment had taken a beating and the sandbags which we had put on the floor of the Amtrac for protection from mines were literally full of fleas. While we were in Okinawa, I took my platoon and some enlisted tank personnel out on an exercise to conduct infantry training. One of my men was bitten by a habu, a poisonous pit viper. We needed some medical help asap, so I used my PRC-25 radio to get a Medivac. I kept calling and finally someone came on and I gave him my coordinates. He kept asking me where I was and finally yelled, "Where the hell are you?" It turned out that my radio, which usually has a 30-mile range, had been answered by someone in Vietnam! Apparently, the signal was bouncing off clouds and the ground and made it all the way to Vietnam. Fortunately, we were able to get our Marine evacuated and he survived.

The habu snake which bit the young Marine is found almost exclusively on some Japanese islands. It is very aggressive, and its bite can cause serious injury. Most have heard of the habu due to its use in making "snake wine," a supposedly medicinal concoction which has an entire snake immersed in a bottle of rice wine. It is alleged that the ethanol content in the rice wine denatures the snake's venom. Some claim that it is possible for the snake to go into a form of hibernation and actually bite the unfortunate consumer as the bottle is opened! There are several stories to this effect online.

When we landed back in Vietnam with our equipment, we were moved north from Da Nang to Cua Viet to operate in the DMZ area. We received some fire up there on an almost daily basis, mostly mortars and snipers, but we were never hit while I was there. My only real firefight was crossing a rice paddy when we were opened up on by a .50 caliber machine gun. My unit was also attacked once in Da Nang at night by satchel charges which were used to go after some of our Amtracs parked there. It turned out that the attackers were several of the Vietnamese barbers who worked on the base during the day! It was difficult to tell friend from foe. I spent only a few weeks in the DMZ region because I had only 6 weeks to go on my 13-month tour in Vietnam.

As soon as I arrived back in the states, my next assignment was Executive Officer of the Marine detachment on USS CORAL SEA (CVA-43). And guess what? It was headed straight to Vietnam and Yankee Station. The job of my contingent of Marines was to safeguard the "special weapons" on board, to guard the brig, to man some of the gun mounts, and a few other smaller tasks. We were one of three carriers in the Gulf with a rotation of 60 days on Yankee Station, five days in Subic Bay, and repeat. Even though I was a Marine, I stood bridge watches and qualified as the senior Officer of the Deck (OOD) underway. One time our Marine detachment was put on alert to be inserted into North Vietnam on a mission to rescue a Carrier Air Group Commander whose plane had been shot down. He was on the ground but not yet captured. Just before we were to go, it was called off, apparently by Washington. As far as I know that senior aviator was not rescued. We went to General Quarters once when a rocket went off in the assembly area. This killed several people and started a major fire. All of our Marine blue uniforms were destroyed. They flew me back to the U.S. to ensure that all of my men had blue uniforms for a change of command of the ship when it got back to port. I have no idea how much this cost. Because of the Pueblo incident, the CORAL SEA was extended at sea for over two months, so I ended up with all that extra time free from any duties. But I had all those new uniforms waiting when the ship finally arrived.

USS PUEBLO was a refurbished and re-configured WW II light cargo ship. It was re-fitted with state-of-the-art intelligence and communications gathering equipment. Because a hostile attack was considered low risk, it had very few defensive weapons. Although its stated mission was oceanographic research, PUEBLO was very much a vessel dedicated to spying. In mid-January 1968 PUEBLO was on a mission in international waters off the coast of North Korea. Its orders included maintaining radio silence, but when sensing threatening activities by North Korean vessels, informed superiors. This message was not read until 24 hours later. On January 23, several North Korean ships approached PUEBLO and encircled it. When one of the Korean ships fired on PUEBLO, the Commanding Officer, Lloyd Bucher, ordered all classified material to be destroyed and requested immediate help from higher authorities. As the North Koreans came alongside and attempted to board the ship, one American sailor was killed. When additional Korean forces, including two MiG aircraft arrived, Commander Bucher heeded orders to follow a Korean boat toward port. Following another futile skirmish, PUEBLO was seized, its crew members tied up, with the ship piloted into the port of Wonson. Over the course of the following year, the PUEBLO crew was imprisoned under harsh conditions, while the North Koreans extracted every bit of possible propaganda shaming the U.S. The crew was not released until December 28, 1968, nearly a year later. The ship was never returned. Several retaliatory measures were prepared for President Johnson, but he chose only to send a large naval force into the area, including three carriers (including CORAL SEA), as a show of force rather than risk a second war on the Korean peninsula. Whether or not Johnson made the correct decision has been argued for years.

My next set of orders was to Headquarters Marine Corps in D.C. for 18 months, followed by orders as Legal Officer at Treasure Island in San Francisco. This led to my interest in law. I stayed in the Marine Corps and went to Law School at Hastings in San Francisco. I remained in the Corps as an attorney until I retired after 21 years in the service.

Following his retirement, Mike joined a large law firm in San Francisco and specialized in labor law. He later joined a smaller firm in the Bay Area and did mostly insurance work until his retirement. Although Mike's experiences in Vietnam did not expose him to as many hazards as his Marine peers who were infantry officers, it was still dangerous. Daily worry about mines was a reality never far from one's mind in Vietnam.

John Thompson

New Orleans, Louisiana
"I had a lot of dead friends"

After hearing that I wanted to talk to an A-4 pilot, several classmates suggested that I talk to John Thompson. I interviewed John via computer from his home in Dallas where he lives with his wife, Nina. Like several of our classmates, John is suffering from Parkinson's disease, possibly due to exposure to Agent Orange. Nina supplemented John's thoughts with several comments throughout our talk. Married since 1967, Nina's memories of each of John's deployments were still vivid. During our talk I learned that Nina has amazing recall of dates, places, and events. John spoke slowly, but clearly, and was very enthusiastic.

My father was a Supply Corps officer in the Navy during WW II. He was on USS BARNSTABLE (APA-93), an attack transport ship. He was thrown overboard into the sea during a kamikaze attack on the ship and ultimately received a medical discharge. Although I never had any particular inclination for the Navy, in my senior year of high school in Lubbock, Texas, Dad showed up at class one day in my senior year and asked me if I wanted to go to the Naval Academy. I remember my exact words, "Well, I guess." Apparently, our local Congressman was in town and Dad had met him. All I know is that three months later I was at Annapolis.

At the Naval Academy, I did Brigade Boxing at 147 lbs. I fought for the championship but lost on points. One of my roommates was Laughton Smith who was serving aboard USS SCORPION (SSN-589), the submarine which was lost in the Atlantic in May 1968. I had learned earlier from my summer cruises that I did not want to be on submarines or surface ships, so when service selection came around, I definitely chose to go Navy Air. Following graduation, I went through all the routine flight training and was able to go jets. I wanted to fly a single-engine, single-person plane, the A-4 Skyhawk. After getting my wings, I was assigned to squadron VA-195 at the Naval Air Station in Lemoore, California. After all the workups and training, we deployed to Vietnam on USS TICONDEROGA (CVA-14) with Carrier Air Wing 19 from San Diego on Dec 27, 1967. It was an older carrier with a wooden flight deck. It had been commissioned in 1944 during WW II and now had an angled flight deck. In addition to my squadron of A-4C's, our air wing had two squadrons of A-4F's, and two F-8E Crusader fighter aircraft squadrons. All of the A-4's were attack aircraft with a mission to carry weapons to the enemy. There were other reconnaissance and support aircraft aboard and a squadron of helicopters. We had plenty of aircraft!

Here Nina added her memories.

John was home on leave at Christmas, 1966, and I had a date with another fellow. My date asked me if it would be OK if we stopped by to see one of his friends named John because "He's gonna get shot and killed over there in Vietnam." Anyway, the other fellow went back to his school, and I started to date John. He proposed on our second date. We were married a few months later on June 9, 1967, exactly two years after his graduation from USNA.

John and Nina both laughed as John continued his memories about flying in the war.

Once we arrived at Yankee Station, we immediately began flying one to three missions every day. We basically flew around looking for trouble. Each of these missions was about an hour and a half long. It would generally take me about 20 minutes to get over North Vietnam. One of my first assignments was to bomb an airfield near Vinh with 500 lb bombs. As I was climbing out of a 45-degree dive bombing run, I noticed that my plane was not climbing well. Fortunately, my wingman called over to me and told me that I still had my speed brakes out. That was embarrassing - a stupid new guy mistake! My plane was not supersonic, but sometimes when I had time to kill on the way back from a mission, I would climb up to 30,000 ft, point the plane straight downward at full throttle and reach the speed of sound just for grins. We would also practice dogfighting with the F-8 fighters on our ship to prepare each other in the event that North Vietnamese planes ventured out.

Just as our squadron was getting accustomed to flying missions over the North, the U.S. halted bombing north of the 19th parallel, so I never got to do missions around Hanoi. I was in one Alpha strike targeting the North Vietnamese airfield at Vinh. Our A-4's were doing primarily dive bombing which makes you very vulnerable to ground fire. We had learned from prior experience that if you don't pull up at 3000 ft, you can be in serious trouble below that. That's what happened to the first American POW, Everett Alvarez. He didn't pull up his A-4 until 1500 ft and was shot down. We all knew about him because he had already been a POW for over three years. When we did this type of bombing, our targets were mostly artillery sites and trucks. We would also strafe targets on the ground with our guns, and when we had missions over the south, we would strafe areas around our guys to help them.

Everett Alvarez's A-4 was shot down on August 5, 1964. He ended up spending over 8 years in the infamous "Hanoi Hilton" as a Prisoner of War (POW). For the first year of his captivity, he was the only aviator POW and was beaten and tortured during interrogations. Subsequent A-4 pilots had been briefed on the pitfalls of pulling out of a bombing dive too late. I recently met Porter Halyburton, another POW, who had spent over seven years in captivity with Alvarez. To understand the trauma, both physical and psychological, which the 591 American POWs endured while in North Vietnam, I recommend Halyburton's book, *Reflections on Captivity.*

We received a lot of anti-aircraft fire - a bunch. I recall one time we were going in to bomb something important. There were a lot of us on that strike. We were taking turns rolling in and dropping bombs, but as I rolled in, the enemy had me on their radar. I knew from experience that for every six bullets, there was one tracer. There were so many tracers flying around me I felt like I was in a shower. And I could not see the bullets, just the tracers!

**John approaching the carrier in his A-4 for a landing.
Note tail hook extended and destroyer plane guarding
aft of the carrier. Insert is John in front of his plane.**

*We used to do a lot of crazy shit. One time on the way back to the ship,
I was in a formation of four planes and decided to move up and roll my
plane over the skipper's plane. I did a similar roll over the ship and got
into a lot of trouble with the CO of the ship. One of my good friends,
on an earlier deployment, was with his wingman and had dropped their
bombs over Hanoi. On the way back to the ship they decided to take off
their helmets and smile for each other's cameras. They were not paying
attention to where they were and suddenly realized that they were now
flying over the Chinese island of Hainan. They were very lucky not to
have been shot down which is what happened to another plane up there
earlier in the war.*

*On one mission over the southern part of North Vietnam we were
heading back to the carrier and just as we got to "feet wet"* (this term
refers to leaving land and going over water) *I get the word that there are
two Air Force guys on the ground after they had been shot down and
that they were now surrounded by bad guys. We were told to refuel from
an Air Force KC-135 and help out. A flare had been dropped near the*

downed airmen so that we knew where they were. I was now with several other aircraft and was using an emergency frequency to communicate. As soon as we got our fuel, we rolled in to strafe all around the flare. We kept doing this while three helos came to try to pick up the Air Force guys. Unfortunately, the first helo was shot down and all three aboard were killed. Then the second one tried, and it also got shot down. The third helo was successful and the airmen on the ground were saved. But we lost 6 men saving the two. It was brutal. I never learned where the helos came from, but it let us know that we were not going to leave our people behind.

I have a lot of dead friends. We did not lose many from our squadron on our first cruise, but on our second deployment we had A-6's with us on the carrier and they had several losses. They were getting shot down all over the place. There were some bad days. I was involved in a mission providing protection for an F-8 Crusader photo bird, which was flying real low to take photos for damage assessment. All of a sudden, there was a loud explosion just behind me. A missile had hit him, and the plane just blew up into pieces. On the last day of our second deployment, the XO of the ship was flying, and as he took off, I watched his plane go straight into the water in front of the carrier. We lost him also and never really knew for sure what had happened. We even had a tragedy when we returned from deployment. My roommate on TICONDEROGA, Clarence Miles, a classmate of ours, had a terrible accident on the first workday after we returned to the states following this Vietnam deployment. He somehow flew into some electrical wires and died.

Here Nina added her perspective.

Whenever John was deployed, I trained my kids to try to sleep as late as possible in the morning. I did this because us wives at the base at Lemoore had learned that the black limo with the CO of the base and the chaplain would always show up early in the morning to tell the wife that her husband had been shot down or was missing. I figured that if we slept late, we could be assured that the rest of that day would be safe. It was always ever-present in my mind. Even when John was home, when I kissed him goodbye for a day of flying, there was always the reality that he may not come home. The only time John was deployed that I heard his voice was whenever they went into port where he was able to call me. Of course, we wrote letters and also sent audio tapes to each other. I don't think that he mentioned it, but the TICONDEROGA staterooms had no air conditioning. When John came back from that first cruise, he was skin and bones and had lost 25 pounds.

Following his second deployment to Vietnam, John resigned from the Navy and began a career as a pilot for Delta Airlines for "32 years and 2 months." John told me that he sometimes had thoughts when he was firing weapons against the enemy, but that it never lingered because "they were trying to kill me....it was war and I knew that they were killing innocent people."

It was interesting to hear Nina's perspective as a wife with small children anxiously awaiting word from John that he had survived yet another mission. It is not only the warriors who are under stress. The misery of war is never confined to the battlefield.

I find it remarkable that those continuously in harm's way, whether Marines on the ground or aviators flying dangerous missions, having seen friends perish the previous day are able to get up the next day to push the envelope of risk.... again.

John Wroten

Shreveport, Louisiana
"I wasn't sure if we should get up"

One of John's fellow Marines recommended that if I wanted to learn about artillery, I should talk to John Wroten. I was able to connect with John via computer from his home in Fairview, Texas, where he now lives with his wife, Leahray.

My dad was a schoolteacher before he went off to the war. When he came back, he ran a Western Auto store in Winfield, Louisiana. There were only 7500 people in the town, but we had three governors, including Huey and Earl Long, come from our town. Because my father was enlisted in the Navy in WW II, he had kept "The Bluejacket's Manual" which I used to read as a kid. I also watched "Men of Annapolis" so I wanted to go to the Naval Academy. The first year I applied, I was an alternate from our congressman, so I went to Louisiana Tech for a year, and then got his principal appointment the next year.

The Bluejacket's Manual has been given to every enlisted Navy recruit since 1902. It is the "bible" about Navy procedures and contains a wide range of topics every sailor should know. It is still printed and was last updated in a 25th edition in 2017. *Men of Annapolis* was a fictional television series based on life at the Naval Academy that lasted only two seasons (1957-58) but seems to have been seen by nearly every one of our classmates while they were in their early impressionable teen years. Many of us cite it as one of the reasons we wanted to attend the Academy.

While John and I were talking about the infamous Governor Huey Long and Robert Penn Warren's famous novel about him, *All the King's Men*, we laughed that both of us had seen the acclaimed stripper and Burlesque artist, Blaze Starr, who was one of Long's not-so-secret "girlfriends." Starr was a regular at the Two O'Clock Club in Baltimore where she landed after an impoverished childhood in the hollers of West Virginia. Her flaming red hair and outlandish props made her an instant favorite and a magnet for many Navy midshipmen and sailors from around the world during liberty in Baltimore. The 1989 movie, *Blaze*, featuring Paul Newman, recounted her life and included Starr in a cameo role.

While I was at Navy, I found that not too many things about ships excited me. I even threw up while we were on one of those YP's (a small training ship) *they put us on to go down the Chesapeake Bay to a football game. I became attracted to the Marine Corps early on and that's what I wanted to do. I graduated from Marine Basic School in January 1966. I didn't really care which part of the Marines I was going to, but chose artillery. I was sent out to the Army base at Fort Sill in Oklahoma to learn about these weapons, and they then flew me into Da Nang. My assigned artillery battery was Echo-212, but I was deployed as a Forward Observer with Echo-29, an infantry unit with the 9th Marines, for much of my 13 months in Vietnam. My job was to call in artillery fire for the infantry company. I went out on foot patrols with them every day, almost always south of Da Nang. I could call in gunfire from Navy ships offshore or get air support from Navy and Air Force, even B-52's. What I could call in for help depended on availability and what we needed at the moment. You had to know where you were and hoped that those firing the artillery knew where you were. Miraculously, while I was doing this, we had no incidents of friendly fire.*

A lot of the foot patrols south of Da Nang were through minefields which had been laid by the Viet Cong. It was bad. After one guy would get hit by one of these mines and get taken away by a Medevac helicopter, we would barely get up before another guy would get hit. The platoon I was with one day was walking single file through these rice paddies and behind me was my radio operator. There was a South Vietnamese interpreter behind him. We were sitting down while a Medevac helo was taking off. As soon as I took two steps, the ARVN fellow stepped on a "Bouncing Betty" mine and it blew his legs off. What saved me and my radioman was that most of the shrapnel hit his radio on his back. The blast knocked both of us down. I was still in my first month in Vietnam and wasn't sure if we should get up or what to do. Of course, we did keep moving, but those patrols were dangerous. We had some young Marines shoot themselves in the foot so that they wouldn't have to go out again. When these patrols were during the wet season, we were sleeping in the rice paddies and would often wake up with leeches all over us. Other times those paddies were dry. While we were out there on these patrols, I would often be ordered to call in some artillery fire for H&I during the night. There wasn't a lot of sleep.

Artillery fired at random intervals throughout the night to designated locations was called Harassment and Interdiction (H&I). The purpose was to not necessarily hit a known enemy concentration, but to pound a designated location in an unpredictable manner to keep the enemy guessing when moving at night. Most Marines I have spoken to have told me that they quickly became adjusted to these loud noises and were able to sleep, probably because of their own exhaustion.

After several months of these operations south of Da Nang, our infantry company started moving north and eventually got up to our 105-mm howitzer battery near the DMZ. One night we got mortared and I caught a piece of flak in my left leg while trying to crawl into a foxhole. The hospital corpsman with us patched it up and I just continued on. Once we got north of Da Nang and out of the minefields, it wasn't too bad. I had to fire my .45 a few times from my foxhole to keep the bad guys away. Our company was engaged in fire fights only a few times. Most of the problems were from snipers shooting at us from small villages as we passed by. My job was not to be a platoon leader but to be with the company of Marines to call in fire support.

I didn't get to conduct artillery fire myself until my last few months when we reached the battery location near the DMZ. I was stationed in the fire control center where I was in charge of a battery of six 105's. There were several Marines operating each weapon. While we were up here, we would occasionally get some incoming from a lone mortar. We slept in tents and lived pretty well compared to others up there making patrols. We even had a bar with Playboy pinups. The Air Force would trade us a case of beer for our Marine "Ka-Bar" knives. I went to Bangkok for my

R&R; most single guys went there, and the married guys went to Hawaii to see their wives.

A "howitzer" is a short cannon used to fire projectiles on high trajectories and at low velocity. A cannon fires shells at a flat trajectory; a mortar fires at a high trajectory. The term "howitzer" now generally refers to any type of artillery piece that attacks targets by "indirect fire." In other words, you are not aiming directly at the target but are lobbing ordnance at it. Due to its mobility and versatility, the 105 mm howitzer was used in Vietnam both by the Army and the Marines. The firebase where John directed the fire of these weapons was located just south of the DMZ and was intended to keep the North Vietnamese from infiltrating across the DMZ into the south. It was a relatively light-weight towed weapon and was typically used in a battery of six. The 105 was an older weapon which had first been built in the 1920's and used extensively in WW II. The 4 to 6 Marines manning it would set the number of propellant charges based on the range to the target. It could fire a variety of ammunition, such as high explosive, white phosphorus, smoke and even an anti-personnel round which could shoot 10,000 flechettes. The maximum range for the howitzer was about 7 miles. The gun had been initially used in Vietnam both by the French and the Viet Minh and was also used by the North Vietnamese against the U.S.

105 mm howitzer

The Ka-Bar knife mentioned by John is a legendary piece of equipment worn by every Marine in combat. It was first issued in December of 1942 and has been a trusty companion of Marines since that date, both as a weapon and as a general-purpose tool. It has been used to dig foxholes, open C-ration cans, and slit enemy throats. A caption on a photo of one of the Marines in action during the landing on Iwo Jima has the slogan, "Ka- Bar was there."

One humorous event happened while I was there. The mother of a young Marine in one of the platoons I was with was the secretary to the actress Ann Margaret. Like many other single guys, I was in love with her. His mom would send a lot of photos, the 8 1/2 x 11 glossy pin up shots, to us. We loved it! He pre-arranged with his mom that I was going to have dinner with Ann Margaret when I left Vietnam and returned to San Francisco. It was going to be a big publicity event, you know, a popular actress having dinner with a returning vet. Of course, just my luck, it didn't happen, because about a month before I came back to the states, she married the actor Roger Smith, and my dream was crushed!

My next assignment was in San Diego at the Marine Corps Recruit Depot training new Marines. I then received orders to "Junior School" in Quantico for new Captains, but the joke was that the diploma you received was actually orders back to Vietnam. I had no desire to return, so I resigned from the Marine Corps, got married, and went to work for a small company in Dallas called EDS - all in the same week. That marriage didn't last, but my job did. I stayed with them for the next 37 years. I was working for Ross Perot and had to go to Ross to ask his permission to marry my current wife because she was also working there. When Perot decided that he was going to leave EDS and start his own company in 1982, he asked me to go with him, but I chose to remain with EDS.

John told me that he did not regret going to Vietnam because, at the time, he was a firm believer in what we were doing, but by the time he left he was beginning to feel that a lot of young men were being killed for no reason. Many of our classmates ended up in Dallas working for Ross Perot's EDS (Electronic Data Systems) when they resigned from the service in the early 1970's. Perot, himself a 1953 graduate of the Naval Academy, had founded EDS in 1962 after being a salesman for IBM. His initial niche was to train personnel to operate new computer equipment which many corporations were purchasing. EDS would take over the computing and data processing tasks for a client company allowing it to focus on what it did best. Perot adopted many of the IBM employee schemes with conservative dress and strict rules for personnel behavior. He preferentially hired many young military officers who had recently resigned and filled most positions from within.

John had a long and highly successful career with EDS and remained in the Dallas area. He and his wife, Leahray, also spend time at a home in New Mexico.

Jere Harper

Pittsburgh, Pennsylvania

"It was pretty quiet for us in 1966"

I wanted to interview Jere (Jerry) because he had been on an unusual temporary assignment in early 1968. I interviewed Jere via computer from his home in Lemoore, California, where he lives with his wife, Jo Ann.

I was a swimmer in high school and wanted to attend the Naval Academy. I was the second alternate for my congressman's appointment, but both one of my high school classmates and I were accepted. I am not sure why, but my high school coach kept telling me that my swimming helped get me in. When service selection came around, I picked destroyers and met my first ship, USS HOLDER (DD-819) in Genoa, Italy. My job was the assistant Damage Control Assistant. I always remember our passage through the Atlantic back to our home port of Norfolk because we had to pass through a hurricane. Everyone aboard was sick, including the Captain.

We stayed in Norfolk getting ready for a long deployment the following summer. HOLDER sailed with our entire squadron of eight destroyers in DESRON 18 via the Panama Canal. After stops at Pearl Harbor and Guam, six weeks later we ended up on Yankee Station with several carriers. Most of what we did there during 1966 was gunfire support for U.S. units ashore in South Vietnam. We were firing our 5"/54 guns mostly during the night based on target information received from ashore. We did not interdict any small boats. It was pretty quiet offshore in the summer of 1966. On our way back we returned to Norfolk "the other way" via the Suez Canal and the Mediterranean Sea with the entire destroyer squadron.

My next assignment was in San Diego where I was assigned to the Naval Athletic Facility. This job involved a series of temporary assignments on ships throughout the Pacific Fleet. One of the ships I was assigned to was a LPH (Landing Platform Helicopter) off the coast of Vietnam where it *was being used as a hospital ship. Our main role was receiving bodies of Marines and Army troops who had been killed or wounded during the Tet offensive in early 1968. It was gruesome and sad duty, but very necessary due to the high number of incoming casualties.*

Jere resigned from the Navy in June 1970. He spent the following 25 years in sales with AT&T. He then taught for 5 years in public schools in Lemoore, before retiring while continuing to do frequent substitute teaching at the high school two blocks from his home.

Jere was not the only one of our classmates who found himself on ships receiving wounded, dying, and dead members of American fighting forces. It was important for morale that those risking their lives knew that they would receive excellent medical treatment, and in the event of death, that every effort would be made to bring their remains home for a proper stateside burial. No one wanted to be buried in Vietnam.

Steve Fabry

Evanston, Illinois

"There were no computers"

I heard that Steve and his family were stationed in the Philippines and had lived in Olongapo sometime during the war. Since so many of our classmates passed through that city while on various assignments during the Vietnam War, I was interested in hearing why Steve was there and what his experiences were. I interviewed him via computer from his home in Bremerton, Washington, where he lives with his wife, Betty.

I was born in Evanston, Illinois, in November 1941, just prior to WW II beginning for the U.S. My dad was already in the Army and served in the Army Signal Corps during the war. I was raised in Albert Lea, Minnesota, about 20 miles from the Iowa border. I attended high school there, but had no funds to pay for college, so I enlisted in the Navy immediately after graduation. I became a Hospital Corpsman and several of the doctors I was working with began pushing me to try to go to the Naval Academy. There were 150 slots or so reserved for enlisted personnel, and the doctors were convinced that I could get in. I applied and was selected, but first I had to spend a year at the Naval Academy Preparatory School in Bainbridge, Maryland. When I had my eyes examined during our youngster (slang for sophomore) *year at the Academy, I found out that I needed glasses which meant that at graduation I had to go to a staff assignment. On one of my training cruises, I started to hang out with the Supply Officer on a destroyer and knew right away that I wanted to follow that route.*

My first assignment after six months of Supply School in Georgia was on USS HENRY W TUCKER (DD-875) homeported in Yokosuka, Japan. I arrived in March 1966, and it was absolutely painful. As Supply Officer I was a Department Head, but still got a lot of bad jobs because all other officers were senior to me. I had a lot of men working for me, including all the cooks, disbursing clerks, ship store and food service personnel, and storekeepers, but none of these guys had been trained in Navy schools. I had to get men from the deck force and train them. We simply did not have many senior enlisted men in my department. I did have a Storekeeper who was a Chief Petty Officer, but he mostly stayed in the Chief's Quarters and didn't come out much. I ended up having to do almost all the paperwork in so many different areas. As I said, it was painful.

TUCKER spent a lot of time on Yankee Station plane guarding for the carriers. This involved us following the carrier to be in position to pick up any aviators who ended up in the sea due to an aircraft accident. But we also went down south and did shore bombardment of targets inside South Vietnam. In fact, I believe that our ship was the first U.S. ship to do shore bombardment there. During one evolution, we fired 5000 rounds from our 5"/38 guns around the clock at coordinates provided to us. As far as I could determine, we were never firing at known enemy locations. The purpose was only to disrupt and confuse Viet Cong ground forces.

We pulled into Da Nang once for briefings, but generally we were always being resupplied at sea. All of our ammunition came from AEs, which were ammunition ships. We also received provisions and stores from AFs which carry refrigerated food and dry stores. They modified some of these to be AFSs, which are combat stores ship. They carried food and lots of parts, but not much fuel. AOs were the oilers which carried fuel. We were the first ship to refuel a hovering helicopter at night, and we also did frequent refueling of helos during daytime. Land bases such as Da Nang and Cam Ranh Bay received supplies mostly from commercial cargo ships which had been chartered for the war.

I did two Vietnam tours on TUCKER doing much the same, except on the second deployment when we did several MARKET TIME operations inspecting small ships which were transiting up and down the Vietnamese coastline. Most of the time when our ship was at General Quarters doing firing operations, I was in the crypto center decoding messages. I

145

was transferred off TUCKER to the Naval Supply Center at Bremerton, Washington, where my work involved transportation and distribution. I married Betty during this tour, and we started a family. The Navy then sent me to further training in Oakland to become a "transportation expert." I did not know that finishing first in the class meant that you were going to be automatically sent to Naval Supply Depot Subic Bay in the Philippines, THE hub of all Navy transportation involved with Vietnam. This is where all the planes and supply ships headed to Vietnam were loaded.

I arrived in the Philippines in 1970. All repair parts and supplies came into Subic Bay via airplanes from the States or merchant ships, which were usually large container ships. I had 80 sailors working for me and half were probably on opium. I also had a large number of Filipino contract stevedores who did the loading and unloading of the ships. We were constantly transferring supplies from merchant ships bringing in materials to Navy ships heading back over to Vietnam. This is why I contend that we were the greatest Navy in the world - and still are. No other country has the ability to sustain this level of logistics around the globe - no one. My daughter, who became a Supply Corps Admiral, had the honor of being the logistics officer for the entire Pacific Fleet a few years ago. She had the challenge of ensuring that the U.S. still had the capability of managing all these parts and supplies to supply battle groups, even in the event we lost satellites. Of course, when we were doing all of this during the Vietnam War, it was all on cards using pencil and paper. There were no computers - just a ton of paper. There were also several organizations throughout the Pacific with the responsibility of figuring out where each of the ships were located and how to get supplies and repair parts to each of them. It was a constantly challenging task.

My family was allowed to join me in Subic Bay. Upon arrival, we learned that there was no longer any housing available on the base. In short, it was an absolute disaster for us. I had to go out into Olongapo, the Philippine city next to the base, to search for a place for us to live. I found a small house, in a relatively safe area. But drinkable water was a problem. Every morning we had to fill 5-gallon jugs of water from a hose on the base near the gate, carry it to our car, then drive those jugs to our home. You did not want to drink the local water! Betty had to wash our clothes in a bucket, including diapers for our two-year-old baby.

I drove our only car to the base, so Betty had to use Jeepneys to get around town. There was no telephone, and most nights we had brown outs when the electricity went off. Those lucky enough to be living on the base had no idea what we were going through living off base. Several of the Filipino women who lived near our home were working as "dancers" in the bars and would bring sailors home for the night. There were frequent gunfights near our home because President Marcos had not yet declared martial law. We had bars on our windows and even put broken beer bottles in cement on the top of our exterior walls. Frequently, as Betty was cooking, power would go out and she had to finish the meal on a Coleman stove. We often tried to visit friends living on base for dinner so that we could bring along our sheets to wash at their place. Once, during a typhoon, the Olongapo River backed up and was coming into our home via a floor drain. Betty was upset and I told her to stop crying, at least until we moved my new stereo equipment to the second floor. That was not well received! On our wedding anniversary we decided to go out to the one restaurant in town which had drinkable water. After dinner Betty asked me to show her some of the sailor bars in town where the "ladies" were working. It was an interesting night. Betty talked to some of the young girls who proved to be very friendly and outgoing. We even did some dancing with them. Sometimes when I was driving home from the base, I would see a gunfight along the side of the road. If I saw a sailor nearby, I would pick him up and drop him off in a safer place. Olongapo was not a great place to raise a child.

Most public transportation in the Philippines during this era consisted of a multitude of "Jeepneys" – small, motorized vehicles converted from American jeeps left after WW II. Most were covered all over with garish, and often outlandish, painting. Passengers sat inside facing each other, or simply hung on to the back. When a Jeepney came by, you simply hopped on and then hopped off when close to your destination. I do not recall the exact fare, but it was very low. In the midst of all the other dangers in Olongapo, I always felt safe in the Jeepneys.

Like most ships assigned to duty in the Western Pacific, my submarine, USS GURNARD (SSN-662), came to the Naval Base at Subic Bay on several occasions for supplies and repairs. The facility had capabilities to repair ships of all sizes and types, including both aircraft carriers and nuclear-powered ships. The surrounding region also hosted Cubi Point Naval Air Station and Clark Air Force Base. With so many sailors and airmen arriving replete with cash following long deployments, there was a ready market for all forms of "entertainment." The atmosphere was indeed akin to the Wild West. Many local men carried guns; it was certainly not safe to walk any of the back streets after dark. On a trip I took from Olongapo to Manila on a "Victory Liner" bus, we stopped in the middle of nowhere for a bathroom break. As everyone piled off the bus, I noticed that every man on the bus had pulled out a handgun to protect us from Communist Huk rebels who controlled much of the region. The bathroom was the side of the road for both men and women.

The Olongapo River was one of the most notorious sewage systems in the world. Steve even mentioned to me how he could see blue toilet paper from their home floating in the river shortly after flushing the toilet. The river had a distinctively foul odor. Everyone I talked to who had crossed the bridge over this river immediately cringed at the memory of the unique smell. To make matters worse, Filipino children were almost always swimming in the river under the bridge while imploring sailors to toss coins which they would then dive for. It was surreal. I cannot imagine how a young American wife like Betty survived Steve's tour of duty at Subic.

Prolonged war cannot take place without solid logistics - especially when the war is on the other side of the world from the homeland. None of the weapons of war, nor the personnel using those weapons, can be sustained without an intricate and reliable supply chain. Steve was part of that chain.

Following his tour at Subic Bay, Steve attended graduate school at Michigan State and served in a succession of positions within the Supply Corps, rising to the rank of Captain prior to his retirement.

Mike Hester
Honolulu, Hawaii
"Mine Mike"

A mutual friend recommended that I talk to Mike about his experiences as a Marine platoon leader in Vietnam. In addition to my initial interview with him via computer, I had several other follow-up phone conversations with Mike. He and his wife, Linda, live in an apartment in Norfolk overlooking the WW II battleship, USS WISCONSIN (BB-64).

I was born in Honolulu early in 1942. My biological father was a Supply Officer in the Navy at Cavite in the Philippines when the Japanese invaded. He and a number of Army guys and Australians escaped and later took off in a motor sailboat for Australia. They were captured nine months later off an island in the Pacific and became POWs. He died in captivity in August 1945. My mother came back to the U.S. and later married my stepfather, who was a Marine, at the base at Parris Island, South Carolina. I went to high school at Admiral Farragut Prep in Florida, and then spent a year at Columbia Prep in D.C. before I received an appointment to the Naval Academy. I had always wanted to go to USNA; my grandfather on my mother's side had been out of the USNA class of 1911. At Navy, I was on the rifle team and went to the National championships one year.

I wanted to be a Marine based on my stepfather's career and other family connections. He had been a Marine captain stationed in Peking, China, at the U.S. Embassy prior to our entry into WW II. On December 8, 1941, their detachment surrendered to the Japanese and became POWs for the duration of the war. He didn't talk about this much, but I admired him. Also, my Aunt Amy was married to a Marine General. At service selection, there were 70 slots available to go Marine Corps and I was able to get one of them.

There is more to Mike's story concerning his father and stepfather. His biological father, who was captured with the Australians, suffered terrible treatment; he was one of the over 400 out of this group of 500 who died while in captivity. His stepfather, who survived after being imprisoned in China, was part of the "North China Marines." U.S. Marines had been stationed in China since the Boxer Rebellion of 1900. Their role was to guard the American Embassy in Peking and other official enclaves in other Chinese cities. In late November 1941 the men in the 4th Marines in Shanghai were evacuated to the Philippines, with the men of the North China Marines scheduled to leave China on December 10, 1941. The day after the Japanese bombed Pearl Harbor, all 203 of these Marines became POW's. Fifteen were officers (including Mike's future stepfather) and 188 were enlisted men. During the next 4 years of the war, these POWs were moved by boxcar to various prison camps in China and ultimately to Hokkaido and Sendai on the Japanese mainland to work in coal mines. Mike told me that because his stepfather was an officer, he was ordered to supervise the enlisted men digging coal. When ordered to teach his men Japanese, his stepfather complied, but only by teaching one number a day. When liberated at the end of the war, these Marines had been prisoners for 1,376 days. Amazingly, of the 203 interned, only nine died from starvation and brutal treatment. More information is available online by searching "North China Marines."

When I asked Mike if the POW fate of both his biological father and stepfather was in his mind as he flew toward his first assignment in Vietnam, he quickly replied, "Of course!" But it was his mother who was most concerned. As Mike was leaving she said to him, "Here I go again."

At Marine Basic School I knew that I wanted to go infantry. There were about 250 2nd Lieutenants in my class. I broke my leg in the first month of training at Quantico. As a result, I did not graduate until June 1966. The battalion to which I was assigned was formed from several units; we trained in California for eight weeks before packing out for Vietnam and boarding a group of amphibious ships with all our vehicles and equipment. Our entire infantry battalion was loaded on an APA [an attack transport ship] *and arrived at Dong Ha in October 1966. There were roughly 1000 men in our battalion. I was 1st platoon commander in Mike Company, 3rd Battalions, 26th Marines. When the 2nd platoon commander was killed, I took over that platoon.*

At Dong Ha we were sent to what later became Camp Eagle halfway between Dong Ha and Hue. We initially formed a perimeter protecting our tanks and the artillery battery. Because bad guys were continuing to come down jungle paths near Route 1, we were tasked to set up ambushes to try to intercept them. The enemy was a mixture of Viet Cong and NVA. To set up these ambushes, we would go out as a company. All three platoons would walk out for eight to twelve day missions carrying all our food, water, and ammunition. This was quite a heavy load for these young Marines to carry. In addition to carrying his M-16 rifle, he would be wearing a flak jacket and helmet, up to 10 days of C-rations, two canteens of water, a trenching tool, and a poncho with liner. He would also have 75-100 rounds of ammunition for his weapon. The C-rations came in metal cans which added to the weight. Many of these were left over from the Korean War and some from WW II. Most men would also bring extra pairs of socks to try to ensure that their feet would be dry. Also, you would bring along a poncho to cover yourself in the rain and an inflatable mattress. I would estimate that each Marine was initially carrying at least 55 pounds when beginning to walk on these missions.

Protective clothing, weapons and supplies were always a weight challenge for infantry. A comparable list of the gear and weights carried by Army infantry soldiers can be found in the first chapter of *The Things They Carried* by Tim O'Brien.

We would pick a spot along one of the numerous trails in the surrounding jungle, set up an ambush, and wait. You didn't talk, smoke, or even urinate. Typically, the enemy would come in groups of 10-15 as they walked down trails from the hills heading to friendly villages on the other side of Highway 1 to get re-supplied. We would take up a hidden position in the jungle maybe 8-10 yards off a trail allowing us to be well concealed. We could hear them coming because they were usually talking, often during daylight. It would generally be over in 2-3 minutes. After the shooting ended, we would collect any weapons and then search the bodies for paperwork which they had been carrying. We always saved this to give to our intel people. The writing was, of course, in Vietnamese so we had no idea what was on the papers. We weren't even sure if it was important, but we gathered it. Most of the enemy were carrying AK-47s; a few had single shot weapons. After our attacks, there was never any enemy left. After collecting their weapons and paperwork and anything else of interest, we just left the bodies and moved on to set up a new ambush. Occasionally, we would return to a site and find that all the bodies had been buried.

Marines setting up for an ambush

Mike's description of ambushes may sound cold and impersonal to someone who has not been exposed to the realities of war. The object of the war at this time, as dictated by the Commander of U.S. Forces in Vietnam, was to win by "outkilling" the Communist forces (Viet Cong and North Vietnamese). There were few attempts to capture territory; hills taken during a battle were typically abandoned the next day. "Score" was kept by enemy body count. The theory was that if the U.S.

and its allies could "eliminate" sufficient enemy, the opponents would surely eventually sue for peace or at least begin negotiations. The job of Mike and his platoon was to find and kill enemy forces with as few losses as possible. For both sides in this tragic war, it was indeed a filthy way to die. Mike words to me were, "Once we set up for an ambush, it was gonna happen."

The U.S. would run convoys of 100-150 trucks carrying supplies up Route 1 from Da Nang to U.S. posts near the DMZ. One of our other jobs was to provide security for many of these convoys, which were called Rough Riders. At other times, we worked with the South Vietnamese in combined action platoons consisting of 8-10 Marines and 10-15 ARVN troops. These Vietnamese soldiers often lived in nearby villages. Some of the ARVN troops I later worked with in the hills near Khe Sanh were Montagnards.

The Montagnards were indigenous Vietnamese who lived mostly in the mountains. They were excellent fighters and were a great help to the U.S. Special Forces. It is estimated that close to 40,000 Montagnards fought side-by-side with the U.S. out of base camps in the Highlands of Vietnam and in the mountainous region around Khe Sanh and in Laos. As Mike recounts, they also fought alongside U.S. Marines.

When I first went in country, all together I had 62 men in my platoon which included a machine gun unit, four guys with rockets, and two hospital corpsmen. There were so many enemy mines causing us to lose Marines. I ended up with only 18 men! Most were not killed, but many lost limbs due to injuries from "Bouncing Betty" mines. One night we were on top of a hill and a Bouncing Betty went off near me, but it went straight up and never exploded. If it had blown, all of the officers in our company who happened to be nearby would probably been killed or seriously wounded. On that operation, we had about 20 guys who had to be medevaced. Our Mike Company had such a problem with these mines that we were often called "Mine Mike."

We kept doing these operations until March 1967 when we went to Phu Bai and the area near the Imperial Capital of Hue. We later learned that the North Vietnamese had begun to mass nearly 10,000 troops in the area in preparation for a future assault, but we had found few of them while we were there. Our battalion was then flown over to Khe Sanh to do fighting on Hills 881 and 861 in that region. These were called the "Hill Battles." I was told to have our unit lead the charge up one called Hill 689, but there was little resistance and we suffered few casualties in that operation. Later, in July 1967 when I was still at Khe Sanh, I took over a group called Sub Unit Five which put me in charge of 200-250 Marines running the mess hall, the medical facility, and generally doing all the things to keep the base running. The young Lieutenant who took over my platoon was killed one week later.

Khe Sanh was important for both the U.S. and North Vietnam if only because of its strategic location near the Laotian border and the Ho Chi Minh Trail. Because American forces had been using Khe Sanh to launch operations against supplies and troops being sent down the Trail, it became a prime target for the NVA. The siege of Khe Sanh began on January 21, 1968, roughly three months after Mike left the area. This was one of the few times the North Vietnamese chose to extend a battle past a few days. Fighting went on for over two months with the Marines, U.S. Special Forces, and South Vietnamese allies under intense shelling and frequent attack. During the two-month battle, U.S. forces at Khe Sanh numbering 7500 men were fighting at least 25,000 North Vietnamese. One day during the siege, over 1300 shells hit the base. Throughout all of March 1968 there was an average of at least 150 shells per day being fired at the Marines. It was not until April 9 that land access to Khe Sanh was achieved, and the siege ended. Numerous books have been written concerning this lengthy battle.

In October 1967, I was at Khe Sanh beginning my 13th month in Vietnam when two infantry officers were killed nearby close to the end of their tours. As a result, if only to prevent yet another Marine getting killed at the end of his tour, the authorities sent me on a helicopter back to Phu Bai. From there I was sent to Da Nang and put on an R&R flight to Hawaii. I was ultimately assigned a seat on a plane back to the states.

Mike's experience as a Marine infantry officer in Vietnam took place during a particularly dangerous and brutal phase of the war. His Marine Corps Basic School class graduated 500 Lieutenants; 33 were killed in action (KIA). The classes following his fared even worse. Of the 498 graduates in Class Six-67, 50 lost their lives in Vietnam - a staggering 1 out of 10. Mike talked soberly about these numbers. He was acutely aware that many of the deaths were random. You were either near a mine when it went off, or you happened to be lucky that day. And how did one platoon escape being victims of an ambush when another was decimated?

Following Vietnam, Mike served in a series of assignments for the Marine Corps throughout the world, both afloat and ashore. He obtained a Master's degree in operations research and served in Japan, Korea, and Saudi Arabia prior to retiring as a Colonel in 1991. Mike told me that he had never spoken to his family about much of his experience in Vietnam, but now wanted to share that phase of his life. He said that he did not have nightmares or conditions now called PTSD (post-traumatic stress disorder) but had simply internalized the horrors. I am not certain that I could do the same.

Phase II, late 1967 – late 1969

American casualties during the Vietnam War rose dramatically in the years following the arrival of the 3500 Marines in the Ninth Marine Expeditionary Brigade on March 8, 1965. Once the Marines waded ashore on the beach at Da Nang, additional U.S. forces soon followed. Missions quickly expanded from a defensive posture to offensive operations throughout South Vietnam. With General Westmoreland now directing American forces, the strategy became one of using overwhelming forces against the Viet Cong and North Vietnamese troops, along with bombing of North Vietnam in a war of attrition. By 1968, U.S. forces reached a peak of 535,000. American losses also grew steadily from 1,863 in 1965 to 16,592 in 1968. Injuries and wounds were much higher. U.S. offensive strategy throughout this period continued to be focused on "body count," that is, conductng operations designed to engage and kill as many enemy troops as possible, but not retaining control of ground. After bloody battles were waged to capture strategic hills, Americans would withdraw from the same hills as higher level planners were content with having high body counts of dead enemy forces. As you will read in many of the following stories, this policy was questioned by those Americans who were actually involved in these bloody battles.

Westmoreland continued to deliver optimistic reports to both the media and the U.S. Congress throughout 1967 and even bragged that under his leadership American forces "won every battle." However, public perception in the U.S. changed quickly following the massive Tet Offensive launched by communist forces throughout South Vietnam in early 1968. Although Allied forces successfully fought off these attacks with heavy losses inflicted on both the Viet Cong and the North Vietnamese, Westmoreland's prior assurances that the war was being won by his strategy of attrition were now viewed as hollow. President Johnson discontinued further buildup of American forces and soon relieved Westmoreland by naming General Creighton Abrams as his successor.

Throughout this period, the Soviet Union and China continued to pour weapons, advisors, and supplies into North Vietnam to bolster their war effort. The communists had obviously not lost their will to fight.

American political leadership continued to tightly control bombing operations to avoid Chinese or Soviet troops directly entering the war. "Sanctuaries," areas where American bombing was forbidden, were created around Hanoi and Haiphong harbor at various times and on March 31, 1968, Johnson ordered another bombing halt north of the 20th parallel in North Vietnam in the hope that this would entice the communists to come to the peace table. This halt coincided with an increase in U.S. bombing and artillery operations south of the 20th parallel in an effort to concentrate on enemy forces and supplies crossing the DMZ into the south. When Richard Nixon won the Presidency in the fall of 1968, he promised to end U.S. involvement with "peace and honor." But American troops continued to die - over 11,000 in 1969. Although the long-time leader of North Vietnam, Ho Chi Minh, died in September 1969, his successors were equally committed to pursuing the war to a successful conclusion. The war was far from over.

Skip Gunther

Riverside, California

"Mustang Sally"

Skip telephoned me to ask if I had interviewed any I Corps Swift boat guys. When I told him that I had spoken only to "Swifties" who had served in the Mekong Delta, he responded, "I bet none of them were ever bracketed by friendly fire." I replied, "We have to talk." A week later we were chatting via computer. Skip was in his Ford F-350 pickup truck in Kennesaw, Georgia. His wife, Nancy, was in their RV travel trailer behind Skip's truck. They had been on the road for the past four years and were back in Georgia where they occasionally return to pick up mail.

I was born in Riverside, California, and was the oldest of five. Dad was a professor at the University of California, Riverside, where he was a specialist in insect toxicology. In fact, one of his major jobs was to analyze DDT for the government. He made several trips to Belgium to work with European scientists on this insecticide. As a kid I watched all the "Victory at Sea" episodes and became interested in the Navy. Also, one of our neighbors was a Naval Academy grad, so in my final years of high school I wrote to my congressman and received his appointment. Both during high school and throughout my four years at the Academy I played the trumpet. It was, by far, my favorite thing to do; I played in several bands while at USNA. In fact, that is how I got my nickname, Skip. In our first summer at the Academy, I was playing in a concert we were giving at Hood College, which was, at the time, an all-girls school. I was the featured soloist during one of the songs, "Trumpeter's Lullaby." I knew that song like my own name, but as I looked out at all those girls in rather skimpy summer outfits, I totally skipped one of the sections. Of course, none of the girls noticed it, but everyone in the band did. They immediately started calling me "Skip," and that's what I have been ever since!

I wanted to be a pilot, but early in our last year at USNA I found that I no longer had 20/20 vision. I opted to go down to D.C. to be interviewed by Admiral Rickover for selection into the Nuclear Submarine program. My interview with Rickover lasted maybe six seconds until I was told "get the #### out." I was ushered to a small closet where I had to "think" for at least the next 20 minutes. Nonetheless I was accepted and upon graduation, off I went to Submarine School in Groton, Connecticut. While I was there, I realized that I didn't want to serve in subs. It's a long story, but I managed to get out of submarines and was assigned to USS CONE (DD-866) in Charleston, South Carolina, as the Main Propulsion Assistant (MPA).

Skip's interview with Admiral Rickover was not unusual. When a senior from the Naval Academy or other university was "invited" to apply to be trained to serve on nuclear-powered submarines or surface ships, he was transported to the Office of Naval Reactors in Washington, D.C. to be interviewed by three senior engineers (who may, or may not, have been naval officers). Following these technically oriented interviews, the midshipman was escorted into Admiral Rickover's office for the final "go-no go" interview. These sessions are infamous; many recollections can be found online. Rickover's apparent goal was to put the interviewee under stress, often by having you seated in front of him in a chair with shortened front legs. Nearly always, the interview ended with a stream of profanities from Rickover directed at the young man being interviewed. As in the case with Skip, my interview also lasted under 10 seconds and was also told "get the #### out." That was the first of my numerous interactions with "the kindly old gentleman" over the course of the following 16 years while I was in submarines. (Many actually used "KOG" as an abbreviation for Rickover). I exacted some small measure of payback by being involved in Rickover being fired by Secretary of the Navy John Lehman in late 1981. That, of course, is a book-length "another story."

The CONE had been built during an 8-month period at the end of WW II and was not in great material condition when I arrived aboard in late 1965. As MPA I was in charge of much of the engineering equipment which included the distilling plants that make water for the ship. They had numerous leaks and were always a problem. When I told the captain about the seriousness of the problem, he sent all of the engineering department down to the engine room and told to us to stay there until the problems were fixed. By the time we reached port in Piraeus, Greece, he was so angry that he restricted all of my enlisted engineering crew to the ship for the first two days while we were in port. On the third day, I had duty aboard ship, but when my men came back at the end of liberty call, they coaxed me to drink some ouzo. A few drinks later, I was marching the entire group out into town to "The Anchor Bar" where we all drank until 4 AM. I always traveled with my trumpet and played the entire night with the local band. I then marched them all back, and we got underway a few hours later. I always joked that I could now lay claim to having led a mutiny. The captain was furious and restricted me to the ship; two months later he told me that my actions were "the best example of naval leadership" that he had seen. We remained friends for years.

At the end of my tour on CONE, I volunteered for Swift boat duty in Vietnam. After training with my crew at the Naval Amphibious Base in San Diego, we all arrived in Da Nang in October 1967. I was the Officer-in-Charge with a crew of 5 enlisted men. We often had a Vietnamese Liaison Officer who was presumably in training to ultimately take over the boat. We soon learned that following the pre-patrol briefing assigning us to a patrol area, if the Liaison dude showed up, it was going to be a safe patrol. If he was a no-show, we knew that we better be ready for action. Coincidence? I think not.

My boat was PCF-21. We operated out of Da Nang for the first six months making patrols up and down the coast of I Corps. My call sign was "Mustang Sally." I got that because, in the lyrics of that song it says, "I guess you gotta put your flat feet on the ground." That's exactly what my reputation was because I would sometimes be the only Swift boat commander who would go out in high seas. Big waves never bothered me. My feet were always on the deck even though the weather up there during monsoons can be pretty bad. Although I wasn't a Captain of the ship, but was the "Officer-in-Charge, the crew called me "Skipper." I never would let them call me Skip….it had to be skipper.

There were about 20 PCF patrol areas up and down the coast of I Corps. Many involved river entrances, such as at the Cua Dai River. The south entrance to that river was infested with Viet Cong. Every time we went up that river we were ambushed and got into a fire fight. We thought that there was an underground VC hospital on the southern entrance. We often took some hits on the boat, but none of us were wounded. We also did patrols on the Perfume River heading toward Hue, but never got that far upriver. I once took an Admiral to the PBR base up that river, but the weather was beginning to get real bad from a typhoon that was coming. On the way back to Da Nang I had to order the Admiral to get in the aft of the boat to keep him alive. He didn't like being ordered around, but I told him that I didn't care if he was an Admiral and that I was in charge of the boat. When we got back safely to Da Nang, he came to the pilot house. I didn't know what to expect, but he thanked me and said, "Lieutenant, you were right. And that was great boat handling!"

Skip's Swift boat, PCF-21, (Patrol Craft Fast) was built for Vietnam warfare. It was constructed in Louisiana by Sewart Seacraft. The 50 ft aluminum hull had a beam of 13 1/2 ft and a shallow draft of just under five ft. Two 475-horsepower diesel engines gave it a speed of close to 30 kts, but Skip told me that he generally cruised at 15 kts. The twin screws (propellers) made the boat extremely maneuverable. Skip mentioned that during the typhoon adventure with the Admiral he was steering strictly with the engines and screws. The armament was twin .50 caliber machine guns on top of the pilot house with another .50 mounted aft over an 81-mm mortar. During the Vietnam War, 125 PCFs were built; 104 ended up being transferred to the South Vietnamese Navy. Although originally intended primarily for use in offshore waters, Swift boats were increasingly used from 1968-70 in the rivers both along the coastline of South Vietnam and in the waterways of the Mekong Delta. Skip spent considerable time in hazardous rivers; four Swift boats were lost in combat. Of the 3600 who served on Swift boats, 500 were wounded and 50 were killed.

We did a lot of crazy stuff and while at Da Nang, called ourselves the Ben Hai Raiders. There are two rivers near the DMZ. The Qua Viet River flows into the South China Sea maybe three miles south of the DMZ, and the Ben Hai is about the same distance north. The Ben Hai has a large opening into the sea, maybe five miles wide, and on the north side there are cliffs with caves. We learned that the NVA had dug tunnels with big howitzers on rails which they would roll in and out to attack U.S. ships. Even though we were not supposed to do so, one of our favorite things was to go up there. In the middle of the night, we would cruise up past the DMZ and head for the mouth of the Ben Hai River. I would swing the boat in a large arc at high speed near shore while my crew fired mortar and machine guns into those caves. We would then zig zag out of there. One night as we were on our way out, we were getting shot at from the cliffs. Nothing real close, but all of a sudden, something big went off just off our starboard side. It raised our boat five to ten feet out of the water. All of us yelled, "What the hell was that??" A few seconds later we had another one on our port side just as close! I quickly realized that we were getting shot at by ships on the Navy gun line which was further offshore. They didn't know we were there. I got on the radio and started yelling, "Cease fire! Cease fire! Friendly, friendly!" I thought that I was probably going to get court martialed because we weren't supposed to be up there, but we still did this at least three more times. I was always surprised that no one ever spoke to me about this. Not a single soul said anything. Hell, there were maybe 12-15 boats at Da Nang then, and a bunch of us did it anyway. As far as I know, no one got into trouble doing these nighttime operations and it really helped the morale of our crews.

When Tet began in early 1968 we were doing patrols in Da Nang Harbor 24/7. From the sea we could see the fireworks from enemy attacks on the base, but we never encountered any threats in the harbor area. Pretty soon it died down and we resumed our normal operations.

We did see a lot of action throughout my tour in Vietnam. I was involved in 33 separate firefights, some in the north I Corps area, but several major ones took place further south near Coastal Group 16 off the Batangan Peninsula when I was operating out of Chu Lai. The South Vietnamese base on the Buc Dac River where Coastal Group 16 was located was overrun at least 3 times by the NVA. During one of these events, I drove my boat up on the beach and picked up the two American officer advisors and their two enlisted guys. We didn't pick up any Vietnamese forces which were still fighting. That night we went through all of our ammo, both machine guns and mortars, while making runs *back and forth off the beach. After things calmed down in the morning, I went ashore and found an AK-47 that had been left behind by the VC. It even had notches on it. I shipped it back to San Diego via a buddy on an LST and picked it up when I got back to the states. That Coastal Group 16 was a very dangerous place. The senior Navy advisor that we picked up was killed the next time they were overrun. In fact, while I was in Vietnam no senior Navy advisor completed his tour at Coastal Group 16.*

These actions occurred later in my tour when we were operating out of the base down the coast at Chu Lai. We had five to eight Swift boats there and would tie up to a small pier. It seemed like every time we were in Dung Quat Bay - which is how we got into and out of Chu Lai - we were shot at. It was a real no man's land.

Occasionally I would visit some Army detachments by hitching a ride on a Huey helicopter in order to coordinate upcoming actions with them. A couple of times I flew into Landing Zone Dottie for a meeting with an Army Colonel to plan for a joint operation near My Lai.

We had very little supervision when we were at Chu Lai. We would trade steaks for the use of Army jeeps. Often we would take their guys on patrol in return for getting some Army helo flights into combat with them. Sometimes on these helo flights we would swoop down next to a Vietnamese hooch and look inside to scare them. It was just crazy stuff. None of us expected to come back alive, so we didn't worry too much about rules. Sometimes we would be in a hooch there at Chu Lai playing poker when some incoming rounds would be hitting not too far away. Usually, we would just keep playing and have another beer. I guess no one wanted to leave money on the table while diving into a bunker.

One of the quartermasters on my boat was a Second Class Petty Officer who had served on PT boats in WW II; he was a good man with lots of experience. My engineman was a Second Class Machinist Mate; he was a great mechanic, but he was always drunk. He replaced five different engines when I blew them up. I never knew where the replacement engines came from, but he always had them on the dock waiting for us.

I used to frequently hang around in Chu Lai with Bob, an Army Intelligence officer. I got to know him because he was my contact for turning over detainees we had captured from VC boats. His people would interrogate them. I never asked what happened to them after that. One day I took Bob and three of our crew out to this island off the coast just to see what was out there. We had heard that it had a small air strip. When we arrived, we found a Vietnamese guard who told us "two doctors and two round eye women" were hiking up the trail ahead. We said, "Round eyes?!" As soon as we heard those words, we raced up the trail to meet them. They were American nurses working at an AID [Agency for International Development] *hospital in Quang Ngai and had flown out there on a helicopter to take a hike in a safe place. I started dating Judy, one of these nurses, and on days off I would take a jeep about 20 miles down Route One to Quang Ngai to see her. There were six to eight American nurses working there and they all lived in one house. I had to dodge big potholes on Route 1 and occasionally swerved the jeep into rice paddies to avoid suspicious groups. Once I got stuck in a rice paddy and knew that if night came with me still there, I would be dead. Luckily, an American helo came over and saw me and called for a truck to tow me out so I could get back to Chu Lai. On that drive to Quang Ngai, I always had to pass My Lai, where the massacre had taken place in March 1968. That whole area had always been a major VC stronghold, so I was careful whenever in the vicinity. The massacre had taken place shortly after Tet and there were lots of rumors while I was there about what had taken place, but I was focused on my own problems. I never talked to my Army friends about what they knew or did not know.*

Most readers with knowledge of My Lai might bristle at Skip's apparently casual reaction to those terrible events. The massacre of everyone in the hamlet was indeed barbaric in every sense. The number killed still remains uncertain, but most agree that it was between 347 and 504 unarmed civilians. Some of the women were gang-raped before being mutilated, including girls as young as 12. To make matters worse, if such is possible, several senior Army officers attempted to cover up the massacre. When the public learned of the incident over a year later, there was world-wide outrage along with increased American opposition to the war. Each online description of the My Lai events sickens the stomach. Yet most of us have not been thrust into the daily horrors of war - particularly a war when you are equally at danger from what appear to be innocent villagers. Many Viet Cong combatants were women who raised children and did chores during daytime but became black pajama fighters at night. Skip - like most other American soldiers embedded in Vietnam - had seen such situations and had built-up anger against anyone who may be trying to kill him and who had killed his friends and shipmates. When horrors surround you, it becomes easier to ignore the horrible.

We continued to do a lot of "irregular activities" while I was at Chu Lai. I even took Judy out on my boat on a patrol once. I ran my boat up on a beach only to find that it was infested with Viet Cong, so we got out of there fast. I ended up marrying Judy, and Bob married the other nurse, Wendy. My marriage didn't work out, but Bob's did. Unfortunately, Wendy died of cancer a few years ago.

I left Vietnam in October 1968 and received orders to Destroyer School, but in early 1969 I put in my resignation from the Navy to get out in June. Instead of letting me out, I was sent as Operations Officer on USS COLONIAL (LSD-18) which was headed to Vietnam! So there I was coordinating a large amphibious landing with 1000 Marines south of Da Nang. Later we picked up the same Marines as the U.S. was beginning to draw down forces in 1969.

Skip left the Navy in June 1969 and obtained both a M.A. and a Ph.D. in Operations Research at University of California, Berkeley. He then worked for Bell Labs for 10 years and later became a partner with Booz Allen Hamilton doing consulting until 1995 when he went cruising on a sailboat for the next 5 years. He now travels the U.S. with Nancy in their truck and trailer.

Skip's portrayal of Swift boat activities in Vietnam may seem to some as material for a "MASH" TV series, but it was deadly serious and danger-ous duty. He was fortunate to have survived with no significant injuries to himself or his crew (with some of whom he still stays in touch). His memories do help to portray both the chaotic nature of war and the ac-tions which men take to stay sane in an insane environment. Placing young men into a strange, dangerous environment with death lingering in the air promotes actions and decisions not readily understood, or ac-cepted, by those who have never been there.

Skip Orr

Brooklyn, New York

"On my first day we lost one aircraft"

Skip has always been one of our classmates whom we all envied. Although he was the star wide receiver on the Navy football team, it was not those exploits which gained our attention - we had a lot of great athletes in that Class of 1965. No, it was how in our later years, Skip never appeared to age. Here we were, all showing signs that time had not been kind to us in terms of our appearance, while Skip still looked as if he was ready to go back onto the football field and star for any pro team. To make matters worse for the rest of us, he is also one of the nicest persons I have ever met.

Skip still looks great, but like several of our other classmates who served in Vietnam, he is struggling now with Parkinson's disease. One thing that has not changed is his personality; he remains a cheerful, exceptionally pleasant friend. I interviewed him on the computer from his home in Reston, Virginia, where he lives with his wife, Merry.

My dad was a policeman in New York City before he went off to war. He got that job back after he returned and completed his 20 years for the city. When I was in high school we were now living in Levittown, a planned community for returning WW II veterans on Long Island. I always had to laugh years later when we played Army in football because their quarterback, Rollie Stichweh, went to the public high school right across the street from Chaminade Catholic High School where I was the quarterback. Our teams often walked across the street and scrimmaged together. Small world! I was recruited by Navy as a quarterback, but was third string my first year behind Roger Staubach, a future Heisman Trophy winner, and another fellow who was ahead of me on the plebe team. Our sophomore year the coaches switched me to wide receiver, but I didn't even get to suit up that year. I began our junior year as 4th string, but by our first game, I was now the first team wide receiver - we called that position, flanker. Early in that first game, Roger threw a pass to me, and it was the first one I had ever caught in my entire football career at all levels!

Skip and I went on to discuss his Navy football career. He spoke modestly about his success. In that junior year, Skip caught 35 passes and set a Cotton Bowl record with nine pass receptions. He also reminded me that most of our players at that time played both offense and defense, so when Navy was on defense, he was at the safety position. He also played baseball and basketball while at Navy.

At service selection, I chose to go Navy Air because I had enjoyed our summer aviation training during second class summer. Funny story, during my first three years at the Academy, I had only 20/30 vision and was not qualified to be a pilot. But first class year, they started using a machine to test our eyes, and now I was suddenly 20/20 and eligible to be a pilot. That machine changed my life.

Instead of going directly to flight school, I received orders to stay at the Academy as an assistant football coach for six months. I really enjoyed working with the younger players before reporting for flight training at Pensacola in December 1965 right after I got married. While I was at Pensacola, I also played football for our Navy team called "The Pensacola Goshawks." We actually had our own stadium and were well supported by the town. Our team was pretty good and played mostly mid-major college teams. One of the most memorable Goshawk games for me was against a team from the University of Mexico. We played them in Mexico City and won in front of a crowd of 35,000.

The Pensacola Goshawks (pronounced gos-hawks) were named after a bird of prey. From the end of WW II until the early 1970's several military units had competitive football teams filled with ex-college players now in the service. I was unable to find a definitive history of the Goshawks, but there are several online stories about individual games against teams such as McNeese State. Skip was not alone. Following graduation, many of us played on various military sports teams while still performing our duties. I played on fast pitch softball teams on both coasts while ashore during submarine training assignments.

At Pensacola, I was not sure about a Navy career. I thought that maybe I would ultimately become an airline pilot, so I thought that I should choose multi-engine aircraft instead of jets. Even though we would not be landing on aircraft carriers, we still had to carrier qualify before going to Pax River to learn how to fly the P-3 aircraft.

"Pax River" was the nickname for Naval Air Station Patuxent River. It is located 70 miles southeast of Washington, D.C. on the Chesapeake Bay near the mouth of the Patuxent River. In addition to being the training facility for the Navy's anti-submarine aircraft, it was also home to several other commands, including the Navy Test Pilot School.

After I completed P-3 training, I put in to be stationed at a squadron at Pax River, but found out that I had been assigned to "NSP." I had to ask what this was and quickly learned that I was going to VP-26, a squadron of almost brand-new P-3's at Sangley Point in the Philippines. The plane was a four-engine, long range turboprop with a crew of 12: pilot, co-pilot, navigator, tactical coordinator, and 8 enlisted men who did jobs such as radio operator, ordnance men (they dropped sonobuoys to detect submarines), and decibel operator.

Lockheed P-3 Orion in flight

Having learned that Sangley was located across the bay from Manila, where the average temperature was in the mid-80's, I could never understand why I was sent to survival training in Rangeley, Maine in the middle of winter! We were wearing snowshoes while tromping through the Maine woods trying to evade capture. The nearest jungles were a thousand miles south!

Right after we arrived at Sangley, the USS Pueblo (AGER-2) had been recently seized by the North Koreans, so we were immediately deployed to Japan to conduct increased seaborne patrols in the region. These turned out to be totally uneventful. but we did get to do a lot of flying and become very comfortable with the aircraft.

Our squadron at Sangley was divided up so that about one-third would deploy to U-Tapao, Thailand, while the other two-thirds would be flying out of Sangley to conduct missions to support aircraft carrier battle groups at Yankee Station. Our job with the carriers was to conduct airborne surveillance of shipping anywhere in the vicinity of the task group. It took us 2 1/2 hours to fly there from Sangley, allowing about six to seven hours on station before the long flight back. Almost all of these missions were at night. In addition to our electronics equipment, we had powerful searchlights to inspect shipping. We would often fly as low as 200 feet to get close to these contacts; we also carried flares to light up contacts if required. We didn't carry any weapons; our job was simply to provide information on possible threats to the carriers from long range. If we did find a threat, they had plenty of protection from ships accompanying them or from their own aircraft.

When we went to U-Tapao, a base in Thailand also used by Air Force B-52 bombers, our assignments were totally different than when our planes were protecting carriers. It was located about 75 miles south of Bangkok on the coast of the Gulf of Thailand (also called Gulf of Siam) not too far west of the Cambodian border. We would spend three to four weeks there doing Market Time missions looking for ships running supplies to the Viet Cong operating in the Mekong Delta area. On the first day I arrived at Sangley, we lost one P-3 on a mission out of U-Tapao. Our USNA classmate, Mike Travis, was in the flight crew on that plane which crashed into the sea during a Market Time operation. I had been under the impression that Market Time missions were not that dangerous for P-3's, at least in terms of enemy fire, but Mike's death was sobering and certainly made us more cautious.

Operation Market Time had been established by the U.S. in 1965 to try to stop the flow of troops, war materials and supplies from North Vietnam and Cambodia to the Viet Cong in the south. It involved ships and aircraft of the U.S. Navy and Coast Guard, South Vietnam, and Australia. Most Americans were unaware that 26 Coast Guard cutters were shipped to Vietnam and were involved in Market Time. One of the four coordinating centers for the Market Time missions was at An Thoi near the Cambodian border. The goal was to have continuous, round-the-clock air coverage of the 1200 miles of South Vietnamese coastline. The P-3 patrols for Market Time were long and mostly monotonous, fair or foul weather, day and night.

Later, when I was at U-Tapao, a second P-3 was lost. This time we knew what had happened. This second plane lost had also been on a Market Time operation in the Gulf of Thailand. They were flying near Dao Phu Quoc Island, which is just off the coast of Cambodia, but belongs to Vietnam. U.S. Swift boats operated out of there. The island had a short dirt landing strip on the southern end. While that plane was on patrol over the Gulf of Thailand, they were told to investigate a small ship headed toward Ha Tien, a Vietnamese city on the border with Cambodia. We later learned that this vessel was a Cambodian ship, a small WW II vintage utility boat that had some anti-aircraft weapons added to it. When our guys approached this craft to investigate at low altitude, the Cambodians opened fire and hit our plane just outboard of number four engine which caught on fire. Soon the entire wing was on fire leaving them three options: try to climb up to allow the crew to bail out over water; try to ditch in the ocean while they were still had some control; or attempt to go back 10 miles to that small dirt strip on Phu Quoc. They chose the third option, got to the strip, flew over it, and were making the final turn to attempt the landing. Unfortunately, the fire burned through the aileron cable causing them to lose control and crash into the water. Everyone on board this plane was also lost.

I was on alert when that second P-3 was lost. We were sent out immediately to continue Market Time operations because continuous coverage was a top priority. Another one of our planes was sent for search and rescue. They found the wreckage and the bodies which were recovered and identified. None of the first plane which had Mike Travis aboard was ever found.

As part of the investigation of this event, the Navy concluded that the earlier P-3 was probably lost due to a similar incident, namely that it was also shot down by the Cambodians. Prior to the war, Cambodia was led by Norodom Sihanouk, a western-leaning prince who is said to have loved Elvis Presley music. He had been pro-American, but when the U.S. Marines landed in Vietnam in 1965, Sihanouk began to favor the communists in China and broke off diplomatic relations with the U.S. Although Cambodia was officially neutral during the war, it allowed North Vietnam to move vast quantities of troops, arms, and supplies through its territory. It is not known if the Cambodian government, or even its military, gave permission for its naval units to fire on the P-3's, or if sailors on the boat simply opened fire on their own. The U.S. apparently chose not to retaliate for the losses of these two planes and 24 crewmen. When President Nixon ordered the bombing of Cambodia in 1970, nearly 3 million tons of explosives were dropped on the country, mostly by B-52's. Once again, there are few rules, but terrible suffering, once a war begins.

We continued our Market Time operations out of Thailand with no further incidents. There was no uptick in activity during the Tet offensive, at least for us, because we never flew in-country - in fact, we were not allowed to. Due to the loss of those two planes we had to have another crew join us from our base in Brunswick, Maine. Our squadron left the war zone in June 1968; while we were staying overnight at Moffett Field in California on our way home, Bobby Kennedy was shot. It was not a happy time. During my three years flying P-3's, I was deployed 18 months. Once our squadron was back on the East Coast, we did mostly anti-submarine (ASW) missions against Soviet submarines. While operating out of Lajes in the Azores, we spotted a Russian sub on the surface. As we flew down to inspect it at a low altitude, we saw an oil slick behind the sub. We identified it as a "Charlie" class and obtained the first U.S. photos of this new class of Soviet sub. Based on the oil slick, we assumed that the Charlie sub was having a bad day.

I remained in the Navy until I resigned in 1970. While in VP-26, I had been deployed over half the time and when those P-3's were lost, my wife couldn't find out quickly if I had been aboard. As a civilian, I immediately obtained a job with Eastern Airlines and flew four different planes until they went out of business in 1991. I liked the DC-9 the best. I then went into commercial real estate working for my quarterback buddy, Roger Staubach, at his company for the next 20 years.

Looking back now, the U.S. created a situation in Vietnam where there was no clear, or realistic, end game. I have no regrets about my duty there and am happy that I was lucky to survive.

John Collins

Washington, D.C.

"I had to take over command"

John is another of my monthly USNA Class of 1965 luncheon buddies. He tends to be one of the less raucous participants and always has great insights. I interviewed John via computer from his home in Silver Spring, Maryland, where he lives with his wife, Rosemary.

I was born in Washington, D.C., where my father worked in railroad maintenance. My mom was a secretary for one of the local newspapers, The Washington Star. While I was at St. Johns College High School, I became interested in attending the Naval Academy when a midshipman came to our school to give us a briefing. I received my appointment to USNA through my local congressman in Maryland. I always wanted to be on surface ships and was able to do so at graduation. My first ship was a fairly new destroyer, USS EDWARD McDONNELL (DE-1043), which was homeported in Norfolk. During my tour on McDONNELL, I had jobs as Damage Control Assistant (DCA) and Combat Information Center (CIC) Officer. In April 1967, while our ship was making a port visit to New York City, I received a postcard from the Navy telling me that I was going to be sent to the Coastal Surveillance Center in Cam Ranh Bay in Vietnam. No phone call, no telegram, just a lousy postcard!!!

I left the ship in June 1967 and traveled to San Diego for training. While I was there, I learned that I was now headed to the Riverine Assault Force in the Mekong Delta. After six weeks of training on old WW II LCMs (Landing Craft Medium) in the marshes and streams around Vallejo, California, I flew to Saigon. There was then a short plane ride to a base at Dong Tam down in the Delta, just west of My Tho. I arrived in early December 1967. The base was on the northern bank of the Mekong

River and was shared by Army and Navy units. I was still a Lieutenant (junior grade) and became the Chief Staff Officer (essentially the Executive Officer) of Riverine Assault Division 92. Our Commanding Officer was a Lieutenant.

Our division had several types of boats. The most important were modified LCM's; each could carry a platoon of Army troops which we could put ashore via a drop-down platform in the bow. We also had two Assault Support Patrol Boats (ASPB's) which were fast gun boats. The ASPB's had various armament, but most had two Mk-26 gun mounts with either a 20-mm cannon or a .50 caliber machine gun, a grenade launcher, various small arms, and minesweeping wires. Two ASPB's would be in the lead of a column of 10-15 troop-carrying LCMs with two heavily armed "monitors" in the column (called monitors due to the similarity in appearance to the original Civil War boat, MONITOR). With a rotating gun turret on top, 40-mm cannons, 81-mm mortars, and two different caliber machine guns, the monitors had considerable firepower. There was also a Command and Control boat and a refueling boat on most missions. Sometimes, we would have another ASPB in the rear. When I arrived, the boats were moored at Cam Tho alongside USS BENEWAH (APD-32) where we berthed and ate. Various LST's from the fleet would bring in supplies; sometimes we tied up alongside them. On large missions, our Squadron Commander, a Navy Commander, would join us in the convoy.

A monitor underway....note the firepower!

Our mission was to ferry Army troops to conduct assault operations up the myriad rivers and canals of the Delta. Nearly all of this territory contained Viet Cong, sometimes in heavy concentrations. These operations were generally one to four days in duration; most were *within 20-25 miles of Dong Tam. My CO would be in the first boat in the column. As the second in command, I would be in a boat in the middle, about eight boats behind. Each boat was driven by an enlisted man, an E-6 or an E-7, along with three to four other enlisted crew. The boats had twin diesel engines and a shallow draft of two to three feet. In a typical mission, we would be transporting a battalion of Army troops who were carrying M-16's and other light weapons. We would drop them off in a designated location where intelligence had indicated the presence of VC and then pick them up in another pre-determined location a few days later.*

The Mekong Delta has over 3000 miles of waterways and was the home to one-third of Vietnam's population. Because 75% of Vietnam's food was produced there, control of this area was obviously critical. General Westmoreland, the U.S. Commander in Vietnam, was searching for a way to combat Viet Cong activities in the Delta. By 1966 the VC were conducting at least 1000 attacks each month in this region. Westmoreland had plenty of Army troops but due to the swampy terrain, he could not get them to most locations in the Delta except by helicopters. The Navy was initially ill-prepared to assist because its ability to operate and fight on shallow and inland waters (called "brown water") had atrophied in the 20 years following WW II. Westmoreland huddled with Navy leaders and ordered the buildup of a Mobile Riverine Force (MRF) using Navy resources to project Army power into all areas of this swampy region. The plan was to modify old WW II landing craft to insert units of the Army's 9th Division into the Delta on a frequent and unpredictable basis. Navy Task Force 117 was located at a new location at Dong Tam created by a massive reclamation project to fill in a swamp. The MRF boats were not fast but were heavily armored. When fully loaded, an LCM could make only six knots with 40 soldiers aboard. To escort the LCM's, the Navy developed the ASPB's. They could do 15 knots and had considerable firepower but lighter armor.

When we landed the Army troops at a designated location, we would initially remain in the vicinity to be able to re-load the troops and to provide support if needed. We could often hear firefights and frequently would be involved ourselves. For the first two months in late 1967, there was not much action in our patrol areas northwest of My Tho. All hell broke loose in late January 1968 during the enemy Tet Offensive. We had intelligence that something was about to happen, but we had no idea of the magnitude of the fighting which was to come. When My Tho, Ben Tre, Vinh Long, and Can Tho were overrun by the VC, our orders were to recapture these cities. We landed Army troops in a cemetery near My Tho and in a few days regained control of the city. We then went to the next city and were ourselves involved in firefights in each of these battles. Both our men and the Army suffered casualties.

LCM underway carrying Army troops - note ramp in bow to discharge troops

My first CO had finished his tour and was relieved by a new Lieutenant who was killed on his first mission in an ambush near Rach Ba Rai in an area we called "Snoopy's Nose." The VC had set up bunkers and were firing RPG's (rocket propelled grenades) which hit his boat. I was still a Lieutenant jg and took over command. An Army helicopter flew in to take off the CO's body.

When John told me of the death of his new CO, I told him of a Lieutenant I had run into in Vallejo, California in early 1968. He was a year in front of me at USNA, and we had dinner together the week before he flew to Vietnam to take over one of the Riverine divisions. I later learned that he had been killed during his first week in-country. John explained that his CO was not an Academy graduate and that my friend had to have been a different casualty. I wondered how many others suffered a similar fate on those rivers shortly after their arrival.

Credit for the liberation of Can Tho and other nearby cities during the VC Tet offensive should also be given to ARVN forces (Army of the Republic of South Vietnam). Although many were on leave during the Tet holidays, they were heavily involved in the fighting to liberate Can Tho in four days. Most historians concur with John that the Riverine Forces and the U.S. Army were the deciding factor in regaining control.

We did most of our missions in the almost limitless canals and small streams off the Mekong River. We often gave names to locations where there was almost always fighting. One particularly nasty canal we called "Route 66." On a typical day, we would load Army troops at 4 AM and try to reach the objective area around 7 AM to offload them. The firefights varied in time; some were brief while others went on for hours. We did have one of our boats sunk from enemy fire, but we were able to get the troops off before it went down. We also took a rocket hit on my boat, but it hit aft and fortunately didn't ignite any ammo. We were able to get that boat back to the base. Occasionally we took prisoners, especially during night operations with Navy SEALs. During most missions, there was a Vietnamese interpreter aboard to help us to interact with friendly villagers. We found that we could trust few civilians in the villages because there was no way to ensure that they were not VC or VC sympathizers.

In August 1968, I took R&R in Sydney, Australia. The Opera House was new, and I thoroughly enjoyed those few days away from the war.

When I returned, our boats went upriver to about 10 miles from the Cambodian border where there was considerable action. On one mission, we went ashore into a small village which had been hit by a B-52 strike the previous night. Several fish were still floating in the canal due to the shock waves from those bomb explosions. I felt really bad when I saw a young Vietnamese woman emerge from her damaged hooch appearing to be disoriented and helpless. She was carrying a small baby which was crying hysterically. The "collateral damage" from these B-52 bombings had to be considerable. A few times I was close enough to feel the shock waves generated by these bombs. It was unsettling and appeared to me to be a lousy way to win the hearts of the Vietnamese who were not VC.

Because of the danger of malaria, mosquitoes were a continuing problem. There were also a lot of snakes in the river; some were poisonous. One actually got onto one of our boats. A crewman from the Philippines knew just what to do with that snake: he had it for dinner!.

We received a lot of support from both Army and Navy gunships whenever we got into bad situations. We also had Air Force support, but they were always called in by the Army guys we were carrying. I rarely fired weapons myself because my job was to direct our column of boats and to do coordination with the Army. I felt very fortunate not to be injured during my year in Vietnam.

I left Vietnam in early September 1968. Things had begun to quiet down then, but shortly after I was out of country, one of the LST's that we moored alongside was attacked. It didn't sink but had significant damage. Our classmate, Phil Ferrara, came to our squadron in July 1968. We overlapped a few months but didn't do any operations together because he was in a different division.

Following my time in Vietnam, I had a tour in the Pentagon and married Rosemary in 1973. I then went to Destroyer School, and then following an assignment on DEG-4, went to post graduate school before a series of assignments, all on the East Coast

John continued his career in surface ships and had command of USS JOHN HANCOCK (DD-981) prior to taking command of Destroyer Squadron 14 in Mayport, Florida, from 1988 to 1990. He retired after 30 years of service in 1995. John told me that while he was in Vietnam his most difficult moments were when his enlisted personnel were wounded or killed. He hoped that innocent Vietnamese civilians were not being killed, but there was no way of telling who was who. As soon as he was engaged in a firefight or an ambush, his thoughts were strictly on the mission at hand.

When our class graduated from the Naval Academy in June 1965, none of us, other than those becoming Marines, envisioned being in combat roles more akin to infantry than serving as sailors at sea. Yet, within two years, several members of our class, such as John, found themselves using rifles, machine guns, and mortars in deadly firefights from small craft in narrow rivers and canals. To the credit of these young men and the large number of enlisted sailors who served with them, they not only adapted to the challenge, but were instrumental in contesting control of the Mekong Delta region during this phase of the war. It was, of course, a short-lived success due to later political decisions affecting the overall conduct of the war.

Don Bonsper

Olean, New York

"A terrible firefight"

Many of our classmates are already familiar with the experiences of Don Bonsper in Vietnam based on two excellent books he wrote in 2015. Entitled *Vietnam Memoirs, Part 1 and Part 2*, his collection of memories provides a riveting journey of his first-hand experience as a young Marine First Lieutenant thrust into an intense, and deadly, battle environment. The first book, subtitled *My Experiences as a Marine Platoon Leader,* recounts his time as 1st platoon leader of E Company, 2nd Battalion, 9th Marines in the area just south of the DMZ. Upon arrival he was greeted with the news that the previous platoon leader had been killed the day before. The Battalion adjutant had even worse news, "Actually you will be the 13th platoon leader of the 1st platoon in the last six months. They've had a hell of time with their lieutenants. The other 12 were killed or wounded." In less than a week, Don found himself and his platoon involved in a hellacious fire fight where he came close to being number 13.

Don's second book, subtitled M*y Experiences as an Advisor with the Vietnamese Marine Corps*, details the second half of his year in Vietnam when he was embedded with a battalion of the Vietnamese Marine Corps (VNMC). This was an entirely different experience from E Company, but no less dangerous. On several occasions Don was again exposed to life-threatening combat. He soon learned that his role was not so much an "advisor," as a coordinator of support for the Vietnamese troops during battles. I strongly recommend both books if you are interested in the gritty details of how ground warfare was conducted in Vietnam.

I certainly felt the mud, the blood, the terror of combat while reading Don's memories.

In both of his books, Don credits his wife, Pam, for her strong support throughout his time in Vietnam. To understand a wife's perspective of coping with her husband being in harm's way on the other side of the world, I recommend Chapter 6 of Don's Part 2 book and the book which Pam has written, *Sempre Juntos*.

I interviewed Don via computer from his home in Carmel Valley, California, where he lives with Pam.

I was born in a small town, Olean, New York. It is in the western part of the state just north of the border with Pennsylvania. My high school, Portville Central School, was also small and was located in a nearby town. There were only 60 students in my class, and I played on all the usual sports teams. I was looking for the greatest challenge after high school, and although my family had no military background, I applied to the Naval Academy through our local congressman whom I never met. He accepted applications from everyone who applied and had his staff pick who they thought were the top six. They then sent those names to the Academy and told them to make the final selection. I ended up getting his primary appointment. At the Academy I did baseball as a plebe but ended up playing rugby for the next three years. When service selection came, based on our training cruises, I decided that I wouldn't have enough room to move around on a ship, and liking the outdoors, I chose the Marine Corps. I was fortunate to receive a Fulbright Scholarship to study in Costa Rica for a year after graduation. While I was in Costa Rica, I used our December to February three-month break from school to hitchhike around South America. When I reached Brazil I met a young girl, Pam, who would later become my wife. She was staying with a family with whom she had lived as an exchange student earlier in high school. We immediately "clicked" and decided to hitchhike together back to San Jose, Costa Rica. She returned to her home in Minnesota but joined me back in San Jose to drive to Marine Corps Basic School in Virginia, where I began training in the summer 1966. We got married when I finished Basic School and are still together.

My first assignment was in Vietnam. I arrived there in June 1967 and was the Platoon Leader of 1st Platoon, Echo Company, 2nd Battalion, 9th Marines. Because of my year of study in Costa Rica, I was a year older than most new platoon leaders. I met my platoon in June 1967 at a Marine base at Cam Lo which is just south of the DMZ. We were doing "search and destroy" operations sending out a platoon or a company of Marines to find enemy troops. I was worried because I didn't know the names of each of the men in my platoon, and we were heading out on a company-size mission the next day. Our objective was to capture Hill 179. We left our base in the late afternoon and walked all night only to run into an ambush early the next morning as we approached the hill. We spent the day lying in the sun on the side of the hill trying to advance to the top. We were under considerable fire from the enemy and getting nowhere, so the Company Commander called in air strikes which literally took off the top of the hill. We suffered casualties from that bomb debris which had been thrown up in the air and came down hitting us.

Eventually, we got to the top of the hill. We found an aiming circle, three or four bodies, some equipment, and an outpost which could see all the way to Cam Lo. It had been an excellent position for them to see everything and to direct fire from their artillery north of the DMZ. We then received orders to walk back to Cam Lo. My platoon had no one killed, but our company suffered casualties during this Hill 179 operation. The bodies we found on top were either North Vietnamese or Chinese - I later heard that there were some Chinese involved in these operations. In these ambushes, the enemy would generally not shoot the first man they saw but let others continue to approach and then shoot. When our cry came out, "Corpsman up," they would then try to shoot the corpsman and any others who came to help. The Hill 179 battle, I learned, was a typical operation for us. We would take a hill or a position, often while suffering considerable casualties, but then leave it behind. We never tried to hold a place.

Americans referred to specific hills by the height in meters. A few battles were so difficult or bloody that the name became famous among American forces (e.g., Hue and Khe Sanh), but most were known simply by numbers. Don's frustration was easy to understand. "Search and Destroy" involved putting your men (and yourself) in what was an essentially endless operation in a region where enemy troops could continuously infiltrate replacement soldiers across the DMZ nightly. Capturing these hills was nothing more than a very short-lived pyrrhic victory destined to be repeated ad infinitum. Injuries due to "debris" ejected by bombs dropped by friendly forces added to the Kafkaesque nature of these operations. Listening to Don, I found myself imagining huge boulders, torrents of dirt, pieces of weapons, and even human body parts falling on his men desperately hugging the ground. Also bear in mind that Don's young Marines generally walked to and from combat carrying heavy loads in a tropical climate. In addition to weapons and ammunition, each Marine infantryman carried equipment for digging a hole to protect against mortar fire, sufficient water (at least two canteens), C-rations (all in metal cans), helmets, a poncho, a sleeping mattress (called your "rubber lady"), and a flak jacket. The overall weight varied, but was easily in the 45-55 lb. range, not counting your weapon. And during the monsoon season (usually several months long) you were doing this in rains, often torrential. The platoon radioman, who never left the platoon commander's side, was also carrying a large radio (the PRC-25) of perhaps 30 pounds. Often in the field you might not wash for weeks.

What you did not want to do when fighting the North Vietnamese was to stay in one place too long. During one operation near Con Thien, just south of the DMZ, we were there fighting three to four nights. We got mortared terribly every night and took 85 casualties. The Battalion Commander and his XO were both wounded and had to be evacuated. Their replacements came in immediately, and we never stayed in one place more than one night after that. When we stopped to establish protection during the night, we would set up a defensive perimeter of perhaps 100 yards diameter. Our platoon would be in individual foxholes inside in a circle of maybe 25 yards. The Marines guarding the perimeter are out there all night; one is a listening post (LP) and the other an observation post (OP). There are four Marines in each of these with one guy awake while the other 3 sleep. If you cannot reach these fellows on radio, our company policy was that the Platoon Commander had to go out himself to investigate.

When I had this situation develop one night, I went out with one PFC [Private First Class] and as we got close to the LP, I called out the name of one of the Marines in the LP. My voice startled the four and two instinctively started firing at our direction. The PFC with me took three rounds and lost his eye and part of his chin. All four of my Marines had fallen asleep. The one young Marine who was supposed to have been awake was sent back to the base at Dong Ha. I don't know if he was disciplined. No one ever mentioned the incident to me. I was far too busy with other issues to be concerned. It was just a terrible accident amidst the daily horror of war.

I had a great relationship with my Staff Sergeant. He was a rather quiet Black man, and he really helped me. In many situations I had to lean on him for support, especially since I was so new that I didn't initially know the strengths and weaknesses of the men in my platoon. On the other hand, I did not have a particularly good relationship with my Company Officer. He was, of course, my boss and outranked me. A day or so after some intense fighting, he called me to his area for a briefing and then, on my way out, he admonished me for wearing VC tire tread sandals (I had found these in an enemy base camp which we had captured) around "his" area instead of Marine boots. I explained to him that I was simply trying to let my feet dry out. Then he said, "Lieutenant, I also think that you're too familiar with your men, especially your radio operator. I heard you use nicknames when talking to several of your men." My attempt to explain my rationale went nowhere. He simply dismissed me with, "Don't argue with me. Just do what you're told." We had a bad relationship on several levels.

After I was there for several months, the XO of our company left, and I was assigned his job. A 2nd Lieutenant arrived to take my place as platoon leader but was killed almost immediately, and I took back my old job as 1st platoon leader while still being XO. Not long later, our battalion was ambushed in a large operation near the DMZ. There were about 50 killed and at least 100 wounded, but most were in another company. While I was there as XO, I developed real bad infections on my hands and arms. The corpsman would clean my sores every night, put on antibiotic, and wrap me up. Then the next day I would go out and get all sweaty and sore again. We were near the DMZ during the monsoon rainy season, causing large amounts of water to build up along the roads. We were walking back to Cam Lo and had just crossed a culvert in ankle deep water. Right after my platoon crossed it, the water suddenly washed the culvert away and three of our Marines in the next platoon were swept away downstream. Two drowned and one survived. We couldn't find one of the bodies until the next day.

**Dead U.S. Marines being evacuated during
Operation Buffalo, July 2, 1967**

Operation Buffalo is chronicled in many online articles. It was a 12-day battle in early July 1967 between U.S. Marines and the North Vietnamese 90th Regiment. The Marines lost 159 men with close to 1000 wounded. Estimates of NVA losses range from 1300 to 1800. Navy ships offshore and a host of planes and helicopters provided gunfire support. It was a brutal battle. All of it took place in the proximity of Cam Lo, Con Thien, and Dong Ha near the DMZ. These were the three Marine bases from which Don's company conducted most operations.

My first six months were a continuous slog of search and destroy patrols. On a few occasions we did operations with tanks. One was during that battalion operation near the DMZ that I just mentioned. There were five tanks, and one got buried so deep in mud that we had a real problem getting it out. We were ordered to walk all night in the brush providing security for the tanks on the road to avoid an ambush. The plan had been to circle back via a road along a river, but the tanks couldn't get through the road ahead, so battalion leaders decided that we all had to go back the way we came in. Marine tactics 101 says that is never a good plan. I hated doing ops with tanks because they are incredibly noisy and belch smoke. The enemy always knew where the tanks were. As we started to go back down the road, the VC had hung a heavy artillery round in a tree and exploded it remotely just after our company went past it. This was obviously a signal for their mortar units to begin firing. Suddenly we were in a terrible fire fight. The enemy rushed infantry units along the road to engage the rest of our battalion. The tanks started going back and forth to remove our bodies which were piling up. We were able to go on, but the rest of the battalion was hung up in that location. The next morning, the rest of our forces got out. That was Operation Buffalo. All of us eventually got back to Dong Ha for a memorial service, and I was one of the readers.

In November 1967, I learned that I had been promoted to Captain and was being reassigned to a Marine Advisory Unit as an advisor to the Vietnamese Marines. Apparently, someone had figured out that I had attended some Vietnamese language training and wanted to fill the vacancy from someone in-country. The Vietnamese Marine headquarters were in Saigon and their units operated in both the III and IV Corps area. There were two American advisors for each Marine battalion. We weren't actually advising because these Vietnamese Marines knew what they were doing and did it well. We were there to call in U.S. fire support when needed. Our job was to obtain support and then talk to the pilots to direct them as to where to fire. Most of the enemy were VC except during Tet when they were clearly North Vietnamese. Shortly after I had reported to my new duty, I was able to take my six days of R&R in Hawaii with Pam near the end of January 1968. It was great. On the way back, Tet started. I flew into Tan Son Nhut airport amidst the fighting and had to hitchhike into the city. All of us American advisors had been given rooms in the Splendid Hotel to use when we were not in the field with the Vietnamese Marines.

Interestingly, one of the more popular hotels in Hanoi is now the Splendid Hotel and Spa (pronounced Splen-deed with the accent on deed). How times change!

We had several major battles when I was with the Vietnamese Marines. During one event south of Saigon in the Delta, we flew helos into a hot landing zone. We were under constant fire in a rice paddy as I was controlling a multitude of air strikes using U.S. Army and Air Force planes. These Marines took casualties but were superb fighters. The enemy was in a tree line, and we were in ditches in that rice paddy. Each time I would come up to look, there were countless rounds of fire suddenly directed toward us. It took me a while to figure out that although the enemy couldn't see us, they could easily spot the long antenna of my radio operator's radio. I realized that we had to switch to a short antenna. That miserable day was a stalemate.

We also did operations with the U.S. Riverine Force in the Delta while working with U.S. Army units. The Navy would take us in boats to a location and drop us off. One time we were sent to assist a U.S. Army unit that had taken terrible casualties to help them retrieve their dead personnel. What was strange was that the Army still had hot meals and ice cream flown in while this was going on. We all got mortared the next morning. War has insane moments.

The good news was that mines were not as much of a problem as in the north. Down there in the Delta we had pretty good intelligence and were able to take the fight to the enemy better than our search operations near the DMZ. There we generally had no idea where the enemy was located.

When "Tet 2" began in May 1968, our Vietnamese Marine unit was called back to protect Saigon. We were sent to Cholon, the Chinese part of the city, to ensure that it would not be taken. We stopped the attack cold and killed over 200 North Vietnamese who were attacking. These enemy troops were just inexperienced young kids who had apparently been told that it would be an easy victory. After the battle we found bodies, whereas when I was up north with our Marines you would hardly ever find a body. Up there the North Vietnamese had "body snatchers" with tools like ice picks to drag bodies so that they could be pulled out of the ongoing fight and later buried.

When Don came back from Vietnam, he spent two years at the Naval Post Graduate School in Monterey, California. Upon completion he received orders back to Vietnam, but when he reached Okinawa, he learned that because the Marines were now pulling out of Vietnam, he would spend no more combat time there. Don was then assigned to be a Company Commander and following several other assignments, he returned to Monterey as a faculty member. In 1985 he retired from the Marine Corps and remained teaching at the Post Graduate School until retiring in 2013. As with several of our classmates, Don is suffering prostate cancer, possibly due to the effects of exposure to Agent Orange.

Some of Don's experiences in Vietnam makes for uneasy reading. The constant life-threatening danger - constant - had to have been difficult for all of these young Marines, many still less than 20 years old: living in grime, eating endless meals from cans, starved for sleep; kill or be killed. Even those of us in other military situations had no feel for the extent of the horror. Nightly television news may have captured some of these moments for Americans at home, but those were, by necessity, simply edited snapshots of the ongoing nightmarish hell of war.

Ted Nanz

Grand Rapids, Michigan
"They were happy to
see our helicopter"

Ted is a neighbor in Virginia. We did not know each other at the Academy but have become good friends due to mutual interests developed while driving together for events in Annapolis. Ted and his wife, Meliza, live only a few miles away, so he drove over to my home for an interview.

I wanted to go to the Naval Academy all my life. My uncle had wanted to go there, but it didn't happen. He was one of my heroes because he went into the Coast Guard and during WW II his ship rammed and sunk a German U-boat on the surface. During high school we moved to south Florida and I was fortunate to receive a congressional appointment to the Academy. During service selection at the Academy, I chose to go into the surface Navy. I wanted an assignment on a ship out of Mayport, Florida, near my home. Fortunately, I received orders to USS WILLIAM V PRATT (DLG-13), a guided missile destroyer. In spite of having been sent to guided missile school before reporting aboard, I was assigned to be the ASW (anti-submarine warfare) officer - typical Navy logic!

I met PRATT while it was in the Mediterranean. Following another Med deployment, we were sent to Vietnam in the summer of 1967 via the Panama Canal. Once on Yankee Station, our first assignment was "North SAR." This meant that we were the northernmost U.S. ship doing Search and Rescue missions in support of aircraft flying off the carriers on Yankee Station during missions over North Vietnam. We were west of the Chinese island, Hainan, and sometimes just 12 miles off the coast of North Vietnam. Our ship had the SH-2 Kaman Seasprite helicopter aboard that we used to pick up Navy and Air Force pilots who had been shot down over the Gulf of Tonkin. In August, a Navy A-6 Intruder attack aircraft was shot down over China; this caused quite a stir among our carrier group, and those of us on the scene never knew why the plane was there or what happened to the crew.

This A-6 incident happened on August 21, 1967. It was actually two A-6's and it is still unknown why they had wandered over "southern China." It is not clear if this was the Chinese island of Hainan, or mainland China. U.S. intelligence reports, now unclassified, confirm that they were definitely shot down by Chinese MiG fighter aircraft. One of the U.S. pilots, LCDR Robert Flynn, spent the next five years in a Chinese prison. The other member of his crew, the weapons officer, died in the MiG attack. The two aviators in the second aircraft also did not survive. Throughout the war the Chinese vigorously defended their airspace, both around Hainan and the mainland. Most of these incidents which did occur, and there were several, were not publicized by the U.S. before or after the war due to the sensitive diplomatic relationship with China.

While on North SAR we did successfully pick up two F-4 Phantom crews, one Air Force and one Navy, who had been shot down over the Gulf of Tonkin. All four were wet, but not seriously injured. I assure you that they were happy to see our helicopter and to be taken back to our ship. In November 1967 a major typhoon came through the Gulf of Tonkin. There were several PBR boats near the shore and they were floundering in the high seas. We were called to try to rescue the boats. As we were in the process of trying to launch our helo, a large wave suddenly swept over the fantail. We were able to rescue two of our crew but lost two others to the sea. This event cast a somber pall over our entire crew.

PBR's (Patrol Boat Riverine) were small fiberglass boats used primarily by the Navy for operations in the Mekong Delta. The Navy deployed 140 of these to Vietnam during the war, with most being used in the Delta. Some were assigned for duty off the coastline of Vietnam to check the cargo of small boats moving along the coasts, but they were not designed for the high seas encountered in typhoons. Ted did not know the fate of the PBR's which reported being in trouble.

The "fantail" is the rear aft deck of a ship. On PRATT it was a flat open area from which its helicopter operated.

USS William V. Pratt (DLG-13) at sea December 1967

One night while on SAR we were tracking aircraft. We could often see them over North Vietnam. I was in CIC (Combat Information Center) *as the watch officer, and we saw some fast approaching boats doing maybe 40-50 knots heading toward us. These were solid blips on the radar scope. Then they suddenly disappeared! This caused me to believe that the 1964 Gulf of Tonkin incident may have involved similar anomalies due to atmospherics.*

While on North SAR, we would spend 30 days on station. Every third night we would go south to Yankee Station to refuel with the carrier group. We were always relieved up there by another DLG - someone had to be there at all times during flight operations. Those typhoons were serious. Fall was the typhoon season. We would take 40-45 degree rolls and often our bow would go under causing the whole ship to shudder. When I was the Officer of the Deck during those storms, I would grab a cable that went across above us and swing like a pendulum. I swear that my fingerprints are still on that cable!

We began our return in December 1967 and returned to Florida in January 1968. As soon as we got back, I received orders to USS FOX (DLG-33), also a guided missile ship, but larger than the PRATT. It was homeported in San Diego, but as soon as I got there, the ship immediately headed to Vietnam. The call sign, RED CROWN, was what was used for air traffic control over all of North Vietnam. Our job was to keep track of everything in the air over land and water. RED CROWN saved a lot of aviators during those missions using our strong air search radar. Our position was south of North SAR and north of Yankee Station, so we had a good radar vision of everything going on. FOX would move location about 100 miles south into South SAR on a rotating basis with other ships. While in the south, most of the air missions were also over North Vietnam but in the southern sector near Vinh. We would occasionally go into Da Nang for supplies, but my only time on shore was sitting on the pier. I would often hear mortar fire while there. My roommate on FOX was Bob Woodward, who later, of course, was the Watergate reporter with Carl Bernstein. He was a good shipmate.

Upon FOX's return to San Diego in May 1969, Ted submitted his resignation but received orders in July to an east coast ship, USS TATTNALL (DDG-19). Four months later he was released from active duty and began a civilian career in communications and electronics. He served as President of American operations for SPOT Image, an Earth observation company, from 1990 to 1999.

Courtland Gray
Monroe, Louisiana
"There's no practice for that"

Courtland was another of our exceptional track athletes in the Naval Academy Class of 1965. Because he was one of only a few of our classmates to become a Marine helicopter pilot, I wanted to hear his experiences in Vietnam. I interviewed Courtland via computer from his home in Navarre, Florida, where he lives with his wife, Pat.

I was born in Monroe, Louisiana, in 1944. I believe that I am one of the youngest members of our class. In high school I began running track during my sophomore year. The football coach had just started the track team and preached that we had to "run on our toes." He didn't know much about track, but he did give all of us a pair of spikes and made us run a long distance in them. Most of us had trouble walking the next day! I specialized in hurdles and won the state championship in both low and high hurdles. We also had a very successful relay team.

My dad was the one who wanted me to go to the Naval Academy and actually used some of his connections with our local Congressman to obtain an appointment for me two years before I even got there. The track coach at the Academy had never heard of me and didn't know I was coming so he was surprised that I was pretty fast. I became successful in track at Navy and competed several times at the Penn Relays. One year, Bill Cosby was the honorary starter; he was spending more time trying to make jokes than starting us properly. In the summer before our first class [senior] year, I raced at the NCAA track meet at Berkeley, California. After this, I had my summer cruise on a destroyer but didn't have a good experience because it was a very dysfunctional crew. This caused me to decide to go Marine Corps.

After Basic Marine Corps Training, I arrived at flight school at Pensacola, Florida, in June 1966. The pipeline for fixed wing aircraft was jammed and was not an option for me. So, all of us Marines flew basic training aircraft like the T-34 and T-28 and then transitioned to learn to fly helicopters. I completed training in May 1967 and received orders to the Marine Air Station at New River, North Carolina. On the day I checked in, there had just been a mid-air collision of two helicopters. One helicopter, a CH-53, was landing and a Huey, a UH-1E, was taking off. Because both pilots on the Huey were killed, I became one of the replacements. This was fine with me because I preferred to be a Huey pilot rather than flying the CH-46.

I was at New River until November 1967 and was then assigned to Vietnam with Squadron VM-01. Two days before I checked in to my squadron at Da Nang two helicopters hit a mountain and the four pilots were killed. Because of this accident, instead of going north to a squadron near the DMZ, I was kept at Da Nang to replace them in VM-02. We were located just east of Da Nang at a helo base called Marble Mountain. The first day I flew I was the co-pilot for the flight leader. It was a troop lift with us as a gun ship escorting the troop-carrying helicopters, the CH-46s. I flew 8.4 hours that day and saw four CH-46s go down in flames. When we got back, I said to myself, "I can't do this. If this is normal and I have to do this every day, I'm gonna shoot myself." It turned out that those 8.4 hours in one day were the most I ever flew again in one day in Vietnam. Also, I never again saw that level of carnage among our troops. Of course, we were taking fire ourselves during that initial mission and later during many others. In training, they can teach you how to fly, but they can never teach you how to react when you are getting shot at. There's no practice for that. My helo was hit several times and we had a crew member get wounded. I was just lucky I didn't get hit myself. We typically flew four days a week, enabling me to log over 980 hours of flight time in-country. Although we got shot at a lot and our aircraft was hit occasionally, I was never wounded. Unfortunately, several others were not so lucky, and we lost a lot of our squadron mates.

We also did VIP missions, including transporting the Secretary of Defense when he would come in. On these, we would fly a "SLICK" which meant that it didn't have guns on it. The enemy knew that whenever they saw a Slick flying by, it probably had a VIP aboard, so they would generally take a pot shot at us. I think that some of the VIPs actually liked this - as long as we didn't get hit - so that they could have their own war stories.

Mock-up of USMC Huey

A "Huey" is a single-engine, two-rotor Bell UH-1 "Iroquois" helicopter. As Courtland so graphically described it, "the big rotor gets you up in the air, and the little vertical rotor in back keeps you from spinning in the opposite direction caused by the torque of the big rotor." The Huey has a pilot and a co-pilot; in Vietnam the two other crew members were door gunners. You normally were the co-pilot for the first six months, and then the pilot for the rest of the time in country. The door gunners both used M-60 machine guns on swivel mounts; there were also four forward-firing machine guns controlled by the pilots. The swivel mounts had stops which kept the door gunners from shooting the cockpit or the tail rotor. Courtland talked to one pilot whose helicopter didn't have these stops; one of his gunners actually shot down his own aircraft. Hueys were first used by the Army in Vietnam in 1962 and became a symbolic image of the war. They had a wide variety of missions: cargo and troop transport, medical evacuation, search and rescue, and ground attack. Hueys were used not only by the Army, but also other branches of the service. This helicopter could also be fitted with rockets and grenade launchers. It continued to be called a "Huey" because of its original designation, HU-1, even after it was later changed to UH-1. These helicopters were used post-Vietnam until 2015.

We had all sorts of missions when I was flying out of Da Nang. Most of my missions, however, were gunship escorts for troop movements. Our gunners always had to get the pilot's permission to fire. Often, we would be tasked to do Marine recon team inserts with us in charge. That way all the CH-46 pilots flying with the Recon Marines had to do was to concentrate on landing the 14 or so Marines on board. Sometimes we would call in Navy support aircraft to drop bombs or napalm in an area prior to landing the troops to improve its safety. Most of these missions were in the jungle out west or southwest of Da Nang. During close air support we would begin firing at about 1200-1300 ft and then go down to 500 ft. When we were directing fixed wing aircraft, the A-4's and F-4's, those Marine pilots would decide which altitude they would bomb from. When the A-6's would come in from Da Nang or Chu Lai, they would bomb from 2500 ft. The Air Force pilots we worked with would never come in low.

We would always plan ahead for a troop insertion and have the support planes there to assist. If we had an emergency need for help, those planes could get there in less than 10 minutes because they were on stand-by. Occasionally, some of our missions took us over Laos but we were never allowed to talk about this. During the siege of Khe Sanh, I flew several VIPs to locations near there, but I myself had no missions into the besieged area itself.

On one flight, I had total engine failure and landed on wet sand on China Beach which is northeast of Da Nang. We had learned from a previous incident that when landing on this type of surface you just come straight down of else you can have problems. The maintenance guys came out and replaced the engine right there on the beach in just a few hours. Then I flew it back.

There were frequent enemy rocket attacks on Da Nang. In fact, we had one during my first night there and I spent the night in a bunker. Ironically, on my last night in-country I was also in a bunker for the same reason. Rocket attacks were a rather continuous feature of life in Da Nang. They would only last maybe 10 minutes. Most of us got so used to these attacks that when we heard "incoming" and learned that it was on the other end of the field, we wouldn't even react. One time we were in the Officer's Club and there was incoming. We all hit the deck next to the bar, but as soon as it was over, everyone resumed drinking *and the band immediately started playing, usually, "We Gotta Get Out of This Place."*

When I returned to the States after 13 months in Vietnam, I went back to New River as an instructor pilot. I resigned in 1970 and obtained an M.B.A. at Harvard Business School. I then began work for Bell Helicopter and became head of international marketing. I went to China at least 15 times; the first time I was there in 1978 the Chinese treated us like rock stars. I hired a translator to go with me and he stayed with me for 20 years. In my work for Bell, I had the opportunity to travel all over the world. It was a great experience.

Courtland was not flippant when he discussed his combat experiences. It was obviously traumatic to see friends lost when their helicopters were shot down and knowing that but for the grace of God you might be next. He told me that during his post-war days at Harvard he had some empathy for the anti-war movement but did not regret doing what was necessary to provide fire support for fellow Marines. Wars are morally complicated.

Aaron Spurway

Kellogg, Idaho

"It was gruesome"

Aaron is a life-long friend. We were in the same company during our final year at the Naval Academy and spent many weekends together. We became close friends during the fall of 1965 while attending the Naval Nuclear Power School in Vallejo, California. The Navy sent us in different directions, but we have stayed in touch on a regular basis for the past 55 years. Aaron went on to serve in Vietnam aboard an amphibious landing ship while I was on submarines. I interviewed him via computer from his home in Deer Park, Washington, where he lives with his wife, Coco.

I was born in 1943 in Yakima, Washington, where my mom was working in a cannery. I never knew my father. As I was growing up, we moved a lot, and I attended many schools. My mother met my stepfather who had later adopted me. They were operating restaurants and bars with slots machines in small towns all over north Idaho. During the summer before my 8th grade, we moved to Kellogg, Idaho, where my stepfather got a job at the Bunker Hill, a large zinc mine. My four younger stepbrothers and I had a paper route which began at 4:30 A.M. I would usually get to high school around 8:30. In high school, I played baseball and basketball and also played American Legion baseball during the summers. Although I always did well academically, I wasn't sure that I would be able to attend college because we had no money. I became interested in the service academies listening to a friend, Ronnie McCoy, who wanted to go to the Air Force Academy. The more I looked, the more I saw the service academies as an option. I received an appointment to the Naval Academy because of my membership in DeMolay, which is an offshoot of the Masons for boys. The fellow who was our Counselor for DeMolay was an attorney who was politically connected to one of our senators. That connection got me the appointment. I had never seen a ship except during war movies.

Aaron told me that his friend, Ronnie McCoy, did attend the Air Force Academy, but after Ronnie's graduation, he was killed in an aircraft accident during his first solo flight. Aaron was not alone in our class in seeking an appointment based on his family's lack of funds to pay for college. There were several members of our class who knew that college was not financially an option. But we soon learned that none of the service academies was a free lunch; graduates had a commitment for four years of service (which was extended to five years for most of us).

At the Academy I played mostly intramural sports. When service selection came around during our final year, I chose to go nuclear submarines. After graduation I was sent to Mare Island, California, for six months of classroom lessons on nuclear reactor operation. The next phase of training consisted of six months of hands-on learning to operate a naval reactor. This took place at a reactor "prototype" located in the desert outside Idaho Falls, Idaho. While I was in this phase of my training, I realized that I was not a good candidate and asked to be dropped from the nuclear submarine training pipeline. This request was not well-received, and I immediately received orders to Gunnery School in San Diego before an assignment to USS VERNON COUNTY (LST-1161) homeported in Yokosuka, Japan.

"Not well received" is a major understatement. Aaron's senior officers were furious. If the U.S. had not been in the middle of the Vietnam War and desperate for officers to serve there, Aaron may well have been cashiered out of the Navy, or even faced disciplinary action. If his superiors thought that Aaron's new assignment was punishment, they were very wrong. Sending a bachelor to Yokosuka, Japan at that time was akin to going to heaven. LSTs (Landing Ship Tank) were developed by the U.S. for use during WW II to support amphibious operations for landing troops, cargo, tanks and other vehicles ashore. VERNON COUNTY had been built in 1953 and saw considerable action during the Vietnam War.

Like many U.S. warships, VERNON COUNTY was ultimately transferred to a foreign Navy, in this case, Venezuela, in 1973.

My initial assignment on VERNON COUNTY was Gunnery Officer. We had three 3-inch mounts with two guns each; two were forward, and the other aft. We also had .50 and .30 caliber machine guns. I arrived during the summer of 1966, and we deployed to Vietnam in September. Our ship had conducted missions in Vietnamese waters previously, so our Captain and Executive Officer had considerable experience conducting MARKET TIME operations. This involved patrolling along the coast to interdict enemy boats attempting to move people or material south to help the Viet Cong. At this time, we were not tasked to do harassment or interdiction firing of our guns supporting troops ashore - that came in later deployments. Most of our assignments consisted of checking out junks that we encountered and providing supplies (mostly food and ammo) for Swift boats and PBRs. We made occasional incursions into a few of the rivers in order to serve as a Swift boat haven. These boats constantly needed fuel and provisions. Essentially, we were a supply ship for them. But most of this first deployment was MARKET TIME. We didn't receive enemy fire on this deployment.

Swift boats (PCFs) were basically small gun boats with no sleeping quarters. LST's, such as VERNON COUNTY, often acted as "mother ships" providing mooring and accommodations for crews of both PCFs and other small boats such as PBRs (Patrol Boat Riverine). These were smaller than Swift boats but had comparable speeds and much shallower drafts which made them ideal for missions on the Vietnamese rivers and canals.

I did five deployments on VERNON COUNTY. We would load up on supplies in Yokosuka and head to Vietnam, often via Subic Bay in the Philippines. For most of the summer of 1967, we were operating just south of Da Nang but then headed to the Mekong Delta for search and destroy operations. We cruised up the rivers and did a lot of assignments involving transporting Army and Republic of Korea (ROK) troops. We also supplied the U.S. Riverine forces. One of my new duties now was Helo Officer; we conducted nearly 800 helicopter landings during these ops. The helicopters were cycling back and forth from firefights taking place inland, but not far away. We could hear and sometimes see the action. The Army (and a few Marines) had a "Graves Registration Unit"(GRU) aboard who worked on the tank deck of our LST. Their job was to collect dead bodies, arms and legs, and various other body parts. It was problematic because the helicopter (mostly Hueys) could stay only a brief period. I was in charge of a group of sailors who had to quickly offload bodies and body parts from the helo onto a pallet next to the landing pad. The pallet was then winched down to the tank deck below. Down there, the GRU people would collect everything and try to ID the body, or parts, and tag them. It was gruesome. The GRU then put the bodies or parts into body bags, zip them up, and put the bags back onto pallets. We would then winch the body bags up to where I was and load everything onto other helicopters which came in. None of us knew where the bodies went from there, but I assumed that they ultimately were returned for proper burials in the U.S.

Aaron was visibly upset as he recounted this experience with the GRU. It was obviously a difficult assignment for not only the personnel in the GRU, but also for the young sailors handling bodies and human fragments. Aaron said that his CO would not allow any of his crew to interact with anyone on the GRU in order to minimize harm to crew morale. I cannot imagine being assigned to a GRU, or to be involved in any phase of these operations. Accounting in as dignified manner as possible for those who have made the ultimate sacrifice is an aspect of war fighting rarely discussed. The assignment was obviously difficult, but absolutely necessary.

USS VERNON COUNTY (LST-1161) underway

I saw a lot of courage by the spotters who were flying the helos hovering above these battles. The spotter's role was to call in air and artillery strikes and assist in directing assistance for the ground forces. These guys would fly to our ship for a quick lunch while we patched up their helicopters. I noticed that the armor under the seat on the helo was often heavily damaged from enemy fire. Then they would return immediately to the action. One spotter with whom I frequently worked while we were on the rivers eventually get shot down. I visited him later in a hospital in Saigon and he seemed to be absolutely nuts. He was burned up real bad, but all he wanted to do was to get back in that helo and do more spotting. I don't remember if he was Army, Navy, or Marines.

We left these river operations in late summer 1967 and went back to Yokosuka for very needed repairs. We then headed back to Vietnam but had to turn back because of a major typhoon. By this time, I was the First Lieutenant. I took the place of an officer who had taken a bad fall down a ladder aboard ship. Our assignment was to patrol in the South China Sea from Da Nang north to the DMZ. VERNON COUNTY was in port in Da Nang when the enemy began the Tet attacks at the end of January 1968. We were offloading supplies and taking on damaged equipment to be refurbished when all hell broke loose as the base came under attack. The authorities ordered us to get under way immediately. We had a damaged helo on deck that was not secured, and the Captain told me, "Get rid of it!" I ordered one of my men to hop onto a forklift and push that helo off the deck right into the harbor. By this time, there were quite a few rounds coming at us; the ship was hit, but there was no serious damage and no personnel injuries. We got to sea safely, but I always wondered if that helicopter is still on the bottom of Da Nang harbor.

After an overhaul, we took some ROK troops back to Korea; while we were there, we trained placing pontoons to provide a haven for Swift boats. Upon our return to Vietnam, we joined Mobile Riverine Force Alpha and offloaded supplies and equipment up north at Quang Tri very close to the DMZ. We then went south to the Mekong Delta where we worked with Swift boats. We could swing our new pontoon down alongside our ship, use our winches to load it full of supplies, and have the Swifties come alongside and quickly load up. We were now doing ops in all the rivers down there. In three weeks, we traveled nearly 600 miles on those rivers. We also were firing Harassment and Interdiction rounds every night into the jungle on both sides of us. In these rivers it was necessary to always guard against enemy swimmers and sappers, so most nights we would drop grenades into the water alongside the ship at random intervals. We felt relatively safe once we were at a location, but when we were moving to a new location, it wasn't as safe, so we were always at General Quarters (GQ). Our draft was 17 feet, so our ship was often scraping along the bottom of these rivers. During GQ my job was to always be on the bow in combat gear looking in the river for mines. While up these rivers, we did go into Cambodia at least once, but to me it was just dangerous water far from the safety of the South China Sea.

One time we were guarding the exit of a river into the South China Sea when there was a serious firefight near the shore. Our 3-inch guns would not reach the shore, so the CO ordered us to fire our guns anyway and try to skip the projectile off the water onto the shore. Those of us doing the firing were grumbling that the only reason we were doing this was so that the CO could get a medal. We later learned that both he and the XO did receive a Bronze Star for this ridiculous operation. That summer up the rivers was really hot, but we still wore mostly proper uniforms. Another LST that we relieved up one of these rivers had been there for some time and everyone on that ship was in white underwear, had long hair, and was unshaven. They had obviously lost all discipline.

My final Vietnam deployment on the LST was again with Riverine Forces in the Vung Tau area southeast of Saigon. This was not as dangerous as our previous river assignments. I was now the senior OOD and had to frequently bail out our new CO who was not a good shiphandler. We were now mostly a "support LST" tasked to provide assistance to Riverine forces boats. My last river adventure was up in the Dong Tam region. By this time most of the officers aboard were pretty jaded and kept wondering about the efficacy of our even being there. When we heard that General Westmoreland was now requesting 200,000 more troops, our morale, which had previously been quite high, plummeted. I was glad to receive orders in October 1968 to USS CHARLESTON (LKA-113), an amphibious cargo ship which was just completing construction at Newport News Shipbuilding in Virginia. The ship had been built specifically to carry a new advanced type of tank in its hold, but when *we first tried to bring it aboard, it wouldn't fit! I was on CHARLESTON until December 1969 when I resigned and was discharged.*

The use of LST's in the Vietnam War is an example of "going with what you got." These WW II ships were designed to conduct amphibious landings on islands in the Pacific. Aaron's ship, the VERNON COUNTY, made zero amphibious landings while he was aboard, but was used in a variety of roles to support the riverine operations of smaller boats, to conduct gunfire support to troops ashore, to be a helicopter hub for inland battles, and to do surveillance along the coastline.

After leaving the Navy, Aaron became a licensed surveyor in Montana. He later launched a weekly newspaper in Spokane, Washington, which continues in operation today. During much of his post-Navy days, Aaron and his wife, Coco, lived on a ranch breeding Tennessee Walking horses. He now spends much of his retirement attempting to "shoot his age" in golf.

John Flynn
Holdensville, Oklahoma
"I was very lucky"

John was another of our superb athletes in our USNA Class of 1965. His sport was fencing, specializing in the epee. As one of the oldest members of our class, John had a much different view of Naval Academy life than most of us "kids." I interviewed him by computer from his home in Bradenton, Florida, where he currently lives with his wife, Lisa.

I was born in Oklahoma in 1939 and was the second oldest member of our USNA class. I was a Native American, a member of the Chickasaws, but my family moved to a city in west Texas called Big Spring where I went to high school. After graduation, I attended Texas A&M for two years as a Physics major. My father worked for the railroad, and after my second year at A&M, he got me a job working the night shift on the railroad. My job was putting together freight trains; it was a paperwork job where I had to figure out which car went on which train. My buddy and I liked to watch a TV series about submarines and soon we went to the local Navy recruiter to sign up for the Navy nuclear submarine program. We went through a year of training before I ended up as an electrician on USS SARGO (SSN-583) in Pearl Harbor. The Chief of the Boat [the senior enlisted man aboard] *on SARGO looked at my background and recommended that I apply to the Naval Academy under what I think was called the "Seaman to Admiral" program. So I applied, was accepted and sent to the Naval Academy Prep School (NAPS) in Bainbridge, Maryland.*

While I was at Texas A&M, I had taken up fencing. I continued this during my enlisted time and also while I was at NAPS. In fact, the

Commanding Officer of the base there, Captain Steele, happened to be an excellent fencer, and I met him at a local tournament. We became fencing buddies, and he arranged for me to participate with him in local fencing tournaments. Being at NAPS, I was not guaranteed going to the Naval Academy because a number of "Napsters" were also sent to NROTC units at various universities. When I told Captain Steele that my name was on the list of those going to Purdue University, he immediately picked up the phone and directed the head of NAPS to change my assignment to the Naval Academy. He wanted me to be on the fencing team there, so in June 1961 I ended up being sworn with you in as a midshipman in Tecumseh Court.

I continued to fence while at the Academy. The epee was my favorite of the three weapons used in fencing. In our senior year I was at the Olympic Trials in New Jersey where I placed 7th. This enabled me to compete at Nationals both as an individual in the epee and on a team of other older fencers.

I had a private pilot's license before I arrived at the Naval Academy and expected to become a pilot. But in our senior year, my eye exam showed that I had "some" color-blindness, disqualifying me for flying. My initial orders were to USS KITTY HAWK (CVA-63), not as an aviator, but as Asst Machinery Division (M-Division) Officer. Within two months my boss, a "Mustang" Lieutenant retired, and I became the M-Division Officer with 210 men working for me. The best part of this was that as an Ensign I was able to walk around the carrier with a rather prestigious jacket saying "Main Engines Officer."

I had stayed in regular contact with my USNA roommate, Al Jones, who was in flight training at Pensacola. He told me that the Navy was in desperate need of pilots and that I should apply. I wrote a letter to the Navy stating my pilot's license background and requesting flight school. To my surprise, I quickly received orders to flight training at Pensacola. But when I arrived, they again rejected me for pilot training and put me into the Naval Flight Officer (NFO) program which allows you to specialize in airborne weapons or sensor systems. I did well in Flight School and was able to receive my first choice to join a SIGINT squadron, VQ-1, in planes full of electronics flying out of Atsugi, Japan.

I joined them toward the end of 1967 and began flying the Lockheed EC-121M Warning Star. My first job was as an Electronics Evaluator monitoring all of our electronics equipment. The officers aboard my plane typically were two pilots, a navigator, myself, and sometimes a linguistic officer. There were also a considerable number of enlisted men. On most missions, we had additional intelligence specialists who were always referred to as "spooks." Basically, we were an intelligence gathering (a.k.a. spy) platform doing patrols off the North Korean, Russian, and North Vietnamese coasts. On April. 15, 1969, one of our EC-121's was shot down on such a reconnaissance mission by two North Korean MiG-21s. All 31 Americans aboard were lost. Instead of flying that day, I was the duty officer, and in retrospect, was very lucky because I had often flown with that crew.

This tragic EC-121 incident took place over the Sea of Japan approximately 90 miles off the North Korean coast. The plane, call sign Deep Sea 129, was an adaptation of the standard Lockheed Super Constellation which was in wide service in the airline industry. It was capable of long flights and was packed with electronics surveillance equipment. On this mission, code-named Beggar Shadow, the plane was on a mission nearly identical in routing to 200 others flown by VQ-1 and Air Force planes during the previous three months. In addition to the regular crew, there were nine Naval Security Group cryptologic technicians and linguists aboard. In spite of having massive retaliatory forces (many brought from Yankee Station) staged in the Sea of Japan to punish North Korea, President Nixon, who had recently come into office, chose not to retaliate. He did, however, secretly order the resumption of bombing of Cambodia, apparently under the theory that it did not matter where he was killing communists in retaliation. There is also conjecture that neither he nor the Joint Chiefs wanted to precipitate a second war in the Far East. The U.S. soon resumed reconnaissance flights. There is considerable information online concerning this incident and the associated debates which took place within the U.S. government.

When I arrived at Atsugi, my squadron had already been flying patrols off Vietnam. We would send a detachment down to Da Nang, and they would operate out of there for about a month. We would fly every day, seven days a week, along the coast or sometimes over Laos. For a crew, it was a month flying out of Atsugi, and then a month flying out of Da Nang. I flew well over 200 missions in this rotation. We stayed in barracks in Da Nang and ate in a general mess hall. There were frequent mortar attacks while we were in Da Nang. When the warning siren went off, we would run to our bunkers. One attack hit our barracks but no one was injured because the round hit the corner of the building. I was sleeping in the building at the time. During another attack, a rocket hit our tool shed on the flight line and put some holes in one of our parked aircraft. Sometimes, at night, we could see the rockets being fired from just outside the base.

The actual EC-121 aircraft shot down by the North Koreans

We lost one EC-121 on a landing when it went off the runway. Most aboard were killed. We also frequently took small arms fire when coming in to land at Da Nang. While inspecting our plane we would find all sorts of bullet holes. Although we did a lot of flying over Laos, when we flew off the North Vietnamese coast, we always observed the 12-mile limit. On all our missions in Vietnam, we were monitoring both the North Vietnamese and their Russian advisors. We used our base in Thailand for overnights when we flew the Laotian missions.

My actual job on a typical EC-121 mission was to monitor all our intercepts and evaluate both the ELINT (electronic intelligence) and COMINT (communications intelligence) to tell the pilots where they needed to fly and to decide what information needed to be immediately relayed. We were monitoring MiG frequencies and SAM (surface to air missile) sites to be able to send out warning to U.S. pilots that a missile was either being launched or about to be launched against them. I also flew a few EA-3B's off carriers performing the same types of missions. I would pick up these "rides" when one of the EA-3B's flew into Da Nang.

A 3-star Admiral from the National Security Agency was making a tour of Atsugi about the time I was due to rotate out of Vietnam. I was the Briefing Officer; when he learned that I was ready to rotate, he offered me a job as his Military Aide back in Washington. One of my jobs was to always be on the phone with him whenever he received a call. When he was promoted to a 4-star Admiral as Commander-in-Chief, Pacific, I stayed at NSA and became part of an outfit called "The Musketeer Group." In this job we went all over the world doing special operations using vans that we shipped ahead containing all types of specialized intelligence equipment. Sometimes I would go on submarine special operations, and other times we would be on the East German border gathering information. I later became CO of VQ-2 flying EC-121's out of Rota, Spain. I then had two other assignments before retiring in 1986.

John's career often involved working with the highest levels of American classified material and equipment to gather vital intelligence. Having served on U.S. fast attack submarines during the height of the Cold War, I had the opportunity to participate in this form of important intelligence gathering against the Soviet Union while working alongside officers like John. The success or failure of war often depends on which side has the best ability to gather and disseminate intelligence for use by decision makers, war planners, and combat units. Far too often, as John's experiences illustrate, those tasked with obtaining this information are thrust directly into harm's way.

Doug Burgess

Hartford, Connecticut

"You're not going to shoot these people"

Several of my Naval Academy classmates spent a year or more at a prep school or college prior to attending USNA. One of my close friends who attended The Bullis School (commonly called "Bullis Prep") in Potomac, Maryland, recommended that I talk to Doug who was one of 40 students there with him who ended up at the Naval Academy. He told me that Doug had some challenging experiences on Swift boats in Vietnam. I located Doug at his home in Swampscott, Massachusetts where he now lives with his wife, Sue. I interviewed him by computer.

My dad worked for Quaker Oats for 42 years. I spent my first three years of high school in Arlington Heights, Illinois, a suburb of Chicago, before Dad was transferred back to Connecticut. I spent my senior year at Amity Regional High School in Woodbridge, which is just outside of New Haven. I wasn't a great athlete but did participate on the swimming and basketball teams, primarily because it was a small school of only 200 students. You didn't have to be that good to get on the teams. I had watched both TV shows, "Men of Annapolis" and "West Point Story," and knew that I wanted to go to a service academy. My first choice was the Coast Guard Academy, but I couldn't get an appointment there. I did, however, during my year at Bullis, get appointments to both the Air Force Academy and Annapolis. I took the Naval Academy offer and never regretted it.

At the Academy I played intramural sports and when service selection came, I chose to go Surface Navy. My first ship after graduation was USS NORRIS (DD-859) operating out of Newport, Rhode Island. It had been built near the end of WW II but had been modernized as a FRAM 2 ship - that's Fleet Rehabilitation and Modernization. Basically, the ship was upgraded with more modern weapons. The day I reported aboard we departed for the Mediterranean. I was the First Lieutenant in charge of the deck force. After we came back, we soon sailed to Vietnam via the Panama Canal with the usual stops in Pearl Harbor and Subic Bay. We arrived in Saigon where my Captain took me along for several meetings with senior officers ashore. During my time in Saigon, I was able to see Vietnamese life and appreciate the culture more than most destroyer sailors at sea. NORRIS was then vectored north to do gunfire support operations along the coast. Spotters with units ashore would call for us to use our 5"/38 guns on inland targets. We also did a lot of plane guarding for carriers conducting flight ops at Yankee Station. During our operations near Da Nang, I became fascinated by the Swift boats which often refueled from us. I was invited to go on patrol on one and when I got back, I told the Captain, "I gotta do that." He told me that he would make it happen. When our ship got back to Newport, I had orders to Swift boats.

Following three months of Swift boat training at Coronado, California. I flew from Seattle non-stop to the Philippines and on to Can Ranh Bay. We had to find our own way to the Swift boat Division in Da Nang; it was now November 1967. I was the Officer-in-Charge (OIC) of Swift Boat PCF-19. I wasn't the Commanding Officer, but OIC, because it was not a commissioned ship, but a boat, Patrol Craft Fast. I had a crew of five sailors and one Vietnamese Navy Petty Officer who was our liaison and translator. Of the three of these, two spoke little English but the other was well-educated and very fluent in English. We operated out of Da Nang in the South China Sea up the coast 90 miles north to the DMZ and then 20 miles south of Da Nang to the Cua Dai River where Coastal Group 14 (CG 14) was located. Our classmate, John Lehman, was the U.S. Naval Advisor there to the South Vietnamese Navy at that time. On one occasion his base was in danger of being overrun by Viet Cong and he called us to come to extract him. It was always tricky going into the Cua Dai River because the sands were always shifting. Upon arrival, we were greeted by several shots, but none hit us. Apparently, the South Vietnamese Navy forces who were there with John were able to fend off the attack, so after getting assurances from John that he was okay, we returned to Da Nang.

The South Vietnamese Navy had "Coastal Group" bases in several locations along the South China Sea. These were actually small outposts
which used wooden junks to patrol the coast and inland waterways. A
U.S. naval officer was attached to call in American support when needed
and to provide liaison with American military forces. This year-long assignment was regarded as one of the most dangerous roles for a naval
officer in Vietnam; many advisors were killed or seriously wounded.
The harrowing experiences of another of our classmates, Bob Andretta,
during his later tour as an advisor to this same CG-14 are told in detail in
his book, *Brown Water Runs Red.*

*Our typical patrol was 24 hours; sometimes we had to watch our fuel to
make sure that we didn't run out. This was an ongoing problem whenever
we went up to the DMZ because it was 90 miles each way. Our boat
had three .50 caliber machine guns and a 81 mm mortar. During high
seas, aiming that mortar was a challenge, making it imprecise at best.
Our orders were to do whatever was necessary to interdict the flow of
men and weapons from North Vietnam to South Vietnam. We were very
successful in this mission, so much so that the North pretty much stopped
trying to do this.*

*While I was there, Swift boats out of Da Nang were not supposed to go up
the rivers because they were not designed to do this. This policy was later
changed. One assignment I never cared for was doing psychological ops.
This meant that we would patrol near the coastline using a loudspeaker
to blare some phrases in Vietnamese saying, "Come on over." The usual
response we would get was a few shots fired at us from shore. A couple of
times we even got into some firefights during these operations. Never did
we have some Viet Cong swim out to us asking for asylum. I'm not sure
what we would have done! None of us wore any ear protection during
these operations or when we were firing our guns. I suspect that my
current hearing loss may have begun on those patrols.*

*I did have thoughts about killing innocent people when we were firing.
I liked the Vietnamese people and found the country to be beautiful. I
was on patrol one night in an area that had been designated a "free fire*

zone." *Anybody you see there is presumed to be an enemy and you are authorized to shoot them. This was a flawed concept because anyone who had served in Vietnam learned that there were always innocent civilians in every one of these areas. I was on patrol near the coastline one night and we came across a number of sampans which are small double-ended boats used by Vietnamese fishermen. I got a call from an Army helicopter which had seen the lanterns on the sampans. He told me on the radio to clear the area because he was going to shoot all the fuckers. I became angry and yelled back, "No, you're not going to shoot these people. They're just fishing." It soon turned into a confrontation between him and me. I told him, "I'm not leaving the area. If you start shooting, we are going to shoot at you." Finally, he left without attacking the sampans. I got somewhat of a reprimand over this because our radios conversation had been monitored. However, my CO was understanding and told me, "Maybe next time you might find a better way to defuse the situation other than threatening to shoot one of our helicopters." I remain proud of my decision that night.*

I was involved in another dicey situation when I was on patrol up near the DMZ. It was nighttime and there was not much boat traffic. We eventually saw one sampan heading north. I hailed the boat and told them to stop so we could check them out. He kept moving so we blew our siren, but he ignored it and kept moving north. This made him an evader meaning that we were authorized to shoot him. We started to chase him into North Vietnamese waters and were prepared to open fire, but something about this whole situation made me uneasy. It didn't feel right. I decided to fire some .50 caliber across his bow. That made him stop. We went alongside and boarded the boat only to find a middle-aged man and two cute little girls with him. There were no weapons aboard and the man had correct papers. I still think about how close we came to shooting them. I have been thankful ever since.

Another time we were doing some psychological operations while transporting a South Vietnamese officer to a location south of Da Nang. We were shot at from somewhere on the shore near a local community. The Vietnamese officer aboard kept insisting that I call in an airstrike on that village. I refused to do so because we would be wiping out a large number of civilians because one guy shot at us. I couldn't believe that this fellow wanted so bad to kill his own people.

Here Doug paused to tell me how much he and a number of fellow Swift boat officers detested John Kerry, the future Senator from Massachusetts, Presidential candidate, and Secretary of State. Kerry had been a Swift boat OIC who returned to the U.S. early after receiving three Purple Hearts during action in the Mekong Delta region. When Kerry arrived back in the U.S., he asserted that most Swift boat crews were killing civilians. Doug insisted that this was simply not true. He added that there were certainly a few overly aggressive Swift boat officers, but most didn't want to kill innocent civilians and were very careful about it. Every Swift boat officer to whom I spoke echoed Doug's views. Most also had very critical remarks questioning the circumstances surrounding each of Kerry's Purple Hearts enabling him to be eligible to return to the U.S. after only four months of service in Vietnam. There is voluminous discussion of Kerry's Vietnam service online.

My close friend, John Davis, was another OIC of a Swift boat in Da Nang. Both of us took our crews up to the DMZ in my boat, PCF-19, during an operation where we would be working with a Coast Guard cutter. The plan was for one crew to do a patrol, then refuel the boat so that the other crew could immediately do another 24-hour patrol without having to keep returning to Da Nang. This way we could maintain continuous coverage and allow the "off-crew" to get some food and 24 hours of rest on the cutter. Both John and I were very tired when we arrived, and he volunteered to take his crew on the first patrol. They were patrolling that night close to the shore when suddenly the boat was hit by high explosives and blown to smithereens. Everyone aboard was killed except John and one of his crewmen. Both were picked up out of the water by another cutter in the area. The official investigation concluded that it was a friendly fire incident from an Air Force jet which thought that it was attacking an enemy helicopter. Apparently, the Air forces guy thought that he was shooting at an enemy helicopter because his radar blip was moving fast. The plane's first missile missed the boat, but the second one was a direct hit. John was badly injured. For the rest of his life, he had bad vision and walked with a limp. Back in the states

I frequently visited him and was godfather to his son. John passed away about 10 years ago.

After a year on the Swift boats, I received orders to Destroyer School in Newport, Rhode Island, followed by orders to another destroyer. Sue and I were married in April 1971, and I resigned from the Navy to attend graduate school at the University of Massachusetts. I then worked the next 25 years for an engineering company in Boston. Later I had my own engineering consulting firm.

Doug's experiences graphically reflect both the fog of war and the moral ambiguity associated with rules of engagement. Each day as he took his PCF on patrol there was uncertainty about whether the small boats they interdicted were enemy or were simply Vietnamese civilians trying to eke out a living fishing these same waters. No one knows for certain how they might react when placed into the situations which Doug and his crew encountered. Add to this delicate balance the threat of friendly fire and the natural dangers of the seas. Swift boats were notoriously unstable in high seas and were dangerous to operate in the monsoon seasons in Vietnam. Several crews paid the price of being at sea on these small boats during bad weather. Doug told me that it has taken a long time, but he has come to terms with the circumstances associated with the loss of his boat, the death of several crew members, and the life-long injuries suffered by his close friend. War wounds are slow to heal.

Bob Elder

Bloomsburg, Pennsylvania
"This ship is going
to have a riot "

I have had the pleasure of having lunch with Bob in Annapolis on several occasions during recent years, but I conducted this interview by computer from his home where he now lives in Valdosta, Georgia.

Although I was born in Pennsylvania, our family moved south to Georgia after WW II. Dad was in Navy aviation during the war. He worked on some Top Secret projects involving two-engine drones. These were carried by TBM's which were torpedo bombers. Once released from the TBM, the drones, which were filled with explosives, were radio-controlled from aboard the plane. It was like a Kamikaze without a pilot. In the Pacific this system was deployed initially to the Marianas late in the war; once the atomic bombs were dropped, they were no longer needed. There was a different version, also Top Secret, in the Atlantic. These involved a drone B-24 Liberator bomber loaded with explosives. It was a crazy plan because the pilot would fly the plane and then had to bail out. From that point on, the B-24 would be radio-controlled by another plane to direct it to its target. Joseph Kennedy, the older brother of President Kennedy, died while involved in this project.

The TBM's were basically the same aircraft as the Grumman TBF Avenger except that they were made by General Motors. These two aircraft were the most widely used U.S. torpedo bombers during the war and were credited with sinking Japanese battleships and numerous other vessels, including 30 submarines. The drone programs in which Bob's dad was involved were kept highly classified long after the war ended. Joe Kennedy, Jr. was also a naval aviator. He had gone to Europe

217

in late 1943 to fly with the British on numerous combat missions. He volunteered for the program Bob mentioned which, in the Atlantic, was code-named Operation Aphrodite. His mission was to fly the Liberator toward a German V-2 rocket site in August 1944, but electromagnetic interference caused the bomb he was carrying to prematurely explode before he was scheduled to bail out. This accident caused the Atlantic program to be terminated.

After I graduated from high school, I entered the NROTC program at Georgia Tech but chose to go to the Naval Academy as soon as I received an appointment through a competitive exam. Based on my dad's experience, all I wanted to do was be an aviator. During flight school I chose multi-engines and ended up flying the anti-submarine P-3 aircraft. My squadron was stationed at Moffett Field in California, but we soon deployed to the Marine Corps Air Station at Iwakuni in Japan. Our mission there was essentially anti-submarine warfare (ASW). We would fly ops around the perimeter of North Korea, China, and the Soviet Union - we would also be collecting signal intelligence. There were many occasions when the Soviets would send out planes to "greet" us. We would return "hand signals" in response to their mooning us.

In late spring 1968 we deployed to Vietnam, primarily Cam Ranh Bay, and Thailand. We stayed in barracks at Cam Ranh surrounded by sandbags. There were bunkers nearby for us to dive into when the base was being attacked. Our flights were supporting MARKET TIME operations looking for small ships along the coast which were supplying the Viet Cong. We never found any on our flights.

When I left the VP squadron, I had a tour at the Navy postgraduate school. Once I obtained my Master's degree, I was assigned to be the Flag Secretary to the Admiral in charge of Carrier Group Three. One of my assignments in this job required me to take a helicopter over to USS RANGER (CV-61) to conduct a "race relations evaluation." I looked at all the pertinent paperwork, talked to the chaplain, and asked questions with sailors on the mess deck. The chaplain told me, "This ship is going to have a riot." At 0600 the next morning there was a rap on my stateroom door, and I was told, "The Captain wants to see you NOW." His face was red as he yelled at me, "You guys started a riot." I left there and went back to the other carrier where our staff was located. My admiral told me not to worry about it, I was just doing my job. RANGER had two other riots not long later. It was a bad environment aboard that ship.

There were several serious race riots aboard U.S. aircraft carriers in the early 1970's. One of the worst occurred in October 1972 on USS KITTY HAWK (CV-63). It began while the ship was in the South China Sea after having been deployed for nearly 8 months. There had been a demanding period of flight operations. Of the 4500 sailors aboard, 302 were black. Because there was considerable unrest back in the U.S., racial tensions aboard were high. Although accounts differ, apparently an incident began in the galley in a dispute over a sandwich. A fight broke out and black sailors began to roam the ship's passageways using broom handles, pieces of metal, and other makeshift weapons to attack white sailors. Over 50 sailors were injured, some seriously. Subsequently, there were other race riots on USS CONSTELLATION (CV-64) and an oiler. Amazingly, the day after the KITTY HAWK riot, the ship launched combat sorties on schedule, and according to the Navy Times, then continued round-the-clock combat flight operations for the next 28 days. There were indeed racial incidents throughout the military during the Vietnam War. None of the services were immune from such incidents. It was a difficult time for America, both at home, and on battlefields and ships.

Bob went on to a 23 year career in the Navy after switching from aviation to aeronautical engineering. After his retirement from the Navy, he worked for several corporations and the Federal Aviation Administration before moving back to his hometown of Valdosta, Georgia.

Mike Brown

Lawrenceville, Illinois

"Brown's Run"

Mike was another of our top athletes at the Naval Academy. He was one of the best collegiate pole vaulters in the U.S. and competed at the national level. I met Mike during our first year when we were members of the 13th Company. The 4000 midshipmen are arranged in "companies" having approximately equal numbers of all four years of students. The seniors, called first classmen, pretty much ran the day-to-day routine. At that time, there was considerable hazing of the freshmen who were called plebes. It was somewhat akin to college fraternities, without the drinking. Following our graduation, Mike and I chose different professional paths within the Navy and did not see each other again. His career began on surface ships; I was on nuclear submarines. I interviewed Mike via telephone from his home in Ellenton, Florida.

I was born in a small town in southern Illinois and actually began, almost by accident, pole vaulting when I was eight years old - long story. In high school, I competed in various events in track, including high jump and pole vaulting. The highest I ever vaulted in high school was 12 feet. I was not recruited by the track coach at Navy, but one day early in our plebe summer, I was sort of goofing off over on the track and picked up a fiberglass pole someone had left. I started to jump with it and began clearing increasing heights. When I reached 11'6", I noticed an older man with a fedora hat watching me. When I cleared 13'6", he came over and said, "You just broke the Navy plebe record. Who are you?" Being a new plebe, I braced up and replied, "Midshipman Brown, 4th Class, Sir!" He laughed and said, "Midshipman Brown, you're now on the Navy track team." I went on to considerable success in track while at the Academy jumping 16' 4 1/2" and having the opportunity to compete at the Penn Relays. Post-graduation, my best ever was 17 feet, both in 1968 and 1974 at some "all-comers" meets.

I wanted to be a pilot, but I had poor vision in my right eye. My next choice was to go Marine Corps, but there was a quota depending on class standing that kept me out. So, I ended up in the Surface Navy aboard USS GALVESTON (CLG-3). I joined the ship in Japan immediately after graduation. We did some operations in the Gulf of Tonkin then headed back to our homeport in San Diego. We had too many junior officers aboard, so I was transferred to USS OKLAHOMA CITY (CLG-5), also in San Diego. I had put in to go to Swift boats but was told that Ensigns were not eligible.

In February 1968, right after I had done one of those 17 ft jumps at a meet in Los Angeles, I received orders to Swift boat training in San Diego. After training, I was sent to Cam Ranh Bay, before being transferred in April 1968 to a detachment of Swifts at Phu Quoc Island in the Gulf of Thailand. We operated from a floating pier with 14 Swift boats. Initially I was sent on patrols with an experienced officer named Bob. On my first patrol, I heard a "PSSST" sound and yelled, "What the hell was that?" Bob yelled back, "Just some guy shooting at us. They never hit anything." Soon, I got my own boat, PCF-93. I was the Officer-in-Charge and had five enlisted crew members: an engineer, a gunner's mate, a radar operator, a quartermaster, and a boatswain's mate. We generally brought a Vietnamese interpreter along. In addition to the normal armament of the M-60 machine gun mounts and an 81-mm mortar, I scrounged around and picked up two belt-fed Mk-19 grenade launchers that had 25 rounds in a belt. We could reach 400 yds with that weapon.

At that time, we were never supposed to go into the rivers, just do coastal patrols looking for enemy boats carrying goods or weapons. Our boat had a draft of just under five feet, and because there were numerous sandbars, there was a legitimate concern that the boats could go hard aground and be in danger of attack from shore. For example, the entrance to the major city of Rach Gia, on the west coast of the Mekong Delta, not far from Cambodia, had sand bars in front two and a half to three feet deep. But we would watch sampans, and even large junks, routinely go into the river without a problem. So, I said to my crew, "If they can do it, so can we." Soon, I was following a junk into the river for about a half mile. We turned around and went back out without a problem. As we headed out, a U.S. Coast Guard cutter came alongside yelling, "You can't go in there." It turned out that an Army Major aboard another Coast Guard cutter had been killed during a recent ambush in this same area.

I always asked my crew if they wanted to go into the rivers. They would always reply, "Let's go! That's where the shooting at us is coming from." Almost all of the entire lower section of the Ca Mau Peninsula was controlled by the VC and the NVA which had infiltrated from Cambodia. My boat was involved in at least 15 separate firefights on canals and rivers. There was a significant enemy outpost about three to four hours south of Rach Gia on the coast and every time we passed it, we would throw our mortars in there. Once I dumped 50 rounds of 81-mm mortars on them, some with flechettes. I got into trouble for some of our incursions into the rivers. Some busybody Coast Guard officer wanted to court martial me for disobeying orders, but when they talked to an Army Colonel ashore at Rach Gia, he told them that he wanted to give me a medal. They let it go.

Flechettes were essentially small metal darts assembled in a "beehive" fashion inside the shell. Mortars loaded with 2000 flechette rounds were a particularly nasty anti-personnel weapon.

While these types of formal restrictions on our operations were in effect for the first three months, I had been operating out of Phu Quoc. The Task Group Commander came down to visit, and said, "Hey, Brown, how many VC did you kill today?" I told him, "As long as we were restricted so much, none!" A week later, there was a message to all Coastal Patrol units allowing us to now be in the river business. Here is the bottom line as I saw it: during the first three months with restrictions, nada enemy dead. Over the following six months, we were allowed to operate without restrictions, and we inflicted tremendous casualties on the enemy.

This success was not without pain. We suffered 186 wounded, two killed, and two boats lost during those six months. Fortunately, my boat, PCF-93, never had anyone killed or wounded. I always flew a blue pennant with a white B from our boat; we had the "B" because we were the Bravo crew for that boat. It must have been our good luck charm because we were engaged in maybe 20 firefights and never had one bullet hole in that boat.

However, I was wounded twice while me and my crew were on another boat, PCF-38. We had been doing patrols near the tip of the Ca Mau Peninsula, which is the southern-most point of Vietnam. The area was full of VC and had been designated a free-fire zone, meaning that we were authorized to shoot anyone and anything. On October 4, 1968, we were there with another boat in what was called "Square Bay" at the entrance to the Song Cau Lon River. The other Swift boat had been there previously and knew how to get past the sandbars and into the river. Before leaving the area, they showed us how to get in. I asked my crew if they wanted to go into the river, and each guy said, "Hell, yes!" So, in we went. We had orders not to go past this place called "Fish Island," but when we saw a boat with two men in it ahead, we went toward it to investigate. As it turned to run away, we fired a warning shot, but it kept on going. I told my gunner's mate to fire, and we pretty much tore up the boat. We looked but never found those men who had been in the boat. Up ahead we saw some grass hooches but no sign of any people anywhere in the area. There was a Viet Cong flag flying next to it, so we went ashore to investigate. All we could find were pigs and chickens. We set the hooch on fire and killed the animals because they would be food for the VC. There was still no one in view.

Hooch with VC flag prior to destruction by Mike and his crew

We decided to go further up the river. We found more hooches, but again no one was there. We used my signal pistol and our Zippo lighters to set all the hooches on fire. Next, we saw a lookout station on the other shore and took it out with our mortar. As we continued upriver and rounded a large S turn in the river, we were startled to see what appeared to be a good-sized city. Again, it was deserted! I knew from having previously seen charts of the area that this city had to be Nam Can. We threw some mortars into the city, but probably did no serious damage. We were able to destroy close to 100 boats by shooting the motors with our pistols and burning many of them. Still, we saw no one. Where the hell had they gone? It was now getting later in the day, so I had to make a decision. We knew from experience that we would almost certainly be ambushed if we tried to return the way we had come in, so I asked the crew if they wanted to continue up the river to try to find the Bo De River, which I had seen on a map of the Delta area. Each of my crew agreed that we would possibly be killed if we did the return route. So, we continued on. I had no chart of the river, and it was getting late in the day, but after maybe four more bends in the river, we came to a wider river. It just had to be the Bo De, which I knew emptied into the South China Sea. We turned right and headed downriver, not sure how far we had to go to get to the ocean. Everything was going good until we were maybe 2000 yards from the sea when someone started to shoot at us with an AK-47 from the northern shore. My Quartermaster was driving the boat and got hit in the leg. He was knocked out of his chair and fell on the deck. Just as I jumped into his seat to steer, a round hit the radar next to me, sending shrapnel into my left arm and the side of my face. We went full speed to the sea where two Swift boats from up north at Vung Tau were patrolling. It was now dark; they had to shine lights on us to make sure we weren't enemy. Thank God that they didn't shoot first.

We then headed back around the tip of the peninsula toward our base at Phu Quoc but met a Coast Guard cutter near Square Bay. They patched us up enough to return to our base. I filed my "after-action" report by radio on the way back. We were met by my CO who was threatening to court martial me for disobeying his direct order not to go past Fish Island. Fortunately, by the next day, Admiral Zumwalt in Saigon had read my report and told my boss that he was personally coming down to congratulate me and give me an award.

Mike's "adventure" as the first U.S. boat of any kind to transit Vietnamese rivers through Viet Cong territory from the Gulf of Thailand to the South China Sea became known as "Brown's Run." It was written up in the book, "Swift Boats in Vietnam," and became somewhat legendary. A shorter version can be found online. Mike was not the first Swift boat skipper in Vietnam to disobey orders. Boats operating in the North also ventured into areas "off-limits." There is often a fine line between being court-martialed and receiving a medal. The U.S. also sent clandestine operations into North Vietnam, Laos, and Cambodia, while publicly proclaiming that it never happened.

My other time being wounded happened on a multi-boat operation on a canal off the Son On Doc River. We had received intelligence that there was a meeting taking place on a lake there involving VC and NVA troops. We took four boats and searched all over that lake but found nothing. As we were returning and about to re-enter the river, someone ran out of a hooch and threw a grenade at our boats. It exploded in the air near my boat and knocked me down. One of my crew ran over and told me to stay down. I had blood all over my face and left arm (again)! I still have a small fragment in my head near my left ear.

On one occasion, the CBS reporter, Liz Trotta, and her photographer were embedded with us. This was a later mission in that same area near Square Bay. As four of our boats were headed up the Song Cu Lon, the two boats in front of us came under heavy fire with several casualties. Liz got a first-hand taste of what was going on in our part of the war. I don't know if any of her experiences with us made the CBS Evening News, but I heard later that she won at least three Emmy awards during her career.

In January 1969, I was assigned to be an assistant in Cam Ranh Bay to the Commander of Riverine Forces. My job as the advisor for all riverine missions entailed travel to a lot of various Navy units in-country, but I was no longer involved in combat situations. When I was due to leave Vietnam in April 1970, Admiral Zumwalt offered me two months leave in the States if I would stay in Vietnam as his aide. I thought about taking his offer, but declined because I was planning to resign from the Navy to do other things. As it turned out, once I was at my next assignment in Puerto Rico, I decided to stay in the Navy and ended up in various assignments until I did resign in 1978. I stayed in the Reserves and retired with 25 years of service in 1990.

After he left the Navy, Mike worked as a consultant in the Washington, D.C. area for several years before moving to Florida to work as an accountant. He became a very successful golfer and even attempted to qualify as a professional for the PGA Senior Tour. Although he did not succeed as a golf professional, Mike still routinely shoots his age in golf.

Reading Mike's experiences on Swift boats, it might be tempting to be critical of some of his actions burning hooches and boats and killing livestock. These actions all took place in free-fire zones where everyone and everything was considered hostile. Denying food and lodging to enemy forces attempting to kill Americans was standard policy. War has few rules associated with civil society, and even those rules disappear in the heat of battle. The lesson is that war must be avoided. It is cruel, filthy, and abhorrent. And it does not stop at termination of hostilities. For those who survive - combatants or innocents - memories linger.

Bill (Fuzzy) Erickson

Portsmouth, Virginia
"Our job was to build things"

Fuzzy did not graduate with our Naval Academy Class of 1965 due to a serious injury, but stayed at USNA and completed his studies the following year. Our tradition is that no matter when or whatever happens, if you began with our class, you are forever a member. I wanted to hear Fuzzy's memories of his time in Vietnam because he was stationed near the DMZ with a Seabee battalion. I interviewed him via computer from his apartment in Annapolis.

I was born at the Naval Hospital at Portsmouth, Virginia. Dad was a Civilian Engineering Corps (CEC) officer and had a degree in civil engineering. Because of his degree, he was involved in the early stages of the Navy's nuclear power program. He also worked for the CIA after the war building radio towers in the Philippines. During our moves I went to various high schools but spent my senior year at Franklin High School in Seattle. When I applied to our local congressman for an appointment to the Academy, he told all of us who applied that he would give the appointment to whomever scored highest on a civil service exam. Next thing I knew I was taking the oath of office in Tecumseh Court with you and over 1200 others.

I got the nickname, Fuzzy, because my older brother had gone to the Academy and used to cut hair in his room for his roommates [cutting another's hair was technically illegal at the Academy, but there were several such "barbers" around to provide an alternative to the midshipman barber shop]. *Because of his style of haircutting, my brother became known as "Fuzzy." When I arrived and it became known that I was his younger brother, the upperclassmen started to call me "Little*

227

Fuzz" which over time became "Fuzzy." At the Academy I played rugby, but injured my knee so much that I was declared "Not Physically Qualified" (NPQ) for commissioning. This setback meant that I had to "turn back" to the Class of 1966. When I graduated, I was sent to a Medical Board which allowed me to be commissioned as an officer, but in the Supply Corps. I graduated from Supply Officer School in June 1967. Because Dad had been in the CEC, I volunteered to be assigned to a Seabee Battalion in Port Hueneme, California. We began an 8-month deployment to the Dong Ha combat base in Vietnam which was located just south of the DMZ. In addition to being the Disbursing Officer, I ran the galley, the mess hall, and the retail store for the 800 Seabees stationed there.

The Seabees are truly combat engineers. Before we left the states, we spent three weeks of combat training with the Marines. Everyone had to be able to fire a M-16 and to throw grenades. While we were there our base was under fire from both mortars and rockets at least five times. The worst occurred in early 1968 during the Tet offensive. We lived in elevated plywood hooches with trap doors that allowed us to dive into trenches underneath whenever the base came under attack. We lost four Seabees in our camp during these attacks; at least two others were killed during operations outside the base.

Our job was to build things. By the time we arrived, other Seabee units had built up Dong Ha into a functional base. It had a landing strip and a field hospital. Our job was mostly to build a lot of roads. One of our major efforts was to help relieve the Marines under siege at Khe Sanh. We were tasked to build a large helicopter landing pad out in the jungle maybe 4-5 miles away from Khe Sanh. We used bulldozers to knock down trees and lay down metal pads to make landings possible. We had most of the necessary equipment to do this because all the bulldozers and road building gear in Vietnam were passed down from one Seabee unit to another and stayed in Vietnam while the battalions rotated in and out.

As Disbursing Officer, I would hold payday before reveille at the camp, then get in a helicopter to fly around to pay all the Seabees at various detachments in the region. On several of these helicopter flights *we took enemy fire but were never hit. The men were paid in Military Payment Certificates (MPCs) to keep greenbacks out of the hands of the Vietnamese to protect their local currency. I always kept about $200,000 of MPCs with me to do payroll. Before each payday, each Seabee wrote down how much of his pay he wanted in MPCs; the rest of his pay would stay on his pay record (which was like a bank account). If a Seabee wanted to send money home, it had to be done through an allotment which I could set up for him.*

Our hospital at Dong Ha was really nothing more than a MASH unit; all serious casualties were airlifted to hospital ships offshore or to Da Nang. There were no Vietnamese allowed to work on our base due to security. We also could not leave the base after 8 PM. It was far too dangerous. There were few safe areas in Vietnam.

Fuzzy mentioned the presence of a MASH (Mobile Army Surgical Hospital) unit at Dong Ha. This hospital facility may or may not have been a MASH unit because Medical Unit Self-Contained Transportable (MUST) units were also established in Vietnam. These were expandable, mobile shelters with inflatable ward sections. These could also be expanded for radiology and a pharmacy. Several MUST units were hit by mortar fire in the Tay Ninh region. One hospital commander was killed in an attack.

Our battalion came back to Port Hueneme in late July 1968, but I was in an "after party" of four officers cycling back and forth between Da Nang and Dong Ha to ensure that all was prepared for our next deployment. We had been lucky; none of our officers had been killed during this deployment.

I was detached from this Seabee assignment in December 1968 and was able to obtain a great assignment at the Naval Communications Station at Northwest Cape, Australia. In 1973 I was stationed at the Texas Instrument plant in Dallas as a Defense Contract Administrator. I stayed there until I resigned from the Navy in 1976. I remained in the Reserves and went back to work as a civil servant in the same job for the Navy. I retired from the Reserves in 1996.

About five years ago I returned to Vietnam as a tourist. When I was in Hue, I paid a local fellow to ride me up to Dong Ha on his motorcycle. I asked him to take me to the site of the American Combat Base there. He quickly replied, "There's never been a base in Dong Ha." I laughed and asked him to find "someone old." Sure enough, he found an old man who was a life-long resident of Dong Ha. He took us to a location and said in Vietnamese, "This is where it was." We were standing next to a 12-story skyscraper. How things change!

Fuzzy's experiences as a Supply Corps officer with the Seabees provide an insight into an aspect of war that is frequently overlooked. Not only does a fighting force require a complicated, functional logistics chain, but also a highly trained engineering component which can build and maintain facilities necessary to support the fighting force. The Seabees have a storied history dating from WW II. Their motto, "We Build, We Fight," sums up their mission. If you have not seen the 1944 John Wayne and Susan Hayward movie, *The Fighting Seabees*, it may be worth your time, if only for the overly dramatic scenes of Wayne driving a bulldozer to attack Japanese soldiers.

Phil Ferrara

West Roxbury, Massachusetts
"I remember their names to this day"

Phil is perhaps the most organized man I have met. He drove to my residence in Virginia from his home in Annapolis, Maryland, bringing heavily marked charts, photographs, log books, after-action reports, ship newsletters, and other "stuff" associated with his tour in Vietnam. He began by explaining why he wanted to attend the Naval Academy,

I was born in a hospital in the shadow of Fenway Park but grew up nearby in West Roxbury, Massachusetts. Like a lot of our generation, I watched the television series, "Men of Annapolis," every episode. Several members of our family had served in the military, and by the time I was in high school, going to Annapolis had become my dream. Although both my parents were dyed-in-the-wool Democrats, I was able to obtain an appointment through a Republican congressman. They got a big kick out of that.

Following our four years at Navy, I was selected to go into nuclear submarines. Immediately after graduation, I went to six months of submarine school in Connecticut which I liked quite a bit. The Navy then sent me to Bainbridge, Maryland, to attend classes on nuclear power plants. Things were going well, but after about two months I became deathly sick with mono. I was hospitalized for several weeks and ended up missing over a month of classes which caused me to fail one of the mid-term exams. They sent me back to Annapolis to explain to a senior officer why I had failed, but apparently being sick wasn't a good excuse. When I learned that their plan was for me to repeat the school from the start, I told them that I didn't want to do nuclear power anymore. They were not happy, and I received orders to report to USS TRUCKEE (AO-147), an oiler in Norfolk, Virginia.

I was the Petroleum Cargo Officer on TRUCKEE. I was responsible for getting all the oil onto the ship and then off to all the other ships we were assigned to refuel at sea. After I was aboard and had qualified as OOD (Officer of the Deck), the Navigator got orders to go to the Riverine Forces in Vietnam, and although I was very junior, the Captain asked me to become the Navigator. I enjoyed this assignment, and soon we went for a deployment to the Med. While we were there, the Arab-Israeli War started in June 1967, putting the entire Med fleet on high alert.

I detached from TRUCKEE in May 1968 upon receiving orders to Vietnam. I first had to undergo a week of survival training at Whidbey Island, Washington, and then five weeks of training at Mare Island, California, on Armored Troop Carriers, the boats we were going to be on in Vietnam. These were actually converted Landing Craft Medium boats (LCM) and had twin-engine V-8's. While I was in the middle of this training, I got called in to see the Commanding Officer of our squadron, who told me, "I need to make a change. I want you to take over as CO of River Division 51." This put me as a 25-year old in command of 200 men and 21 boats. We trained as a unit and then flew together to Tan Son Nhut Air Base near Saigon. We then flew east to Vung Tau, a city on the coast of the South China Sea, in order to meet the freighters which were bringing us all new ATC's. We had to wait a month in Vung Tau aboard three ships until the freighter arrived with our boats from the states.

The ATCs were often called "Vietnam Ironclads" because they had a visual resemblance to the Civil War monitors. The ones which Phil's squadron received at Vung Tau were all brand new and had been built near Seattle. Most of the 21 boats under his command had a maximum speed of 6 knots and a shallow draft of 3-4 feet. Each of the boats had a crew of 10-12 enlisted men with a Chief Petty Officer in charge. Phil would generally ride in one designated the Command Control Boat (CCB) which had more communication equipment than the others.

All of us boarded the cargo ship there at Vung Tau and rode it with all our boats up the river to Nha Be, the main base for what was called "The Brown Water Navy" - the boats which were patrolling the rivers and canals throughout Vietnam. If you had seen this Mekong Delta water, you would understand why it was called "The Brown Water Navy!" As we rode that freighter up the river, I was shocked and appalled to look at the entire east side of the river, which had once been a swampy jungle. After being defoliated by U.S. forces with Agent Orange to deny hiding places to enemy forces, it was now totally obliterated into a dead moonscape. It was surreal...and sad. That image has stuck with me all these years.

At this time in mid-68, Vietnam was still in chaos due to the Tet Offensive a few months earlier. We were told that the main threat to boats on the rivers and canals would be B-40 rockets fired from concealed locations in jungle along the shore. Once we got our boats ready, we took them to what would be our main base at Dong Tam just upriver from My Tho which was about 45 miles southwest of Saigon. Whenever we were here, we would use larger Navy ships (LST's and APL's) to feed and house our personnel. The good news was that, because our boats were new, we had few engineering problems. Our enginemen were young, but learned quickly and could fix almost anything.

Our initial base was at Nha Be, about 5-10 miles south of Saigon. It was now August 1968. The next step was to outfit the boats, learn everything about them and their weapons, and get them ready for combat. One weapon I was not familiar with was a flamethrower which we had on two of the boats. They were called "Zippos" based on those small metal cigarette lighters by that name which everyone had at that time.

We began operations in late September and soon learned that we would be working all over the Mekong Delta area, a region of roughly 16,000 square miles. Our first assignment was in the Manh Thit-Nocolai Canal for a three-week operation supporting the 9th ARVN Division. We had all sorts of assignments: patrols, ferrying U.S. Army and ARVN troops, providing security for the larger ships at Dong Tam, and fire suppression for units engaged in battle. We captured our first prisoner in mid-October. Unfortunately, one of my boats got ambushed at the end of October with four B-40 rockets. Two of our sailors and 14 of the U.S. Army troops aboard were wounded. We killed several Viet Cong during these initial operations but were ambushed several times resulting in wounded sailors.

A shipboard flamethrower

Most Americans, including the troops fighting there, did not know the history or the geography of the Mekong Delta. The Mekong River, which originates in Tibet, runs over 3000 miles through six countries before emptying into the South China Sea via a vast network of waterways, some large, others small. It is difficult to define the land area of the Delta because it constantly varies as water levels change based on the seasons. During the French control of Vietnam, numerous additional canals were constructed to improve rice production and transportation. It is truly a maze of waterways.

It is believed that human settlements in the region began as early as the fourth century B.C. There is evidence that sites in the Delta were used for extensive trading with India and other Southeast Asia locations for a thousand years during this early period. Different ethnic groups came and went, and various rulers gained control until French colonists took over in the 1860's. By the time Phil's riverine forces arrived in the Delta, the population exceeded 10 million. Most were farmers, scrambling to make a living farming and fishing. Also, a large percentage were distrustful, if not openly hostile, to the South Vietnamese government in Saigon. Hence, the Delta was fertile recruiting ground for the Viet Cong who found widespread support among the indigenous population.

I was a Lieutenant, and my XO was a Lieutenant (junior grade) (LTJG). My Ops officer was also a JG. Generally, one of them might be taking seven boats on a mission in one place, and the other guy would take eight boats somewhere else. Or I might take all the boats myself. Our operations were all driven by the Army, 3rd Brigade of the 9th Infantry Division, which was also based at Dong Tam. They told us where to take their troops. The 25th ARVN Division was also down there in the Delta, and we worked with them. Basically U.S. intelligence would decide where we would go and what we would be doing.

The canals we went through had all been built by the French and were straight as an arrow. You had to be a map guy, or you would get lost in the Delta. If you did not hit the correct turn, your boats would be lost. These canals were about as wide as a suburban street and were all lined with palm trees and other dense vegetation so you could not see much of anything on shore. Fortunately, my experience as Navigator on the oiler helped me quite a bit to avoid getting lost. We carried all our own supplies; if we were short of fuel, they would send out a helicopter to bring us more. When we were moving troops, I would often have an Army captain with me on my boat. On these missions, we would load an entire company of Army troops, maybe 150 soldiers, with about 20-25 troops on each of the boats. The Army guys had all their own supplies and weapons. We just ferried them to drop points. We would load them at 4 AM and make an insertion maybe around 7 AM, depending on the tides. They had everything with them, and helicopters could be called in if they needed any additional supplies. Our job was to get them there so that they could engage enemy troops wherever it was thought they were located.

We were often under fire - almost always. Out of my 200 men, 105 were wounded. Four were killed. I remember their names to this day: Tom Gaudet, Iris Harrington, David Land, Jose Campos. I took it as a pledge that someone had to remember how they died. The enemy fire always came from the shore, usually B-40 rockets. Two of my guys were killed by these rockets. Your constant fear/paranoia was riverbank rockets. You never knew when they were going to hit you. You just don't hear it. During one attack, I got hit in the legs by shrapnel below my flak jacket. Compared to others who had been hit during ambushes, my wounds weren't that bad. I was bleeding heavily, and it looked terrible, but wasn't life threatening. My legs felt like they had been hit by a porcupine with a lot of its needles sticking out, except the needles were shards of metal. One of our three hospital corpsmen, Chief Phillips, happened to be aboard my boat at the time, so he put me down on the deck and started pulling the needles out. I was lucky; two of our four deaths came from rockets, and almost all of the 105 men who were wounded were hit by this same type of rocket.

The B-40 RGP-2 rocket is basically a 40 mm Bazooka which was designed in the early 1950's in the Soviet Union as an anti-tank weapon. The North Vietnamese and Viet Cong quickly realized its potential to attack U.S. vessels in the narrow waterways of the Mekong Delta. The tail fins roll over to allow a soldier to insert it into a firing tube. It is shoulder-fired and has a range of just under 500 feet. Although the total length of the weapon is close to four feet, it is ideal for jungle warfare because the launcher and weapon together weigh less than 10 pounds. One soldier could easily carry it to an optimum hidden launch location. In fact, this same weapon is still in use today by the North Koreans and many other countries which obtain weapons from Russia, China, and other arms merchants. Because it is relatively easy to re-load, a group of Viet Cong equipped with extra shells could do extreme damage to the type of boats Phil's division was using. The projectile uses a shaped hot charge on initial contact to easily penetrate several inches of the steel hull of the boat. Once this hot charge penetrates the hull, a separate explosion occurs when the round hits the far wall of the craft. Large amounts of shrapnel then hit everyone and everything in the vicinity. The shrapnel can be deadly if it hits the body in areas not protected by a flak jacket or flak pants. This weapon was feared by everyone on U.S. vessels operating in the narrow waters of the Delta. As with the "Bouncing Betty" mines ashore, the damage was both physical and psychological.

The B-40 rocket

Our other two deaths were due to a mine blowing up one of our boats, the T-151-5, on January 14, 1969, on the Rach Cai Nhut. It was our first boat lost. We were almost certain that it was a device that the VC detonated as our boat went over it. We believed that they took an unexploded 750-lb B-52 bomb, put it in a mud bank, rigged it up with a wire, and then detonated it by wire command. Losing these two men was my most harrowing experience.

Let me explain a typical operation. We would load up troops at 4:00 AM and send the boats seven miles up a river, then turn left up into an unnamed canal for maybe 10 miles, then turn right into a creek and drop off a company of 100 troops one mile up that creek on the left bank. It was a maze and a very dangerous one. You also have to understand that the Mekong Delta has tides, sometimes 5 to 6 feet. We had to time it so that the Army troops didn't arrive at low tide when they might have to climb up a five-foot mud bank to get ashore. There was a lot of planning involved. Most of these missions would last 3-13 days. The Army guys never slept on our boats, but we obviously had to make do with some bunks aboard and C-rations. Remember, none of these ATC's usually had officers aboard. The officer-in-charge was a senior enlisted man, and most of his crew were in their teens or twenties. Obviously, they grew up fast in this situation.

After a while I learned to use my four ASPB's (Assault Support Patrol Boat) to help sweep mines. They were a totally different type of boat than the 13 ATC's I had. My command had 21 boats consisting of 13

ATC's, one CCB (Command Control Boat), two monitor howitzers., one Zippo flame monitor boat, and 4 ASPB's (Assault Support Patrol Boat). Everything except the ASPB's were built on LCM (Landing Craft Medium) hulls and were used to carry the troops. This last group, the ASPB's, could go 15 knots, much faster than our other boats. I learned to use these to help sweep for mines in the rivers and canals. I would run them close to the banks and drag a cable to cut any wires attached to command detonated mines in the middle of the river. It was a learning curve on how to use these assets. Of course, the boats were totally exposed to small arms fire and rockets from Viet Cong hiding along the shore. It did not provide perfect protection because we still had two near misses from mines.

Sunken T-151-5 blown up by mines on Rach Cai Nhut

In November '68, I got a call saying that I was going to have company in about 30 minutes. It was going to be Vice Admiral Zumwalt who had recently assumed his role as Commander of Naval Forces, Vietnam. He was very personable and was liked by most of us because he took great effort to visit and learn what our problems were. He arrived ashore via helicopter and talked to the Army CO. He then came aboard my boat and talked to me for at least five minutes. He was very attentive. The Admiral talked to each of my senior petty officer boat captains and many of our enlisted men during his visit. I would describe him as "endearing." Of *course, it was his tactics which resulted in many of our casualties, but at least he seemed concerned.*

One of our scariest moments happened in January 1969 while trying to land two companies of Army troops on a mission. After dropping them off, we were supposed to go through a series of canals and creeks to establish a blocking force for any Viet Cong attempting to escape. I had been briefed that there was going to be a three-plane B-52 strike in the area at 0905 one mile away. At 0905 and one second, the whole earth erupted. However, in addition to those explosions, three bombs fell short hitting all around us. We were in one of these creeks and one of the bombs hit right in the middle of a small village of maybe five to six hooches. The second one hit in the water about 100 yards in front of our lead boat creating a wave that almost swamped it. The third bomb exploded in a rice paddy again only about 100 yards to our west. Everything there went up in pieces, including some water buffalo. It was horrible. Our operation was wiped out; the landing was cancelled because the entire village had been demolished. The Army sent in doctors and medics to try to tend to the villagers. They also brought money to give to the surviving villagers. I almost cried as I watched those three planes turn and head back to Guam to do another mission the next day. It was a horrible day.

The B-52 bomber was a devastating weapon of war. It could carry 84 500-pound bombs and also 24 750-pound bombs on its wings. Of the nearly 7 million pounds of bombs dropped on Vietnam during the war, B-52's operating out of Guam and Thailand carried roughly a third of this fire power. To put this into perspective, the B-52's in Vietnam dropped about the same amount of ordnance as all of the Allied forces during WW II. A formation of six B-52's, dropping their bombs from 30,000 feet, could devastate an area 1/2 mile wide by 2 miles long. As Phil can attest, accuracy was often an issue, particularly if the tail fins on the bombs were damaged as they were dropped. Countless innocent Vietnamese were killed or injured by such malfunctions. Farms were destroyed, animals killed, and lives forever disrupted. It was a cruel, often indiscriminate, weapon. For the Vietnamese victims, it was a filthy way to die.

We never had to bring back bodies of deceased Army troops. They were all taken out by helicopters. The bodies of our own sailors who were killed by the mine were not discovered until two days later. We took them back to our base to be sent home. Whenever the Army would bring prisoners aboard our boats, they would be interrogated through an interpreter and then turned over to the ARVN. I never wanted to know what happened once they were in custody of the South Vietnamese.

While we were on patrol, we were dressed in green uniforms with a flak jacket and usually flak pants. Although I carried a .357 magnum, we never went ashore on these missions. We were ordered not to do so because if you got injured ashore, who was going to run the boats to take the troops back? Fighting ashore was Army business, but we were often involved in firefights with enemy on the banks or in the jungle. We had two men with 30 and 50 caliber machine guns to open fire to suppress shore fire. We also could use the Zippo if one of those boats was in the area.

Phil actually understated the daily dangers faced during his time in command of River Assault Division 151. Here is one paragraph of the official command history for his squadron:

"On 24 December 1968 the boats of River Assault Divisions 151 and 152, with the 2nd and 3rd Battalions, Vietnamese Marine Corps, commenced a new phase of OPERATION SEALORDS, pushing into a section of southwestern Kien Giang Province where no government forces had entered in over five years. The area proved particularly difficult to subdue, as the Marines were unable to maintain contact with the Viet Cong and the boats were subject to a number of highly accurate ambushes. A total of 36 personnel were wounded in the course of the 14-day operation. The boats faced the longest sustained ambush as the result of a Viet Cong multi-company action on New Year's Eve that extended three kilometers and lasted over an hour. The boats returned to base on January 6 after having been ambushed 10 times. Fifteen Viet Cong were killed in action and sixteen captured, along with a large enemy hospital complex destroyed and several hundred pounds of hospital supplies captured."

Operation SEALORDS (an acronym for Southeast Asia Lake, Ocean. River, and Delta Strategy) was conceived by the Commander, Naval Forces, Vietnam, Admiral Elmo Zumwalt. The purpose was to disrupt supplies being sent by the North Vietnamese from Cambodia to Viet Cong forces in the Mekong Delta region. The program was turned over to the South Vietnamese in 1971. It is difficult to assess the effectiveness of this strategy. Large numbers of enemy troops were killed, but at a heavy cost to U.S. and Vietnamese forces. By 1971, all of the boats operated by Phil and his colleagues had been turned over to the South Vietnamese Navy as part of the American policy of the "Vietnamization" of the war. Ironically, just four years later, with the fall of Saigon, each of the remaining operational boats became property of the communist government of Vietnam. In spite of heavy losses during and after SEALORDS, the communists retained control of most of the Delta region throughout the war.

One of the tasks which we actually enjoyed was to protect the larger ships, an LST or APL, that we tied up alongside in Dong Tam. We were assigned this duty about once a month. We would have some of our boats patrolling around the ships to use our cables to cut any wires attached to mines which might have been placed in the water to float down the rivers. We would also throw concussion grenades into the water at random intervals to deter enemy sappers (swimmers) in the water.

My XO, Pete, was married and went on R&R to Hawaii for a week about mid-way during our tour. When he came back, he was totally changed. He was now like a deer in the headlights and was now terrified about getting killed during the next five months before he could leave Vietnam. He had seen heaven and was now back in hell. I saw this change and decided to wait until my tour was almost over before I went on my R&R because I didn't want to be like Pete. When I left Vietnam, we were already in the process of turning everything in our division over to the South Vietnamese. When I got on that plane to leave, we flew to Tokyo and then Travis Air Force Base in California. I flew in my green uniform, and as soon as I was at Travis, we were told to go into the men's room to change clothes. I took off those greens, threw them in the trash can and put on civvies. I then got on a plane to visit my girlfriend in Illinois and then to Boston to visit my family. I honestly feel that I closed a chapter, encapsulated it, and left it behind. I have never had nightmares or PTSD. Others, like my brother, still have issues. In retrospect, I was numb to all the horror around me. While attending a school in Newport, Rhode Island, for my next assignment, I was able to sail a lot and to relax; that was really cathartic for me. I still vacillate back and forth about our involvement there in Vietnam. It was a bad mistake, but we tried to fix it as best we could. I sometimes think, "Why did we do this?"

Following his tour in Vietnam, Phil went to USS TRIPPE (FF1075) as ASW Officer, but resigned in May 1972 to pursue a career in business. He spent the next 25 years in executive positions with Mobil Oil. He and his wife, Linda, are extremely active supporting the Naval Academy and arranging Class of 1965 activities.

Doyle Borchers

Boerne, Texas

"I knew that it was just awful."

I interviewed Doyle via computer from his home in Napa, California. As we began our conversation, he told me that he was born on a ranch outside Boerne, in the hill country of Texas. His parents soon moved to Clifton, a small city near Waco. Doyle laughed as he told me that at the time it was always called "the Norwegian capital of Texas" due to a heavy concentration of Norwegians who had settled there.

During World War II Doyle's father had been in the Army Air Corps as a waist gunner in a B-17 making bombing runs over Germany. He had the misfortune to have his plane shot down on a top secret mission and spent the remainder of the war as a prisoner of war. He was injured badly and had to wear a brace for the rest of his life. Doyle later told me that this memory sometimes popped up in his own mind when he was making bombing raids and other missions over North Vietnam, 25 years after his dad's ordeal.

When I asked how he ended up being a Naval aviator, Doyle paused and said that it was complicated.

As a youngster, I had watched a television show about the military academy at West Point and always wanted to go there. One of our family friends was the local congressman, and he gave me an appointment to the Naval Academy. I told him that I wanted to go to West Point, but he firmly told me that I could get the best education at Annapolis and also the most career opportunities. I even asked him about going to the newly opened Air Force Academy, but he said, "You're going to Navy, that's it." But there was a problem. When I took the physical, I was disqualified, believe it or not, because I had a massive underbite! But I had a scholarship from Texas A&M to play football, and a Navy football coach came down to see me and told me that if I went to New Mexico Military Institute and played football there, we can get you in. Also, a Naval Reserve officer in Dallas had heard about my jaw and set me up with a famous oral surgeon who chopped my jaw in half and reconstructed it so I could now be physically eligible. I played right offensive tackle at New Mexico, and we had a helluva team. Roger Staubach was our quarterback, and we won all of our games except one. Roger went on to become our Heisman trophy winning quarterback at Navy, won two Super Bowls with the Dallas Cowboys, and is in the Pro Football Hall of Fame. Unfortunately, I injured both shoulders in my last game and that ended any football career. At least one of us did pretty well in football!

Even though I was no longer a football prospect, the Naval Academy kept their word and on June 28, 1961, I was sworn in as a midshipman with the Class of 1965. Although I was initially inclined to become a Surface Warfare Officer, as soon as I went to summer training at the Pensacola airfields, that did it - I was determined to be an aviator. After graduation, while in initial training at Pensacola, I did well and was able to select jets as my specialty. Later there were six of us in one of the advanced training sections, and all were later killed in aircraft accidents or combat except me. No idea why I was so lucky.

The naval aviation pipeline is necessarily long in order to ensure that pilots are fully prepared when they reach the fleet. The initial 12-week "ground school" at Pensacola is always the first step where students learn meteorology, navigation, human physiology, and other aviation-related topics. They then begin actual flying lessons in two-seat planes (a T-34 propeller plane at that time) with an instructor. After 12 training flights, they go up alone in a "solo" flight. Because Doyle was selected for jet training, he spent the next six months at the Naval Station in Meridian, Mississippi, learning to fly the Buckeye, the T-2A twin engine jet. Then pilots return to Pensacola to practice carrier landings on a shore-based landing strip before doing six daytime landings on a carrier in the Gulf of Mexico. If all has gone well, the jet pilots then are assigned to advanced training at another Navy air station, this time at Beeville, Texas. Here

Doyle learned to fly one of the fighter airplanes, the F-9 F "Panther." It was not until completion of all this training, in February 1967, that Doyle was awarded his Navy wings signifying that he was now a Naval Aviator. Because of all these challenging and lengthy steps in learning to fly, the aviators in our class did not reach the Vietnam theater of operations for over two years. Even though Doyle had his wings and was assigned to fighter squadron, VF-33, in Virginia Beach, Virginia, he was regarded as a "nugget" - a newbie who still needed to learn how to become proficient landing both night and day on an aircraft carrier.

Our squadron was assigned to Carrier Air Group Six (CAG-6) which was then on USS AMERICA (CVA-66), a recently commissioned Kitty Hawk class aircraft carrier. We left Norfolk in early 1968, sailed around Africa, and arrived on Yankee Station in May. When we arrived, USS LEXINGTON (CV-16), an old Essex-class carrier built during WW II, was already there - it was a short-deck carrier that carried different planes than AMERICA. They did most of the daytime missions, and we did mostly nights.

"Yankee Station" was an area in the South China Sea where the U.S. could safely launch air strikes on North (and South Vietnam) from Task Force 77. This large group of ships typically was composed of 2-3 aircraft carriers with a large accompanying force of support ships providing protection, fuel, and supplies. Each carrier would usually spend 20 days "on the line" conducting air operations, then depart for Subic Bay in the Philippines or other support (and liberty) ports. The departing ship would be replaced by another carrier. Most of the support ships rotated in and out. When Doyle arrived on AMERICA on 30 May, the central coordinates of Yankee Station were 17-30N, 108-30E. This location provided sufficient room for carriers to steam into the wind to launch and recover planes, then reposition for the next strike while remaining a safe distance from both the Vietnamese shore and the Chinese island of Hainan. By early morning the day after his arrival, Doyle and many of his fellow pilots were being launched on missions to strike the enemy. U.S. carriers operated in Yankee Station for the length of the war.

While we were on Yankee Station, I would be averaging over one and a half flights each day. My plane, the McDonnell Douglas F-4 Phantom, was a two-seater. I was in the front of the cockpit piloting the plane, and my RIO (radar intercept officer) sat behind me controlling the radar and providing both visual and radar information. Normally the Navy tries to balance the pilot and RIO in terms of experience so that if the pilot is new, the RIO has had a lot of experience. Well, that wasn't our case, because my RIO, Jim Bowen, was even greener than me. He was a great guy and was black. At that time, it was unusual to have black officers as Naval aviators, and I'm sorry to say Jim did receive some harassment on board. He became a close friend as we flew together so often.

We had many types of missions on Yankee Station. One was called BARCAP (Barrier Combat Air Patrol) where we flew for just under two hours north of the carriers looking for North Vietnamese MiGs coming down to attack planes or units in our task force. Another mission, both day and night, was to escort our bombers during strikes to protect them from MiGs. Often on those bombing missions we would provide flak suppression against enemy anti-aircraft sites. We would usually fly in ahead of our bombers, and when the anti-aircraft guns opened up, we would try to "suppress" them with these 5-inch rockets filled with thousands of small cluster bombs. Then the bombers (A-6's and A-7's) would come in to do their attack bombing missions. We also did bombing sorties ourselves carrying six Mark-82 500 lb bombs.

Doyle in his F-4 Phantom in flight

I never had a visual encounter with a MiG, but we did have many radar intercepts. Our rules of engagement (ROE) were demoralizing and terrible. We were given a latitude cut-off line beyond which we couldn't go further north chasing the MiG's. Of course, the communists knew this and would sometimes set up a "MiG trap." The CO of our sister squadron on AMERICA and his RIO were killed by a MiG due to this insane policy. They were chasing one MiG north but had to turn around due to the ROE. Unbeknownst to them, there were two other MiGs waiting way down low close to the jungle where he couldn't see them on radar. As soon as he turned around to head back, they popped up and shot him down from behind. He died, and his RIO parachuted to the ground where he was captured and killed. Apparently, they were not taking POW's that day. His wingman made it back, but there was considerable talk on the ship as to what he had done, or not done, to assist his CO when he was attacked.

The MiG designation began with Soviet Union fighter aircraft originally designed in 1939 by two Russians whose last names were Mikoyan and Gurevich. The "i" is the first letter of "and" in Russian. The aircraft being flown by the North Vietnamese at that time were variants called the MiG-17 and the MiG-21. The 17's were old and not as much of a problem for us, but the 21 was a very capable fighter plane which had been introduced in 1959. It was the most-produced supersonic jet in history. Its NATO nickname was "Fishbed" and it was manufactured in the USSR (later models were produced in several other countries). The MiG was often credited with being more maneuverable than the Phantom because it weighed nearly half as much, but the electronics and weapons systems on the American planes were far superior. One characteristic of the Phantom was the large, easily visible smoke trails from its engines, making it easy to spot from a distance in a combat situation. On the other hand, all the MiGs were difficult to acquire visually.

Doyle's F-4J Phantom was a state-of-the-art aircraft, but did not have cannons or any guns normally mounted (an option was available, but infrequently used). Its anti-aircraft weapons were typically two Sidewinder missiles and two Sparrow missiles. The Sidewinders were heat-seeking and had to be fired behind the target to lock onto the enemy's engines; the Sparrow could be fired at any orientation and used radar to acquire the target. In most aerial dogfights between Phantoms and MiG's, the U.S. plane was victorious. Because of this large discrepancy, the North Vietnamese MiG's rarely came out far enough from their base to initiate action. It was essentially suicidal.

Doyle became very somber as he spoke of the loss of a good friend.

My roommate, Eric, with whom I was very close, was killed shortly after we had arrived on station. His plane had been seriously damaged by 37 mm anti-aircraft fire on a mission over the North near Vinh. A hydraulic fire broke out on his F-4 and burned through cabling. He could no longer control many aspects of the aircraft, including the speed of the plane. Eric managed to get back over water and was headed to the carrier, but his airspeed had now increased to around 600 knots. His RIO was able to bail out and was picked up from the water by a helo, but he had severe injuries that ended the war for him. Eric still had communications with the ship throughout all this mess and told us that his ejection system would not work due to the high speed. We all listened in horror while he continued to talk to us as his plane hit the water at 600 knots. To make matters even worse, Eric's wife was pregnant. I later became a surrogate dad for the family. The one good part of this tragic loss was that over the next two weeks we were able to use Eric's description of the problem to develop a new procedure to use to be able to slow down the plane so that the crew could bail out if this ever happened again.

Everyone knew that Eric and I were very close friends, so, rather than having me resume flying immediately, they gave me a few days off and sent me as a passenger on a COD (small airplane) to the Philippines to pick up a replacement aircraft to bring back to the ship. While I was there, in early June 1968, I learned that one of my heroes, Robert F. Kennedy, had just been assassinated. The bad news was not yet over, because in flying the replacement F-4J back to the carrier, my plane was hit by lightning in a bad thunderstorm causing me to lose both generators. I could now see virtually nothing but was able to make it out of the thunderstorm clouds by flying a few feet away from the rear stabilizer on the plane I was making the transit with. Once we broke into clear skies, I was able to get the generators re-started and return to the carrier. It was a difficult start for my first weeks of combat.

In fact, we had a large number of casualties during that deployment on AMERICA. Our wing, VF-33, consisted of two fighter squadrons of F-4's, two light attack squadrons of A-7's, one squadron of medium attack bombers, A-6's, and a squadron of supersonic RA-5C Vigilantes which were used for reconnaissance. We called them "Viggies." Out of the 200 pilots in our air wing, we lost 40 pilots and RIO's who were killed, captured, or had aircraft accidents coming to or going from the carrier. Part of the problem, in my opinion, was that our wing commander was, for lack of a better word, insane. Most of us felt that his tactics were all wrong....and deadly for us. He had no prior combat experience and would make us go in low to our targets and then, worse, have us make multiple runs on the same target. We were sitting ducks the second time around, and really easy targets for the North Vietnamese gunner on a third run. Even worse for me, when he decided to fly F-4's, he also chose me to be his wingman. On one run, when we were going into a target for the third time on a mission, we had 37 mm and 57 mm all around us. It was like a wall of flak. Not sure how we survived that one!

The Wing Commander on an aircraft carrier was, at that time, a senior officer usually with the rank of Commander (O-5). Each of the individual aircraft squadron commanders reported to him, and he was responsible for all flying aspects of the aircraft and personnel. Most of these wing commanders flew each of the planes in his squadron and would simply decide on a daily basis which aircraft and which mission he would fly on a given day.

One of my assignments was to occasionally provide cover for the Viggies doing photo reconnaissance over targets which we had bombed the previous day. Needless to say, those who were still around those targets on the ground were upset and looking for us. The Vigilante could fly far faster than my Phantom, and usually took photos from 8000 feet. My job was to stay behind him to warn about MiG's or anti-aircraft fire. For some reason, the North Vietnamese always shot behind the Viggie; we could never figure out why they did not lead them. I saw a lot of anti-aircraft (AAA) flak on these missions. We could tell what they were shooting by the color of the puffs as the ordnance exploded near us. The 37 mm had white puffs, 57 mm was yellow, and 85 mm, the really dangerous stuff, was black. They would carpet areas with flak. Amazingly, I never had one hole in my aircraft.

On our own bombing missions, we would have designated targets....if we could find them. That was often an issue due to weather. I would roll and come into a target at a 45 degree angle with six 500 lb bombs using just an iron bomb sight. When the RIO told me to release, I would pickle the bombs and pull up at 3500 feet to get out of there. We would often see tracers from anti-aircraft below come close to us, and frequently had flak burst all around, but again we were never hit.

It is difficult to overestimate the danger that Navy (and Air Force) pilots faced on bombing missions over North Vietnam. On a typical bombing run, they first had to dodge surface-to-air missiles, then face heavy AAA units, then light AAA, and even small arms fire when close to the target. After releasing their bombs, the pilots then had to worry about MiG's taking advantage of them being distracted by all the AAA fire and the fact that they were now flying at a relatively slow speed. And they did this day-after-day and night-after-night, often after losing friends on these same assignments.

One time our mission was to find some trucks to attack to interdict their supply chain. We would work with aircraft we called "whales" (A-3's) which were flown by Navy pilots out of the airbase in Da Nang. Our job was to drop flares near the target, then have the whales attack the trucks to wipe them out. One mission was on a beautiful moonlit night, and as I returned to AMERICA, I noticed that I was down to 2500 lbs of fuel. My plane burns 100 lb a minute, but they put me in a holding pattern due to a problem on the ship. Just as I was cleared to land, the ship disappeared in a terrible thunderstorm. I told the ship that I might have to eject alongside as I was almost out of fuel. Fortunately, at the last moment, I was able to get refueled above the carrier and then land when the weather broke. Every night landing was an adventure, but this one was "special."

The A-3 "Skywarrior" was initially designed to be a strategic bomber for the Navy carrying nuclear weapons on essentially one-way, suicidal missions against the Soviet Union. The Vigilante was the only other carrier-launched aircraft with this capability, but when these missions were curtailed, both planes were assigned other tasks. Because the A-3 was the heaviest operational aircraft to operate from a carrier, Navy pilots (either affectionately or sarcastically) called it "The Whale." During Vietnam the A-3 was outfitted with an arsenal of deadly firepower, including machine guns and cannons, and even artillery guns carried in the belly. Due to its capability to carry large amounts of JP-5 jet fuel, it became highly valuable for refueling other planes in flight.

Another night there was a malfunction so that I couldn't drop my bombs. In this situation, it is too dangerous to land on the carrier, so I was diverted to Da Nang. As I approached the control tower, they refused to give me permission to land because the base was under mortar attack. Assessing my choices, I decided to land anyway. 120 mm rockets were going off all around us, but neither my plane nor myself was hit.

One other mission we occasionally had was to look for junks which were carrying ammunition and supplies along the coast from the north to the VC in the Da Nang area. We called these boats "wiblics" which stood for waterborne logistics targets. We actually had no way of discriminating between fishermen in their junks and wiblics and may have killed innocent civilians. There was no way of knowing.

What bothered me the most about our role in the war was that almost all the targeting assignments came from "McNamara's Boys" back in Washington. They would analyze photos back there and tell us what to hit, and what not to hit. Even worse, they would send us in and not tell us where the SAM (surface-to-air missiles) were located! I had been "gung ho" when I arrived at Yankee Station, but after seeing what was really happening, the light bulb came on, and I knew that it was just awful. In fact, and I am not ashamed to say this, on the last mission for me and my buddy who was piloting a Vigilante photo mission, it was iffy on weather, and as we approached the coast on the way in, we gave each other a thumbs down, turned around, and went back to the ship. It wasn't worth it to take the risk.

Control of the war from Washington was a common complaint from most of those I interviewed. Robert McNamara had been a businessman and President of Ford Motor Company before being selected by President Kennedy to be the Secretary of Defense in 1961. He had an arrangement with Kennedy that he could run the Defense Department "his own way." His primary management tool was systems analysis using some of the early computers. The people (primarily from the Rand Corporation) that he brought in to help make decisions based on this approach became derisively known as "McNamara's Whiz Kids." Whether or not this group, or others using a similar approach, was responsible for mandating targets for the carriers and other U.S. forces is not clear. What is certain is that Vietnam aviators had the impression that they were pawns being manipulated by officials in Washington who had no clue about the realities of the war.

Doyle talked to me for several hours and also in subsequent conversations. Although he considered getting out of the Navy after his Vietnam tour, he chose to accept an assignment to the Navy Post Graduate School and ultimately became a lead test pilot. He later became CO of an F-14 fighter squadron, and ultimately the Commanding Officer of the nuclear powered carrier, Carl Vinson (CVN-70) - an assignment of enormous responsibility given to only a very few Naval officers. In his career Doyle made over 800 carrier landings, many at night. He told me several times what I have heard from other naval aviators about night landings on a carrier, "Daytime landings are almost fun, but for the night ones, the last one is just as hard as the first." If you have never seen a jet airplane land on a carrier, I encourage you to look online for as many videos of this amazing feat as possible. It is inherently an extremely dangerous evolution, not only for the pilots, but also for the five thousand working on the ship to make it happen.

When I asked Doyle about his thoughts of flying combat missions when so many friends around him were dying or ending up as POW's, he told me:

It's sort of like a prize fighter entering a ring. You have a job to do. We would look under our stateroom door each day for the flight schedule and jokingly ask each other, "How are they going to try to kill us today?" But once my plane went inland over the beach, it was all business. At the time, there were no thoughts of collateral damage. Years later I think about it and am sorry, but then it was simply kill, or be killed.

Ken Andrews

Cleveland, Ohio

"So many areas were all brown"

I knew Ken at the Naval Academy as a teammate on the plebe (freshman) squash team, but our paths never crossed after graduation. Later I heard about his adventures on Swift boats during the Vietnam War. After locating him via our alumni database at his home in Cornelius, North Carolina, where he lives with his wife, Connie, I conducted our interview via computer.

My father was a criminal, and after getting out of prison, eventually became a truck driver. I was raised mostly by my mother who struggled to provide for us. I went to Cleveland South High School where I played one year of baseball and football. When I graduated, I had no money and no plans, so I enlisted in the Navy. After boot camp, I was trained to work on airplanes at a base outside Memphis. While I was there, I was encouraged to apply for one of the programs that sent enlisted men to the Naval Academy. I was accepted and found myself in Bainbridge, Maryland, at the Naval Academy Prep School. The timing was great, and in June 1961 I was sworn in as a midshipman.

I had hoped to become an aviator, but during one of my physicals I learned that my eyes were bad, meaning that I was disqualified for flight training. Following graduation, I received orders to USS BAINBRIDGE (DLGN-25), which was initially homeported in Charleston. They had first sent me to missile school, so my first job was Guided Missile Officer. We departed Charleston and sailed around South Africa with another nuclear-powered surface ship, USS ENTERPRISE (CVN-65). We were headed to Yankee Station off Vietnam, but a sailor fell overboard off the deck on ENTERPRISE in the Indian Ocean during the transit. We looked for three days, but never found him. When we arrived at Yankee Station, we assumed air control duties for the carriers. We were also on the lookout for enemy high-speed surface craft, but none ever came out toward us. Both ships then sailed back to the U.S. with a stop in the Philippines. Our new homeport was Long Beach, California. One of our missions had been to prove the utility of nuclear-powered ships. We certainly did that because out of the entire time from when we left Charleston and arrived in Long Beach, we had spent a grand total of 11 days in port!

When we made that stop in the Philippines, I had seen a Swift boat and decided that I wanted to be on one of them. I put in for this assignment, and instead the Navy sent me to a new ship, USS BIDDLE (DLG-34), which was under construction in Bath, Maine. I was made the Missile Systems Officer. The ship was commissioned in January 1967 and did all the usual "shake-down" exercises in the Caribbean. By the time we reached our homeport in Norfolk, I had orders to Swift boats in Vietnam. I was sent to the Swift boat school in San Diego for training. My initial orders were to Cat Lo, in the south, near Vung Tau on the coast; I arrived there in early 1968, not long after the Tet offensive had begun. The base was located on Ganh Rai Bay which is the opening in the South China Sea leading toward Saigon. My boat was PTF-23; as the Officer-in-Charge, I had a crew of 6 and also usually a Vietnamese interpreter. When I arrived, our boats were mostly doing MARKET TIME operations patrolling along the coastline. We had strict limitations allowing us only to do other patrols in "river mouths and estuaries." In other words, we were not supposed to go up any rivers. These restrictions were later lifted. Our patrol area was north to Phan Thiet and south all the way to the tip of the Ca Mau Peninsula. I didn't go up any of the rivers, but my future brother-in-law wasn't the kind of guy who followed orders. He did patrols in the Delta area up some of the rivers and was eventually shot up pretty bad. On my patrols we encountered a lot of small boat traffic, even during the northeast monsoon season which produced crazy seas. During these monsoons, we would often find a fishing boat in high seas with a family grilling a meal on a small hibachi! Whenever we found any boat in a "free fire" zone, we would inspect it, and if all was OK, we would tell them to get the hell out of there or we would have to shoot them.

Free fire zones were a controversial aspect of the Vietnam War. The term was defined as "a specifically designated area in which any weapon or weapons systems might fire without having to coordinate with main headquarters." The concept was that all friendly forces had been cleared and any remaining people were hostile. The obvious problem was disseminating this information to Vietnamese civilians to ensure that they would not be unintentionally killed. It was particularly difficult to do this at sea where local fishermen often had no prior knowledge that they were in now prohibited waters.

Most of our patrols took place at slow speeds. The northeast monsoons were very difficult for Swift boats because the swells had been building since Hawaii. On several occasions in heavy seas, we had fish land in our boat. Several Swift boats actually flipped over in the monsoon conditions. A Naval Academy officer who graduated a year after us drowned in one of these accidents. I always felt that during the time I was there, it was more dangerous patrolling in these kinds of seas than going up the rivers and risking enemy fire. My boat did get shot at from shore on a few occasions, but no one was injured.

Routine patrols ended for me when I became Maintenance Officer for our division of about 25 boats. I was later transferred to Cam Ranh Bay as the Squadron Maintenance Officer to develop an in-country overhaul capability for all Swift boats in Vietnam. I decided that we could best do these overhauls at sites in Cat Lo and Cam Ranh. The boats over in the Gulf of Thailand at Phu Quoc Island were maintained by an LST which rotated in and out of there. While I was at Cam Ranh Bay, I was required to fly frequently in small planes to various Swift boat sites. What I noticed on these flights was the terrible deforestation which had been done by Agent Orange. So many areas were all brown, particularly along the rivers. The defoliants definitely worked, but at what a cost to the countryside and the livelihoods of the Vietnamese farmers! I cannot imagine how badly their health was later affected.

I left Vietnam in March 1969 and initially had orders to the shipyard in Mare Island, but a friend had my orders changed to Philadelphia

Naval Shipyard. I resigned in November 1969 and married. My friend and I started a company in Camden, New Jersey, providing services to the Navy in terms of software and procedures for missile systems. I did this for a few years but ended up as an FBI agent where I specialized in electronics, such as tapping phones. I spent the next 25 years as an agent for the FBI and sometimes found myself having to fire weapons at other humans just as I had dome in Vietnam. In both situations, I always thought about it and did not take it casually.

Ken's assignments did not place him in harm's way due to enemy fire as much as other Swift boat skippers, but his experiences are testimony to the inherent dangers of being on the high seas during bad weather. It was of little consolation to a family if their loved ones were lost due to wounds or drowning. Ken spoke to me at length about the dangers he and his crew experienced during the monsoon seasons.

Jon Lazzaretti

San Francisco, California

"It was impossible to land"

Our Naval Academy class has a chat group dedicated to discussing "life." Although it was initially established as a "WARDROOM" where controversial topics such as religion and politics were forbidden, it quickly evolved into a free-for-all where just about anything goes. There was a general rule on most Navy ships that the area where officers eat meals, the Wardroom, should not be used for discussions on issues which might create enmity. It is challenging enough to live together at sea for extended periods, so these informal rules evolved: professional topics, OK; weather, OK; sports, OK; movies, OK; sexual conquests and failures, OK; religion and politics, NOT OK. During various chats in our online group, helicopters sometimes come up as a discussion point. In these cases, our main go-to-guy was "Lazz." If you had any questions about helicopters, ask Lazz. So, when I needed to learn about helicopters in Vietnam, I contacted Jon Lazzaretti. I interviewed him via phone from his home in Capitan, New Mexico, where he lives with his wife, Cynthia.

I was born in 1943 in San Francisco; my dad was a liquor salesman and Mom was a housewife. Dad had been a prospective big league baseball player, but the war intervened, and he never made it to the bigs. In his later years Dad became an excellent golfer, even as he reached 100 years of age. The 16th green at Presidio golf club, where he had three-holes-in-one, still carries his name. I attended Sacred Heart High School just outside the Tenderloin District. It was a Catholic all-boys school. I played various sports there but wasn't varsity level. Most of my classmates became either cops or lawyers. I became interested in attending the Naval Academy because of a double scoop of strawberry ice cream. This retired admiral came in every day to an ice cream store where I was working to order that double scoop and we became friends. He invited me up to his apartment to meet his wife and urged me to try to go to the Academy. I also had been watching the television series, "Men of Annapolis," which interested me. I applied and received an appointment through my congressman.

At the Academy, I decided that I wanted to go aviation and really fell in love with helicopters during our summer training at the Naval Air Station in Pensacola. On my final training cruise, I was on USS TOPEKA (CL-67) in the Pacific, and the gunnery officer sent me to work with a helicopter pilot who was flying out of Cubi Point in the Philippines. That really cemented helos for me. At Pensacola I did all the fixed wing stuff, but at the end when we had to choose which type of aircraft, I put my preference as helicopters. We trained at Ellison Field which is near Pensacola, and I received my wings around Thanksgiving 1966. My first assignment was to HC-1, a helicopter squadron at Imperial Beach, south of San Diego. No one else wanted to fly the big helicopter, the UH-46, which was good for me because that's exactly what I wanted to fly. It was designed for vertical replenishment of ships at seas. We could do about 125 kts and go up to about 12,000-13,000 ft, but most of our work was at low levels. The 46's were assigned to work with the Navy supply fleet. We first deployed to Vietnam in April 1968 on USS NIAGARA FALLS (AFS-3). Each detachment consisted of 2 aircraft. On missions, we flew with a command pilot, a second in command, and an enlisted crew chief to handle the cargo. Much of our work in Vietnam consisted of transferring supplies to the carriers and their surrounding ships at night. We were definitely busy; during my two tours in Vietnam, I had 1200 hours of flight time.

The UH-46 flown by Lazz was also operated by the Marine Corps to provide all-weather, day-or-night transport of combat troops, supplies, and equipment. It was a medium-lift tandem-rotor helicopter with a set of counter-rotating main rotors, each with three blades. It was powered by two turboshaft engines; if one was lost, the other could still power both rotors. Lazz told me of the loss of one engine at 3000 ft with 20 sailors aboard; he was able to make a successful shipboard landing although "it was dicey." There were several fatal accidents involving this helicopter during the Vietnam War, due both to enemy fire and mechanical issues. The aircraft flown by Lazz, the UH-46A, was simply a variant of the more ubiquitous, CH-46A, flown by other services.

**Boeing Vertol UH-46D Sea Knight doing
vertical replenishment operations**

One of my most interesting missions happened during a re-supply of the carrier, USS CONSTELLATION (CV-64) during the tail end of a typhoon. The seas were so high that we couldn't land to refuel on our ship, USS WHITE PLAINS (AFS-4). We could hover above to pick up supplies from WHITE PLAINS but couldn't land, so we had to refuel on the carrier. We did this all night long from midnight to 7 AM carrying 8800 lbs of cargo each trip. We also picked up supplies from the Marine Base at Da Nang to take out to ships at sea. Ironically, we had to supply the Naval Supply Center in Da Nang from our ship at sea also. This was crazy because, for reasons I never understood, they couldn't get supplies from the Army there. It was so insane. We were flying ice cream from our freezers to the shore facility! We also flew into most bases along the Vietnamese coast and even supplied some of the 'brown water" guys all the way down to Phu Quoc on the border with Cambodia. Our ship would sail down there around the tip of the Ca Mau Peninsula and up into the Gulf of Thailand to supply the LST's which were the mother ships for the Swift boats operating there. Our own ship would re-supply in Sasebo, Japan, or at Subic Bay in the Philippines and then come back to Vietnam.

After my two tours in Vietnam, I resigned in August 1970. I wanted to emigrate to Australia to do civilian helicopter work, but I instead found a job with a small outfit doing mining operations in New Guinea. After a few months, I brought my wife and kids over to join me there. This company had a relationship with Columbia Helicopter, and I ended up working for Columbia for the next 46 years all over the world doing logging, fire work, mining - you name it.

Although Lazz was never shot at during his tour in Vietnam, his work flying supplies to men, ships, and aircraft involved in warfighting provides insight into aspects of war frequently overlooked. Without a functioning supply chain, wars cannot be waged. Fulfilling logistics requirements for a war half-way around the world was a continuing and challenging task. As I mentioned earlier, flying the UH-46 had its own hazards due to various engine and rotor failures. There were few safe assignments in the Vietnam War.

Fred Vogel

Annapolis, Maryland

"I was mooning an entire NVA regiment"

In 2006, a Mexican beer, Dos Equis, began a very successful marketing ploy with ads featuring a distinctive-looking actor, Jonathan Goldsmith, who was claimed to be "The Most Interesting Man in the World." Dos Equis was wrong. Without a doubt, our classmate, Fred Vogel, is THE most interesting man in the world. Not only has Fred been involved in remarkable scenarios around the world, but he served 3 1/2 years in the Vietnam War, conducted over 30 "Black Operations" into enemy territory, flew on a strike mission off a carrier over North Vietnam (although not a Naval Aviator), did covert work for the CIA, was a wanted criminal in Malaysia, was goosed by a yak while climbing to 18,000 ft on Mount Everest, made over 300 parachute jumps in Thailand to raise money to build rural schools, worked as a Foreign Service Officer all over Europe and Asia, and rode the Trans-Siberian Railway and a side link from Moscow to Beijing in the dead of winter. This is only a partial list of Fred's adventures! He is, among other things, a qualified military diver, a jumpmaster, a private pilot, and a 2nd degree Black Belt in Taekwondo. Fred is fluent in several languages and is one of the most well-read friends I have. He can quote the eulogy for Sir Lancelot, describe ancient Germanic culture, and provide minute details of the geopolitical history of numerous nations around the world. He will tell you that his most important accomplishment has been raising three beautiful daughters with his wife, Donsiri, a nurse whom he met in Thailand.

I interviewed Fred on two occasions at his home in Northern Virginia.

I was born at the Naval Hospital on the grounds of the Naval Academy. My father was a Naval Aviator who had graduated from USNA in the

Class of 1936. Dad flew F-4F's in WW II but was shot down and killed in August 1950 during the Korean War after having just blown up an enemy bridge. My mom moved us back to Annapolis from the West Coast to live with her family. I attended school at St. Mary's High School where I played football and lacrosse. I skipped my senior year of high school and spent a year at Purdue where I joined the NROTC and enlisted in the USMC Reserves. Because of my dad's service, I received a Presidential appointment to the Academy.

I always wanted to be a Marine and immediately after graduation began The Basic School at Quantico, Virginia. Upon completion in December 1965, I chose infantry because I had completed both jump school and scuba training while at the Academy. My first assignment was not in Vietnam, but as a Platoon Commander at Camp Lejeune in North Carolina. In December 1966, I was sent for additional training at Camp Pendleton in California. Five months later our entire battalion was loaded onto an APA [a transport ship] *headed to Vietnam.*

We reached Da Nang in June 1967. I was now a 1st Lieutenant and was sent to Division Headquarters on Hill 327 outside Da Nang where my job for the next few months was to brief the General each morning on intelligence matters. My next assignment was with 1st Force Reconnaissance Company located at the base of the same hill. I was the XO (Executive Officer) of the company; our role was to go out in small groups to find enemy troops in the hills and jungles to the west. The mission was not so much to engage the bad guys by ourselves, although we did so many times, but to call in airborne firepower to take them out. UH-34 helicopters would take six to eight of us to a landing zone and pick us up four to five days later, not necessarily at the same landing zone. It seemed like every time we were out there, we were wet and hungry by the time they picked us up.

Our helos (and us) often came under fire during attempts to drop us off. Sometimes the enemy fire was so heavy that we had to abort the mission and try again somewhere else. Pretty soon our opponents got clever and learned to wait until we landed to start firing at us. If we quickly found ourselves in a heavy fire fight, we would try to get the helo back to extract us. If the enemy fire from their AK-47's and .50 caliber machine guns was too intense, we would run for the jungle and try to disappear. We initially carried M-14 rifles and then received M-16's, but they had some problems. One of my Marines was killed while trying to clear his M-16 which had jammed. I also had an M-16 jamming problem myself while we were in a helo trying to land. When it jammed, I pulled out a .45 and just started shooting at wherever I saw a flash below.

On more than one occasion, we had a Marine killed while he was still in the helicopter before we landed. As soon as we were dropped off, we would clear datum (get away from the landing area) asap and try to locate the route we were supposed to follow. We carried our maps in plastic sleeves to keep them dry. While I was there, we never made a nighttime drop; it was tough enough doing it in daytime. When nightfall came, we would find a "harbor site" with heavily overgrown vegetation where we could safely remain for the night. I was the only officer in our recon team, with about 7 enlisted Marines. In addition to our M-16's and .45's, our team usually carried a M-79 grenade launcher, a M-60 machine gun, and plenty of ammo. One of our key members was the radioman. There were always mosquitoes, leeches, and some snakes on these patrols. One of our units had a tiger come walking through. It was killed and skinned. I didn't hear how it tasted.

It was hit or miss if your group made contact with the enemy during these recon patrols. On my first mission when I was going along for orientation, we set up on a hill when all of a sudden, our Marine with the M-60 starts firing on a group of NVA coming down a trail. As our guy rolled to his right, the NVA kept firing where he had been. He killed several NVA; their bodies were dragged off by other enemy soldiers.

Another assignment on these patrols was to do BDA (Bomb Damage Assessment), mostly for Air Force B-52's which were doing Arc Light bombing missions out of Guam. The craters they created were surreal. On one of these BDA missions, we were jumped by NVA and had to call for a helo to get us out. As it started to come in, the helo was being peppered by NVA shells and had to abort the extraction. We managed to escape but had to spend a couple more days on the run while avoiding the enemy. Another time we were on the side of a hill moving around in a bunch of large rocks below where the NVA had established a perimeter *around their camp using bamboo stakes. Suddenly, we started receiving heavy machine gun fire. One of our Marines had a bullet hit a grenade on his belt and split it in half without blowing up the grenade and him! We then had a foot race to get out of there. Basically, we were jungle fighters during these missions. We learned to stay off trails because most had booby traps and mines hidden along them. I made at least 30 of these missions but was never wounded.*

Although I made only one combat jump while in Vietnam, I did have the opportunity to do numerous practice jumps. These experiences served me well later when I was in Thailand after the war. In addition to doing jumps, I was also the Diving Officer for our battalion. My Marine team spent a lot of time in rivers searching for enemy explosives (and finding several).

In December 1967, I was moved north to Phu Bai just south of Hue to do advance work prior to our recon unit arriving. Two days after I got to Phu Bai, I was in the Combat Operations Center listening on the radio to a Marine recon unit which was under attack by a NVA force and in bad shape. All of a sudden, the radio went silent. The next day we went out to where they had been and found eight dead. One Marine had survived because he had been hit in the head and blown down the side of a hill. He didn't have to "play dead" to avoid being killed; he was close to dead. What baffled us was that the NVA didn't bother to take any of the Marines weapons. In retrospect, they didn't need them because they were armed to the gills with their own weapons in preparation for the upcoming massive Tet offensive.

Once the Tet Offensive began in January 1968, during the battle for Hue, infantry Marines had moved into the city and wanted to cross the Perfume River into the Citadel to reach the Imperial City where the enemy was firmly lodged. The NVA had occupied 3/4 of Hue; but an ARVN force had managed to hold out in one remaining part of the city. There was still heavy fighting when my dive unit (me and 3 other divers) was tasked to check the Silver Bridge over the river for underwater explosives. We rode in a truck convoy to get there and had one infantry platoon to provide cover for us. The previous day a convoy taking the same route had been ambushed with many Marines killed. When we reached the bridge in a jeep with our gear in a trailer behind, we were still under heavy small arms and mortar fire. We jumped out and ran to the river's edge wearing only swim shorts and scuba tanks. The water was really cold, and we weren't wearing wet suits. We set up two teams of two men each in the water, one low and one high. The enemy was lobbing mortars at us, but they weren't using delayed fuses, so the explosions were above and didn't harm us. We checked out each of the bridges but found no booby traps. There was some NVA guy firing at us a lot when we came out of the water, so we used our M-79 grenade launcher to take him out. My biggest problem on this mission was making sure that my hyper-aggressive Marines didn't charge across the bridges to take on the NVA. They would probably have been all wounded or killed. We returned to our compound with no casualties, but the infantry Marines continued to take heavy casualties during street fighting in Hue.

When I got back to Phu Bai, I learned that one of my bosses, a Major, wanted to have me relieved because he had not given me permission to do those diving ops in Hue. A general intervened and stopped that nonsense. While I was there, the Army noticed that some unusual activity was taking place near the south gate of Phu Bai and pre-positioned these Quad-40's and Spooky (C-47) gunships. Three nights later, the NVA attacked in human waves but were slaughtered. In the morning we found over 300 bodies....who knows how many others had been dragged off?

Another incident at Phu Bai that is seared in my memory is when one of our recon units came back with four Marines carrying four dead. They were met by this same crazy Major who started to berate them because they had not properly cleaned up their hooch before they had gone on patrol. About an hour later, one of the Marines was carrying a grenade and heading toward the Major when he was stopped by his First Sergeant. The good news is that the Major was relieved for cause and sent back to the U.S.

I left Phu Bai in June 1968 and took over as Company Commander of a recon unit back on Hill 327. I extended for three months to do this. Our recon teams initiated plenty of contact, but we lost several men, mostly due to small arms fire and machine guns. I now had to write letters home to their families, which was difficult. One of my worst memories concerns my best sergeant, named Johnson. He had been transferred to another unit, but I wrote a letter getting him back with us. Soon, he was out on a patrol and became involved in a close-encounter firefight with each side throwing grenades at the other. One of our men spotted this American who had red hair fighting for the NVA. We knew about this guy because he always wore a red sash so that the NVA wouldn't inadvertently kill him. Lance Corporal Herrera took him out, but then his machine gun jammed, and he was shot through the head. Meanwhile, Sergeant Johnson had survived this horrific battle and as his team was being extracted by a CH-46, he was shot in the head while on the helo. Later, while I was a Reservist assigned to the Embassy in Bangkok in the mid-1970's, I saw some U.S. Marines playing football and heard a Hispanic kid being called Herrera. It was the Lance Corporal's younger brother. I talked to him and told him what a superb Marine his brother had been and asked him to write to his family to relay my feelings.

Fred broke down in tears when relating these difficult memories. He still feels personally responsible for Sergeant Johnson's death.

In May 1968, there was a huge battle on top of Hill 327 when a NVA sapper battalion attacked. It was being defended by our battalion band which managed to drive them off the hill. Two other Marines were in a bunker and had killed several NVA. When a NVA corpsman came up to drag off dead and wounded, the two Marines didn't shoot him and allowed him to do his duty. When the NVA corpsman finished, he turned and saluted the two Marines before he walked off.

We were involved in several other intense fights with the NVA. One particularly brutal fight occurred when the NVA came up Route 1 and captured Hoa Vang, a small city. My company's job was to guard the bridge at the end of the town. This battle involved not just our Marines, but also a group of ARVN in armored personnel carriers who joined the fighting against the NVA troops. The first thing I saw when I came into town was the head and hands of a NVA soldier on the road, with no other body parts. I watched as one of the personnel carriers drove right over them. I then met a Marine officer who was carrying a .45 in one hand and a dead Marine in the other. It was terrible – just terrible.

I remained Company Commander until December 1968 when I decided to extend again and took extension leave. As a reward for extending, the Marines would give you a round-trip plane ticket to anywhere in the world. Because I had just read Michener's "Caravans," I chose to go to Kabul, Afghanistan. It was a fascinating experience.

As soon as I came back to Vietnam, I was on my last patrol with my recon unit when we become involved in a major sound and light show on what we called "Charlie Ridge," a plateau with a heavy concentration of NVA and VC just west of Da Nang. We were on one side of the hill and could hear them just above us talking. I called for an emergency extraction to get us out of there. A bunch of F-4's showed up dropping bombs and napalm. The bombs hit so close to us that we had to dig our hands into the ground to keep from getting thrown into the air. One of my men was seriously injured, but the rest of us got out safely.

In February 1969, I was detached to join the Phoenix Program at a compound near Hoi An. I was the CO of a CIA team involving a Provincial Reconnaissance Unit (PRU) which consisted of a group of Vietnamese civilians and some former military. The CIA fed, housed, and paid each of the Vietnamese members of the PRU. Our mission was to kill or capture local VC political leaders who were attempting to take over villages. For example, two young Vietnamese came to us saying that the VC had arrived in their village. We took our PRU forces and surrounded the village at night. We then covered up these teens so that they couldn't be identified and took them in to point out the VC for questioning. Our Vietnamese would "interrogate" these fellows with some rather brutal methods, including waterboarding, and then remove them as POWs. Sometimes we were able to identify a VC propaganda person and then go into the village and take him out. Another time we were operating with an Army division near Goi Noi in a running gun battle with a large NVA force. There were not a lot of rules in the Phoenix Program.

The Phoenix Program was indeed brutal and lawless, but generally deemed to have been effective. It was developed by the CIA and is alleged to have killed over 25,000 Viet Cong and their sympathizers. It was in operation from 1965 to 1972, although the CIA relinquished control in 1969. Some sources claim that this program "neutralized" nearly

82,000 suspected VC or VC supporters in an effort to destroy the political infrastructure of the Viet Cong. The interrogation centers and PRU's were developed by a CIA Station Chief in Saigon under the premise that "counter terror" was a legitimate strategy in unconventional warfare. Some called it an assassination squad.

I did this PRU work in the Hoi An area until September 1969 when I went back to Virginia for Defense Language School training in the Lao language. After nearly a year, I received orders back to Vietnam which I had requested. I was assigned to the Military Assistance Command in a Naval Advisory Detachment east of Da Nang as the Field Operations Officer. We went on clandestine missions conducting black operations in North Vietnam. We wore NVA uniforms and went out in a group of 12-14 called Sea Commandos. My counterpart was actually a North Vietnamese officer who had come south as a youth around 1954. There were just two Americans in our group, which operated out of a combat outpost at the mouth the Cua Viet River just south of the DMZ. We would go up the coast at night in a junk to set up an ambush ashore. I would always wear black pajamas like the VC because the objective was to surprise enemy troops. One time 14 of us saw an entire NVA regiment and my Vietnamese Petty Officer started firing at them. Apparently, the NVA had been planning to conduct their own surprise operation and decided to withdraw even though there were so few of us. As this was going on, I suddenly realized that the bottom of my pj's was now down around my ankles, and I was mooning an entire NVA regiment!

On these ops, we were often in waist deep water and that same Vietnamese CPO got a parasite which entered his penis; he became violently ill and eventually died. As a result, I got a new South Vietnamese gunny sergeant who came up with the idea to walk the McNamara Line south of the DMZ. We coordinated with the Army to take us on a helicopter to a point called Alpha-1 to set up an ambush in the DMZ while we were wearing NVA uniforms. We had someone walk us through the American minefields. This mission wasn't terribly successful , but we did catch a couple of bad guys. At other times we would take a Swift boat north of the DMZ, then swim in from a thousand meters offshore in order to set up an ambush using AK-47's, which worked even when wet. We would stay overnight and come out before daylight.

Fred on a mission with friends

During this tour, I flew out one day to USS ENTERPRISE (CVN-65) to visit my brother, Tim, who was an A-7 pilot, because brothers were allowed to visit each other in-country. While I was there, I was given the opportunity to fly in another plane (an electronics countermeasures plane) during Tim's bombing mission over Hanoi. I preferred taking my chances as a Marine.

I came home from Vietnam in February 1972 and decided to leave active duty to take a position with "the Firm" [CIA] assuming that I would be sent back to Vietnam doing more covert ops. Instead, I was assigned to Headquarters for a year before being assigned in 1974 as a Case Officer in Bangkok, Thailand. For my first year there I was a full-time language student. I had remained in the USMC Reserves and became active in Thailand raising money for an education foundation by doing parachute jumps. I did well over 300 jumps while I was there, helping to raise a lot of money. I did go on one mission with Thai forces fighting the Khmer Rouge who had kidnapped women to take back to Cambodia. This was violent warfare involving terrible battles. If the Thais captured a Khmer Rouge soldier, they would sometimes actually cut out his living heart and eat it. One of the Thai Marines told me, "It tastes like pork."

Fred's adventures continued following his tour in Thailand. He left the CIA after receiving an offer from the State Department to become a Foreign Service Officer. His subsequent assignments took him to London, then back to Bangkok where he met and married Donsiri in 1983. He became a Colonel in the Marine Reserves in 1986 before being on the American team negotiating a Chemical Treaty in Geneva and later the Nuclear Non-Proliferation Treaty. After his retirement from the State Department, Fred did occasional work for State monitoring elections in 12 countries around the world, including Russia and Ukraine.

Some might describe Fred as a professional warrior who lived for the thrill of combat. Having had the opportunity to know him, I would disagree. I believe that Fred honestly felt that he was helping to stem Communist aggression and a probable takeover of all of Southeast Asia. Although he readily admitted, "I killed a lot of people," Fred insisted that he did not feel hate. "They were simply opponents who were trying to kill me and my fellow Marines." By twice volunteering to extend his tours in Vietnam, Fred was actually saving other less experienced Marines from being exposed to the insanity of this deadly war.

When we send our youngsters to fight wars for us, there is inevitably a terrible cost. Far too many come home in body bags, or, even worse, in the Vietnam War, many were lost forever in jungles, canals, or mud with loved ones uncertain of their fate.

Gary Rezeau

Chicago, Illinois

"It was then their guns versus our guns."

I interviewed Gary via computer from his home in Melbourne, Florida. He told me that he wanted to be an aviator from his early days watching films of airplanes and aircraft carriers. During service selection in our final year at Annapolis, he selected aviation and began training at Pensacola Naval Aviation Station in late summer 1965.

I did fine in all the initial phases of flight training. The instructor for my check ride had no fleet experience, but he was a nice, interesting guy who had flown the SPAD airplane. After I had successfully completed my check ride, we had extra time, so he showed me a lot of cool stuff which impressed the hell out of me. I immediately wanted to become a SPAD guy and actually gave up jets twice to try to get into SPADs. Unfortunately, just as I was about to get my wings, the Navy decided to close down its only SPAD RAG and had begun to give the planes to the Vietnamese Air Force and our Air Force. With the SPAD option gone, I chose to go to a S-2 squadron. It was a good plane and I enjoyed flying it. I was able to get some really good flight and carrier landing experience during a 7-month deployment to the Mediterranean.

"SPAD" was the nickname for an older plane, the Douglas A-1 Skyraider attack aircraft. It was a single-engine plane with a 4-bladed propeller and could carry a lot of ordnance. It came into service right at the end of WW II and was involved in considerable combat in Korea. It is understandable why Gary wanted to fly the SPAD because it was, by all accounts, a "fun" plane with just a single pilot. The nickname came from a French biplane fighter used in WW I developed by Societe Pour L'Aviation et sea **D**erives. Over 3000 A-1's were built by the U.S. until production ended in 1957. It was the main attack aircraft used on carriers during the Korean War and all were painted dark blue. Because the engine had incredible torque, some pilots had difficulty controlling the plane after aborting a carrier landing, leading to several fatal accidents. A large number of Navy and Marine SPAD's (128) were lost in the Korean War, 101 in combat. The A-1 was used off carriers in the early days of the Vietnam War to carry out strikes against North Vietnam beginning in August 1964. In fact, the first "kill" of a North Vietnamese plane was done by a SPAD in October 1966. With the introduction of the jet-powered A-6 Intruder attack plane, the A-1 was phased out by the Navy just as Gary was hoping to fly it. The "RAG" (Replacement Air Group) is a squadron which serves as the final training stop for a particular aircraft. Pilots go to the RAG to gain proficiency on their assigned aircraft prior to deploying.

The S-2 Tracker aircraft, built by Grumman, was a twin-engine propeller plane designed to fly off carriers on anti-submarine missions. It had two pilots and two enlisted ASW (anti-submarine warfare) technicians. It came into service in 1952 but was replaced in 1974 by a jet-powered ASW plane, the Lockheed S-3 Viking.

In response to the Pueblo incident in January 1968, we deployed with our S-2 squadron on USS YORKTOWN (CVS-10) to the Sea of Japan. YORKTOWN was an old Essex-class carrier built in 1943 for service in WW II. It had been put back into service in 1953 and was one of the older carriers in operation. In March, YORKTOWN was sent to the Gulf of Tonkin to conduct operations against North Vietnam. The water was too shallow for a credible submarine threat so we were given other missions, such as surveillance and gunfire support. That is how I first got shot at. Our flight pattern would generally take us along the coast, but sometimes we were sent inland which was not a lot of fun. Fortunately for us, the North Vietnamese gunners were used to trying to hit the fast movers, the jets, and they never got the range right on us because we were only moving at 140 knots and down low, 1500-3000 ft. Our naval gunfire from ships offshore was going over the top of us! One day on a typical flight over the North, all of a sudden, these puffies (anti-aircraft flak) were going off just above us. I took some evasive maneuvers and headed out to sea. We got shot at several times on that deployment. There was some dicey stuff going on that spring of '68. We didn't have any attack aircraft on that carrier, mostly ASW planes.

I was enjoying flying the S-2, but one day when we were back in the states after our Vietnam deployment, our Executive Officer asked for pilot volunteers to fly in a new squadron of OV-10's that was going to be formed. It would be for close air support in combat in Vietnam. I volunteered and began training at North Island (San Diego) in October 1968 in the new squadron, VF-41. The Navy took 18 new OV-10's directly from the factory, left four at North Island for a RAG, and took 14 overseas in two detachments of six each, giving us two spares. They put them on an old WW II Jeep carrier to send them to Vietnam. We arrived in Vietnam in March, and the planes got there a few weeks later. We were flying combat by mid-April 1969.

The Rockwell OV-10 Bronco was a twin-turboprop light attack and observation plane specifically developed in the early 60's for Vietnam operations. Its primary missions were counterinsurgency and forward air control (FAC), because of its ability to loiter on station for three to four hours. The prototype was actually built by a Marine aviator and an engineer in a garage at China Lake Naval Air Weapons Station in California. It was designed to be able to take off and land on dirt roads and even on clearings in jungles if at least 600 feet long. The OV-10 armament was varied, but always included machine guns.

We set up two bases; mine was at Binh Thuy on the Mekong River along with some Air Force and Vietnamese planes. We also had a detachment down at Vung Tau in III Corps on the coast. I flew my first five months at Binh Thuy and my last seven at Vung Tau. At Binh Thuy I was flying at least twice a day carrying 4400 lbs of ordnance on each OV-10 mission.

We would always launch two planes at a time and work as a pair. We were called a light attack fire team. Targets were never a problem because something was always going on. Not long after we were in the air, we would get a call from a FAC (Forward Air Controller), "Hey, Black Pony, are you busy?" Black Pony was our call sign. They would then give us coordinates and we would fly over and kill some bad guys to help out our friends on the ground who were in trouble.

OV-10 Bronco in flight

The OV-10 had two pilots siting tandem in each plane with two ejection seats. The front-seater was the pilot. Our missions lasted about 2 1/2 hours. By that time, we had expended all our ordnance and it was time to come back. Our squadron did this day and night, 24 hours a day. At night we would use ambient light; our young eyes could see well enough to do very accurate attacks and read our charts. We had flares, but never liked to use them unless the customer insisted because it destroyed our night vision. Each plane carried between twelve and twenty 5-inch Zuni rockets - they were deadly. We would load these with different fuses depending on the mission. For example, we had bunker busting ones to punch down into the bunker before exploding and also some anti-personnel ones. The lead plane had a Mark 4 20 mm cannon on its centerline - a Gatling gun. It could fire 400 rounds a minute. The other plane had a 7.63 mm Gatling gun pod on its wing. We carried 1500 rounds each and would fire these in short bursts. Both of these guns were very effective. Those rounds carried a lot of energy and could inflict serious damage.

One day I flew six missions due to the high level of activity. Most of the action was in the Delta, and we often flew all the way down to the tip and along the coast in the Sea of Thailand up to the Cambodian border. We flew missions in most of III and IV Corps and also into Cambodia, especially the "Parrot's Beak" section. Of course, none of those missions in Cambodia "happened." We supported everyone.....Army, USMC, ARVN, Australian, USN - whoever needed us. If they called us, we came.

We were shot at on essentially every mission. As we got better at jinking, we only got hit about every third mission. Whenever we came back, our ground crew would inspect where there were holes to see if anything important had been hit. If not, they just put tape over the holes and off we went for the next one. I even had a canopy shot away during one mission. I was training a pilot and was in the back seat. We were taking fire from an old French fort near Rach Gia on the Gulf of Thailand. Mike was in the front seat while we were making multiple runs on the target. I could see tracers all going by us, and all of a sudden, it got very noisy and very windy because my right side canopy got shot away. I got a little ding on my shoulder, but it was not much. Unless you took a round in the hot section of the engine, it would keep running.

The Parrot's Beak section of Cambodia, which Gary referred to, was essentially a land peninsula between two rivers reaching roughly 25 miles into Vietnam about 50 miles west of Saigon. It was heavily infiltrated with North Vietnamese Army troops which had transited south along the Ho Chi Minh Trail or through Cambodia from the east along the Sihanouk Trail. During most of Gary's tour in Vietnam, neither American nor South Vietnamese forces officially conducted operations in Cambodia. In reality, as Gary's air and ground experiences showed, the border was essentially a porous membrane that both sides ignored. For the Viet Cong and NVA, Cambodia was a convenient, mostly safe sanctuary. On April 28, 1970, President Nixon ordered U.S. ground troops to invade Cambodia. With sentiment against the war already building, Nixon's order created such a backlash that, three years later, the U.S. Congress passed the War Powers Act limiting the scope of the President to declare war without congressional approval. Subsequent U.S. Presidents all found ways to get around this law.

We would normally cruise in the OV-10 at 140 knots but could get up to 200 in a dive. It was a pretty quiet airplane, and the enemy could not hear us until we were 1-2 kilometers away. We learned from Army intelligence that the Viet Cong had a huge bounty for anyone who could shoot down a Black Pony. They told us that the bounty on Huey (helicopter) *gunships in our fellow squadron was maybe 400,000 piasters* (Vietnamese currency, about $1500), *but that it was 750,000 (*about $2750) *on us.*

We knew we were effective. Basically, if I could see an enemy's muzzle flashes, he was dead.

When I later went over to fly at Vung Tau, we had similar missions, but we were also supporting the Aussies. They were crazy. They would go out on patrol in the bush wearing shorts, boots, no shirt, dog tags, hat, rifle, canteen - and no flak jacket! Like I said, they were crazy! That whole province was heavily NVA and VC. Many of the VC in this area were rice farmers during the day and VC at night.

I also did about 3 weeks on our boats on the rivers with some of our PBR crews as sort of an exchange tour. This all came about because our boss, the CO of River Patrol Force, CTF-116, a Navy Commander whom I shall not name, decided that all his boat drivers should get air medals. This was, of course, insane, but nonetheless, he ordered us pilots to swap with the officers who were in charge of PBR's on the rivers. They would fly in the back seat on some of our missions to collect points for air medals, and we would ride the PBR's. On these ops we would sometimes work with "Ruff Puffs" who were friendly South Vietnamese who may or may not have been VC. We were always on guard when around these guys; you just never knew.

A PBR is a "Patrol Boat Riverine" and was built specifically for use in the "brown water Navy" shallow water operations in the Mekong Delta. These boats were initially built in 1965 by a yacht company in North Carolina! They had twin 50-caliber machine guns forward and a 30-caliber gun mounted aft. There were also mounts on the sides for grenade launchers and another machine gun. The crew carried additional weapons, usually M-16 rifles, grenade launchers, and hand grenades. The only protection provided was ceramic armor installed in a few places. It was powered by twin diesel engines and water-jet pumps enabling it to do 25 knots. It had a design draft of 8 inches but fully loaded it was closer to 20 inches. The hull was made of fiberglass so that rockets might puncture the hull but usually would not explode because there was nothing solid to hit. It had a four-man crew typically led by an enlisted Chief Petty Officer. It was dangerous duty; one of every three PBR sailors was wounded during his tour on PBR's.

On these patrols we would go into a village, and they would raise the Vietnamese flag. We would then always talk to the Chief. We had South Vietnamese translators with us along with some other Vietnamese we called our "Kit Carson" scouts. If these guys got a bad feeling about the village, we would send in special forces at night to do some "housekeeping."

The enemy would generally hide in the occasional cluster of trees in the Delta at night. So we would also hide and try to catch the NVA guys if they started to move. We would push our boats into the banks of the river and were absolutely quiet...total radio silence too. The NVA would come down to the riverbank but could not see over the raised embankments. So, they would make little balls of mud and throw them over the embankment toward the water. If they heard a plop from them hitting the water, they knew it was probably safe. But if they got a thunk sound, they knew it hit something other than water and we were probably there. They would shoot an illumination round and the fire fight was on. It was then their guns versus our guns. We usually won because we had superior fire power. We got into a lot of fire fights during those nights in the Delta. Some of our people in another boat had two killed and five wounded in one of the battles. The wounded guys were ultimately able to get back to their boats.

While I was on the PBR's, we sometimes would switch over to some Army ACV's (Air Cushion Vehicles) which could do 70 mph across that shallow water in the Plain of Reeds near the southeast corner of the Parrot's Beak of Cambodia. We would "prep" areas with 20 mm cannon fire which would kill most of the bad guys we hit within 3/4 mile. We would then go up there and count the bodies and get intel off their uniforms.

A lot of the areas I waded in were booby-trapped. Sometimes when I was in some of these marshes and rivers, I was carrying three weapons: an M-16 rifle, a .45 pistol, and a snub nose .38 pistol. I remember one time while wading in neck-deep water in a river in the Parrot's Beak in Cambodia, I was carrying my rifle over my head. I never worried about the pistols getting wet or muddy because they always worked. If you captured an AK-47, they were great because you could rinse it off and *start shooting. I did this brown water stuff for about three weeks and then went back flying.*

While flying at Vung Tau, we got scrambled around 10 AM on a Thursday to help two Aussie platoons of about 80 guys who had engaged an entire 450-man battalion of NVA who had heavy weapons. They were in a massive fire fight that they were not going to win. We scrambled out there and watched some Vietnamese SPADs doing some awesome bombing of the NVA. Then we took over. We ran about 12 OV-10's out there in groups of two and broke up the NVA while killing a lot of them. We were back in the bar watching movies the following night and all of a sudden, here come the Aussies all bandaged up. When they learned that we were the guys who saved them, they brought in cases of lagers and ale under their arms and the party was on. We drank about eight cases of beer that night....living large!

I never did operations with the South Koreans. They were mostly up in II Corps. It would have been interesting to work with them. They had deliberately built a reputation for being ruthless. They would actually take scalps and various body parts - ears, tongues - during battles. None of the enemy wanted to fight them.

We supported anyone who needed us. The Coast Guard Swifties (both the Navy and the Coast Guard had Swift boats in Vietnam) *loved us because we always hit what we aimed at. There were also a lot more Marines than I expected who were advisors to the Vietnamese Marines; we helped them too.*

When Gary's Vietnam tour was up, he returned to Texas as a flight instructor in the same squadron in which he had received his naval aviator wings. He soon transferred to jets and became an A-6 Intruder pilot. Gary went on to fly an entire range of Navy aircraft in his career before retiring in 1988. He then had a second career as a pilot for Delta Airlines for the next 15 years.

In our conversation, Gary was very candid about duties requiring him to "kill bad guys." He did not relish this assignment. Having seen "how the communists treated their fellow Vietnamese," it was clear to him that we were supporting allies under duress. "I didn't take my job lightly, and I took no pleasure in taking lives." For Gary, it was not a scorecard exercise counting kills, but actions to support our forces needing his help while under attack - and always at considerable danger to himself. There is no way to know for certain, but Gary may have been fired at in Vietnam on more occasions than any of our classmates.

Phase III, Late 1969 – Summer 1973

Although the U.S. was withdrawing troops from Vietnam, the war was not over. Death and injury continued, not only for all combatants, but for tens of thousands of innocent civilians. American deaths fell, but were still close to 12,000 in 1969, the second highest year of carnage for the U.S. in Vietnam. It was not until 1972 that American deaths were under 1000. Even in 1975, when the war concluded with the capture of Saigon by North Vietnamese forces, 161 Americans died in Vietnam.

Throughout 1970, the U.S. conducted over 100 designated operations, not only in South Vietnam, but also in Cambodia and Laos. The American plan throughout 1970-72 was to place an increased burden on ARVN ground and naval forces in a strategy called "Vietnamization." In early 1971, ARVN troops, supported by U.S. assets, invaded Laos in an attempt to cut off the Ho Chi Minh Trail but were repulsed and suffered heavy losses. In early 1972, North Vietnamese troops launched a large-scale "Easter Offensive" in several regions in the south against both ARVN and U.S. forces. The effort gained more territory for the communists but did not deliver the decisive blow which the North had hoped to achieve.

American ground forces had been reduced to under 60,000 by the end of 1972 when President Nixon ordered a concentrated air attack on the Hanoi and Haiphong regions to force the North Vietnamese to negotiate a peace treaty. The resulting loss of life and damage suffered by the North apparently convinced the communists that it was now in their interest to conclude an agreement.

Although peace talks in Paris had been underway since May 1968, the treaty, called the Paris Peace Accords (officially the Agreement on Ending the War and Restoring Peace in Vietnam), was not signed until January 23, 1973. The governments of North Vietnam, South Vietnam, the U.S., and "The Provisional Revolutionary Government of the Republic of South Vietnam" (the Viet Cong) were signatories. The agreement included the removal of all U.S. forces and the end of direct U.S. involvement.

Fighting between the Vietnamese resumed almost immediately. Although the South Vietnamese had nearly one million men in their armed forces opposing just over 200,000 communists in the south, the North Vietnamese had assumed control of considerably more territory by the end of 1973. Using a massive offensive in 1975, the communists overran Saigon and assumed control of the entire country. Two of their first acts were to change the name of Saigon to Ho Chi Minh City and to rename Tan Son Nhut airport Tan Son Nhut Airport. The official reunification of all of Vietnam took place on July 2, 1976, with the establishment of the Socialist Republic of Vietnam.

Paul Bloch

Berwyn, Illinois

"I felt like we were in the middle of The War of the Worlds"

I had several classes with Paul at the Academy and remember him well. Following graduation, we chose different professional routes. He ended up in aviation, while I was in submarines. We did cross paths 16 years after graduation when both of us were on USS CONSTELLATION (CV-64) during a deployment in the Indian Ocean, but neither of us was aware of the other being onboard. Paul was then the CO of a squadron of A-6 aircraft, and I was the anti-submarine warfare officer for the Carrier Group Commander. I interviewed Paul by phone from his home in Mercer Island, Washington, where he lives with his wife, Sherlyn.

My dad had been an upholsterer in a small town west of Chicago when WW II began. He shifted jobs to wartime industries making machine gun bullets and then working in a B-29 aircraft factory. When I was in 5th grade at our local Catholic school, we read a book, "These Are Our People," which had a story profiling the Naval Academy. I decided at that early age that I wanted to go to the Academy. I tried to receive an appointment from my congressman in my senior year, but he didn't have one that year. Instead, I went to the University of Illinois for a year; I applied again and got the appointment. While I was at the Academy, I spent all four years in the sailing squadron. Following graduation in 1965, I stayed at USNA for six months teaching sailing and being a Division officer for the small craft facility. I then began aviation training at Pensacola in December. I loved flying, but once I was assigned to an A-4 squadron on the West Coast, I found out that I was not very good at landing the aircraft on a carrier. I decided it best that I turn in my wings.

283

I received orders to USS STERETT (DLG-31) where I was assigned to be the Assistant CIC (Combat Information Systems) Officer.

Shortly after I reported aboard in the fall of 1968, STERETT shifted its homeport from Long Beach to Yokosuka, Japan. We were soon doing SAR (Search and Rescue) operations east of the North Vietnamese city of Vinh for carriers doing flight operations on Yankee Station. With our radars, we were helping pilots flying missions over North Vietnam south of the 19th parallel. Because of my prior experience, I knew many of the pilots flying missions with A-4's. Using our electronics warfare suite, we could pick up enemy radars, including the Spin Scan radar used by MiG-21 aircraft. Because of slight differences in frequencies, we could even tell how many MiGs were out there. The North Vietnamese would often try to set a trap for our F-4's by having two MiGs up high as bait, while two others were hiding in a valley where we could not see them on radar. When our F-4's showed up to go after the bait, the other two MiGs would sweep up behind and attack them. One F-4 did get shot down in this type of action, but it may have been due to friendly fire. We also lost an A-4 due to ground fire. I remember hearing his wingman on the radio yelling, "Fireball and a chute!" We immediately launched our two helos and were able to successfully pick up the pilot while the wingman kept track of where he was.

During my tour on STERETT, I decided that I really preferred aviation and put in to become a NFO. These are officers who fly with the pilot while performing other duties such as navigation or directing the bombing. In August 1969, I reported to Glencoe, Georgia, for training, and soon received my BN (bombardier navigator) wings. I was assigned to VA-128, a RAG (Replacement Air Group) training squadron in Whidbey Island, Washington, flying A-6's. After completing this training, I joined VA-52, also at Whidbey, which deployed to Vietnam aboard USS KITTY HAWK (CV-63) in October 1970.

The Grumman A-6 Intruder is a two-seat, twin-engine attack aircraft designed to conduct carrier-based operations in all weather conditions day or night. As bombardier/navigator, Paul sat to the right of the pilot. His job was to spend much of his airborne time under a hood concentrating on the pre-loaded navigation and targeting displayed on the scope in front of him while the pilot maneuvered the aircraft. On attack missions, the BN provides steering information to the pilot who follows a presentation on a screen which is often described as "cartoonish." There have been instances of an A-6 lost by hitting mountains due to the BN looking outside rather than keeping his eyes glued to the scope.

When we arrived on Yankee Station in Fall 1970, our missions were conducting bombing over Laos on and around the Ho Chi Minh Trail. Most of these assignments were at night trying to disrupt the steady stream of trucks bringing NVA troops and supplies to the south. One series of night missions was called "Commando Bolt." These raids took place after Navy P-3 aircraft dropped motion and acoustic sensors on the trail to detect movement. The signals from these devices were picked up by an orbiting Air Force EC-121; it would then send that info to a data center in Thailand which then forwarded target coordinates to us called DMPI (Desired Mean Point of Impact). It was always difficult to assess the effectiveness of our strikes, even the following day, due to the heavy vegetation cover along the Trail.

The Lockheed P-3 Orion aircraft was designed for anti-submarine warfare but was used during the Vietnam War for surveillance of boat traffic along the coast and to conduct these "Bolt" operations. Wartime flights in an aircraft were not without risk. At least two P-3's and their entire crews were lost during the war. The Lockheed EC-121 Warning Star was originally deployed in the early 1950's as an early warning and signal intelligence gathering platform. They were used extensively in Vietnam in a variety of missions.

Our daytime missions were called Commando Nail. Here we would do "buddy bombing" with A-7's off our carrier. Our targets were determined by Air Force spotter planes, OV-1's and OV-10's, which would be flying low to drop smoke flares near targets. They would call us with instructions such as, "Drop your bombs 500 meters north of my smoke." The job of these FAC's (Forward Air Controllers) was incredibly dangerous. One thing we learned was to never make multiple passes on the same target. I had a good friend shot down in an A-6 by AAA (anti-aircraft artillery) before I got to Vietnam because his pilot did just this.

This deployment on KITTY HAWK ended in July 1971 and our squadron headed back to Whidbey Island. I was married that fall before we deployed again on KITTY HAWK in February 1972. This was a quick turnaround for the carrier because the powers in Washington wanted another carrier there "now." When we arrived, the buzz was that there was about to be another enemy offensive, probably around Easter. Nothing unusual happened at first; we were doing the same type of Laos missions. On Easter, the ship was back at Subic Bay in the Philippines when we suddenly got word to "get down to the ship." We sailed immediately and began conducting missions over South Vietnam supporting South Vietnamese forces which were under heavy attack. We conducted an Alpha Strike (nearly all planes on carrier) near Dong Ha.

A few days later, we received orders to begin bombing the North. We began by working our way up the North Vietnamese coast with initial runs on Vinh, and then on April 16 on targets in the Haiphong area. These targets had not been bombed in four years and were very heavily defended. We were working in coordination with Air Force B-52's doing high altitude bombing while we were concentrating on SAM (surface-to-air missile) sites. On these missions, it looked to us like everything in the air was coming at us. On one night mission south of Haiphong, there were so many missiles and AAA in the air (we could see the AAA tracers at night) that I felt like we were in the middle of the 1953 movie, "War of the Worlds," based on the H.G. Wells novel. In addition to 500 lb bombs, we were dropping Mk-20 Rockeyes. This was a cluster weapon containing 247 orange armor-piercing bomblets. Each Rockeye could cover the area of a football field. We encountered no MiGs during these runs but encountered a lot of SAMs and AAA flak. On another mission near Hanoi, we came in low and, after releasing our bombs, banked sharply to the right to get out of there. We were so low that I looked out and was able to see a guy below loading artillery! We hit all types of targets: rail lines to China, truck repair facilities, roads, bridges. We did lose one A-6 crew which ran into a mountain east of Haiphong and also two A-7's which were shot down. We didn't lose any A-6's to enemy fire during this campaign.

On April 16, 1972, President Nixon, angered by the North Vietnamese spring offensive, ordered the resumption of U.S. bombing of Hanoi and Haiphong and surrounding targets. His Secretary of State, Henry Kissinger, had begun back channel negotiations with North Vietnam in February 1970 but hoping to gain an edge in the talks, the communists sent a force of over 120,000 men to attack South Vietnam on March 10, 1972. Nixon was enraged because he felt that this action might threaten his reelection in the fall. By October 1972, following the bombing campaign in which Paul participated, North Vietnam made sufficient concessions allowing Kissinger to announce, "Peace is at hand." The American bombing was halted. However, the South Vietnamese President, Thieu, demanded changes and talks again collapsed. Following his reelection, Nixon became frustrated with the stalemate and on December 13, 1972, ordered massive bombing of the north to spur all sides to the negotiating table. One month later, on January 23, 1973, talks were concluded with the signing of the "Paris Peace Accords." Both Nixon and Kissinger were able to declare that they had achieved "peace with honor" and American prisoners of war were soon headed home. Although the U.S. hope was that the South Vietnamese would now be sufficiently strong to hold off the North, such was not to be. The last U.S. troops left Vietnam on March 29, 1973, but fighting continued throughout South Vietnam. American bombing of Cambodia did not halt until August 14, 1973. With Nixon now involved in the Watergate scandal, he felt that he had no remaining political capital to offer military assistance to the South Vietnamese. Following Nixon's resignation in August 1974, it was only a matter of time until the South Vietnamese army crumbled. When Saigon fell to communist forces on April 30, 1975, South Vietnam ceased to exist.

When we returned to Whidbey in November 1972, I had orders to study Operations Analysis at the Naval Postgraduate School in Monterey, California. I later was assigned to a squadron on USS MIDWAY (CV-41) which was homeported in Japan. I ultimately was assigned command of a squadron of A-6's, VA-165, and deployed on USS CONSTELLATION (CV-64) during operations in the Indian Ocean.

Following his command tour, Paul spent several years as a Department Head at the U.S. Naval War College in Newport, Rhode Island, and at the Naval Post Graduate School. He retired in August 1991 and later worked for Boeing in Seattle in their Military Concept Development Analysis group. During his military aviation career, Paul completed 355 missions and made over 1000 carrier landings as an NFO. Although aviators do not feel the "closeness" of enemy death experienced by many of our Marine and Riverine Force classmates, Paul told me of watching truck targets engulfed in flames creating certain casualties. He explained to me that his reaction to such was tempered by the realization that nearly all targets were enemy military who were intent on killing Americans. I suspect that losing friends in battle erases much empathy for the enemy. War often dehumanizes many who are involved.

Jim Stark

Washington, D.C.

"I was always exhausted"

Jim is a close friend and former roommate at the Naval Academy. Although our Navy careers took us in different directions, we have remained in contact. Our homes are within 10 miles of each other, so it was convenient to interview him at his residence in Fairfax, Virginia, where he and his wife Rosi reside.

We began by discussing the Tonkin Gulf incident. Jim and I were both still at the Naval Academy when this event took place in the darkness off the coast of North Vietnam in early August 1964. Neither of us realized at the time how much this incident would affect Jim's subsequent naval career, nor how it would accelerate U.S. direct involvement in the ongoing war between North and South Vietnam. What is certain is that there was a confrontation between North Vietnamese naval forces and U.S. ships on August 2. The USS MADDOX (DD-731), an American destroyer, was conducting operations in international waters in the Gulf of Tonkin when three North Vietnamese torpedo boats approached at high speed. MADDOX fired warning shots in an attempt to dissuade the Vietnamese from attacking. In response the Vietnamese launched torpedoes and commenced machine gun fire. In the melee that followed, all three torpedo boats were damaged, with the loss of four Vietnamese sailors and another six wounded. One American plane from the nearby aircraft carrier, USS TICONDEROGA (CV-14), was damaged and MADDOX had one bullet hole.

Two days later, based on sonar and radar information, both MADDOX and another U.S. destroyer, USS TURNER JOY (DD-951), believed that a second attack was about to take place. Their initial report to U.S.

authorities in Washington, coupled with what proved to be erroneous intercepts of North Vietnamese communications, precipitated immediate action by the Johnson administration to escalate and intensify military actions against North Vietnam. Subsequent information obtained years later from both U.S. and North Vietnamese sources proved that no actual attack had taken place. However, in what some termed "the fog of war, President Johnson went immediately on national television to announce the attack. He and his cabinet then prodded the U.S. Congress to pass a joint resolution on August 7 titled "The Southeast Asia Resolution" granting Johnson authority to conduct military operations without an actual declaration of war. This piece of paper, now known as the "Gulf of Tonkin Resolution," led to 11 years of fighting in and around Vietnam and the death of millions. Jim discussed his current views on the entire situation based on his access to multiple reports and analyses in the years following the events.

The first incident involving the patrol boats was definitely an actual attack by the North Vietnamese. The second one was a situation in which the ships there genuinely believed, based on their sensors, that an attack by the Vietnamese was imminent. What I found when I was in the Gulf of Tonkin on ships from late 1968 to early 1969 and from April to September 1970 was that you will sometimes see things on radar that look like actual contacts that appear to be moving too slow to be aircraft, but still going fast enough to be some form of threat. I saw this myself both when I was on USS JENKINS (DD-447) and USS HIGBY (DD-868) in the Gulf of Tonkin. The radar blips would then just suddenly break up and disappear. Maybe it was a flight of geese....who knows?

My first ship after graduating from the Academy in 1965 was USS BRONSON (DD-668), a Fletcher class WW II destroyer homeported in Newport, Rhode Island. BRONSON was one of the oldest ships in the Navy at that time. This was basically a temporary assignment as it was headed to Europe for a Northern European goodwill cruise. I got off in Copenhagen, Denmark, to travel to the University of Vienna where I had a Fulbright Scholarship to study history and German. After a year of classes in Austria I received orders to USS WILKINSON (DL-5) in Newport where I was the CIC officer (Combat Information Center) from December 1966 to May 1968. I then volunteered for duty in Vietnam and thought I was going to a Swift boat but received a call sending me to Destroyer School for six months. Upon completion I received orders to JENKINS which was homeported in Pearl Harbor, Hawaii. It was deployed, so I picked it up in Subic Bay in the Philippines.

We sailed to the Tonkin Gulf to plane guard for the carriers. We also had assignments doing North and South SAR operations. There were always about three to four destroyers assigned to support each carrier on Yankee Station. There was a "bombing pause" of North Vietnam at the time, so all the aircraft missions were over the south. It was very challenging trying to maintain station at 25-27 knots alongside, or 1200-1500 yards behind, a carrier at night. Our Captain was very aggressive and wanted us to get in closer to 500 yards. I never understood why he wanted to be so close. It was, in my opinion, unnecessarily dangerous.

Whenever aircraft carriers are conducting flight operations, at least one support ship, usually a destroyer, is assigned "plane guarding" duty. Their role is to be near the carrier to be in a position to pick up aviators who have had to bail out while trying to land, or whose aircraft has had an accident in the vicinity. "SAR" is Search and Rescue. During these missions the destroyers had the responsibility to be ready to locate and pick up U.S. aviators in the sea who had to parachute out of a damaged plane following missions over land.

We did see a lot of Wiblics - what we called the waterborne logistics craft - off the coast of both North and South Vietnam. These were small boats which were attempting to carry supplies down the coast to the Viet Cong. We would sometimes fire at these. One situation in particular I recall occurred on JENKINS when we identified a larger than normal fishing trawler that looked suspicious. Our immediate on-scene commander was a senior Coast Guard officer who told us to station snipers as we approached to 500 yards and take the boat under fire. I was designated to lead a boarding party in a motor whaleboat. I told my crew that if anyone on that trawler did any shooting at us to make sure that we killed every one of them because I didn't want any of us killed by a wounded guy shooting us in the back. For whatever reason, right at the last minute, we received orders from the the Commander in Chief of the Pacific Fleet in Hawaii, CINCPACFLT, to back off and not provoke the boat. Fortunately, the trawler turned around. It obviously understood that we would not let it go further south.

Sometimes when U.S. diesel submarines would come into the Tonkin Gulf, we would do anti-submarine training exercises with them. There was one time in 1968 when a Soviet Echo class submarine came into the Gulf and that had created quite a stir. However, the entire time we were in the Gulf, we never saw or heard any other non-U.S. submarines there.

We also did gunfire support operations off South Vietnam. We would go in close to shore, sometimes just a few hundred yards off the coast and receive target coordinates from a gunfire spotter at the scene where the fighting was taking place. Our 5"/38 guns had a 55 lb projectile with a 20 lb powder charge. A typical mission would be 100-200 rounds over the course of a morning. These locations were up and down the coast in all the I, II, III, and IV Corps areas. Our max range was 26,000 yards for rocket assisted weapons, and 18,000 yards for our guns. We were absolutely exhausted doing these operations because every three days we had to pull out 50 miles or so to rendezvous with an oiler to take on fuel. It almost always seemed to take place around one in the morning. We would then race back to the gunfire support mission just off the shore. I was one of our two gunfire liaison officers talking to the spotter ashore and directing our fire, so I was always exhausted. We would also take on ordnance from an AOE which carried both fuel and ammunition. We would also have to rendezvous with a stores ship to receive food and fresh vegetables. Each of these operations required careful shiphandling because both ships would be at sea moving alongside each other.

When Jim said that he was exhausted, it was due to often having to be involved both in these supply rendezvous during the night and then the gunfire liaison duties most of the day. Sleep was a premium throughout most of these deployments for both officer and enlisted personnel. The Mark 12 5"/38 caliber gun was a workhorse weapon that had been introduced in 1934. The 5" designation meant that the projectile fired was 5 inches in diameter; 38 caliber means that the barrel length was 38 "calibers" long, where the caliber is the diameter of the muzzle of the gun. In this case, that translates to a length of 190 inches. The gun was intended for both surface and air targets. In the Vietnam operations which Jim describes, essentially 100% of the usage was against surface targets on land. With a well-trained crew, it could be fired at roughly 15 rounds per minute, that is, one every four seconds. The barrels could not last indefinitely and had to be replaced approximately every 4500 rounds. There were four different types of fuses available; the appropriate one was selected based on the target. The system was also capable of firing several different variants of projectile, such as white phosphorus used to create a smoke screen to assist troops ashore. The 5"/38 was a remarkably accurate gunfire system and was used extensively throughout the war.

We would also do Harassment and Interdiction operations from offshore. These were called "H and I" missions. Here we would be told to fire 10 rounds into the coordinates of some crossroads during an hour of our choosing during the night. We were told that there would be "no good guys" there at that time, so we always tried to do this sometime when we were not showing a movie to our crew, which I might add, was always the high point of the day for our sailors who had little entertainment while at sea. I never had concerns about doing shore bombardment because we were trying to help our troops ashore who were in danger. We never fired intentionally into a village, just coordinates of enemy locations supplied by the spotter. When we had targets in the mangrove swamps in the Mekong Delta area up near the Cambodian border, the spotters told us that they could not see where our rounds hit. We quickly surmised that the projectiles had simply burrowed into the mud with the point-detonating fuse going off deep in the ground and creating a muffled "puff." So, when we were down there, we began to use time fuses to cause air bursts so that they could be seen by the spotters who could then tell us how to adjust our fire to hit the targets. Our 5'/38's were old and often broke down; even though we had high priority for spare parts, we often had to wait to do repairs. Our sailors did great work keeping those guns going.

When JENKINS returned to Pearl Harbor from Vietnam in May 1969, the ship was inspected and promptly slated for decommissioning as soon as we went on to San Diego. One of the inspectors actually put several holes in the forward deck with a hammer! JENKINS was a very tired ship!

I received orders to USS HIGBEE (DD-806) homeported in Long Beach. It was a much newer ship and had just returned from a tour in Vietnam. I replaced the Weapons Officer who had lost his leg in an accident over there. I intentionally did not ask how that happened. After training and inspections, we returned to Vietnam where we did mostly operations with the carriers on Yankee Station.

On this deployment I did get ashore once via a Swift boat. We then went on a helicopter to an Army base in Bong Son Valley where I talked to an Army general who discussed where he wanted us to fire. It was New Year's Day 1970; I was able to have a warm beer with dinner there. When I returned to the ship, we received targets down around Vung Tau in III Corps, on some high hills where we could see old French tanks in an area now completely controlled by the Viet Cong. We came in close and actually could see the caves we were firing into. The spotters were in helicopters and could direct our fire as little as five yards right or left to put projectiles right into the caves.

On HIGBEE we had a helicopter deck where both Army and Marine Huey helos would refuel from us while they hovered over our ship. We kept JP-5 fuel in a separate tank for this purpose. It would take 15-30 minutes for them to refuel. We did not have our own Huey but did have a DASH unit which we did not use in Vietnam.

The "Huey" was the Bell UH-1 Iroquois helicopter. It was ubiquitous in Vietnam and had a variety of users from all services. It was developed by the Army for medical evacuation but soon became the "go to" aircraft for moving troops and just about every other mission involving a small helo. It was first used in Vietnam in 1962, and by war's end in 1975, over 7000 had been in operation there. Due to the extremely dangerous conditions in which they were used, more than 3000 were lost or destroyed. The DASH helicopter which Jim mentioned was a small, unmanned vehicle used primarily for anti-submarine operations. It stayed in its hangar during most Vietnam deployments.

Our most dangerous operations, by far, were piloting a destroyer near the carrier during flight operations, especially at night. While the carrier is both launching and retrieving aircraft, it is always maneuvering to be heading into the wind, sometimes with little notice. All the smaller ships, such as ours, had to be continuously aware to be able to respond, but not get hit by the carrier. It was always a dicey situation.

Jim went on to have a very successful career in the Surface Navy. He became President of the Naval War College and attained the rank of Rear Admiral. Following retirement, he worked in London as a marketing executive for Northrup Grumman Corporation.

Conrad Best and Moearii Evans

Kittanning, PA - San Francisco, CA

"They all looked so young"

I learned about an important aspect of the Vietnam War from a class-mate, Conrad Best, who received an assignment to become involved in the management of the overseas R&R periods, and Moearii Evans, the widow of our classmate, Gordie Evans. Moearii was a stewardess on many of the Pan Am flights taking soldiers and sailors to and from R&R locations. Although the current title of this job is "flight attendant," when Moearii was working for Pan Am, she was then often called a "steward-ess." I interviewed both on separate occasions via computer from their homes; Conrad lives in Frostburg, Maryland, with his wife, Judith, and Moearii lives in Winter Springs, Florida.

For most American forces serving in Vietnam, the most anticipated time of their tour was the five to seven day R&R period to give them a brief respite from the daily grind of the war. Each sailor or Marine was guaranteed this one-time leave for "rest and recreation" at some point during his tour. R&R stood for "**R**est and **R**___" with the second R meaning **R**ecuperation, **R**elaxation, **R**ecreation, or **R**ehabilitation. Most would argue that the second R could have been each of those. For many on these flights, married or single, I was told, the second R actually evolved into I & I - Intoxication and Intercourse.

There were several approved destinations: Hawaii, Australia, Japan, Taiwan, Malaysia, the Philippines, Thailand, and Singapore. Air transportation was free and was provided by Pan Am Airways. Some units provided an additional shorter break, usually 3 days, for an "in-country" R&R, usually at a beach in the south at Vung Tau (50 miles east of Saigon), at Cam Ranh Bay, or China Beach in the north (close to Da Nang). Again, in addition to the sand and surf, "booze and broads" were the primary attraction for many.

I do not want to give the impression that I am trivializing, finger-wagging, or celebrating these brief respites which those serving in Vietnam so craved. Attempts to maintain morale among the participants in a war are just as important as providing food, housing, and ammunition. This is particularly true for draftees, many of whom had no desire to be thrust into a distant war in harsh conditions with the constant danger of wounds or death. In the case of my Naval Academy classmates, many had not volunteered for Vietnam duty but were simply carrying out the duty to which they were assigned. Based on the many comments I received during interviews, the R&R periods were eagerly anticipated. I might also add that many of the wives to whom I have spoken looked forward perhaps even more than their husbands to a brief rendezvous during the year-long absence.

Conrad began by explaining how he ended up in Vietnam.

I had a long route to Saigon. I had no idea during my high school years in our small town in Pennsylvania that I would end up in Vietnam. My family didn't have much money for me to go to college, so I started applying to service academies. I didn't even get my appointment to the Academy from our local congressman; he didn't have one, but he found one of his colleagues in Iowa who had one that he wasn't using, and I got that one. At service selection in our final year at Navy, I chose aviation, but once in flight training, quickly decided that I didn't like it. I then received assignments to do mine warfare but developed some medical issues. I eventually got orders as First Lieutenant on USS WILLIAM V PRATT (DLG-13), a guided missile destroyer homeported in Mayport, Florida. While the ship was deployed in the Mediterranean in 1969, I tried to resign, but the Navy said that there was a critical shortage of Lieutenants and gave me orders to go to Vietnam.

I flew into Tan Son Nhut Air Base and reported to Naval Support Activity, Saigon, but it was actually located in Nha Be, about 15 miles south. It was a big command which took care of all services for II, III, and IV Corps areas. We covered most of Vietnam south of the Da Nang area - they had their own support group. I did all sort of things in this job. The building had a big, fenced perimeter with guards, but to some of my classmates involved in combat, I was the classic "REMF" (rear echelon mfer).

Most bases in Vietnam had separate facilities for support. For example, although we were at Nha Be, we had satellite offices supporting all the various riverine forces and Swift boats which primarily operated in the Mekong Delta region. Our job was to support each of these smaller offices. My main responsibility was to run the R&R program for every Navy and Marine individual in II, III, and IV Corps. If anyone wanted to go on R&R, officer or enlisted, they had to submit a request which would come to me. I would put them on a civilian charter plane to one of the designated places, and off they went. Time-in-country is what determined your priority. The longer you had been in, the better your chances for getting your choice. For example, you had to be in-country eight to nine months to get to Sydney, Australia. For Hawaii, it was only about six months. Hong Kong was easy, maybe three to four months. It was my impression that each person spent a lot of time trying to figure out what worked best for him.

My job was to see that the seats assigned to the Navy and Marine Corps on all R&R flights were assigned on a fair and equitable basis. Married guys did not get preference to go to Hawaii to see their wives, although that was, by far, the favorite destination for them because their wives could get there easily. Time-in-country was the only criteria. I was under strict orders to keep every seat full. It was the individual command's responsibility to get their men to the airport for the flight and to get them back to their unit. Sometimes, when someone couldn't make it at the last minute, I would call up the ops officer at one of the bases that had planes and tell them I had an empty seat and to pick out anyone and get them to Ton Son Nhut fast. For the last 2/3's of my tour, I never had an empty seat. We actually used some of the first computers and card punches to do all of this. During my tour, I got to go to Tokyo and Sydney for one-week conferences to discuss the R&R program, which was a good deal. I also was sent to Bangkok to hand-carry our monthly newsletter which was printed there. President Nixon happened to be there on a state visit at the same time and came through on a motorcade. I waved an American flag as he went by.

I also arranged USO tours. One of the famous groups I remember was the New Christy Minstrels. One of their female members got sick, and when we later found out what it was, we joked that it was a "New Christy Menstrual" problem! Another time an actress came through by herself and I flew with her to all sorts of bases. Her main talent was that she was a "round-eyed girl." On a serious note, I also took some bands made up of GIs to some really nasty places up near the Cambodian border. We would fly in on a helicopter, do a 15-20 minute program, and then move on. We had a few close calls doing these adventures. Another thing I did was to pay for bands which played in the various Officer Clubs and Enlisted Clubs on bases throughout Vietnam. I even had to go into Saigon to audition some of these groups; most consisted of young Filipinos. Some had discernible talent. A group of us would rate their skills basically by how well they played "Proud Mary" and if they knew the words to "We Gotta Get out of This Place."

My only close call came while we were there at Nha Be one night when a loud explosion came from a hit near our building. We all immediately ran into the bunker near us. The next morning, we found out that we had almost been hit by Army artillery that had accidentally put in the wrong coordinates when they fired. We almost were killed by friendly fire!

One other interesting thing I had to do was to supply Christmas trees, including lights and decorations, to all the bases at Christmas. I distributed 700 trees to all the commands in our region. I had a budget of $200,000 each quarter from the Army-Navy Exchange system to do these sorts of things. I also bought basketballs, plastic models, glue, playing cards, cribbage boards - even Yahtzee games! I had to make sure to order ahead - for example, I ordered all the Christmas things in July. Fortunately, I had a staff of 10-12 enlisted and Vietnamese personnel helping me. They were great!

After his year in Vietnam, Conrad was allowed to resign. He remained in the Naval Reserves in Pennsylvania and retired as a Commander. In 1975 he and his wife sponsored a Vietnamese refugee who lived with them for 18 months. This young fellow ultimately became a mechanical engineer, attended the University of Pittsburgh, and had 4 children, all born in the U.S. Conrad proudly told me that they all now call him "Grandpa."

A few weeks later after talking to Conrad, I had the opportunity to discuss Moearii's experiences in Vietnam with her. She spoke to me via phone from her home in Florida.

You asked about my name. Moearii is a combination of two Tahitian names and was given to me because of my heritage. I was raised by my grandmother in California and was recruited at a party when I was 19 to work for Pan Am. I was too young to fly, so I started in reservations. Shortly after I turned 23, I interviewed to be a flight attendant. My first base was in Chicago, and I flew all over the world: London, Frankfort.... lots of places. I started doing R&R flights out of San Francisco in 1970. We would go from Honolulu to Guam, then Manila, and finally to Vietnam. We also did R&R flights to Hong Kong and Sydney - Sydney was a long trip because we stopped in Darwin. Sometimes I would get flights that just shuttled between Darwin and Sydney.

During one of our layovers in Guam, I met my husband, Gordon, at a Mongolian barbecue at the O'Club. He was in Guam while his submarine was docked for repairs at the submarine tender on the other end of the island. The O'club was at Anderson Air Force Base where the

B-52's flew from on the bombing missions. I was there that night because two of our flight attendants were dating B-52 Air Force officers.

Our planes were always Boeing 707's. There was no first class; the planes had been configured strictly for R&R flights. Pan Am prided itself on not making money on R&R work. It is my understanding that the only charge per flight to the government was cost plus one dollar. We tried to make these flights as nice as possible by always serving full meals with ice cream as dessert. Because the flights were often short, we usually had to start cooking the meals while still on the ground. We almost never had guys try to hit on us on these flights. The enlisted men usually kept their heads down and wouldn't even glance up at you. They all looked so young! Many had been up a river somewhere and were still trying to adjust to being near a "round eye." The officers generally sat up front and were gentlemen. All of our passengers flew in uniforms and would change to civvies when they got there. I never observed anyone with what we now call PTSD symptoms.

I did the R&R flights from 1970-72. We flew mostly into Tan Son Nhut, Cam Ranh Bay, and Da Nang, but never stayed overnight in Vietnam. When I later did commercial round-the-world flights, those were a 12-13 day trip with overnight stops in Bangkok, Delhi, Tehran, Beirut, Frankfurt, London, and then New York. Beirut had THE best croissants anywhere!

On some of the R&R's we did shuttles back and forth from Taipei to Vietnam. Because we were there a lot, Taipei was always interesting to me. I even went into some of the bars with my girlfriends and met some of the local girls working there. It was just like junior high. All the guys were on one side and the girls with their ID's and medical tags around their neck on the other. They would size each other up and then get together for their whole five days there. Considering the situation, I thought that it was a rather safe and civilized approach.

Our crew always had great fun. While in Honolulu, we would buy Playboy magazines and take the centerfolds out and hide them inside the demonstration life jackets. Then at the beginning of the flights taking troops back to Vietnam, while we were doing the life jacket demo, the topless photos would pop out. We would then announce that because they were headed back to Vietnam, as a special treat, we would be doing a topless coffee service. This was greeted with lots of cheers, and as the guys all waited, suddenly the plane engineer would come out shirtless, wearing an apron, one of our hats, and holding a coffee pot. Lots of laughter! I always felt that it was a privilege to do these flights. All of us felt this way

Although Conrad and Moearii's stories may appear at first to have little to do with the war raging about them, their jobs were an integral aspect of maintaining prolonged fighting. A nation cannot sustain a lengthy war in a foreign land, especially if using drafted personnel, without significant measures to maintain morale. Christmas trees, beach time, and time away from the realities of battle are necessary, if not sufficient, means to maintain performance in a war seemingly without end and often without meaningful goals. Both Moearii and Conrad were exposed to risk. Conrad barely avoided a friendly fire tragedy, Moearii saw explosions taking place below her plane as she approached her first landing in Vietnam. Her experience that night proved to be the first of many flights where the crew could see the war not far below. In fact, each Pan Am crew member involved in R&R flights was issued an identification card with the rank of a junior officer in the event that they were captured to possibly ensure more humane treatment by the enemy. Fortunately, Moearii never had to use hers.

Carter Refo

Lake City, Florida

"I kept wondering why I wasn't hit"

Several pilots to whom I had spoken suggested that I interview an A-7 pilot. The Ling Temco Vought (LTV) A-7 Corsair was a single-seat light attack aircraft developed in the early-1960's to deliver substantial bombing payloads while flying off aircraft carriers. One of the classmates mentioned to me as an "A-7 driver" was Carter Refo. I interviewed him via computer from his home in Warrenton, Virginia, where he lives with his wife, Paula.

I was born in Lake City, Florida, in August 1943. My dad was a 1940 graduate of the Naval Academy and became a Naval Aviator. He flew patrol planes during the war and then other aircraft throughout the 1950's. While Dad was stationed in Japan, my mom and I lived in California. I later went to high school in Alexandria, Virginia, at St. Stephens. Although I had looked at other opportunities after high school, my first choice was to go to the Naval Academy. Fortunately, I received a Presidential appointment and was sworn in at USNA in June 1961 with the Class of 1965.

There are many avenues for admission to the Service Academies. Most entrants receive nominations from their senator, congressman, or the Vice President. The President has 100 slots reserved primarily for children of military veterans who have served at least 20 years. There are also set asides each year for enlisted personnel and children of Medal of Honor recipients. No matter the path taken, all applicants must meet rigorous academic and physical criteria.

While I was at the Academy I participated in the sailing program, which was a good deal because we didn't have to march in the weekly parades. I wanted to become a Naval Aviator like my dad. After graduation, I taught sailing to the incoming midshipmen throughout the summer. Paula and I were married in the Academy chapel in June, and in September we headed to Pensacola, Florida, where I began flight training. I wanted to get into jets so I could be in the middle of all the action in Vietnam. At the end of advanced flight training at Kingsville, Texas, I received my wings. The Navy then sent me to Cecil Field in Jacksonville, Florida, to a training squadron, VA-174, flying A-7's. After we went through the training syllabus to learn how to fly the A-7, I was sent to VA-82, a squadron which was about to deploy to Vietnam on USS AMERICA (CV-66). We sailed around the tip of South Africa straight to Yankee Station in the South China Sea where carriers launched flight operations against the enemy. We arrived there on May 31, 1968, so that everyone aboard was eligible for combat pay for May.

I can testify from personal experience on submarines that the Navy often moved ships in and out of Vietnamese waters to maximize pay for sailors. So long as you spent one day of a month in the combat zone, you were eligible to receive combat pay for the entire month. Also, enlisted personnel who reenlisted while in the combat zone were not taxed on their reenlistment bonus. Although nuclear submarines had no mission in Vietnam (our role was to find and track Soviet submarines), the sub I was on at that time was sent to Vietnamese waters. We arrived late on the last day of the month and departed early the next day, making everyone aboard eligible for two months of combat pay. The term "syllabus" used by Naval aviators refers to the course of instruction during a training cycle.

We began flying missions with targets over South Vietnam and Laos. On the last mission of the first day, one of our pilots was shot down over Laos by a 37 mm anti-aircraft gun. The Air Force did a miraculous job picking him up after he had spent 39 hours on the ground, but they lost a pilot of their own in the process. Another one of our pilots, Fred Lentz, who was our classmate, had problems during refueling and also experienced fuel transfer system problems causing his plane to run out of fuel. He had to bail out, but fortunately, he was picked up in good condition. Search and Rescue (SAR) operations were conducted by both the Navy and the Air Force depending on the location. I later did two SAR operations over North Vietnam below the 19th parallel, but both times we were unsuccessful locating the A-7 pilots. I don't believe that they were captured. However, we were always aware that most aviators who reached the ground alive were often tortured and killed before they could be taken to Hanoi as POWs.

My plane, an A-7 "A-model," had two 20 mm guns on each side and two Sidewinder missiles mounted on the fuselage. We had six weapon stations on the wings. Our normal load was twelve 500 lb Mk-82 bombs with six on each side which made the aircraft operate like a heavy truck when we first lifted off the carrier. We would be over land ("feet dry") in less than 25 minutes. Our assignments were generally strike missions to go after a particular target or searching for targets on a designated section of road. We also did support missions carrying gasoline to re-fuel other planes. There were two flight timeframes: midnight to noon and noon to midnight. We would, for example, fly twelve hours a day on a midnight to noon shift, and one of the other carriers would have the other flight schedule. Our ship would be at flight quarters for about 14 hours a day. I much preferred the noon to midnight because I found it difficult to sleep during the daytime. We would have to refuel the ship and take on ammo about every three days because we were going through ammunition pretty fast. We usually didn't fly on those days.

In addition to our two squadrons of A-7's, we had two squadrons of F-4's, one A-6 squadron, two A-3 squadrons, one E-2A, and one A-5 photo recon squadron. You can imagine how crowded the flight deck becomes during flight operations. There were at least nine of our '65 classmates aboard AMERICA during that cruise; three of us went on to command carriers later in our careers. Everyone had close calls during the missions. Flak would often get closer than you would like. As soon as we were over land on a mission, we would use a checklist to ensure that our weapons were selected and all applicable switches on. We never flew straight for long and were always "jinking." One of us would be low, maybe 5000-6000 ft, and one up high. Our low limit was 3500 ft - you did not want to get below that. On a bombing mission we would roll in at a 45-degree dive, release the bombs at 6000 ft, bottom out at 4000 *ft, and generally pull 4 g's while going back up. If we had a full load of bombs, we would sometimes make a second run. I never encountered any MiG's because we had our own fighter aircraft on barrier patrol to keep them away from us. But we did lose a number of A-7's during this cruise due to enemy fire from missiles or anti-aircraft weapons. Bombing restrictions imposed on us by political leaders in Washington limited us to North Vietnamese targets below the 19th parallel, which is just above the city of Vinh. We couldn't attack any of the war machinery further north around Hanoi which enabled the communists to continue their war effort. Instead, we did a lot of bombing of the Ho Chi Minh Trail, mostly in Laos. Our carrier would be on station for 25-30 days, then cycle back to Subic Bay in the Philippines for supplies and repairs and then return to Yankee Station.*

A-7 Corsair in flight

When AMERICA's deployment ended in November 1968, our squadron went back to Jacksonville, but we were soon re-assigned to an older carrier, USS CORAL SEA (CV-43), which was on the West Coast. We deployed out of Alameda, California, in the summer of 1969 and were soon again on Yankee Station. Now there were no missions allowed over North Vietnam, so we spent a lot of time over Laos. As a "2nd cruise" pilot, I felt that my experience made me a much more effective pilot. However, during one of these missions over a pass between North Vietnam and Laos, I came the closest I ever felt to getting hit. It was a night mission, and I found my plane engulfed in tracers from anti-aircraft fire from below. I kept wondering why I wasn't hit. This was a long cruise on CORAL SEA, and we didn't get home until late March 1970. We had flown off early and the ship itself did not return to Alameda until July. Altogether, on both cruises, I had flown 163 combat missions.

Following his Vietnam tours, Carter was selected for Test Pilot School at Patuxent River Naval Air Station in Maryland and later deployed to the Mediterranean again flying A-7's. He continued to progress through Naval Aviation assignments before commanding USS MILWAUKEE (AOR-2). He was then assigned Commanding Officer, USS INDEPENDENCE (CV-62), a carrier operating out of Yokosuka, Japan. Carter retired from the Navy in 1995 after 30 years of service. As with many aviators I interviewed, he remains upset about the political decisions which limited targets during the war. Aviators were tasked with flying day after day and night after night attacking heavily defended targets which were of limited value - often resulting in their deaths. From December 1967 through January 1973, 100 carrier-based A-7 Corsairs were lost - 55 in combat. No wonder that Carter and his fellow pilots were upset.

Don Brown

Glendale, California

"We flew into a total flak trap"

I interviewed Don via computer from his home in San Clemente, California, where he lives with his wife, Karen. We began our conversation talking about Don's experiences running track in high school and at the Academy. Although I was not a runner in my early years, I later coached cross country and track and am very familiar with respectable times for each event. Based on this background, I knew immediately that Don had been an exceptional athlete before entering Navy. In fact, his high school relay team had set a national record. At the Academy Don ran both track and cross country his first three years but learned that the head track coach was not interested in distance events. In frustration, he quit running in our senior year and turned his attention to a new goal of becoming a Marine aviator.

When service selection came along our senior year, I chose the Marine Corps and began Basic Training at Quantico, Virginia, three weeks after our graduation. I had been chosen for aviation at an earlier Marine Aviation Selection Board and began flight school at Pensacola in February 1966. Marine aviation training is much the same as that received by the Navy guys. We began flying the single-engine prop plane, the T-34, and once our scores in several areas were completed, I had the choice between jets and helicopters. I always wanted to fly jets and was fortunate to be able to do so. Over the course of the next year, I completed training and received my flight wings in May 1967. My first assignment was to the 3rd Marine Air Wing in El Toro, California. I was assigned to Marine Air Group 33 and was trained to fly the new F-4J Phantom in Squadron VMFA 334. In July 1968 we took 15 F-4Js to Vietnam by island-hopping to get there. We arrived at Da Nang after Tet in late July. Tet had occurred a few months earlier so everyone at Da Nang was still on edge.

The McDonnell Douglas F-4 Phantom was a supersonic jet fighter aircraft. It was powered by twin engines and flown by a pilot sitting in front of a Radar Intercept Officer (RIO). It first entered service with the Navy in 1961 but was soon also adopted by both the Marines and the Air Force. By the end of production in 1981 nearly 5200 had been built. The Navy's precision flying team, the Blue Angels, flew the same F-4J during aerial shows throughout the early 1970's. In Vietnam, the Phantom was used for multiple missions, including bombing and photo reconnaissance. The "Tet" offensive refers to a massive surprise offensive operation by the Viet Cong, supported by the North Vietnamese throughout South Vietnam beginning on January 30, 1968. These attacks on multiple cities throughout the south were a surprise because they broke the ceasefire which had been agreed upon for the Vietnamese holiday of Tet celebrating the lunar new year. Da Nang had been hit hard.

My first assignment at Da Nang was to support the F-4 reconnaissance flights over North Vietnam. These were conducted by a specially configured F-4 to take photos to assess damage from previous strikes. Usually, we would use one or two Phantoms to escort these photo missions. Our role was "flak suppression" meaning that we were supposed to attack anti-aircraft fire directed at the photo "bird." This was always dicey because at this time all the missions over North Vietnam were limited to below the 19th latitude, which is roughly near the city of Vinh. By the time we got to Vietnam, the North Vietnamese gunners had a lot of experience firing 37 mm cannon at our planes. The F-4 photo bird would go in screaming at 650 kts from the coastline making an east-west run straight over to the Laotian border, then turn around and make a west-east run back to the South China Sea. While they were taking photos, they were down low. None of our photo planes got hit while I was doing the flak suppression and I didn't get hit either. I can tell you that we saw a lot of tracers and a lot of flak. These were not joy rides,

We also did a lot of work over Laos both day and night. We would check in with an airborne Air Force C-130 who would assign us interdiction missions against trucks coming down the Ho Chi Minh Trail. Most people think that this "trail" was one road, but it had maybe 20 different permutations. Often an Air Force plane dropped flares where we should bomb. On these missions we would carry the Mk 80 series of bombs which ranged from 250 to 2000 lbs. The RIO would provide navigation and targeting information, but I had control of the release of the weapons. We also did considerable work supporting the Marines in the territory south of Da Nang where they were continuously engaged in battle.

A Navy F-4 Phantom in a dive releasing bombs

After 3 months of flying, I was assigned to work on the ground for the next 3 months doing temporary duty supporting a brigade of Korean Marines who were also fighting south of Da Nang. My job was to coordinate tactical air support for them using Army, Marine, and Navy gunfire. There I was, an aviator wearing a helmet and a flak jacket in the field with the Koreans! Most of this took place about 10 miles south of Da Nang. My impression was that the Korean Marines were much better on defense than on offense. No Korean Marine base, to my knowledge, was ever overrun. They would defend to the death. However, when they were trying to capture a position, my experience with them was that they would take some incoming rounds, then fall back in a defensive circle until the enemy left, and then move forward.

I went back to my F-4 squadron in Da Nang in January 1969, just in time for us to move south about 60 miles to a Marine air base at Chu Lai. It had a 10,000 ft runway and was now home to two Marine Air Groups including three or four squadrons of A-3's. One of our new jobs was to provide BARCAP missions supporting the carriers out on Yankee Station. We were tasked to fly up north to help the Navy against any MiGs which might venture out of Hanoi to attack the carriers. On these flights we would carry air-to-air missiles. We were vectored toward some MiGs, but they always turned and headed back north.

Our F-4 squadron was still also doing close air support for units on the ground. We would generally come in at a high dive angle of 30 to 40 degrees from 3000 ft and release a Mark 82 "snake eye" bomb. These had a special fin to provide drag to slow it down before it hit the ground so that we could get away safely before the explosion. We usually carried six of these on a mission. Other times we would be loaded with three napalm canisters which looked like big beer barrels. We received orders through the chain of command located in Da Nang. The response time was actually quick. As soon as a battalion asked for support, unless someone objected, we were headed there to help. Once a week at Chu Lai we would go "hot pad," meaning that planes in our squadron would be ready to fly immediately on either air-to-air or air-to-ground missions. This hot pad stuff rotated daily between squadrons. We would usually get this job once a week or so. It was not uncommon to fly five to six missions a day when on air-to-ground hot pad. In addition, the Marine Corps was tasked to maintain an orbit point over Hue from sunrise to sunset. We could respond to anyone in I Corps needing help in 10-15 minutes. Basically, we were flying around in circles and would refuel from C-130's. When we were coming back to base, the authorities would generally find some target for you to drop your bombs on or direct you offshore to jettison your weapons before landing. Although we could land with weapons, we didn't want to because of the obvious danger.

I did receive some small arms fire from the hills when on missions west of Hoi An. One time we were trying to provide cover for a Marine recon *unit which was being extracted from the hills. We were dropping napalm to assist them, and I got four to five holes in the left side of our airplane. Fortunately, Chu Lai was only about 25 miles away. Our left engine was shot up, so I flew back single engine. The good news was that the Marine recon unit did get out safely. While I was at Chu Lai, we lost a pilot on a bomb run; his RIO was able to eject and an Army helo picked him up.*

When we were flying out of Chu Lai, we were often in Laos day and night. There was a lot of AAA (anti-aircraft artillery) *there coming from 23 mm and 37 mm guns all along the area of the Ho Chi Minh Trail. If you went further north in Laos near where the trail came in from North Vietnam, you could run into some 57 mm cannon fire. Roughly 80% of these flights were in a flight of two with a wingman.*

When we did the BARCAP for the carriers, we would check in with "Red Crown" which was a surface ship designated to essentially act as a coordinator of all the aircraft up there. Although we were Marines, we were there to supplement the carrier's own aircraft. These were three-hour missions: half hour each way to get there and back and two hours on station. We would refuel day and night off a Marine C-130 flying out of Da Nang to maintain fuel load in case they vectored us to chase something to the north. We would normally receive 10,000 lbs of fuel from a hose about 80 ft long behind the C-130. At night we would find the plane on our radar and put our fuel probe into the basket at the end of the hose. There was an indicator light showing that we were connected.

It was difficult for me to accept the nonchalance of Don (and other aviators I talked to) concerning aerial refueling. In Don's case the two planes were flying at 220 kts, often at night, in extreme proximity to each other with Don approaching a lighted probe dangling from the other aircraft. He then had to engage the probe on the front of his plane approximately 5 ft into this "basket." I was even more astounded when Don told me that Navy and Marine aviators do not do this evolution before receiving their wings as aviators. They learn to do this once they get to their first squadron. I am well aware of the dangers which surface ships face when refueling at sea at night from another ship....but doing this airborne at night while flying at well over 200 mph!!!

In September 1969 our squadron pulled out of Chu Lai and went to Marine Corps Air Station Iwakuni in Japan. I was only there three weeks until I received orders back to El Toro in California where I was married in August 1970. Shortly after that our squadron was relocated to the Marine Air Station in Yuma, Arizona.

Don spent the next two years in Yuma in a training squadron as an instructor. While he was there, he spent six weeks in Miramar, California, flying F-4's in air-to-air combat training in the Top Gun School. He later flew with an Air Force squadron before a later assignment at the Navy Test Pilot School, testing various aircraft including the F-18 fighter. Prior to his retirement in 1985 Don was Commanding Officer of VMFA-314, a squadron of 12 F-18's at El Toro. Following his retirement, Don became a test pilot for McDonnell Douglas and later with Boeing when McDonnell Douglas merged with Boeing.

Don expressed mixed feelings about his role in the war. Like several other aviators, he was bitter about restraints on targets. He mentioned one situation in which he was assigned to conduct a 5th strike on the same target, "Of course," he told me angrily, "the North Vietnamese were ready for us. We flew into a total flak trap."

Dave Secrest

Brunswick, Georgia

"We just let it go, we didn't know"

I wanted to hear Dave's perspective because I was told that he had been involved in maintenance activities for boats in the Navy's Riverine Force in the Mekong Delta region. Prior to our talk, I did not realize that he also had other assignments in Vietnam. I interviewed him via computer at his home in Littleton, North Carolina, where he lives with his wife, Christie.

When I was born in 1943, my dad was a Navy dentist stationed at Glynco Naval Air Station near Brunswick, Georgia. After the war, we lived at Camp LeJeune in North Carolina. When Dad was later assigned to duty in Panama, my parents decided that I would be better off finishing high school at the Severn School in Severna Park, Maryland. It was a boarding school, and I enjoyed the experience. I thought that I was going to go to Duke for college. However, at the last minute I received a waiver for my eyesight to gain admission to the Naval Academy, so I opted to go there. While at Navy I did intramural sports, mostly squash and cross country.

Glynco Naval Air Station was the base for the Navy's fleet of airships (a.k.a., blimps) which were used during WW II to patrol the U.S. east coast looking for German submarines. It was established in 1942 and totally revived the economic life of the local counties. Operating from two huge, hastily constructed hangars, the eight blimps also flew thousands of hours performing convoy escort duty protecting ships carrying essential war materials. The unusual name was simply an abbreviation of Glynn County. The airship program was not disestablished until 1959 when the base was converted to a Naval aviation training center. The base was closed in 1974 and is now home to a Federal Law Enforcement Training Center.

Because my poor eyesight disqualified me for aviation, I chose to go Surface Navy. At graduation, I was assigned as Main Propulsion Assistant on a destroyer, USS NOA (DD-841), homeported in Mayport, Florida, but I actually met the ship in the Gulf of Aden. I had to take several military hops to get to Yemen, where I was taken out to the ship on a launch. I was escorted by heavily armed men because of hostilities involving the Brits and the locals. Fortunately for me, the Chief Petty Officers on the ship took me under their wings and taught me everything so that I had some clue what to do. We returned home via the Suez Canal and the Mediterranean. I met my future wife, Christie, in Florida where she was a schoolteacher. My next assignment was to another destroyer, USS THOMAS J GARY (DER-326), a radar picket ship in Key West, Florida. The ship had air-start diesel engines and soon went into overhaul in Jacksonville, Florida. What I remember the most about that overhaul was the Fairbanks Morse diesel tech rep who had the largest biceps I have ever seen on a human. After the overhaul, we did radar guiding exercises with the Air Force who were practicing some highly classified training exercises off the Florida Panhandle in the event that they had to try to extract downed aviators or POWs in North Vietnam.

I volunteered in early 1968 to go to Vietnam. I was sent to the Naval Support Activity in Saigon and arrived in country in October 1968. My first job was the Mobile Riverine Force Project Officer. This assignment got me the use of a Ford F-150 pickup and a Boston Whaler. When Riverine Force boats needed parts, my job was to find them. Fortunately, the fellow I relieved had located a bunch of small Vietnamese shops in Saigon that could produce parts that we needed for the riverine boats. I would drive my truck through the city to one of these shops and pay them in Vietnamese money. These guys could make anything! It was a total black market operation – and it worked.

My next job was Officer-in-Charge of the YR-9, a floating barge which we converted to a repair facility. This barge replaced USS HARNETT COUNTY (LST-821), a Landing Ship, Tank, which had been servicing all the U.S. boats which were operating up the rivers near Cambodia. The LST had been attacked with RPG's several times; the plan was that our YR-9 would be a less valuable target than a "real" ship like the LST. So, the Navy in Vietnam, now under Admiral Zumwalt, built a base at Ben Luc where the barge was to be berthed. We dredged a slip near the bridge where Route 4 crosses the river and slid the barge in. We just dumped all our discharges directly into the river; there were no environmental rules. On March 28, 1969, we came under a mortar attack which blew up a lot of warehouses on the adjacent 9th Army Division base. I was living in a small trailer on top of YR-9. The attack lasted about an hour, and I got hit by some shrapnel before I could run to a nearby bunker. The YR-9 also got hit by a lot of shrapnel, but we were able to repair the damage and were soon in business supporting Operation GIANT SLINGSHOT which began in late 1968.

Operation GIANT SLINGSHOT was a major thrust of the Navy's "brown water" operations. The goal was to eliminate or drastically reduce Communist force infiltration into South Vietnam along the Vam Co Dong and Vam Co Tay rivers flowing out of Cambodia. The tactic was to use small, armed boats to take the fight to the enemy before they could become entrenched in South Vietnam. These rivers (the term brown water comes from the typically muddy rivers of Vietnam, as opposed to clearer sea water) are on each side of a "land peninsula" which juts into Vietnam from Cambodia west of Saigon. Because of its shape, this land mass is referred to as "The Parrot's Beak." The name of the operation was based on the slingshot shape formed by the two rivers. The operation officially began on December 5, 1968, with patrols beginning the next day. GIANT SLINGSHOT was a major effort and involved coordination with both U.S. and South Vietnamese armies and U.S. Special Forces units. By January 1969, Navy riverine forces were engaging the enemy on an average of three times daily. Firefights on the Vam Co Dong River near the Cambodian border became so frequent that the area became known as "Blood Alley." A detailed history of OPERATION SLINGSHOT can be found online under "RiverVet." Dave's vessel, the YR-9, remained at Ben Luc until February 1970 when it was towed to Nha Be a few miles south of Saigon.

Soon we were servicing all of the riverine boats involved in SLINGSHOT. All the men working on YR-9 were senior enlisted guys and Limited Duty Officers (LDO's) who could make pretty much whatever was needed. For example, we installed heavy cyclone fencing around exposed parts of the boats to detonate enemy rockets before they ended up in your lap. We had skilled labor, a lot of clever guys, and a Supply Officer who could get anything, including a decorated tablecloth for Christmas dinner.

**Ben Luc site of mooring of YR-9 in slip
off Vam Co Dong River 1969**

I next became the Maintenance Officer for a new repair facility being constructed at Ben Luc. I stayed aboard YR-9 because I had a great bed which had been custom-built for me. We were now working closely with the Seabees because they had a crane which could lift damaged boats out of the river so we could work on them. The crane went into the river a couple of times, but we always managed to get it out. When the USS WESTCHESTER COUNTY (LST-1167) got hit by a mine set by Viet Cong frogmen, the CO wisely grounded the ship to keep it from sinking. Unfortunately, the explosion was next to a berthing area and some Chief Petty Officers were killed by the blast. I happened to be there shortly after this took place and immediately started to coordinate repairs.

Sometimes I had to improvise to get equipment for the remote pontoons which were being used upriver to store fuel and ammo near the Cambodian border - often by "borrowing" things like fuel pumps from Army bases. When I would drive on local roads to procure things, I had a M-79 grenade launcher with me on the dashboard in my F-150. I practiced firing it a few times but never had to shoot it at enemy forces. Highway 4, which I frequently traveled, had a section just off of it known as Ambush Alley....it was a very bad idea to travel anywhere at night.

The Vietnamese Navy assigned a Lieutenant to shadow me when I was on YR-9 so he could take over when we turned the war over to the South Vietnamese. He was a very nice man, but he had zero English capability. I asked for a replacement, and they sent me Lieutenant Hung who was superb. During that mortar attack, he got hit bad and had blood coming out of his ear. He did have a pulse. We carried him out and he survived. He later sent me a very nice letter following his recovery. I never received a replacement for him.

When my tour in Vietnam ended in October 1969, I received orders to a SOSUS station in Cape Hatteras, North Carolina. I was there a few years before the Navy sent me to Destroyer School. My next assignment was to USS BORDELON (DD-881) where I was the Chief Engineer. It was homeported in Charleston, South Carolina, and believe it or not, I was soon headed back to Vietnam. We went through the Panama Canal, transited the Pacific via Midway Island before heading to Yankee Station in the South China Sea. We were initially supporting Operation LINEBACKER which had begun in May 1972. This was the renewed bombing attack against North Vietnam by Navy aircraft carriers and the Air Force. We sometimes were sent to investigate the position of downed U.S. aircraft. This was sobering because we would find only debris fields floating in the ocean. We never found any bodies, live or dead - just plane debris. Also, when Marines called us to provide support near the DMZ, we would fire our 5"/38 guns wherever the spotters asked us to target. On other occasions our job would be to find and direct fire at a sampan crossing an inland river or running near the coast. We never knew if these small boats were carrying troops or a family. We just let it go, we didn't know. This uncertainty often bothered me....we usually had no idea who or what we were shooting at.

SOSUS stations were highly classified Sound Surveillance Systems designed to process data from hydrophones located far in the ocean to detect Soviet submarines. At the time, even the word SOSUS was classified. The cover story was that these facilities were engaged strictly in oceanographic research.

Just before we were due to come home, we were near the North Vietnamese shore and suddenly received an enemy round hitting in the water just forward of us, then another one just aft. We were bracketed! As we maneuvered to get the hell out of there asap, one of our shafts developed a bearing problem, forcing us to have to leave on one screw. Fortunately, that one screw was enough, or we would have probably been sunk. On the way back to the states, we received great maintenance work in both Subic Bay and at the Ship Repair Facility in Guam.

Following this last Vietnam experience, Dave went to a billet in Cartagena, Columbia, as an engineering advisor for the Columbian Navy. He then proceeded through several other surface ship and shore assignments, including Commanding Officer of the destroyer tender, USS PUGET SOUND (AD-38), before retiring as a Captain in 1994. Dave's experiences illustrate the importance of repair facilities to keep the instruments of war operating in challenging conditions. There could be no effective riverine forces taking the fight to the enemy on the rivers of South Vietnam without a dedicated repair facility staffed with competent mechanics with access to necessary repair parts. He still is uneasy about having to fire at sampans without positive identification. The fog of war often lingers in one's mind for a lifetime.

Frank Corah

East Aurora, New York
"Those are lousy odds"

I interviewed Frank via computer from his home in Coronado, California, where he lives with his wife, Sandy. We initially talked about our respective high school sports experiences. Suffice it to say that Frank was considerably more successful than I was; he lettered both in football and baseball. I, on the other hand, ended my football career in 4th grade with a concussion. My baseball resume was even more pathetic, but I did not get injured. Frank began by recalling his early interest in becoming an aviator.

While I was in high school, I decided that I wanted to fly. I applied to all three major service academies, but Navy recruited me for football and arranged that I could get an appointment. But when I took the entrance physical, I failed because I didn't have 20/20 vision. I was very upset, but when I got home, I had a telegram telling me not to worry because they could still get me in. So I arrived at Annapolis and played Plebe (freshman) football, but had the bad luck to be there when we had the best team in history. I would be, at best, the third string fullback and decided that varsity football at Navy was not in my future. So I played rugby the next three years.

When service selection came around, I chose the NFO option for aviation. When I got to Pensacola, I kept re-taking the eye exam until the hospital corpsman passed me, which put me into the pilot training program. I had good grades in flight school and was able to get selected for jets. Flying the F-8 Crusader was my top choice because it was a sweet plane to fly. I was assigned to my first squadron, VF-111, the Sundowners, which flew off USS INTREPID (CVS-11). It was definitely one of the older carriers and had been built during the middle of World War II. It even had a wooden flight deck. Our squadron consisted of six aircraft; we were the only fighter planes aboard. Most of the others were attack aircraft. I picked the ship up in Norfolk and we sailed to Vietnam via the Horn of Africa. We arrived at Yankee Station in July 1968. We flew an early model of the F-8, and because of our poor radar, we did not fly at night. We were doing missions along the beaches and escorting Alpha strikes. The MiGs were coming down from the Hanoi area about every two weeks, so everyone was very jazzed up about maybe getting into some action with them.

The role of a NFO (Naval Flight Officer) is to operate the weapons and sensor systems in an aircraft. He is not a pilot but does assist the pilot in many mission responsibilities. NFO's are line officers and are eligible to be squadron commanders or to be Captain of an aircraft carrier. Frank's successful transition to pilot after finally passing the vision exam was rare. An Alpha strike is a Navy term for an attack consisting of a large number of carrier aircraft, often against what is regarded as a high value target. Three variants of the MiG aircraft were used by the North Vietnamese and were worthy opponents of Frank's F-8.

On September 18, 1968, my wingman and I were doing a MiGCAP to the west of one of the AAA batteries. There was a valley between North Vietnam and Cambodia called Happy Valley and we heard chatter on our radio that sounded like Vietnamese - which made no sense. My wingman suddenly yelled, "I've got a bogey at 9 o'clock." It was a MiG-21, but when he saw us he made a huge turn and headed north toward Hanoi. He probably thought that he could sneak up and surprise us, but we saw him and began to chase him as he headed away. He headed into a cloud layer and dove down causing us to lose him in the clouds. When we came back to the carrier, the intelligence guys didn't believe us because we were just a couple of JO's (Junior Officers). The next day our CO decided that he wanted to go out for some action and took me as his wingman on the first sortie. No MiGs came out for us, but on the second sortie that day they did come out, and the flight leader did shoot down one of the MiGs. Flying with the CO was unusual for me. We generally tried to keep the same wingman on our missions because we got to know each other's moves and could anticipate what was going to happen.

"MiGCAP" stands for MiG Combat Air Patrol. During this assignment, Frank was responsible for defending carrier aircraft from the threat of MiG attacks as the American planes were going to or from a mission.

Our primary weapon for dog fighting was the Sidewinder missile, but in those days you pretty much had to get behind a plane to use that weapon. The "sweet spot" to use the Sidewinder was about a mile behind the other guy. The minimum range to use the weapon was 1000 ft. We later learned from defectors that the reason the North Vietnamese pilots feared the F-8 was because of our guns which could be used from any direction. The MiGs were coming down from the north about every two weeks that summer, so it was a great time to be a fighter pilot. The F-8's would shoot one down, and the MiGs would go back and re-group.

One of our classmates, Barney Broms, was an attack pilot on our ship. He got shot down over North Vietnam while flying an A-4 on a strike mission. We know that he rolled in to attack but suddenly made a transmission, "There's flak all around me." No one heard from him again. We had three squadrons of those A-4's aboard INTREPID; it was primarily an attack carrier with A-4 squadrons of 12 planes each, our six F-8 fighter aircraft, and 4 photo birds. Those were also F-8's which took all the photos of the damage inflicted. Because these F-8's carried no weapons, we had to escort them on their missions to provide protection.

Just before the 1968 Presidential election in November, President Johnson announced that the U.S. would no longer bomb targets in the Hanoi area, so we were now restricted from the north and had to stay below 19N latitude. This kept us at least 125 miles south of the North Vietnamese capital. As a result of this restriction, we were now flying most of our missions over North Vietnam from the city of Vinh south to the DMZ. This policy meant that we were going after what were essentially low-value targets down in the North Vietnamese panhandle. We were totally frustrated by this political restriction and the fact that most of our targets were being selected in Washington, rather than by our on-scene commanders.

INTREPID was on Yankee Station from July to December 1968 in one month periods separated by returns for repairs and crew liberty, mostly in Subic Bay in the Philippines. While we were in Subic we would always have to get our wooden deck replaced; it was fascinating to see a swarm of carpenters come down to the ship and put on a new deck. On our way home INTREPID made a port call to Sydney, Australia, where I detached and flew back to San Diego. I was transferred to a different squadron, VF-21, which left again for Yankee Station on USS HANCOCK (CV-19) in September 1970. We had new planes, the F-8J, which had a sensational radar enabling us to fly night missions. We were still not doing strike missions over the north, but we were doing frequent photo recon up there. Of course, we provided fighter protection on all these missions, but never saw any MiGs. Apparently, everybody had decided to leave each other alone.

One of our problems was that three of our new F-8J's had "ramp strikes" during night landings on HANCOCK. These accidents took place because the F-8J had been modified to land slower than previous versions. It had not been properly tested before we got the planes. The plane was underpowered for landings, and because of the way it was constructed it was difficult to see over the nose of the plane as you were approaching the carrier. When the plane hit the ramp while attempting a landing, it produced a dramatic scene. There are all sorts of flames with wreckage all over the deck; it is like "Apocalypse Now." All three of these pilots were able to eject safely; each accident took place during low visibility situations, and the pilots were often shot up above the clouds by the ejection seat explosion and came floating down behind the ship. The sailors on the carrier deck were trained to immediately throw their light wands, which they had been using to guide planes on the deck, into the water to mark the spot where the pilot would probably come down because the carrier keeps going at high speed. This way the rescue helicopter has a good chance of finding the pilot. I never had to eject, thank God. I did 57 night landings on HANCOCK and felt genuinely lucky because it turned out that the mean time between ramp strikes with the F-8 was 54. Those are lousy odds.

We had to refuel while airborne essentially every night. These were tricky evolutions, especially if you had to bolt on a landing and needed gas real bad. We would usually refuel from an A-3 tanker with both of us doing about 280 kts. It was all done visually once we got close to each other, even in bad weather. On our missions we would usually launch at night, then immediately get refueled to get topped off with about 2000 lbs of fuel before going off to do our BARCAP during a two-hour flight. The tanker would always be hanging around if we needed help during the landing process. Plugging in to the tanker hose takes some practice, but once you get the hang of it, refueling becomes routine.

BARCAP is an acronym for Barrier Combat Air Patrol. These missions involved fighter aircraft setting up a barrier between the direction of a perceived threat and an aircraft carrier or a Navy battle group. The barrier is established a sufficient distance from the carrier to allow for early warning and intercept of a threat.

When I came back from the cruise on HANCOCK in late 1971, I put in my resignation from the Navy. I was unhappy with the way we were doing the war. It was crazy. We were being sent in harm's way, but could not attack targets which would allow us to win the war. I went to work for Grumman Corporation but soon landed a job flying for Continental Airlines. Not long afterwards several of us got furloughed by Continental, so I went back with Grumman for a job setting up a pilot training program in Iran. My wife and I didn't have any kids yet, so she accompanied me. It was an experience. At times we didn't know what was going to happen; many days when I came home from work, my wife was crying. Fortunately, I was recalled by Continental, but when the airline pilot strike took place in 1983, I got a new job working in Switzerland. Seven years later I was back flying for Continental and flew for them until 2003.

Frank's disenchantment was not so much with the Navy, but with the conduct of the air war. Based on my interviews with other Navy and Marine pilots, he was not alone in this feeling. U.S. bombing strategy was based on policies directed by President Johnson and his Secretary of Defense. Whenever Johnson would halt bombing in an attempt to induce the North Vietnamese to negotiate, the Vietnamese would use these quiet periods to strengthen their anti-aircraft defense and to move more supplies to the south. Navy (and Air Force) pilots were prohibited from striking meaningful targets while being subjected to significantly increased dangers. Watching fellow pilots getting shot down during attacks on essentially meaningless targets while Hanoi and its major supply chains were off-limits was a source of anger and frustration not only for the pilots but also many senior military leaders who were arguing futilely for permission to conduct missions to end the war.

Paul Rogers

Portsmouth, Virginia
"We were in a terrible
location"

A classmate told me that Paul had considerable experience late in the war involving PBR's (Patrol Boat Riverine), the first boat specifically built for the "Brown Water Navy" in Vietnam. These small boats were used from early 1966 until the South Vietnam government collapsed in 1975. Initially, they were used exclusively by Navy personnel, but were later turned over to the South Vietnamese Navy. These fiberglass boats were just over 30 ft long and were fast (over 28 kts) due to water jet propulsion. A yacht company in North Carolina did the initial design. Four enlisted men operated the boat, which was equipped with .50 caliber machine guns, a grenade launcher, and 7.62 mm light machine guns. The crew also had access to handguns, rifles, hand grenades, and even shotguns. Armor and shielding had been sacrificed in order to achieve shallow draft and high speed. It was perfect for the shallow rivers and canals in the Mekong Delta region. I interviewed Paul via computer from his home in Southport, NC, where he lives with wife, Suzanne.

I was born at the Naval Hospital in Portsmouth, Virginia, where my dad was serving in the Navy as a Pharmacist's Mate. During my teenage years, we were living in Annapolis, and I attended high school there. Dad was now an officer and was stationed at the hospital on the Naval Academy grounds where we also lived. I actually had a key to Gate One so I could deliver newspapers outside the grounds each morning. One of my customers was the same Mrs. Marshall who taught all of us how to dance during our Plebe year.

Every midshipman of our era remembers Mrs. Marshall. She was the Academy's "Social Director," whose responsibilities included trying to teach us to dance during our first year. There were no female midshipmen then, so we actually had to dance with each other while learning the foxtrot and other popular dances of the time. We endured this embarrassment in preparation for "tea dances" which were also mandatory. Roughly six times a year, Mrs. Marshall would "import" hundreds of local college girls for us to dance with in a large armory next to our living quarters, Bancroft Hall. Midshipmen preferred to call these events "tea fights" for reasons I will not elaborate. In spite of Mrs. Marshall's best efforts, most of us never became accomplished dancers. However, several classmates ended up marrying young ladies first met at these tea fights.

I had long wanted to attend USNA and was able to receive a Presidential appointment. While I was at Navy, I was a gymnast. My professional goal was to become a line officer driving ships. After graduation I received orders to USS WILTSIE (DD-716), a destroyer operating out of San Diego, which deployed to Vietnam in early 1966. One of my lasting impressions during deployments was the amazing logistics chain required to keep all our ships operating over there for such long periods. We would meet supply ships every few days for fuel and food while we were operating with the carriers at Yankee Station, mostly in the North SAR (Search and Rescue) area in the Gulf of Tonkin. During this duty, one fighter aircraft went into the water 2000 yards from us; he was safely picked up by a helo. On several occasions, our radar showed contacts coming toward us, but we quickly learned that the atmospheric conditions there off the coast produced surface ducting often causing false blips on our radar. This may have been what happened during the infamous Gulf of Tonkin Incident in 1964.

We also did gunfire support for some of U.S. forces engaged in battles further south near Hue. We would fire on coordinates provided to us from spotters. Wherever we were told to shoot, that's where we aimed our 5"/38 guns. We were shooting, day and night, and often weren't sure which branch of service or whom we were supporting.

I then left WILTSIE to spend six months at Destroyer School before being assigned to USS PICKING (DD-685) in Long Beach. Right after I reported aboard, we headed to the Gulf of Tonkin doing much the same as on WILTSIE. We watched as one of the carriers lost an A-6 plane during launching due to a "cold cat." Both aviators aboard were lost.

A "cold cat" refers to a malfunction of the catapult launching system on an aircraft carrier. Several things can go wrong while launching aircraft, such as the catapult not receiving a full amount of steam to enable the aircraft to reach launch speed.

Most of our ops during this cruise involved gunfire support. During the early part of 1968 we were doing a lot of firing in response to enemy movements during and after the Tet Offensive. On our way home, we found ourselves in the middle of a typhoon which seriously damaged our ship. We were concerned about losing it, but we got home OK.

In July 1969, I received orders for three months of PBR training at Mare Island, California, in preparation for duty with a detachment of PBR's in the Mekong Delta. I was now a Lieutenant and was the most senior officer in the class. Upon completion, I was sent to Chau Duc which was up a major river near the Cambodian border. I was the Executive Officer for two divisions of PBR's. We were living on a YRBM (Yard Repair and Berthing Barge) and doing patrols of canals in the area. Each division of PBR's had 12 boats manned by four enlisted personnel each. We would patrol during the day inspecting sampans for contraband, and at night we would go along the canals to set up an ambush on the shore looking for VC or NVA trying to infiltrate into the Delta from the mountains in Cambodia. Our boats would hide on the Cambodian side of the canal, initiate contact, and call in air support. We weren't "bait" per se, and often handled the action ourselves. Unfortunately, we did suffer casualties during these missions. We would typically send out six to eight boats on an operation.

We never lost a PBR, but we did lose some men, mostly due to small arms fire. It was the CO's job to write the letters to the families. I had to do this when I took over command. It is a terrible responsibility. I also went on many of these ops and carried a .38 revolver loaded with tracer shots to direct fire at night. I would call in helos and then direct their fire with the tracers.

The aircraft we called in were the "Seawolves" (UH-1 Hueys) and the "Black Ponies," (Rockwell OV-10 Broncos). Both were loaded with firepower which was very impressive. At this time, they were not allowed to fly into Cambodia and had to fly parallel to the canal to assist us. Insane rules! We were in Cambodia, but they couldn't be. My aim with that .38 was a standing joke among the crews. One of our sailors drew a cartoon making fun of my accuracy using that .38!

After six months, I was tasked to take command of River Assault Division 131, an ATSB (Advanced Tactical Support Base), on the Song Ong Doc River. I had no experience with the "monitor" boats (converted WW II Landing Craft Medium) there, but when I went to Saigon to talk to Admiral Zumwalt, he told me that he was fine with me taking the job. The base was located way down the Delta near Ca Mau. One of our boats had a flame thrower and another a 105 mm howitzer. Both had machine guns. We were in a terrible location and were incredibly vulnerable because the entire region around us was a VC stronghold. None of us went into the local town because of the danger. We were frequently shelled at night and often had a Navy or Coast Guard destroyer anchored offshore to provide gunfire support. On our missions up the river, we frequently took

rocket fire, but I was never injured myself. We did suffer the loss of two of our men during an unfortunate friendly fire episode when we had a Coast Guard cutter offshore to provide support. We had given them a marker with an offset, but for some reason, they didn't apply the offset and hit us with 10 shells before we could send them a cease fire. As far as I know, no one on the cutter was punished for killing our two sailors.

Shortly after I arrived, we began the process of turning over some of our boats to the Vietnamese Navy. I mostly trusted them, but their biggest shortcoming was properly maintaining the boats. Just before I left, there was a major battle in September 1970 at what became known as "VC Lake," which was not far from us. A contingent of South Vietnamese troops had inadvertently located an entire regiment of VC and NVA and were pinned down. When our forces came to help, two Seawolf helicopters were shot down and their pilots killed. There was controversy about the Army's refusal to assist because they felt it was too dangerous. One of those lost was a close friend of mine. There is considerable coverage of this battle available online.

Less than two weeks after I left Vietnam, in October 1970, our base was destroyed when VC mortar fire hit the ammo and fuel storage areas, and the base was overrun by the VC. Two PBR's were sunk during that attack and two Navy sailors were killed. The base was subsequently moved a few kilometers upstream, and all our boats were turned over to the South Vietnamese.

ATSB site at Cau Mau with monitors outboard

After I left Vietnam, my next assignment was at the Naval Academy teaching Seamanship and Tactics. Six months after I was home, my wife, Suzanne, surprised me by joining the Navy! I later went to a cruiser out of Norfolk and, after another assignment, left the Navy in June 1978. Suzanne served four years, and we ended up in northern Virginia where I was working as a consultant. Suzanne and I later ran our own company for several years, but we retired for good about eight years ago and moved to North Carolina.

It is probably safe to say that none of our classmates who opted to become surface officers after graduation in June 1965 dreamed that they would soon find themselves fighting with guns and flamethrowers in the "Brown Water Navy" of Vietnam. Our small arms training at the Academy consisted only of firing the M-1 rifle and the .45 pistol during our first summer. Yet the officers in charge of these small boats, constantly in harm's way, acquitted themselves well by adapting to the challenges. Many were in situations involving hand-to-hand combat in unimaginable conditions. Although most survived, the memories linger.

Laddie Coburn

Marana, Arizona

"I heard a lot of 'Holy Shits' "

When Laddie learned that I was writing about experiences of members of our Naval Academy class in Vietnam, he contacted me to share his story. He surmised (correctly) that I had not interviewed anyone who had flown in the RA-5C Vigilante during carrier operations in Vietnam. He shared with me a presentation, *Vietnam and the Naval Aviation Warrior*, which he has given to groups in Colorado where he now lives. I interviewed Laddie via computer from his home in Grand Lake during a major snowstorm there. Laddie was accompanied by his dog, Obie, during our talk.

I was born in Lansing, Michigan, where my dad was an electrician. Early in my school years, our family moved to Marana, Arizona, northwest of Tucson. I attended Marana High School and played most sports, including football and track. From an early age I wanted to fly, probably because Dad was a pilot for the Civil Air Patrol. We were living near an air base where they trained pilots, and had B-52 bombers from Davis-Monthan Air Force Base flying over our house all the time. I joined the Civil Air Patrol as a cadet; one of the benefits was that all of us got to take a ride in a T-33 jet up at Williams Air Force Base near Phoenix. All of this made me determined to go to one of the military academies so that I could become an aviator. My first choice was the Air Force Academy, but I did not get selected. I had appointments to West Point and Annapolis from Senator Goldwater and quickly chose Navy. West Point was not a consideration.

Although I had 20/20 vision when I entered the Naval Academy, studying under the bed covers with a flashlight for much of plebe year ruined my eyes for being a pilot. At service selection I chose aviation in order to become a NFO (Naval Flight Officer) which did not require 20/20. NFO's train on all types of aircraft. After I received my wings, I was selected to fly the RA-5C Vigilante. Of my five NFO classmates who were assigned to this type of plane, I was the only volunteer because it had a reputation as being dangerous to fly. Since the NFO does none of the flying, as a "back-seater" you are at the mercy of the pilot's skill. We trained at Naval Air Station Sanford in Florida with Reconnaissance Attack Squadron THREE (RVAH-3) for six months before deploying to the Mediterranean in the fall of 1967 on USS SARATOGA (CV-60).

RA-5C Vigilante in flight

While we were in the Med, my pilot and I became involved in what I call "the KIEV incident." The KIEV was a brand-new Soviet aircraft carrier which had just come out of the Black Sea following construction. We were doing a surface ship surveillance flight in the eastern Med when we were assigned to look for KIEV. We were told not to go within three miles if we found it. We found the ship and called our report. There was a miscommunication over whether or not we were allowed to go within those three miles. Our bosses apparently told us that we were not allowed to go in close, but I understood their communication for us to go on in. So, we proceeded to "rig" this new Soviet ship, which means we flew up and down both the port and starboard sides and took a lot of photos. When we returned to the carrier, the Admiral was hopping mad. He was standing on the flight deck waiting for us. He put us in hock, yelling that we had violated the rules of engagement. His version of "hock" was that we were grounded. He was even considering pulling our wings. However, the CAG (Carrier Air Wing Commander) told us he was proud of what we did and got us back flying in three days. It was not a bad hock.

The North American Rockwell Vigilante was originally intended for missions as a Mach 2 carrier-based supersonic nuclear bomber. It was the first bomber to incorporate a digital computer and several other innovations. It even had a gold coating to reflect heat in areas near the bomb bay. Shortly after its introduction into the fleet in 1961, the Vigilante's role was changed due to technical difficulties and a revaluation of the Navy's nuclear strike mission. New models were now produced as strictly reconnaissance aircraft with the pilot and reconnaissance/attack navigator (RAN) sitting in tandem. Note in the photo above that RAN's only windows are small squares above on port and starboard. The aircraft proved to be challenging to maintain and was, as attested to by Laddie, very maintenance intensive.

We next deployed to Vietnam on USS RANGER (CV-61). We flew cross-country from Florida to the West Coast to train out there near where RANGER was homeported. Our squadron, RVAH-9, consisted of three aircraft and five crews. The Vigilante was difficult to maintain, particularly the avionics and photographic equipment, not the engines. We loaded all our logistics on RANGER before she departed. Our squadron flew the planes from Alameda, California, across the Pacific via Hawaii, Midway, Wake, Guam, and finally to Cubi Point in the Philippines where we boarded RANGER. We arrived at Yankee Station in late fall 1968 shortly after the U.S. declared a bombing halt over all of North Vietnam. The Vigilante was an unarmed reconnaissance plane, so we were the only ones on our carrier flying over North Vietnam. This created a situation where the Vigilantes were essentially target practice for all the SAM sites in North Vietnam because we were the only targets for them to shoot at. We always stayed above 20,000 ft to avoid small arms fire or artillery, but this put us squarely in the target zone for the missiles.

All of our intelligence gathering was done automatically by the PECM (passive electronics countermeasures) pod which we carried. It was like an electron vacuum cleaner which would pick up all electronic signals on both sides of the airplane. When we returned to the carrier, that pod was removed, and the information downloaded for all the intel people to analyze. We were gathering photographic intelligence and also had a side-looking radar which was high-resolution providing three ft resolution. That is nothing compared to what is available now, but ours was top-of-the-line for the late '60's. That radar could not only pick up trucks on the ground, but our intelligence guys could tell what type of truck. All of this was from 20,000 ft! To gather these photos, we had to fly straight and level and keep below 450 kts. We couldn't get good resolution at supersonic speeds. Each mission was a 90-minute sortie. If we had all airplanes available, I would fly two sorties a day, one at day and one at night. One of my jobs was Navigator, but fortunately the Vigilante nav system was a state-of-the art inertial navigation system. It would also automatically annotate all photos with the latitude and longitude.

Some of our other missions extended into Laos where there also were SAM sites, but our plane had a warning system to tell us when we were being scanned and locked on. They were using the "Spoon Rest" radar to detect us, and the SA-2 missile systems used the "Fan Song" radar which could track us above 20,000 ft. When we knew that they had launched, we would immediately take evasive actions such as performing a "Split-S" maneuver. This required us to roll over 180 degrees (go upside down), then dive suddenly straight toward the ground making an S-turn while pulling 6-10 g's. From my position in the aircraft, I could usually not see the missile, but the pilot could. I heard a lot of "Holy shits!" One of the planes in our squadron was hit by missile shrapnel with a large piece hitting just 12 inches behind the NFO seat. That plane made it back to the carrier, but it was so badly damaged that we had to crane it off when we got back to Subic Bay to have it repaired in Japan.

The SA-2 surface-to-air missile was developed by the Soviet Union in the mid-1950's. It was a very effective system which had been used to shoot down Gary Powers in the American U-2 spy plane over the USSR in 1960, and then in 1962 another U-2 over Cuba. The North Vietnamese started receiving these missile systems from the Soviets in the spring of 1965. Their sites were well-camouflaged and frequently moved. Most SAM sites were ringed with AAA. A typical site had six missiles on launchers surrounded by support vans, a Spoon Rest acquisition radar and the Fan Song guidance radar. Aircraft could be detected at up to 70 miles, and the Fan Song could guide as many as three missiles at once against one target. North Vietnamese SAM crews could move the entire site in about four hours. This missile flew at Mach 3.5 and had a 288-lb blast fragmentation warhead. It was a formidable weapon.

Often when we were behind enemy lines we would have two F-4 fighters as our escort in case any MiGs decided to come after us. As far as I know, none ever did, at least for us. All of our missions were 90 minutes long. We would often refuel over the ocean from a KA-6 tanker, but we preferred to do this from an Air Force KC-130 tanker because you could get a lot more gas. Like many carrier-based aircraft, we had our share of close calls with running out of fuel. Our worst one occurred on a top-secret mission over North Vietnam doing road recon near the Ho Chi Minh Trail. It was a pitch-black night, no moon, no horizon. We were fired upon and had to do several high-speed evasion maneuvers which burned up a lot of fuel. We desperately needed to refuel to get back to the carrier. We tried multiple plug-in attempts with refueling aircraft but were unsuccessful. Just as we were close to being in extremis, we received some fuel from a KA-3 tanker which was airborne from another carrier.

Although Laddie and his pilots were fortunate not to have been shot down during his 42 missions over North Vietnam and Laos, flying in the Vigilante was risky business. Eighteen RA-5C's were shot down, 14 to AAA fire, three to SAMs, and one to a North Vietnamese MiG-21 fighter. Nine more were lost in operational accidents in Vietnam. It had always been a challenging plane to land on a carrier. On my midshipman summer cruise in 1962 I watched from a destroyer as a Vigilante smashed into the stern of the carrier USS SARATOGA (CV-60) while attempting to land during a routine training exercise in the Atlantic. Both crew members perished.

Laddie left RANGER in May 1969 and managed to find his way from Vietnam to Sweden where he was married. Subsequent assignments took him to post-graduate school where he obtained master's degrees in both Aeronautical Engineering and Electrical Engineering. He continued flying as an NFO in various Navy aircraft and ultimately became an Aeronautical Engineering Duty Officer. He retired from the Navy as a Captain in 1989. Following civilian work at the Navy Air Station at Patuxent River, Maryland, Laddie retired in 2009 to the mountains of Colorado.

Wars can be won or lost on intelligence, based on what you can learn about your enemy. Laddie and his Vigilante buddies flew hours of dangerous missions attempting to put the U.S. at an advantage. How much their work influenced the conduct of the war is difficult to assess because so many decisions in this war were based on politics. There is no doubt that our military had the ability to gain tactical advantage with these intelligence-gathering operations, but most of the effort appears to have been wasted by the highest levels of government.

Bob Shepherd

Tulsa, Oklahoma

"They would hand you a note"

When I asked several Marines if they had any recommendations for a Marine aviator to interview, they all said, "You need to talk to Bob Shepherd." I reached Bob at his home in Conroe, Texas, where he lives with his wife, Paula.

Although I was born in Tulsa, we moved to Fort Worth when I was one year old. My mom was a homemaker, and my dad owned a small dry cleaning and laundry business. When I was a teen, every Wednesday night on TV there were two 30-minute shows following each other, "West Point Story" and "Men of Annapolis." I immediately wanted to go to one of them. When I first applied via my congressman, I didn't get in. So, I went to Iowa State for a year and joined the Air Force ROTC program. When I applied again to Navy, my best friend got the appointment, but I took the physical anyway. I wasn't sure what was going to happen. As luck would have it, my friend broke his elbow, and in early June I received a call from our congressman saying I now had the appointment.

Once I was at Navy for a year, I decided that I wanted to fly, but on my first class cruise on the aircraft carrier USS ROOSEVELT (CV-42) in the Med, they lost seven aircraft due to accidents. Several of my buddies watching this with me said, "You know, Marines also fly, and they don't have to do carrier landings." So, when service selection time came, I chose Marine Corps air. First, I had to go to six months of Marine Basic School at Quantico, Virginia. I then got married to my first wife, Heather, and went to flight school at Pensacola, Florida.

At Pensacola, Marines do flight training with all the Navy aviators. I studied hard, because if a Marine was not in the top 10%, you were probably headed to be a helicopter pilot. I had no desire to do this, so I studied like crazy, and fortunately, I ended up in jets. Once I got my wings in Kingsville, Texas, my first assignment was at Cherry Point, NC, in VMA-AW225. Believe it or not, when I arrived on a Friday, the Gunny Sergeant said to me, "What do you want to fly?" I couldn't believe it. He said I had until Monday to decide. I spent the weekend looking at all their planes: A-4's, F-4's, and A-6's. On Monday I decided on the A-6 Intruder because that plane was the current state-of-the-art. It took me almost a year to be 100% qualified in the A-6 because of all the electronics. Because they held our squadron in North Carolina for almost a year, I became an instructor and flew all different types of planes.

Finally, in January 1969 our entire squadron of 17 A-6's flew together to Vietnam with our planes refueling on the way in the air or on Pacific islands. We were assigned to Da Nang and began to fly every day, often twice a day. When we came back from a mission and there was a bang on the canopy, they would hand you a note while you were refueling saying that troops were in contact with enemy forces and that you had an emergency mission. They would load new ordnance, tell you your new mission, and send you back out.

Our normal load was 28 500-lb bombs; when four A-6's were loaded, they were equivalent to a B-52. We often mixed loads with rockets and even napalm. That was carried in an aluminum tube and would tumble when you dropped it. Most of our bombing runs were at 30 degrees, but with the napalm we would go in flat near tree-top level. Small arms fire was not a problem due to the protection provided by 4 inches of steel underneath us and our bullet-proof canopies. "Triple A," the anti-aircraft fire, was a problem, particularly when we were doing close air support in Laos and at night north on the Ho Chi Minh Trail near Hanoi. Our electronics could tell us when the 23 mm and 37 mm AAA were looking at us and if their radar was locked on. If that happened, we would immediately turn 90 degrees and pull as many g's as we could handle. We saw tracers all the time at night. One evening I was flying with a new bombardier/navigator beside me who was looking at the radar and I punched him to explain the visual difference between the tracers for the 23 mm and 37 mm. He went back to his screen and told me, "Please never show me again."

Due to the electronics on the A-6, we could fly all-weather, in the mountains, at night. I could see the mountains ahead of us on my screen. It takes some getting used to, but we had practiced this in the U.S. in the mountains near Spokane, Washington. When we were in the area over in Laos near the Ho Chi Minh Trail, air control was provided for us by the Air Force. They would give us coordinates for a target and when they wanted us there. I would set it into our computer, and it would tell me how fast I had to go to get to the target on time. We could see enemy trucks at night because our radar could tell us if there was anything on the ground moving over four mph. Even if they pulled over, we also had infrared to see truck engines which were still warm. Normally our targets were ammo dumps and trucks moving troops and supplies. We lost a few aircraft on these missions and sometimes had F-4's to help us if we were getting shot at. The problem was that they sometimes did not know exactly where they were. But I usually liked having them. On one mission, I heard the F-4 say, "Ringneck, break left." The gunners on the ground were getting to be real good; they had started firing behind us and working forward so that we could not see their fire. I broke hard left but still got hit in the rudder, but I made it back. I bought that F-4 pilot, a Marine major, a fifth of whiskey when we returned to Da Nang. Those F-4's and A-4's were being shot down on a regular basis. Another time we got locked on by a missile but being at low altitude really helped because it had to turn around to attack us. We saw it coming on our screen and were able to get away from that one.

We lost two A-6's in our squadron. One was flying under flares, and we think that he accidentally flew his plane into the ground. The other was lost over Laos. All were killed and the bodies not recovered. We often had conversations similar to those in the book, "Flight of the Intruder," where they said, "Why do we do trails every night when we could go to Hanoi and end this thing?" Our position was basically the same. All of us were putting our lives on the line every night; why not do some actual damage?

The A-6 was the only aircraft which could fly regularly during the monsoon season. They shut down the A-4's and F-4's for several weeks. We even had a hook on the tail of our plane to catch a wire on the Da Nang runway, just like doing a carrier landing, except on the ground. Even though the runway was 13,000 feet long, we could still stop with the wire. We were the only ones who could support the Green Berets in the field during the monsoon season. This involved "Beacon Bombing" where the guys on the ground would light off a beacon which we could observe electronically. They would then give us coordinates from that beacon where the enemy was located and all of a sudden, the enemy would be receiving some "mail" from us. We also went up to the DMZ quite a lot because we had a lot of troops working up there.

While I was there, Da Nang was not attacked by mortars so much, but by frequent rocket fire. 'Charlie" would infiltrate the mountains around the base and then place rockets with timed fuses to send those rockets off at 3 to 4 in the morning. We slept in Quonset huts which were surrounded by 50 gallon drums filled with dirt. We always slept with a flak jacket and helmet under our bunk. When the sirens went off warning of an incoming rocket attack, we would just jump out of our rack, roll underneath it, and put on our flak jacket and helmet. Our hut never got hit, but the one next to us was hammered by shrapnel from a rocket. The only damage was that one guy in there lost his new tape recorder. He had just bought it and was pissed.

**Bob in flak jacket and helmet outside hooch
following 1969 attack on ammo dump**

We had a rather famous O'Club. It had been built by Marines and we had Navy, Air Force, and Marine pilots in there every night. It was a wild and woolly place with lots of drinking. Guys would get drunk and start hanging from the rafters. Every once in a while, you would hear a pistol shot! We quickly learned that it was always someone shooting a rat. I don't recall anyone complaining about us drinking and then going out to fly. We had a movie screen set up outside the O Club and often when the lights were turned on to change the movie to the next reel, you would notice that a bunch of the pilots, maybe one-third, would be gone because they had been called out to fly an unscheduled mission. It was a war, and there weren't a lot of rules enforced.

Movies were always a favorite form of nightly entertainment no matter which branch of service. I quickly learned during my initial time on submarines that the junior officer assigned to obtain movies for the duration of a submerged patrol had better bring some good ones aboard or suffer abuse the entire time at sea. The movies were 16 mm and typically consisted of three reels which had to be manually threaded into the projector. When one reel would be complete, the lights were turned on, just as Bob described, for the designated operator to install the new reel and for others to take a head (bathroom) break.

There were some incidents at Da Nang which bothered me. One of the young Marine avionics technicians who was doing work on our A-6's committed suicide. I was assigned to investigate. I found that this kid was scared shitless of perimeter guard duty. Our guys would periodically get pulled out to supplement the infantry troops who were the ones doing regular guard duty for the base. He disappeared on one of these nights and was warned, but he did it again. The Sergeant Major pulled this kid in, stripped him naked, and put him in a bamboo cage all night long in the middle of the squadron area. The next night the kid was again assigned guard duty but went back to his hooch and blew his brains out. In my report I put some of the blame on the Sergeant Major. This was not well received by our Group Commander, a full Colonel. He told me that I was being "a little hard" on the Sergeant Major. I replied that the Sergeant Major was treating our avionics guys the same that he had treated infantry Marines in Korea. I'm not sure if my report went anywhere.

Being a Sergeant Major is a big deal. He is usually the senior enlisted man in the command and has considerable prestige. His duties vary, but frequently he is a confidante to the Commanding Officer concerning personnel matters and is, accordingly, given rather broad latitude. In my opinion, Bob was correct to question the actions of this Sergeant Major. On the other hand, I also understand the reluctance of the Commanding Officer to throw his senior enlisted man under the bus. Leadership is challenging, especially in a wartime setting.

The only other issue was my Commanding Officer, "Black Tom" Griffin. He wasn't Black. He got the nickname because we all felt that his main goal was to make General and that he didn't care about any of us. There was an unwritten rule that when you got to your last two weeks in-country, you could go to the schedulers and request "short-timer" status. This meant that they would not schedule you to fly the dangerous night missions in the north, but you would be given missions in the south. The morning after I did this, Griffin saw me and said, "I'm terribly disappointed in you. I was going to put you in for a medal, but now I don't think so." Griffin was very unpopular; he would hold a lot of daytime inspections when we had been flying all night. Eventually someone fragged his hooch, but he wasn't hurt. I heard that he later died when he crashed a plane back in the states.

The term "fragging" came into use during the Vietnam War to describe a deliberate attempt to kill a fellow soldier, usually a superior, or an officer. As discontent among U.S. soldiers began to increase as the war dragged on, some individuals began to use fragmentation grenades on disliked senior personnel to give the appearance that the senior had been killed by an exploding grenade thrown by the enemy. Soon "fragging" became synonymous with any attempt to use a weapon to kill or harm a superior. I must add that I have no way of determining if the incident involving fragging or the questionable actions of the Sergeant Major were isolated situations within the Marine Corps or were widespread. I can state that no other Marine whom I interviewed was aware of anything comparable.

The enlisted fellows who maintained our planes were great. They were all young guys, but they understood electronics and kept our systems going. They all worked incredibly long hours. Many of them immediately got jobs for the airlines when they left the Marines.

When my Vietnam tour was up, the Marines wanted me to go to Amphibious Warfare School at Quantico for six months. I didn't want to do this, so I put in my letter of resignation. It was at this time that my wife, Heather, and I had a terrible car accident on I-95 near Richmond, Virginia. I was driving on I-95 and we were hit head-on by a drunk driver. I hit the steering wheel and was banged up but survived because of my seat belt. Heather wasn't wearing hers and hit the windshield. She received massive injuries and died that night. The Group Commander called me in and told me that he had lost his son in Vietnam and understood. He said that he was worried what might happen to me if I got out of the service right away in this mental state. If I would pull my resignation, he would send me to the training command back at Beeville where I could fly seven days a week if I wanted to. I took up his offer and built up a lot of flight hours enabling me to be hired immediately by Delta in February 1973 when I left the Marine Corps.

While he was at Beeville, Bob met and married Paula who was teaching in the area. He stayed with Delta Airlines for "one month short of 30 years" ending up flying as Captain of both the 727 and L1011 aircraft. Following his retirement, Bob became a full-time Bible teacher for his local church.

Sonny Harrison

Philadelphia, Pennsylvania
"We've got Indians"

Sonny is a regular at our class luncheons in Annapolis. He is an outgoing friend who enjoys life. Until I had an opportunity to know him better, I would not have guessed his role during the war in Vietnam. He drove from his home in Crownsville, Maryland, to my home in Virginia for our interview. Sonny brought along maps, diaries, and other useful information.

My given first name is Lloyd, but when I was four my uncle started calling me 'Sonny.' Throughout my Navy career, I was always called Lloyd, but to my Naval Academy classmates, I have only been "Sonny." My father was a Class of 1920 Naval Academy graduate. He was still on active duty when I was born in 1940; that makes me one of the older members of our class. Due to Dad's military assignments, our family moved around frequently as I was growing up. I graduated from high school in St. Louis and began studies at Union College in Schenectady, New York. I completed two years of study there in electrical engineering before receiving a congressional appointment to USNA. In addition to playing varsity soccer at Navy, I spent much of my midshipman time as an entrepreneur, selling various items of "contraband" to other midshipmen. One of the more popular items I sold was rubbers (prophylactics), which I obtained from my brother who worked in a pharmacy while he was in dental school. Midshipmen had a difficult time buying them in town then, so I was providing a valuable service. I hollowed out a dictionary and went around to upperclassmen rooms selling the rubbers I had concealed inside. My roommate, Bill, and I also sold booze in small amounts that we had purchased clandestinely from a fellow out in town who bought it for us. In our 2nd Class year, we bought a refrigerator to make ice. We stashed it in a room used for the Naval Academy radio station where Bill worked and covered it with a blanket with a sign on it saying, "High Voltage." We used the fridge to make ice to sell to other midshipmen. Later, we bought cases of beer and hid them in the overhead of that same room. We had parties on many a Saturday night. I also did some occasional studying during my midshipman days.

For my 1st class (senior) cruise, I ended up on a diesel submarine out of Key West. I managed to talk a classmate into switching boats so that I would be on the sub that was headed for Europe. I got off the boat in Spain and traveled all over Europe with a buddy for the rest of the summer. We ended up in East Berlin and somehow avoided being held as spies.

Coincidentally, during leave the previous summer, I also had foolishly ended up behind the Wall in East Berlin. Sonny and I must have had the same gods looking after us not to be imprisoned by the East Germans. The 2015 Steven Spielberg movie, *Bridge of Spies*, chronicled the true story of a young American who exhibited this same type of bad judgement and was arrested as a spy in East Berlin in 1961 creating an international incident.

I wanted to fly, but my vision had deteriorated while I was a midshipman. Instead, I chose to go Surface Navy and received orders to USS JOSEPH P. KENNEDY (DD-850), a destroyer which was operating out of Newport, Rhode Island. I was the Gunnery Officer initially, but later had two other jobs. We steamed all over the world, including spending time in the Indian Ocean. At the end of this tour, the Navy wanted me to attend Destroyer School, but I refused to go because I had already been a department head and saw no benefit. Instead, I received orders to a SOSUS Station in Delaware for 18 months. We were involved in locating the nuclear submarine, USS SCORPION (SSN-589) which had sunk near the Azores in a mysterious accident.

SOSUS was a **SO**und **SU**rveillance **S**ystem which used a string of fixed hydrophones on the ocean bottom to locate and track Soviet submarines. It was a highly classified system given the code name "Project Caesar." Both the name and the system were declassified in the mid-1990's. Among the 99 crewmembers who died on SCORPION on May 22,

1968, was one of our classmates, Lt (jg) Laughton Smith. Although several theories have been advanced for the cause of SCORPION's sinking, none has been officially confirmed.

After I had been at the SOSUS station for 18 months, I received a call from my detailer assigning me to counterinsurgency school in San Diego in preparation for going to Vietnam. In January 1970, I arrived in Saigon. Instead of receiving a M-16, I was assigned a Colt .38 and orders to RAID 75 with the instructions, "The guy you are relieving will pick you up at your hotel at 10 PM." Well, 10 PM was after curfew in Saigon, but the guy, whose last name was Veranda, shows up and takes me to a bar full of "working girls." I will always remember his words when I asked him about the possibility of the Shore Patrol picking us up, "Don't worry. Those guys can't do anything to you worse than where you're going." The next day we drove to Dong Tam on the Mekong River. When we got there, I noticed that it was all Vietnamese except us. I learned that RAID stood for River Assault River Division and that my counterpart was a Vietnamese Lieutenant named Anh.

Veranda and I took a jeep to Long Xuyen where RAID was then located closer to the Cambodian border. On January 15, 1970, as I was in the process of relieving Veranda, he took me into a building which I felt had zero security. As I was trying to get more information, he said, "See ya." On the way out, he told me that we didn't need security because the area was a R&R area for the Viet Cong and "they won't bother you here." I did have a few Navy enlisted guys who worked for me. My command boat was an old WW II LCM (Landing Craft Medium) with portable steel planking attached, but it offered little effective protection. Our job was to use 12 similar boats (which were mostly monitors) to ferry Vietnamese Marines into the surrounding canals and rivers so they could search for VC and NVA troops. One of our boats had a flamethrower on it. The U.S. was trying to turn over most of the fighting to the Vietnamese, so my job was not to fight myself but to call in help from U.S. resources, such as planes and helicopters.

When I came back from a multi-day patrol ferrying the Vietnamese Marines, I found that the Chief Petty Officer who worked for me had converted the first floor of our building into a bar. Upon seeing the situation, I recommended that we move back downriver where it was somewhat safer. Back at Dong Tam, I ended up living in a totally unsafe barracks. When I learned that the huge hole in the middle of the building was due to an earlier mortar attack, I had flak blankets put on the roof and around the walls for some protection. There was always the potential of a sapper infiltrating at night with explosives, so I had our guys set up a small storage unit immediately behind the barracks to use during the night to relieve ourselves safely. On the side, we painted nice lettering saying, "Ye Old Shit House." To greet all the incoming helos, we painted on the roof of the barracks, "COLD BEER, LOOSE WOMEN, WELCOME TO DONG TAM." It was not all fun and games. We received mortar fire essentially every night at around 10 PM. I was even mortared a few times while I was on the shitter.

Sonny (in shorts) and crew on one of his boats

We had two types of patrols. The first was taking Vietnamese Marines up small canals off the rivers to offload them for patrols. Because there was dense jungle (and probably several VC) all around us, the Marines would initially deploy to form two sides of a triangle while we were the third side. Our role on the boat was to randomly fire the M-79 grenade launcher into the jungle on the other side of the canal so that the VC couldn't set up to fire at us from our rear. The second type of operation was to pull up to the bank of a canal and set up an ambush (called a waterborne guard post) to look for bad guys traveling at night. The VC would come down the canal in sampans; our job was to be very quiet in order to surprise them. During these ops we lived and slept on the deck because it was your best chance to live if your boat was blown up. I woke up one morning to see 14 sampans tied up just downstream of us. I was still in my skivvies and a tee shirt. About 80 percent of those aboard were women who were probably VC. They kept staring at me as I relieved myself over the side. My Vietnamese counterpart said that we should let them go because they were just going to market. I think that this was the correct decision.

We were often involved in firefights on the canals late in the day. One instance was when a sapper came down a canal in the water from upstream and put a charge under one of our boats. It blew up the boat and killed everyone in it. When we brought in a crane to salvage the boat, a battalion of VC opened fire on us. They attacked with B-40 rockets from four feet deep holes on shore. When those rockets hit the rebar, which had been mounted for protection on our sides, it exploded into the Styrofoam which we had placed behind it and didn't do much damage. We found that the best way to go after the VC in those holes was to counterattack with flamethrowers because they suck the oxygen out of the holes they are in. During one firefight, a bullet passed by my ear. To get help, I called in the Seawolves, the Huey gunships, telling them, "We've got Indians, can you bring in the calvary?" They showed up and silenced the enemy by pretty much clearing out all the vegetation and everything near it with immense gunfire. We heard nothing the rest of the day.

One of Sonny's boats destroyed by sapper's charge

In April 1970 President Nixon approved U.S. troops going into Cambodia alongside South Vietnamese forces against North Vietnamese coming south through Cambodia. Our unit was assigned to take Vietnamese Marines up the river into Cambodia to seize a ferry landing. To get there, we had to pass through a canyon which was known to have large concentrations of enemy on both sides. Our boats were escorted through this danger spot by two Air Force F-4's which were buzzing both sides of the river which allowed us to get through safely. On the way there, we observed heavy fighting between the U.S. Army and the North Vietnamese. Once we got to the ferry landings, we experienced no fighting ourselves. We stayed in Cambodia for six weeks, and I took the opportunity to visit several Buddhist pagodas before we went back downriver.

One day, an American PBR (Patrol Boat Riverine) came up the river and landed some Army guys. They got into what they thought was going to be a small firefight when suddenly about 500 enemy troops showed up and began firing at them. An OV-10 gunship was called in and started shooting all over the place. The next morning, we found all sorts of NVA bodies. I saw a tall American jumping up and down on the chest of a dead NVA. I went ashore and found his CO and told him that his unit was going to be overrun that night because what his guy was doing was going to enflame the local village. The Vietnamese regarded all bodies, theirs or our, with respect as fallen warriors. Most of these young

American GIs had no clue about the Vietnamese culture. And they were overrun that night.

For bathing, I swam in the rivers but always had a rope handy because of the strong currents. The water was often nasty because, among other things, upstream in Cambodia the locals would tie up dead human bodies in the river to attract fish to catch. Our diet when we were on the rivers consisted of fish (obtained by throwing a grenade overboard) and rice. The locals would cut off fish heads and put them in a salty solution in a barrel which eventually drips out the bottom. The remaining solution becomes a sauce called Nuoc Mam. It really smells terrible; I wouldn't touch it, but the Vietnamese loved it. They also ate a lot of local hot peppers which would melt a Russian tank. Whenever I had one, I had to immediately get a mouthful of rice to temper it.

Throughout nearly all the time I was there with RAID, we were eating mostly fish and rice which caused a lot of digestive issues for us Americans. In September 1970, I developed a high fever, with nausea and diarrhea. I was a mess and knew that I had to get out of there. My enlisted men threw me into a jeep and took me on a long drive to a field hospital at Can Tho. We got there at dark, and they gave me a bunch of drugs. I was yellow (probably due to hepatitis) and had only 17% liver function. I was in the hospital four weeks but recovered.

Shortly after I got back to RAID, I was surprised to receive word that my relief would be arriving by helo in 40 minutes. He was junior to me and told me that he had no idea why they wanted me out of there. I was flown by helo to Dong Tam where I was greeted by a senior Captain, the number two Navy guy in Vietnam, who kept telling me that I am "going to have to work hard." I had no idea what he was talking about. He said, "Didn't you get the letter?" When I told him that I hadn't had mail in a month, he told me, "You've been selected to go back to Washington to be interviewed for the Nuclear Propulsion Program by Admiral Rickover."

I found my crinkled up khakis and flew to D.C. for the interview. My detailer told me I had been selected because the Navy was commissioning several new nuclear surface ships and needed at least 20 new department heads for those ships. Before I left Vietnam, I had applied to become a CEC (Civil Engineering Corps) officer and had just learned from the

CEC detailer that I would be selected if I didn't end up in Nuclear Power. During my interviews with one of Rickover's young engineer henchmen, I intentionally managed to really piss him off. When it became time to see Rickover himself, he quickly kicked me out and ended my interview. I was immediately sent back to Vietnam, but I was smiling knowing that I was going to become a CEC officer when I left.

After Vietnam, I went to grad school at the University of Colorado, and then had assignments in the Civil Engineering Corps (CEC). Along the way, I met my wife, Judy, who was a widow of an Army officer who had been killed in those same battles that I had seen in the fighting when we were headed upriver to Cambodia. I retired after 20 years in the Navy and began work as an engineering consultant.

It would be too simplistic to regard Sonny's Vietnam experience as akin to episodes about the Korean War depicted in the television series, MASH He had found himself in a truly surreal and dangerous situation with few peers to provide support. His predecessor's warning that the shore patrol could do nothing worse to him than where he was going proved to be distressingly accurate. Because of Sonny's rather cavalier attitude toward rules and authority exhibited at the Naval Academy, he was, almost by accident, the perfect fit for a role some might describe as ridiculously surreal…and dangerous. How he survived mentally and physically is a testimony to his innate strengths.

War produces these absurdities on a daily basis.

Jack Musitano

Philadelphia, Pennsylvania

"Holy Crap"

Several of my classmates told me of problems flying early versions of the Vought F-8 Crusader aircraft and suggested that I talk to Jack Musitano. The F-8 was a single engine supersonic fighter aircraft designed for "air superiority." It had been in operation since 1957 and had guns as its primary weapon. It had been used during the Cuban Missile Crisis in 1962 to obtain low level photographs available through no other means. I interviewed Jack via computer from my camp in Maine by computer from his home in Moorpark, California, where he lives with his wife, Terry.

I was born in 1941 less than two weeks after the attack on Pearl Harbor. Beethoven and I were born on the same date, December 16. Later Dad worked in the Philadelphia Navy Yard as a draftsman doing work on the small aircraft carriers during the war. We were living just across the border in New Jersey, and I went to a brand new high school there. It was a small school and I played both offense and defense on our football team. After high school I went to Drexel Institute of Technology and was studying Mechanical Engineering. I always wanted to fly - even in grade school I wanted to be an airline pilot. One of my grade schoolteachers had been a fighter pilot in WW II and was my idol. All along I was trying to figure out how I could become a pilot. This translated into me wanting to go to either the Air Force Academy or the Naval Academy. Our local Athletic Director flew what I thought was a cool airplane in the Navy Reserves and got me in touch with a graduate from the Naval Academy who interviewed prospective candidates. He told me that a 170 lb. guard on a football team was too small for Navy. He recommended that I enlist in the Naval Reserves because each year there are 160 slots to the Academy available for members of the Reserves. I took his advice and enlisted at the Reserve Center in Camden and was sworn in. I then went off to boot camp and was later sent to a Forest Sherman class destroyer operating out of Norfolk. I did two weeks on that ship as a Seaman Apprentice and then came home and did drills with my Reserve unit every Monday evening while I went to Drexel. It turned out to have been a good decision because I received my appointment to the Academy in Spring 1961.

At the Academy I majored in Chemistry. When service selection night came, I was able to realize my dream to begin training as a Naval Aviator. I did well enough in flight training to be the last person in our class to get selected to fly jets. I received my wings at Kingsville, Texas, and ultimately received orders to a F-8 squadron, VF-13, in Jacksonville, Florida. First, they sent me to a RAG in Miramar, California, to be trained for eight months on the Vought F-8 Crusader. This was some intense work. The syllabus was really geared toward the war. You were encouraged to do crazy stuff like they do in Top Gun which was good because it prepared us well for the war. The last part of our training was practicing field carrier landings which simulated actual carrier landings. I still had not landed an F-8 on a carrier.

RAG stands for Replacement Air Group. It is a training unit to prepare aviators to become proficient flying a specific airplane. It consists of both experienced airmen and recent graduates of flight school. The RAG also provides training for mechanics and all members of a squadron with an emphasis on returning to aircraft carrier operations. "Syllabus" is a term used by naval aviators to describe the curriculum followed during training evolutions.

I learned that my squadron was scheduled to deploy to the Mediterranean right away. The CO of the squadron wanted me there the next Monday. When I told him that I was getting married on Saturday in Philadelphia, his response was, "Congrats. But you better be there on the pier in Jacksonville on Monday morning." Terry and I did get married. We drove much of the night and did make it to the pier. Our squadron was deploying on the USS SHANGRI-LA (CVA-38), an old Essex class WW

II carrier which had been converted to have an angled deck with two steam catapults 150 feet long. Our squadron had old airplanes, the oldest operational F-8's at the time. I actually had a leading edge of my wing fall off during an exercise run, but I made it back OK. The F-8 was a true "fighter" aircraft, but there were some known limitations when flying slow. SHANGRI-LA sailed in November 1967 for the Med. I did a lot of flying during this deployment which turned out to be nine months long instead of the planned six. We flew day and night, but there was, of course, no combat in the Mediterranean. I had 150 carrier landings, 35 of them at night. This was ironic because this version of the F-8 was not equipped to be a night fighter.

When the carrier got back to the States, a hurricane came through causing us to take our planes down to Guantanamo Bay, Cuba, which I might add, has a very short landing strip. Finally, SHANGRI-LA came down to Cuba, but I blew both tires on my first night landing there because the new planes we had been given, the F-8H, were very challenging to land on a carrier. It didn't fly well at slow speeds making it difficult to glide when approaching the carrier. I was very upset over this landing and went to the Landing Signal Officer (LSO) to discuss what went wrong. All he said was, "Don't worry, you're OK." The ship sailed back to Jacksonville for more training. We were doing a lot of flying; on a beautiful day as I was attempting to land, my plane came in low and I hit the ramp. [the stern of the ship]. When my plane hit the ramp, the right main landing gear broke off along with the tail hook. I was still at full power as the plane broke in two behind me. A fuel cell ignited causing a huge fire to erupt. All I could see in my three mirrors were orange flames behind me. Essentially my plane was now a huge fireball. By now the cockpit (with me in it) was still moving across the carrier deck. When I saw that we were next to the control tower I pulled the face curtain to eject which literally blasted me upward. Fortunately, my parachute opened while I was still in the air above the carrier deck, or I would have been dead. The chute drifted off the stern of the carrier; I almost hit it. Suddenly I was in the ocean struggling to get clear of the parachute. A helicopter quickly appeared to pick me up, but for some reason they didn't put anyone in the water to help me even though I was tangled up in the shrouds of the chute! I could have used some help, but no one jumped out of the helo to assist. Fortunately, I was a scuba diver and didn't panic while I was in the water. I was wet, but happy to be alive.

Normally hitting the ramp would not be conducive to a long flying career, but in the investigation, most of the blame was placed on the LSO who had never waved F-8's before and had never flown one. I got back into another plane the next day, but my back was in knots from having that seat explode under me. Later in life when I had to have a back fusion my surgeon told me that the damage was almost certainly due to that ejection episode.

USS SHANGRI-LA (CVA-38), note angled flight deck and F-8's parked forward

The LSO, or Landing Signal Officer, is a key component to landing safely on a carrier. The LSO is an experienced aviator whose mission is to facilitate the safe and expeditious recovery of aircraft during landing operations. He is located near the stern of the ship usually a few feet below the deck. In the early days of naval aviation, the LSO used paddles to signal the approaching aircraft as to which adjustments to make during the approach. (Hence, their nickname, "Paddles"). Now the LSO talks to the pilot via a handset advising with respect to position, power change, and other adjustments to assure a glide path for a safe landing. In addition to the verbal guidance provided by the LSO, there is an optical landing system which provides glide information to the pilot. The LSO also holds a "pickle" which controls signal lights to indicate various commands such as wave off (go around), cleared to land. The LSO is obviously a position of great responsibility.

Following this incident, I flew up to D.C. to tell my detailer that I didn't want to deploy to the Med again and preferred to go to Vietnam. My reasoning was that I didn't want to get hurt or killed during any more non-combat flying. If I was going to get hurt or killed, I preferred to do it in combat. He couldn't believe that I was volunteering for combat, but he gave me orders to VF-51, a F-8 squadron in Miramar, California. Terry and I drove across the country and arrived there in November 1968. The squadron had just come back from a deployment and was getting new planes, F-8J's, a much-improved version. These planes were a great improvement because they had been modified to fly well at slower speeds for carrier approaches. Now we would be able to make an approach on a carrier at 130 knots instead of 150, which makes the entire process far safer.

In January 1969 we deployed on an 8-month cruise on USS BON HOMME RICHARD (CVA-31) and went straight to Yankee Station. The U.S. was now in the middle of a bombing halt, so much of our flying was BARCAP (Barrier Combat Air Patrol) making sure that no North Vietnamese planes were coming toward Yankee Station. I did have some missions over North Vietnam and Laos to protect photo reconnaissance F-8's. We would weave above them as lookouts in big S turns. I took one guy in over Vinh and then picked up another photo bird on a mission into Laos. We learned that they were not shooting at us much if we were at high altitudes.

After this cruise I was assigned to be an instructor for the F-8 RAG in Miramar. We then deployed on USS ORISKANY (CVA-34) in February 1972. This time there was plenty of action. We began this cruise on DIXIE station south of the DMZ between Cam Ranh Bay and Saigon. They rigged us with bombing pods and sent us on missions bombing around Quang Tri just south of the DMZ. We coordinated with the Air Force and always flew two-plane missions. My wingman was a pilot I had trained at Miramar. We didn't have any fire control system on our planes, so we did it all manually. Basically, I was the fire control system. They would only assign us targets which were not around our troops - just bridges and stuff like that - because we could not be very accurate. One time I had so much opposing fire coming up at me I thought that I was in rain. The rounds from the 37 mm anti-aircraft guns being used by the bad guys would go off at 7000 ft if they didn't hit something, so several times we would see these white clouds at 7000 ft above us as we were rolling in. You just gritted your teeth and tried to drop your bombs and get out of there.

When we were bombing it became pretty impersonal. Generally, whenever I flew missions, everything below looked to me to be pretty much abandoned except for the guns on the ground. I felt that I was attacking targets more than people. I remember bombing near a 37 mm AA site near Quang Tri and they were shooting up at me every time I rolled in. It was close to a village, but I was pretty sure I had not hit it. On the ship we used to get the "Stars and Stripes" newspaper every day and the next day there was a photo on the front page of women and children running out of a village right in the area where I had bombed. I immediately said, "Holy crap." I knew that our bombing was not very accurate. That photo really bothered me for some time. Fortunately, from that point on, I never had another mission like that.

Later when we were doing missions up north and orbiting Haiphong Harbor, a SAM [surface to air missile] *site was shining on me, and I was pumping out chaff* [small pieces of metal-coated fibers to confuse radar-guided missiles]. *I didn't realize it at the time but one of my buddies told me that I was being bracketed by either a 57 mm or 85 mm AAA with air bursts all around me. I guess that none of those rounds had my name on it. Up north we were flying with the A-7 bombers off our carriers on Target Combat Air Patrol. We would do a weave at 20,000 ft just above them looking for enemy aircraft. When the A-7's went in to do their bombing, they did all sorts of flips and turns to try to fool the gunners on the ground. Once they dropped their bombs, it was a free-for-all. Everyone, including us, would just head back toward the water as quickly as possible. We also flew missions called MIGCAPS, for MiG Combat Air Patrol. On these we would sometimes fly near a MiG base to see if they would come up to challenge us. None ever did, at least while I was flying there. We did have two MiGs come south when I was on BARCAP and were told to go get them. We dove down and flew in just under the cloud cover at 2000 ft where we could see them, but they couldn't see us. We were coming in at them at over 500 kts, but suddenly we were told "Resume." This meant that we had to break off and go back, but then, a few minutes later they sent us back again, but soon got another "Resume." I never knew whether the Admiral on the*

RED CROWN cruiser running this show was playing with us, or if he was really serious. The MiGs were real, but I still have no idea why they called us back.

The ORISKANY had some issues causing us to be deployed longer than scheduled. It had a collision with an ammo ship, and later one of its screws fell off. After repairs in Japan, we went back to Yankee Station, but it lost another screw! When ORISKANY came back to San Diego, we did a 6-month turnaround and arrived back at Yankee Station in 1974. The war was now basically over for the U.S., and we did few combat missions. This was when OPEC cut back on pumping oil, so we were sent to the Indian Ocean in case hostilities broke out. When we were flying there, we never saw land for two months. It was incredibly boring.

My next assignment was a shore job for two years at Point Mugu in California. At the end of this, they wanted to send me back to sea. I would have gone if they put me in a F-8 or F-14 squadron, but that didn't happen. So, I resigned in March 1977 and took a civilian job as a test pilot. I decided to come back on active duty when they said they would send me to Graduate School for a degree in Electrical Engineering. Just as I completed my two years in grad school, the Navy had a Reduction in Force (RIF) and I was again a civilian. I took a job with Northrup at Thousand Oaks, California. Ironically, I also landed a Reserve Officer billet and ended up spending 34 years in the Navy.

Jack ultimately worked for Rocketdyne Corporation for 13 years and then returned to work for Northrup Grumman as the Chief Systems Lead for the Airborne Laser Program. His experiences in naval aviation are indicative of the constant inherent dangers of landing on an aircraft carrier. Every pilot I interviewed always knew two things: his call sign and the number of landings he had made. Almost always the pilot would add how many of these landings were at night. When Jack discussed his feelings about the "impersonal" aspects of bombing, his voice was momentarily broken; he did not recall these missions with pleasure. As with most of the other Naval and Marine aviators I interviewed, the feeling was that they were involved in war and had a job to do. There were no winners on either side, just survivors.

Bill Hart

Queens, NYC, New York
"We fight this war at night"

I heard from several classmates that I should talk to Bill Hart if I wanted to learn about "PBRs." All I knew about PBRs was the name, Patrol Boat Riverine, and that they were used in Vietnam in the Mekong Delta. I interviewed Bill via computer from his home in Pearland, Texas, a suburb of Houston. He speaks with a slight Texas accent. His wife, Nelda, has a stronger accent and supplemented some of his memories.

I was born in Queens, but for most of my early days we lived on Long Island. I attended an all-boys high school, Stuyvesant, which was a very challenging, public, college-prep school in the East Village of MaNhuttan. I had to take a bus and a train to get there, taking well over an hour each way. For a while I was trying to be the best juvenile delinquent possible, but my best friend who was a year ahead of me at Stuyvesant was a very positive influence. I decided to try to go to the Academy for two reasons: I wanted to serve in the military, and, if accepted, my parents would not have to pay for my education and could save for my two siblings. I was not my congressman's principal appointment but was an alternate. I assumed that I was not going to Navy, so I applied for a NROTC scholarship at Illinois Institute of Technology and got it. However, in early June, I received a phone call from our congressman's office telling me that if I could get "there" in two weeks, I could go to the Academy. That decision took me about 20 minutes.

At the Academy I learned that my eyesight was not good enough to be a Marine pilot which is what I was hoping to do. On the night of service selection, I saw the name of USS HARTLEY (DE-1029) on the board, and since that was close to my name, I said to myself, "Why not?" That's how I ended up in the surface Navy going to HARTLEY. After graduation, and still in June, I got a call from the Navy saying that HARTLEY had just been in a major collision and had been almost cut in half. So, they sent me to Portsmouth Naval Shipyard for the next year as Main Propulsion Assistant on HARTLEY while it was being repaired. I was there only until sea trials when I received orders to USS VOGE (DE-1047) which was being built in Bay City, Michigan. When construction was finished, we went through the St. Lawrence Seaway, and I became the Chief Engineer. Soon after we became operational, I talked the Captain into letting me volunteer for PBR's in Vietnam. I was sent to Vallejo, California, where we learned all about PBRs while running them in the sloughs around that area.

The PBR was a fiberglass hull with little armor - all there was between the crew and a firefight was a thin piece of metal and the fiberglass. These were small boats, only 31 ft long, but could reverse direction, turn in their own length, and come to a stop from full speed in only a few boat lengths. Jet streams of water powered by diesel engines were used for propulsion and steering. There were several machine guns: a .50 caliber aft, twin .50's forward, and a M-60 on one side midships, and either another M-60 or a grenade launcher on the other side. The M-60 could fire 400-500 rounds a minute. Basically, it was a fast, maneuverable small vessel with lots of firepower.

My first billet was as a "Patrol Officer" on these boats. In this role I was the Commander of two PBRs which would always go out together; the Patrol Officer usually rode in the front one. Each boat had 4 enlisted men: a Chief Petty Officer or a First Class Petty Officer as the Boat Captain; a gunner, who was usually a Second Class Petty Officer, and two guys stationed with one aft and the other somewhere else on the boat. Sometimes we would have a Vietnamese Navy guy along who acted as an interpreter. We had been flown into Saigon and were transported to the mouth of a large river in the Delta where we had our boats tied up next to USS GARRETT COUNTY (LST-786). We used to call it "The Garrett Maru." The whole purpose of that ship then was to be our hotel where we could eat and sleep. It also had some minor maintenance capability. Our best help came from two Seawolves (UH-1B Bell helicopter gunships) stationed on board which were at our beck and call if we needed them. And we needed them quite often!

**USS GARRETT COUNTY (LST-786) with
PBRs alongside in Mekong Delta**

The Seawolf helicopters (UH-1B) were basically Army helicopters which in some cases had been received by the Navy from Army units already in Vietnam. Many were not in good condition and needed considerable work to be acceptable for Navy use. To make them effective in Navy operations, a radar altimeter was added to aid in operations over the flat ground of the Delta at night or during landing maneuvers on ships. The helicopters did not "belong" to the ship; all were in Helicopter Attack (Light) Squadron 3, HA(L)-3 which was active from April 1967 to March 1972. This was a unique, all-volunteer squadron formed to support Navy Special Warfare operations and Mobile Riverine Forces in Vietnam. In an average year, pilots would fly 320 missions. It was exceptionally dangerous duty for these air crews. While in Vietnam they flew over 120,000 combat missions; many were at night over the featureless terrain of the Delta. Over 200 of these men were wounded and 44 were killed in action. Because the PBR's were essentially unarmored and the crew could not see through the dense vegetation, the Seawolves provided effective air cover and communications linkage. Each Seawolf had a gunner seated on each side of the aircraft with a free-hand, shoulder-fired M-60 machine gun. These gunners were known to often hang out of the helo with one foot on the rocket pod to be able to fire in all directions as the UH-1B rolled in and out during an attack. The Seawolf also carried a 2.75 inch rocket launcher on each side. The crews prided themselves on getting airborne in less than two minutes after receiving a request for assistance from "customers" such as Bill. It was indeed a fearsome weapon, but obviously it was also a prized target for the enemy.

**A UH-1 gunship providing support for a
column of PBRs in the Mekong Delta**

Each River Division had ten PBRs. We always had at least two boats out on patrol and were on the river 24 hrs a day. We would send four boats out at 6 AM until 6 PM, then four more would go out for the next 12 hrs. The other two boats had that 24 hours off. Our major mission during daylight hours was to patrol the rivers and canals. During daytime, we would cruise with a Vietnamese policeman who would interrogate each sampan or fishing vessel that we met and check their papers while looking for weapons or anything suspicious. If we found nothing, we would thank the boat for cooperating. Sometimes they would also give us useful information. Mostly these missions were rather boring, but sometimes a village chief was pissed at some nearby troublemakers and would arrange for an area to be declared a free fire zone so we could whack those coordinates. Nighttime was a little crazier. I might add that our Vietnamese policemen chose NEVER to go out with us at night. We were usually in hostile areas so anything on the rivers after curfew was suspicious. It wasn't a free fire zone, but close to it because the Viet Cong moved at night and would set up ambushes. We were often patrolling where they wanted to cross the water. Whenever they fired on us, we would return fire and call for help from the Seawolves. They could usually get there in 12-15 minutes. We would fire a flare where we wanted them to shoot. It was always impressive because those two helos could fire thousands of rounds in a minute. When that happens, people stop shooting at you. In a sense we were bait being used to tempt the enemy to initiate fire. About every third patrol someone was shooting at us. This led to a lot of firefights.

PBR alongside pier

One patrol was particularly memorable because a rocket hit us and blew off the entire bow of our boat. It happened in the early stages of a nighttime patrol before it was dark. We had been expecting action considerably further up this river, when without warning, WHAM, we were hit. Fortunately, our gunner was not yet at his station on the front gun, or he would have been instantly killed. We still had our engines, so I yelled for us to ground the remaining part of the boat onto the opposite shore from where we took fire. We took off all the weapons and the radar and all five of us jumped out into the mud. We assumed that they would fire another round into the boat to finish us off, but there were no more rockets fired. We were standing there in deep mud with our weapons until we were rescued by one of the other boats that was on patrol with us. While we were there, we watched our boat take on water, roll over, and sink in the muddy water. It had been an unusual patrol because we had four boats on this mission. When a rocket hits a PBR, the big danger is shrapnel. No one was injured in this incident, but I lost three men on other patrols. It's a long story, but when I returned on a helicopter to oversee the salvage of that sunken PBR, I accidentally fell out of the helo from at least 25 ft right into that same river. Apparently, that was not my lucky river! The only thing that was hurt was my dignity. All the other officers there were laughing at my misfortune.

After several months doing these patrols in the Delta from our base alongside GARRETT COUNTY, they moved my boats deep into Vietnam near the Cambodian border. We were at a base camp near Go Dau Ha on the Van Co Gong River at what was called the Naval Advanced Tactical Support Base. This was part of Operation SLINGSHOT. We were living in hooches just like the Vietnamese and did not have a load of security. I arranged to have a bunker built with a lot of sandbags to provide some protection. I was now the Commander of this division and had two junior officers as Patrol Officers. We used generators for electricity and larger ships brought us drinking water. We mostly ate C-rations but occasionally helicopters would bring us "real food." There was a lot of action up there, even more than down south, and we had another boat blown out of the water. I would send out eight boats a day, four in the morning and four at night. I still went out on some patrols but didn't go on all of them. We soon learned that our helo support was not as rapid as down in the Delta. We did occasionally go upriver into Cambodia, especially when the local village chiefs asked us to do so. We were not supposed to go there but I assure you that there were no signs saying, "Welcome to Cambodia." Basically, it all looked like the same dangerous jungle. Our job was to try to slow down or stop the flow of weapons and men which the North Vietnamese were flooding the area with after sending it down the Ho Chi Minh Trail. We felt like we were definitely putting a dent into their supply chain.

When Admiral Zumwalt took over as Commander Naval Forces Vietnam, he frequently visited units to learn first-hand what his forces were doing and what they needed. He was very innovative and would try anything.

He wanted the PBRs to be even more mobile and actually had some of our boats picked up by big helicopters and airlifted to remote areas for two to three days. The helos would then come to pick us up and fly the boats back to our base. We had just been involved in a hairy all-night fight, and the next morning I was sleeping in the command bunker. All of a sudden, I hear a helo arriving and I hear a loud voice asking one of my men, "Where's your CO?" As the voice marched into the bunker, I rolled over and recognized Zumwalt. I greeted him with, "Hi, Admiral!" He then asked me why I was sleeping. I looked him straight in the eye and said, "You know, Admiral, we fight this war at night." He laughed and we chatted for a while, and then he was in the helo and gone.

Operation GIANT SLINGSHOT (Bill referred to it just by SLINGSHOT) was a Navy concept which began in December 1968 to eliminate North Vietnamese infiltration of South Vietnam in the region known as "The Parrot's Beak," a peninsula-shaped part of Cambodia which juts into Vietnam west of Saigon. Go Dau Ha was very close to the Cambodian border and was in a heavily contested region. The famous Cu Chi tunnels used by the Viet Cong were not far to the east. Much of the North Vietnamese infiltration was taking place along the two rivers on each side of this "beak" - the Vam Co Gong and the Vam Co Tay. This was initially a relatively successful operation due to the large number of U.S. boats, including Bill's PBRs, which were heavily involved. There were numerous firefights on the two rivers with significant amounts of weapons seized from enemy boats. However, when the Navy passed responsibility to the South Vietnamese in May 1970, the problem intensified again.

By the end of my tour in mid-1969, we were patrolling mostly safe areas and were no longer looking to start something. I had lost those three men on my PBRs while in Vietnam and didn't want to write any more letters to relatives of deceased sailors. I was content to have us do less provocation because I had come to believe that we were on a mission to nowhere. When my year in-country was up, I flew back to the States. I was supposed to take over PBR training at Vallejo but beginning in July 1969 the decision had been made to turn all the PBRs over to the Vietnamese, so there was no training to be done at Vallejo. I didn't have a job. I had put in my resignation from the Navy just before I left Vietnam, but I wasn't sure when it would be accepted. Most of our classmates had been extended for a year after our initial obligation of four years due to "the needs of the service." When you accept your commission as an officer, you agree to "serve at the pleasure of the President" and can be mandated to serve as long as deemed necessary. But in my case, I had no assignment, so I suppose they figured that it would be too much trouble to send me somewhere for less than a year. At any rate, the Navy let me out in August 1969. I returned to the Boston area and began an IBM training course in September.

Like many of our classmates thrust into the danger and insanity of the war, Bill survived by a combination of luck, skill, and courage. Taking small fiberglass boats up narrow waterways surrounded by jungle placed him and his crew constantly in harm's way. He explained that his boat essentially never initiated fire, if only because they had no way of seeing the enemy. The response of his boats and the supporting Seawolves had to be devastating to anything in the path of their return fire. How many enemy soldiers or innocent civilians that were killed was impossible to determine. There are recorded instances of PBRs and Seawolves decimating over half of a convoy of boats carrying a regiment of North Vietnamese troops attempting to infiltrate the Delta. By the end of his tour in Vietnam in 1969, Bill had seen far too much killing and had become somewhat jaundiced. His final words to me were, "In the end, because of all the restrictions, we were really no more than a nuisance to the North Vietnamese."

Bill spent the next seven years working for IBM before doing motivational speaking across the U.S. He later met his wife, Nelda, while working in automobile sales quality control in North Carolina before moving to Pearland, Texas.

Mike Riley

Rochester, New York

"Why are we doing this?"

Mike played football for Navy during what many consider our glory years of great success, both in national rankings and versus our arch-rival, Army. He was not a starter but played in most games on the offensive line. I lost track of him following graduation but was able to locate him at his home in St. Pete Beach, Florida, where he lives with his wife, Marie. During our talk, I discovered a variant of "6 degrees of separation" in that Mike and Marie attended the same Catholic chapel in Palo Alto, California, where my wife and I were married two years later. I interviewed Mike from his home via computer.

I was born in 1943 in Rochester and attended Aquinas Institute, a Catholic high school. My dad was a politician; he served in the New York State Assembly. He ultimately got fed up and quit. I have always remembered his exact words to me and my brother, "Don't ever go into politics. It's a dirty business." Ever since I was a little kid, I had thought about serving in the Navy because of the great respect I had for my older cousins who had been in the Navy in WW II. I still remember lying on the floor of our living room watching the TV show, "Men of Annapolis," and wanting to go there. My high school guidance counselor recommended that I write to our local congressman to ask for an appointment to the Naval Academy. I did so unbeknownst to my family, and after taking the Academy physical, learned that I was the first alternate for the appointment. The fellow with the principal appointment took it, but one of the Navy football coaches who had talked to my coach got me in through one of their slots.

At the Academy, I played football all four years and enjoyed my time there. At service selection I sat with my roommate and talked over what we didn't want to do, namely be on surface ships, submarines, or in the Marine Corps. That left Navy Air and that's what we both chose. Off we went to aviation training in Pensacola, Florida. Marie and I were married in December 1965. By the time I had to choose which branch of aviation to pursue, we were expecting our first child. I did well in pilot training and didn't want jets, but I was able to get my first choice of flying multi-engine aircraft. I think that everyone else in my class ended up in jets or helos. My first assignment was to VP-40, a squadron in San Diego flying P-5M's. That was the Martin P-5 Marlin, often called a flying boat. Instead of the normal process of training new pilots for a specific aircraft in a Replacement Air Group (RAG), we went directly to an operational squadron. There was no RAG for this aircraft because it was scheduled to be taken out of service very soon. I started out as a Navigator/Third Pilot to learn how to fly the plane. I would get my chance to fly when the pilot got tired and wanted to rest. Most of our operations were Search and Rescue (SAR) and reconnaissance along the California coast. After we retired that aircraft in 1967, I was assigned immediately to a Lockheed P-3 Orion RAG at Moffett Field, south of San Francisco. It was unusual because our entire squadron, VP-40, transitioned at the same time. We flew out of Moffett for six months, and Marie and I were living in Palo Alto.

The P-5 Marlin was built by the Glenn L. Martin Company in Middle River, Maryland. It came into service in 1951 and was powered by twin piston engines. These flying boats were used in Vietnam beginning in 1965 doing surveillance patrols in Market Time operations looking for small enemy boats transporting goods and personnel from North Vietnam to the Viet Cong in the South. These planes operated from a seaplane tender off the Mekong Delta. Mike arrived at VP-40 after the plane's last Vietnam deployment shortly before the plane was retired.

We deployed in January 1969 to Iwakuni in Japan where we operated our P-3's out of a Marine Corps Air Station. Some members of our squadron were able to take dependents with them, but I decided not to do so. This still remains a source of contention between me and Marie who wanted to go with me. Our patrols were in the Sea of Japan to the north along the Russian coast looking for Soviet submarines. Other missions were south down to the Philippines. Up north we would occasionally wave to Soviet fighter aircraft when they came alongside of us to investigate. There seemed to be an understanding that we were both doing our jobs and didn't want to do anything stupid.

Our 1969 Vietnam deployments were out of Cam Ranh Bay. We would be there for 13 days and then fly to the Philippines for one night and then fly back the next day. Our understanding was that we were doing this so that we wouldn't be counted in the numbers of U.S. personnel in Vietnam. This flying back and forth irritated all of us. It was crazy, but so was the whole war. On our patrols out of Cam Ranh, we would fly across Vietnam to Cambodia and then drop down to the coastline of the Gulf of Thailand and fly along the coast all the way around the Ca Mau Peninsula and then north up to the lower part of the Gulf of Tonkin. Whenever we were doing patrols along the coast of North Vietnam, we had fighter escorts from one of the carriers on Yankee Station. Another P-3 job was to practice dropping mines, but my squadron was not tasked to actually mine anywhere. In Vietnam, our job was strictly looking for small enemy boats transporting materials. Our classmate, Mike Travis, was killed on a P-3 mission which was shot down doing this type of operation in the Gulf of Thailand. We became very cynical about these operations because whenever we would find one of these small boats which looked suspicious, we would call in the information, but no one ever came out to investigate the contact....ever. We kept asking ourselves, "Why are we doing this?"

The Lockheed P-3 Orion was a 4-engine turboprop plane developed for anti-submarine and surveillance operations. It was based on Lockheed's L-188 Electra commercial airliner but had a distinctive "tail-stinger" used to track submarines by picking up their magnetic characteristics. Some of these planes remain in operation and rival the Air Force B-52 for longevity. Although its primary mission was to find and locate Soviet submarines, it was pressed into operation in Vietnam to conduct Market Time missions searching for small enemy boats operating along the coastline. Some contend that in terms of cost-benefit, P-3's provided little gain with considerable cost. In view of Mike's experiences and the 1968 loss of two VP-26 P-3's (and the entire crews of 12) in the Gulf of

Thailand (one confirmed to have been shot down and the other due to unknown cause), I would have to also question the use of these planes and crews.

While we were in Cam Ranh Bay, we would be sitting in an amphitheater watching movies and drinking beer while hearing guns going off behind us. When the base was being shelled, we would jump into bomb shelters; often at night I was so tired that I wouldn't bother going to the shelter. The only casualty we had while I was there was a fellow who jumped into a shelter and was bitten by a poisonous snake. Another insanity was that we had to clear customs in Cam Ranh Bay every time we flew back to Vietnam from the Philippines. Our joke was that they were making it hard for us to get into the war! There were silly ways to get around this. Leaving the Philippines, we would fill our bomb bay with San Miguel beer from the Philippines and give a cold one to the customs guy to allow us in with no inspection. The whole experience was surreal!

Our typical flights were 8-10 hours in duration. When we were doing operations out of Japan, we dropped a lot of sonobuoys all over the place looking for Soviet subs. We would occasionally get hits on these and tracked several submarines for short periods. On these missions up north, we would see puffs of smoke as the North Koreans were shooting small arms at us; we were never concerned because we knew that we were out of their range. On one of these missions on what we thought was a typical patrol off the coast of North Korea, we were down low near the water and had no idea that there was a U.S. EC-121 flying above us. Our first indication of danger was receiving a message, "You are under attack." We immediately beat feet south not knowing what was going on. When we arrived back in Japan, our other planes were having active weapons loaded, mostly Bullpup missiles and 5" rockets. The next day we were sent out and located bodies in the water where the EC-121 had been shot down. We reported the location to nearby U.S. ships, but the authorities told those ships to leave because a Russian destroyer was already in the area. When we saw and heard all of this, we were really pissed. Not wanting to leave American bodies in the water, we flew over the Soviet destroyer and had him follow us to where the bodies were still floating. The Russians picked up the bodies, and it is my understanding that they returned the bodies to U.S. forces.

We were scheduled to deploy to Adak, Alaska, in June 1970, but I resigned from the Navy. I felt that we had been doing a "non-job." Also, when my wife was in San Francisco and taking my ill daughter for medical treatment at the military facility at The Presidio, she was pelted with tomatoes and pies by anti-war protestors. When our planes landed in the States after our deployment, we were told to take off our uniforms before leaving the base. The whole scene was so ridiculous that I just felt that I could no longer do this. I simply could not stomach what was going on in our country. Another reason I resigned was my experience with our first Commanding Officer while we were deployed. He was a serious alcoholic, and once when he was drunk, he caused a man to get injured. Although he was married, he had a hooker come to his change of command ceremony there in Vietnam instead of having his wife fly over. He was a terrible human being who really soured me on the Navy.

I was not certain what I was going to do after I left the Navy, but I wrote letters to every airline. I was amazingly lucky because the letter I had sent to Delta asking for a job application was mishandled and they sent me a letter in response telling me to come for an interview! That was how I ended up flying for Delta.

Mike flew for Delta for the next 33 years and retired in 2003 at age 60. He and Marie now rotate between their home in Florida and a summer camp on Lake Ontario. During our conversation, he mentioned some of the absurdities of life in a war zone, not unlike some of the situations lampooned in MASH, the TV series about an Army medical unit during the Korean War. Although he was one of the few classmates I interviewed who mentioned experiencing anti-war activity in the U.S. during the latter stages of the war, it was certainly something which everyone faced, especially military families living off-base.

Charlie Morrison

Bremerton, Washington

"It was terrible"

Naval Academy blood runs through Charlie's veins. His father was a graduate of the Class of 1938; his paternal grandfather, the Class of 1909; and his maternal grandfather, the Class of 1912. Both of his grandfathers served aboard ships in WW I performing convoy duty in the Atlantic. His dad was on USS TENNESSEE (BB-43) on "Battleship Row" at Pearl Harbor in December 1941 during the Japanese attack. His paternal grandfather was also there, but on shore duty. Both rushed to the base to fight the Japanese during the attack.

I met Charlie about 10 years ago at a luncheon of our Class of 1965 classmates. He generally speaks in a soft, comforting voice, which I tend to associate with clergy. I soon learned that Charlie is, in fact, an ordained minister and served as an Army chaplain for many years, including service during Desert Storm in 1991. I interviewed Charlie in Alumni Hall on the grounds of the Naval Academy in Annapolis.

I like to tell folks that I was conceived in Pearl Harbor, but I was actually born at the Naval Hospital in Bremerton, Washington. My father had numerous assignments throughout the world, but our family was living in Virginia while I attended high school in Maryland at the Severn School. I joined the Marine Corps Reserve and had the possibility of two different types of appointments to the Academy, one from the Reserves and the other, a Presidential, but didn't get either. So, I began engineering studies at the University of Rhode Island, where I joined the Army ROTC. I joke that the Marines taught me how to shoot the M-1 rifle, and the Army taught me how to clean it. This time I applied for an appointment to the Naval Academy through a congressman where my grandparents lived in California. When some football player out there didn't take his appointment, I got it.

At the Academy, I was not a great athlete and ended up playing field ball. This sport, (which I still feel is a really horrible game) was being played in only two places, Annapolis and the prison, Sing Sing! I had wanted to be a Marine since I was 12, so at service selection I chose Marine Corps and went directly after graduation to Basic Training at Quantico. My first assignment was to the 2nd Marine Division at Camp LeJeune where I was a platoon commander.

Roughly a year later, in April 1967, I arrived in Vietnam as a First Lieutenant. I was assigned to the "Study and Observation Group" (SOG) in the Military Assistance Command which was nominally out of Saigon. My actual location was up north in Da Nang. SOG was a joint service operation with the Air Force and Army Special Forces. We did "Black PT boats" which used "Nasty Class PTF's" to do special operations north of the 17th parallel. These boats were actually Norwegian and were 65 ft long with twin diesels. They were very fast. The crews were all South Vietnamese and belonged to the "Sacred Sword Patriots League." This was some sort of extreme group which hated the communists. They were commandos whose specialties were making landings in the North to create havoc, directing small arms fire into the enemy locations ashore, and capturing North Vietnamese fishermen. Whenever they captured these fishermen, they brought them back to a "secret island" where they were interrogated, but we were told, not harshly. The idea was to feed them well, treat them medically, and take them back to hopefully be agents to pass information to the South. My role was to be the Security Officer to make sure that none of these boats leaving Da Nang took any info with them which might tie them to U.S. forces. Later, I became the Intelligence Officer to brief the commandos before each mission.

I was then shifted to what we called "The Commando Camp." This unit was located east of Da Nang near Monkey Mountain and had a mixture of Vietnamese commandos, Navy SEALS, and Recon Marines to go on secret missions inside North Vietnam. We started using PBR's to get them there, but we quickly learned that they were too small for our operations. We upgraded to ASPB's [Assault Support Patrol Boat] *which were more heavily armed and allowed us to carry a team of commandos in the cabin aft of the bridge. We would go out only at night to insert these teams. I was aboard and my job was to man the radio while Navy personnel operated the boat. If the team ran into trouble, they would call me, and we would pick them up as they rushed back to the beach.*

My tour in-country ended two months later, and I was assigned as Executive Officer of the Marine Barracks at Annapolis. While I was there, one of my jobs was "Casualty Assistance Officer." This was difficult. A driver and I would go to the door of a family to give them the terrible news that their loved one had been killed. On one occasion there was a young girl about six sitting on the front porch who smiled at us and said, "I haven't seen a Marine in a long time." Her father was a Marine helicopter pilot. Her grandmother came to the door and said, "Is it John? Is he dead?" She then collapsed on the floor before we could answer. I found a neighbor who came over to stay with the grandmother because the Marine's wife was actually in Thailand on her way to visit her husband on R&R. She had no way of knowing immediately that he had been killed. It was terrible. We arranged for a memorial service in their church as the wife headed home. The pilot was buried at Arlington National Cemetery; I was there for support. As I said, it was terrible. I never got comfortable doing this aspect of my job, but my Christian faith and commitment stood by me during these calls. Most of my visits I didn't bring a chaplain with me. Later on, I asked one to come with me, but he was not much use at all, so I did most by myself.

I was at this post in Annapolis for two years and then volunteered to go back to Vietnam. When my wife, Susan, asked me why I did this, I told her that they were going to send me back anyway. I was now a Marine Captain and became E (Echo) Company Commander, 2nd battalion, 1st Marines. It was December 1970, and we were stationed just south of Da Nang at the Marine air base at Marble Mountain. Our camp consisted of tents in the sand. We had 160 Marines in Echo Company and were assigned an area south of the airfield to protect it from enemy 122 mm rockets. The local Vietnamese seemed to be farmers during the day and VC at night. One night the VC attacked in the seam between us and a Korean Marine unit just to the south of us. The attack was in the vicinity of what we called "No Name Lake." We thought we had VC trapped between us and the lake and called for a "basketball," a C-47 that drops flares so you can see what is going on. About 2 AM the VC came out of their holes to try to flee to the south. We killed some of them and took no casualties ourselves. We saw a sampan moving up the lake carrying wounded VC and called on our 106 recoilless rifle to make it go away. We later learned that inside Marble Mountain there was a secret 40-bed VC hospital that they were trying to reach. None of us knew this at the time. Years later, while I was in Germany as a chaplain with the Army, I met a Vietnamese priest from Da Nang who told me about that VC hospital in the mountain. Apparently, it was common knowledge among many of the locals who obviously chose not to share that info with any of our forces.

After we were there at Da Nang for about six months, we received word in June 1971 that we would all be going home to Camp Pendleton in California. I wrote Susan that I was coming home, and three weeks later everyone headed back - except Morrison. They sent me to Okinawa as Company Commander of a service company in the 3rd Marines. I was in charge of a group of non-combat personnel, the fellows taking care of pay, the bakers, etc. After six months I was sent for a tour at Marine Corps Headquarters in Washington. I did this for 3 1/2 years but was passed over for promotion twice - probably because I had never been a battalion staff officer, and because the war was over, the Marine Corps was being drawn down. In 1975 I was discharged and was able to follow my dream to go to seminary in St. Louis. I obtained a counseling degree while I was there and completed studies and residency at a local hospital in 1981.

I had an opportunity to become an Army chaplain and was soon promoted to Major while I was at Fort Hood in Texas. I later had assignments in Panama and Germany and several other bases in the U.S. When I was stationed at Fort Stewart in Georgia with the Army's 24th Infantry Division in 1991, I woke up one morning to learn that we were now on alert to deploy. I was sent to Dammam, Saudi Arabia, on a ship with 100 soldiers and countless military vehicles via the Suez Canal. When we arrived, we were put up on cots in a warehouse. The lights were on all night long and we were fed Saudi meals. Everyone who ate the salads got ill, so we were actually happy to go to the desert when combat began. During Desert Storm, I found myself in a turnip field in Iraq near Basra where our troops had responsibility for a large number of captured Iraqi troops. When the ceasefire occurred, we made our way back to an airfield and returned to Georgia.

Charlie's experiences were unique among our classmates. Although he served two tours in Vietnam as a Marine, due mostly to the time frames involved, he was not personally involved in the same type of horrendous combat experienced by many of his peers. I found his memories of his tour back in the States having to tell families of the loss of their loved ones in Vietnam to be gripping. I am not sure which is worse: having someone die in your arms in war or having to visit a family to tell them of the loss of their husband, father, or son. Both are chilling reminders of the horror of war.

Following Charlie's retirement from the Army in 1999, he served as an associate pastor at several churches in the Annapolis area. He also continues to provide counseling to many of our classmates concerning medical and emotional issues. Near the end of our conversation, Charlie expressed concern for those Vietnam veterans who were exposed to Agent Orange, the defoliant used extensively by American forces throughout the war to kill vegetation where enemy could hide. "It got into everything," he told me. "We essentially were doing our laundry in water containing Agent Orange. I developed prostate cancer in 2014 and am now on disability." Charlie's medical issues, probably resulting from his exposure to Agent Orange, were not unique among our classmates. Several are currently battling Parkinson's Disease, prostate cancer, and other conditions associated with Agent Orange. No one knows for certain how many Vietnamese have been affected, but it remains a horrible legacy for all involved in the war, no matter what nationality.

Bob Stanfield

Santa Monica, California
"His hands were
always sweaty"

Not all of my classmates entered the Naval Academy directly from high school. Bob, for example, joined the Navy reserves following graduation and reached the level of E-3 as an enlisted man on a destroyer. While he was concurrently attending Long Beach State University, an officer at his reserve unit helped him fill out paperwork for various Navy officer programs, including the Naval Academy. I spoke to Bob about his unusual background via computer from his home in Los Altos, California, where he lives with his wife, Kristin.

All of the three Navy programs I had applied for came through, and I chose to go to the Academy. Because I already had two years of college, I didn't have to go to prep school like most of the other prior enlisted. That's how I ended up taking the oath of office with you in June 1961. I wanted to go Navy Air, but my eyes were not good enough. I still wanted to become involved in aviation, so I chose to become a Naval Flight Officer (NFO). We weren't pilots, but you still get to fly. While doing flight training at Pensacola, I chose to go into the four-engine planes which meant P-3 anti-submarine aircraft. Because of a backlog of NFO's at the time, most of us were assigned shore duty for one year. My assignment was to teach navigation at the Navy base at Corpus Christi, Texas. When that was over, I received orders to VP-46 at Moffett Field in California where they were flying P-3B's, the Navy's main anti-submarine aircraft. Our first deployment was to Adak, Alaska, where bad weather was the daily norm. Most of our flights involved doing reconnaissance of the Kamchatka Peninsula where the Soviets had a submarine base. We would pick up the Russian subs as they came out of

Petropavlovsk and try to follow them using our anti-sub gear. In August 1969 we then deployed to Vietnam to the base at Cam Ranh Bay.

Ironically, Bob and I may have been chasing the same Soviet submarines. During this same period, I was a junior officer aboard the nuclear attack submarine USS GURNARD (SSN-662) also operating (covertly submerged, of course) off Petropavlovsk. Our role was to gather intelligence and attempt to follow any newly constructed Soviet subs as they were conducting initial sea trials so that we could monitor their acoustic signatures. We would also follow any sub to see where they were headed. Although we could always determine where the other sub was, we had no way to know its depth. If the two subs happened to cross paths, it could be a deadly collision. There are few "safe" jobs at sea or in the air.

While flying out of Cam Ranh, our main mission was to conduct Market Time patrols searching the entire South Vietnam coast for waterborne logistics craft, which we called "wiblics." When we found a suspicious boat, we could swoop down low to check it out, and at night, light it up with our searchlight. Although we carried Bullpup missiles, we would usually call in one of our surface units who could go out to investigate further and capture or sink them, if necessary. We could go down as low as 300 feet when we surveilled them, but we were generally at 5000 ft. If we saw something doing high speeds, as much as 40 kts, we knew it wasn't a fishing boat. We had to get someone to get it before that boat got into one of the rivers to deliver its goods to the Viet Cong. Usually, we would leave Cam Ranh and fly directly across Vietnam down to where Vietnam met the Cambodian coast at Ha Tien. From there we would begin a lengthy patrol down around the Ca Mau Peninsula and up the coast all the way north to the Gulf of Tonkin. If we shut down two of our engines, we could fly for 14 hours. We did these flights every other day. Because each member of the plane crew had a limit of flying 104 hours a month, they would send us back to the Philippines for the rest of the month. On the long flights we would do a lot of joking with each other to help make the time pass. Once I wrote the direction back to the base on a banana and sent it up to the pilot.

One of my squadron mates, a classmate of ours, Mike Powell, had earlier volunteered for a special mission in squadron VO-67 flying old

P-2 aircraft dropping special listening devices into the jungle near the Ho Chi Minh Trail to hear troop movements of the North Vietnamese as they came down the trail. When his plane was hit and was going down, he bailed out when ordered. Mike survived and was rescued, but after he joined our squadron, he was so nervous about flying that his hands were always sweaty. We talked a lot, and he told me that he would be tossing and turning in bed at night worried about being in the air again. Not too long later, he turned in his wings and was assigned elsewhere in the Navy. I understand that he has since died of cancer.

VO-67 was a squadron of P-2 anti-submarine aircraft converted to perform a secret mission in the Vietnam War from February 1967 to July 1968. Their nickname was the "Ghost Squadron" and all crew members, including Mike, were volunteers. These aircraft flew out of Nakhon Phanom Royal Thai Air Force Base to drop sensors on the Ho Chi Minh Trail in both Vietnam and Laos. The missions were called Muscle Shoals and Operation Igloo. The sensors they dropped were called Air Delivered Seismic Intrusion Detectors (ADSID) which would burrow into the ground to detect movement. Three of the aircraft were shot down and 20 crew members were killed. Although I do not know for certain, Mike was probably aboard the OP-2E aircraft, call sign Sophomore 50, which was hit by anti-aircraft fire over Laos on February 27, 1968. The pilot, Commander Paul Milius, ordered his crew to bail out; seven were rescued. Commander Milius also bailed out, but his body was never recovered. This same squadron participated in providing aerial support of the Marines during their intense battle at Khe Sanh in early 1968.

One night when we were at Cam Ranh Bay, we had a USO show featuring the New Christy Minstrels. After the show was over, we went back to our barracks and about an hour later, the sirens went off to indicate that we were being attacked. This one was mostly mortars and rockets. We all raced to our bunkers and suddenly all of the New Christy Minstrels crawled in with us. I asked them if there were going to sing for us again. They were so scared they didn't laugh! We often went to sleep with lots of machine gun fire all around us. Another night a big rocket hit next to my office; the next morning it looked like Swiss cheese from all the shrapnel which went through the file cabinets and out the other side. The Viet Cong would even send some drugged out teenagers across the bay there in Cam Ranh carrying satchel charges to try to blow up our aircraft. We always had our planes parked with sandbags around them and none were damaged.

My next assignment was a tour at the Navy Postgraduate School studying meteorology. Following that, I was right back in Vietnam in May 1972 as the Flag Lieutenant for the admiral in charge of Carrier Division Seven. We were deployed in the Tonkin Gulf in both USS SARATOGA (CVA-60) and USS AMERICA (CVA-66). While I was there, I became ejection-seat qualified which allowed me to fly in A-6 tankers. These were "gas stations in the sky" providing refueling for all our planes making strikes on North Vietnam. They would give us hand signals for how many pounds of gas they needed.

My first catapult shot off the carrier was "entertaining." The pilot was a young guy who was determined to give me some thrills. He took us down to 50 ft above the water doing 550 kts and then zoomed up to 20,000 ft while pulling 4 g's. Then we flew over along the North Vietnamese coast to see if we could draw some MiG's out so our fighters could take them on, but none came out. We also did some practice dog fights with F-8's and F-4's while we were waiting to provide fuel for planes returning from bombing missions over North Vietnam.

During my time on the carriers, we lost some aircraft on take-offs and landings and also several were shot down by air-to-air-missiles while on missions over the North. Our air crews were very frustrated by the rules of engagement which made them have to get permission from Washington before attacking most targets. We would send flash messages seeking approval but often the permission would come two days later after the targets were long gone.

Bob had 11 years of active duty and then joined the Naval Reserve. He retired as a Captain in the Reserves while spending 17 years in the banking industry. He expressed personal frustration at the direction of the war. "We were saving lives, but we were really pawns on our leaders' chessboard."

Denny Neutze

Baltimore, Maryland

"I needed to do something"

Not all of our classmates served in combat roles in Vietnam. To sustain a prolonged war anywhere, especially on the other side of the world, requires a large support force supplying a steady stream of logistics and services. In addition to war fighting equipment and ammunition, there is a continuous need for food, housing, and a myriad of other needs. Denny's role was to bring his expertise in the legal area to the war.

I interviewed Denny via computer from his home in South Florida where he now lives with his wife, Sunny. Prior to our conversation, in response to a request I had made on our class forum, he had contacted me with information concerning the handling of currency for our troops while they were in Vietnam. I began by asking Denny how he became an attorney in such a short period after our graduation from the Naval Academy in June 1965.

It was not something I had originally planned to do. However, in high school I was in Sea Scouts and decided I wanted to go to the Academy. I enlisted in the Naval Reserves on my 17th birthday and was able to obtain an appointment to USNA via that route. Unfortunately, when time came for our service selection in our final year, my original 20/20 vision was long gone, making me ineligible to be a line officer driving ships or flying planes. My choices to fill our 4-year active duty obligation were CEC (Civil Engineering Corps), NFO (Naval Flight Officer- who is not a pilot), or SC (Supply Corps). My engineering skills were nil, and I didn't want to fly, so....Supply Corps it was. Following graduation,

I attended a 6-month school in Athens, Georgia, learning how to be a supply officer. I was then assigned as Supply Officer on an old destroyer, USS MARSHALL (DD-676), which was now a Naval Reserve training ship in Tacoma, Washington. There I did all the usual jobs associated with this billet, such as obtaining all parts, supplies, and food for the ship; supervising the officer and enlisted messes; running the ship store; disbursing pay to everyone; and most of the other miscellaneous jobs which none of the more senior officers on board wanted.

Although Denny did not use the term, all of us who experienced being the junior officer aboard a ship used the generic term, SLJO, "Shitty Little Jobs Officer" to describe our role. For example, as soon as I reported aboard my first submarine, I was designated the "Movie Officer" whose job was to obtain the 60 or more movies for each patrol. Because I did not always have great success getting the best movies (or even mildly decent ones), I endured considerable grief in this job until someone junior to me reported aboard.

While I was on MARSHALL, I happened to see an article in Navy Times which described a program for officers called "Excess Leave." I saw this as an interesting opportunity for a Navy career in law. I learned that I could remain on active duty as a naval officer but attend law school on my own. To be eligible for this program I had to have been on active duty for at least two years. I didn't meet this requirement, so I applied for a waiver. Much to my surprise, it was granted. I gained acceptance and attended law school at the University of Maryland. While my law classes were in session, I received no pay. During breaks in the school year, I did receive pay while working at a Naval Supply command in Norfolk. I passed the Maryland bar exam in May 1970, but still had several years of required service. I was no longer a Supply Corps officer, but now a member of the Navy JAG Corps (Judge Advocate General). I volunteered for duty in Vietnam and was assigned in December 1970 to the Naval Support Activity, Saigon, which was located at a large Vietnamese base about 20 miles south in Nha Be.

I participated in a lot of trials there, both as a Prosecutor and as Defense Attorney. I preferred doing the prosecuting and was involved in some interesting cases. No matter where sailors and Marines are located, things happen; sometimes violent things happen. For example, I was assigned to prosecute a Navy Chief Petty Officer who allegedly shot and killed another Chief Petty Officer. The shooter was a popular fellow whose nickname was "Sweet Pea." Everyone who witnessed the shooting liked him so they would not freely testify against him. I had to have some of these guys declared "adverse witnesses" which allowed me to ask them leading questions. Because of the difficulty obtaining testimony, it was a tough case and the Chief walked free. I also had temporary assignments in Saigon as the counsel to an investigating officer for a helicopter accident where, due to a mix-up, believe it or not, no one knew for three days that the helo was missing. When they finally realized that no one had seen the crew, they sent out search parties and the Vietnamese found the wreckage (and 4 bodies). The cause was determined to be that the rotor blades had literally come off while in flight. In this investigation I learned all about "the Jesus nut."

The "Jesus nut" was a slang term for the main rotor retaining nut, sometimes called the mast nut, which holds the main rotor to the mast. It is a single point of failure which can cause catastrophic loss of the helicopter. The name originated (supposedly during the Vietnam War due to the considerable use of helos) because if that nut fails, the only option for everyone aboard is to pray to Jesus. Obviously, it is mandatory to check this part carefully before every flight. However, in many combat situations in Vietnam, "things happen" and people die, often due to bad luck or being in the wrong place at the wrong time.

After six months at Nha Be, I was assigned to the staff of COMNAVFORV (Commander Naval Forces Vietnam) in Saigon. I was primarily a military judge in this assignment. We didn't have any Navy brigs for prisoners awaiting trials, so they were always kept in a jail at the huge Army base at Long Binh and shuttled back and forth to our courtroom back at Nha Be. The joke was that they were staying at "LBJ" (Long Binh Jail). This was something of a slap at Lyndon Baines Johnson whose legacy at the time was not exactly popular among many troops in Vietnam after he left office.

One trial that went a while was in August 1971 up at Long Binh. The accused was a First Class Petty Officer whose job was to transport military prisoners back and forth. One day he apparently stopped for a few beers in transit and then hit and killed a Vietnamese man and a passenger who was riding with him on a motorcycle. The Petty Officer's blood alcohol level was high. I was the trial judge in what was a "judge only" trial. The defense argued that there had been no official chain of custody for the blood sample so the results should be excluded. I reluctantly agreed. Because this was the only evidence to convict the Petty Officer of vehicular manslaughter, I could not rule him guilty. However, I was able to do something by finding him guilty of drinking while on duty. I sentenced him to 30 days of restriction and reduced him in rank from E-6 to E-4. That was not a popular decision among the sailors who wanted him to receive no punishment, but I felt that I needed to do something. That motorcyclist and his passenger were dead no matter what the legal issues were.

While I was talking to Denny about his Vietnam experiences, we discussed MPCs (Military Payment Certificates). Most troops in Vietnam were not paid in U.S. dollars while in country. MPCs were paper money denominated in various amounts, from 5 cents up to 20 dollars. Its purpose was to eliminate American currency which could end up in enemy hands and/or distort the Vietnamese economy. MPCs began to be used in Europe following WW II because local citizens were happy to exchange their own currency for U.S. dollars at a much higher rate than the official exchange rate. Merchants had far greater trust in the stability of the U.S. dollar than their own currency. This led to a disruption of the local economy due to a steady inflation of the local currency. The use of MPCs continued both in the Korean and Vietnam wars for the same reasons. The certificates could be used on base for purchases of goods, and I suspect, in many a card game. Of course, they quickly also flowed illegally into the local economy as payment for various services, including many of the local "lovelies." Vietnamese holding these notes had clever ways, all illegal, to convert the MPCs into U.S. cash.

Because of the known fact that MPCs were illegally in the hands of many locals, the U.S. would periodically change colors of the current MPCs to attempt to thwart the local black market types. To do this successfully, there would be, without notice, a declaration of a "C-day" (conversion day), on which all current MPCs held by GI's had to be exchanged for the new color notes. On these days, everyone was restricted to the base while the exchange took place. Any "old" MPCs held after the "C-day" were worthless. Because any Vietnamese in town holding these now worthless notes lost money, there were countless schemes in place to readily convert the MPCs to U.S. cash almost as soon as the locals received them. There were procedures to ensure that sailors and Marines who happened to be in the field on C-days did not lose their money. You could also convert your accumulated MPCs to cash before going out of country on R&R.

Typical MPCs used in Vietnam

Following Denny's departure from Vietnam he was stationed in Naples, Italy. He went on to a series of other JAG Corps assignments both abroad and in the Pentagon before retiring as a Captain following 28 years of service.

Judd Halenza
Richfield, Minnesota
"I lost my wingman"

I had several classes with Judd at the Academy, but our careers took different paths following graduation. I knew that he was an aviator and had flown missions during the war but had no other details. I spoke to him via computer from his home in Del Mar, California, where he lives with his wife, Susan.

My dad was an enlisted man in the Navy during WW II. After the war, we ended up in the Minneapolis area where Dad became an insurance agent. Mom became the first female vice-president of Pillsbury Mills. I went to high school in nearby Richfield where I played football and wrestled. I talked to my counselors and applied to some Ivy League schools. While looking at other catalogs, I saw one from the Naval Academy. It seemed to offer a different type of education and I applied. I received an appointment from a group of senators who had given extra appointments to the Navy athletic department to distribute. At the Academy, I played plebe (freshman) football and wrestling, but for the next three year played scrum half on our new rugby team.

When service selection came during our last year, I had already received an Arleigh Burke scholarship. This meant that I was sent initially to USS DAVIS (DD-937), a destroyer out of Newport, Rhode Island. DAVIS soon deployed to Vietnam in January 1966. I was assigned to be the Ship Secretary which put me in charge of most of the admin on the ship. I always joked that my most important role was being in charge of the ship's Bingo games. During our tour in Westpac, we primarily did two things: plane guarding for the carriers on Yankee Station, and fire support for Marines fighting along Route 1. The forward air controllers were Marines on the ground who gave us coordinates at night indicating where to shoot. While we were plane guarding during carrier operations, there was an A-4 accident with the plane in the water. We were told to "pick up the pieces" - all we found was half of a pilot's helmet.

When DAVIS went into Hong Kong for a liberty visit, a local entrepreneur called "Crazy Mary" would bring a boat alongside. We would trade all our expended brass (from firing countless rounds to help the Marines) in return for her crew to paint our ship for free. Of course, many of us always suspected that same brass found its way back to Vietnam, probably to be used against Americans.

During the war, and for years afterwards, many shady deals took place in liberty ports throughout Westpac where officers on ships would get entangled with local entrepreneurs offering various services. This mentality often led to inappropriate contracts being awarded in return for favors (large sums of cash, expensive gifts, prostitutes) as exemplified as late as the 2000's in the so-called "Fat Leonard" scandal. Seventeen Navy officials were court-martialed or faced federal charges.

While our ship was in Subic Bay, I took a taxi over to the Officer's Club at Cubi Point Naval Air Station where I observed four junior officers each holding a leg of a chair with their squadron commander riding in that chair. They then dumped him into water in the dunk tank. I immediately said to myself that this seemed a much better way to spend liberty time in this war than what we did, or didn't do, on my destroyer. I was now hooked on Navy Air. DAVIS sailed back to the states via the Suez Canal, and I got off the ship in Greece. I did some traveling before beginning Arleigh Burke graduate studies at Stanford in Statistics. While I was there, I applied for Navy Air, was accepted, and arrived at Pensacola for aviation training in Fall 1967. I chose to go jets and trained at Beeville, Texas. My flight instructor was a Marine Corps Captain who told me I was insane if I didn't fly Phantoms, the F-4's. That's exactly what I was able to do.

My first aviation assignment was VF-121, the Replacement Air Group (RAG), which is where I learned to fly the Phantom. After this eight to nine month tour, I was sent to my first operational squadron, VF-114, out of Miramar Air Station near San Diego. Our squadron was assigned to *USS KITTY HAWK (CV-63), but I got married in December 1969, and was sent to Top Gun School before I deployed. This was somewhat unusual because I had not done much of anything in the squadron. I had to cut my honeymoon short to attend Top Gun School; my wife has never forgiven me. Top Gun School was still new, and we were operating out of a trailer. The syllabus consisted mostly of learning how to fight the Russian MiG-21. We did 30 days practicing air-to-air combat over the Pacific. Prior to initiating the Top Gun training, the U.S. Navy had experienced a 2-1 kill ratio in combat against the MiG-21; after the program had been in operation, the kill ratio improved dramatically to 21-1. We learned how to take our aircraft to the absolute limit and how to do close-in fighting.*

VF-114 deployed on KITTY HAWK in November 1970, but we found our time near Vietnam to be relatively benign due to strict U.S. government restrictions on where we could not fly or bomb. On our next deployment, also on KITTY HAWK, in February 1972, we had orders not only to go into North Vietnam, but to gain air superiority and do intense bombing. Our squadron flew 60 days in a row with each of us doing 2-3 flights a day. Initially there was a lot of opposition from North Vietnamese MiGs during our missions against Hanoi and Haiphong, but once we started to shoot a lot of them out of the sky, they tended to come out only occasionally. One pilot in the lead group of planes before us shot down two or three MiGs. By the time I got there, the MiGs had scattered and were nowhere to be found the remainder of that day.

Two Navy F-4 Phantoms in flight

Our biggest concerns were the surface-to-air missiles (SAMs) and 57 mm anti-aircraft artillery (AAA). Both my Radar Intercept Officer (RIO) who sat behind me in the F-4 and I could hear an audible signal indicating the presence of a SAM radar and a different sound when it was locked onto us. When we saw the missile coming toward us (they looked like a skinny telephone pole), we would not maneuver until it was about 3/4 mile away. Then I would execute a hard turn, a real hard turn, pulling maybe 5-6 g's. The SAM couldn't make that type of turn and would explode beyond us. The real problem was when there was reduced visibility because we couldn't see the missiles coming.

Our squadron of F-4's lost two aircraft and their crews during this cruise. I lost my wingman during a bombing mission over the south near Hue. His aircraft was shot down by 37 mm AAA. We were carrying 500 lb bombs and after I dove in at a 45-degree angle to release my bombs, I looked back and saw him get hit in the canopy. His plane went straight into the ground. I saw the glistening glass from his cockpit. I stayed in touch with his widow for at least 15 years. She had continued to work with various groups to attempt to retrieve his remains, but was unable to do so, at least as far as I know. Our other squadron loss was over the North where our XO (Executive Officer) was lost due to a SAM hit on a night mission. He was shot down exactly where Jane Fonda had assured Americans that there were no SAMs. All four of these aviators were KIA.

Targets for most of our missions were determined by planners in Washington, D.C. Our large attack missions, called Alpha strikes, would consist of 20-25 planes all heading toward the pre-determined targets. Sometimes we would find bad weather with low visibility over the target and have to dump our bombs elsewhere. I remember one particular mission when we had been tasked to hit a target in the north over Hanoi, but the weather was impossible there. So then, we were directed to hit another target south near Vinh, but that was also socked in. Suddenly one of our pilots said, "Hey, there's a bridge...let's hit it." So, we all took turns coming in to bomb it. I have no idea if we destroyed that bridge because I was concentrating on getting the hell out of there. On those Alpha missions, our F-4's would always go in first to conduct "flak suppression" before the A-6 and A-7 bombers would arrive to do their bombing. I always believed that although we had to come in first, the

SAM and AAA guys were sleeping, and we could blast them before they knew what was happening. At least that is how I rationalized it. KITTY HAWK also lost other aircraft and their crews during this cruise.

Launching aircraft off a carrier is inherently dangerous. I was sitting on the flight deck hooked up to the catapult waiting to be launched when the plane next to me, an A-7, suffered a catapult malfunction. As I watched, black smoke rose from the wheels as the pilot braked, but the plane still went off the front of the carrier into the water. The pilot was able to eject before the plane hit the water and was safely recovered. As I watched all this, I kept wondering if they were going to now launch me on the other catapult, or if they would stop all operations to investigate what the hell had happened. No, they launched me immediately and everything worked. I was not happy.

When we returned to the states in November 1972, I was transferred to VF-121. I received orders to the Pentagon but decided to resign in early 1974, and joined the reserves. My wife and I moved to L.A. where I joined a friend managing movie star money. I then did real estate work for Coldwell Banker in San Diego for five years before starting my own commercial real estate company in Del Mar, California.

I asked Judd about his feelings in the days back on the carrier after losing a wingman and other aviators during that second Vietnam cruise on KITTY HAWK. He told me, "Of course, you think about it, but most of us were young and feeling immortal. We kept telling ourselves that it couldn't happen to me. If you did dwell on it, you wouldn't be 100% concentrated on your own flying and that would kill you. Flying was my job...dying wasn't."

Bob Andretta

Brooklyn, New York
"Suddenly I heard voices"

Bob has been a good friend for over 50 years. We were both in the 23rd Company at the Naval Academy during our first class (senior) year and often partied together on weekend liberty. Many of these encounters, unfortunately, ended with alcohol-related incidents. I have no idea how we avoided serious trouble. Our journeys in the Navy took us on different paths; it was not until both of us found ourselves living in the Washington, D.C. region in the late 1980's that we resumed contact. I interviewed Bob at my home in northern Virginia.

I was born in Brooklyn but was raised in and around Washington, D.C. Part of this time we lived in Greenbelt, Maryland, which was a planned community first envisioned by Eleanor Roosevelt. My dad worked for the U.S. Government Printing Office and Mom was a housewife. I attended St. John's College High School in Washington and was a percussionist. I had always been enamored with the Navy due to reading a lot of fiction; also, two of my uncles served in WW II. One was in the Royal Navy and the other in the Pacific on USS JUNEAU (CL-52), which was sunk by the Japanese during the Battle of Guadalcanal. He survived in the water for three days before being rescued. I applied to the Academy while in high school but didn't receive an appointment. So, right out of high school, I enlisted in the Navy and went to boot camp before being assigned to USS TURNER (DD-834). While I was standing watch on the bridge, the Captain encouraged me to apply for a program which provided appointments for enlisted personnel to go to the Naval Academy. My main activity at USNA was playing various positions on our new rugby team. One of the highlights was when we beat a group of British midshipmen who were visiting Annapolis on three U.K. frigates. When service selection came, I chose to be on surface ships and received orders to USS CHARLES F. ADAMS (DDG-2).

After I attended Guided Missile School, I joined ADAMS in Charleston, South Carolina, before deploying to the Mediterranean. We had to pass through a harrowing winter storm in the Atlantic to get there, but visited ports all over the Med before returning to Charleston to begin an over-haul of our ship in the summer of 1966. My next orders were temporary duty to USS BORDELON (DDR-881) on a three-week Arctic cruise. Again, this involved horrible North Atlantic weather and we damn near froze to death when we were standing watches on the bridge. I was then assigned to USS JULIUS A. FURER (DEG-6) which was under con-struction at Bath Iron Works in Maine. The ship was commissioned in October 1967 and proceeded to our homeport in Newport, Rhode Island. One of our missions was a sobering one. In May 1968 we were sent to the eastern Atlantic to assist in the search for USS SCORPION (SSN-589) which had disappeared while transiting from the Mediterranean to its homeport in Norfolk. We had to get underway immediately and I was the senior officer aboard (as a Lieutenant); the Captain and all the other senior officers were still ashore. The missing members of our crew, including all the officers, met us halfway across the Atlantic via helicopters. We searched for two days but found nothing. I was supposed to be on FURER for two years, but contrary to what the detailer had told me, I received message orders to Vietnam. I got off the ship in Malta, caught a military hop to Frankfurt via Nice, then flew back to the U.S. to McGuire Air Force Base in New Jersey. A few weeks later, I was in U.S. Navy Advisor School in Coronado, California. I had 11 weeks of Vietnamese language training, but it was, of course, the wrong dialect for where I ended up in Vietnam.

I flew into Tan Son Nhut Air Base in Saigon and made my way to my assignment as the U.S. Navy adviser to Coastal Group 14. This was a Vietnamese Navy base which was on the Cua Dai River. Their "fleet" consisted of several junks which were small wooden boats with curved bows and outfitted with a machine gun. I got to Da Nang and snagged a ride on a small military boat which took me on an overnight trip south 15 miles to Goi hamlet where CG -14 was located. I was soaked from sea spray and quite cold. As we arrived, there was considerable gunfire, some of which hit the side of our boat. I jumped over the side in my khakis and waded ashore in deep mud while dragging all my belongings which were getting soaked with seawater. I was greeted only by Vietnamese sailors. The Lieutenant I was relieving passed me by, yelling, "It's all yours!" He then hopped on the boat I had come in on. That was my turnover. It was now early February 1969.

There were two U.S. enlisted men working for me. One helped with seamanship and weapons. I called him "Gunny." The other sailor was a machinist mate whom I called "Nuts and Bolts." My Vietnamese counterpart was a Lieutenant, a small fellow named Dai Uy Hai who always assured me that he was in charge, and I was only his advisor. My only way to communicate with my boss in Da Nang, a Navy Commander, was via an old Korean War radio telephone. The afternoon I arrived we had a Tet feast consisting of rice covered with some form of fish sauce. It was also covered with a thick coating of black flies.

Later that day, we received a message from Da Nang that a U.S. helicopter had gone down up the Cua Dai River with five Marines aboard. They wanted us to take our junks up the river to help with the search. None of the Vietnamese in our group had ever gone that far up the river, so there was considerable apprehension from my counterparts, especially Dai Uy Hai. He decided to send "volunteers" with me on two junks. I was told that a U.S. Forward Air Observer (FAC) would assist us. As soon as I contacted this fellow on radio, he wanted to change the frequency. He told me several times to switch to "Jack Benny plus three." I didn't know what he was talking about. I quickly learned that formal radio communications didn't exist in this part of Vietnam. The FAC was pissed at my ignorance about Jack Benny's stated age of 39, but we eventually became close friends. He was flying by himself in a small plane that looked to me like a Piper Cub. We didn't take any fire on the way up the river. It was now totally dark, but the whole area was lit up by flares from a U.S. Marine artillery unit. This helped us to see what was going on. Someone else found all of the downed Marines. We took intermittent fire from the shore as we came back down the river to the base. Upon arrival, we were greeted by a crowd of cheering Vietnamese sailors who considered us heroes because none of them had ever gone that far up the river. I still hadn't slept in days.

The boats we were using were called Yabuta junks. They were about 45 ft long with old Chinese truck diesel engines and a single screw. The junks had a .30 caliber machine gun up front and were gray with a red human eye painted on the bow to ward off evil spirits. There was a tiny deck house aft.

Ashore I slept in a hooch made out of 4 x 8 plywood sections with a tin roof. The whole base was built on sand and there were no trees. This had one advantage: no rats, because they couldn't burrow holes in the sand. Our base was next to a small hamlet where some of the families of the Vietnamese sailors lived. There were two other hamlets nearby; in this part of Vietnam, there were typically two to four hamlets to a village. Traditionally, the Vietnamese in this area lived in structures made of palm fronds covered with dirt, but with so many American supplies having arrived in-country, many hooches were now made of plywood. My second night on the base, I was awakened by a clanging sound indicating that we were under attack. We crawled into a command bunker close by and waited for the incoming. We were being attacked with mortars and small arms fire. There was a Marine base further up the river where they would fire 105 mm howitzers, generally toward a nearby island suspected of being a Viet Cong stronghold. When these were fired, it would scare the shit out of us. While we were in the bunker that night, I was thrown across the room and thought we had been hit. When I came to, I immediately threw up like a geyser. It turns out that we had not been hit by a mortar, but during the attack a lightning strike had hit the radio antenna and traveled down the wire to my handset. I had burns on my face, but no other injuries. That ended my second day at CG-14.

Our role was to patrol the inland waterways and the nearby waters off the coast in the South China Sea. Much of the local land was potato farms with women and children doing the work. The men were mostly VC. On one of our missions, we went into these potato fields and saw some women in black clothing, typical of the VC. It was a free fire zone, and I wasn't sure if I should shoot them or not. I chose not to fire and was relieved that my Vietnamese counterpart treated most of these villagers firmly, but politely. We captured a few VC who were hiding in bunkers, but there were no mass shootings. The My Lai massacre had taken place about a year earlier, and we didn't want a repeat of that tragedy. There were several similar missions like this. We would also inspect sampans along the coast searching for contraband, but rarely found any.

Chu Luk command junk

My official title was Senior Naval Advisor for Quang Nam Province. The U.S. Army "boss," a Major, was upriver in a fair-sized city, Hoi An; he was a bit of a prick with immaculately pressed uniforms. We eventually got along, but I always referred to him as "Major Starch." This fellow and my boss in Da Nang wanted us to go places which had never been searched. The other side of the river was totally VC, and my feeling was not to poke the bear. My Vietnamese counterpart was also reluctant, but we took a fleet of six junks, led by a larger one, a Chu Luc, south along the barrier island. One of the Yabuta junks got spun around in the surf and was beached. Dai Uy Hai wanted to leave the junk and its men to fend for themselves, but I refused. I jumped over with a line wearing only my underwear. We were able to use the Chu Luc junk to pull the beached junk off the beach. There was a very strong current and I lost all my underwear. I came back naked, but we had saved that junk and its sailors. On the way back, we passed through a swarm of poisonous sea snakes which the Vietnamese netted and killed for dinner. I chose to pass on this delicacy - or at least I think that I did. I was never sure what I was eating when I joined the Vietnamese for meals.

I had several opportunities to interact with the Vietnamese who lived in the hamlet and on the sampans which they used to fish at sea. Women in the hamlet would start showing up at the market with babies to search for me. The babies had terrible boils on their scalps and their moms asked me to do something to help. I brought out some soap bars, hydrogen peroxide, and a sharp knife. I used the knife to get the core out and then washed the wound with the hydrogen peroxide and gave them a small bar of soap to take home. Some of the women had never seen soap and tried to eat it until I explained its use.

Later we did another operation on a place called Barrier Island and got into an intense firefight with the VC on the shore. I had an M-16 rifle and a holstered .45 pistol and a radio. I soon learned to leave the rifle behind. Once ashore, as we were wading across a rice paddy, we started taking fire. The Vietnamese with me all ducked down into this incredibly foul water, but I couldn't do it. Due to my silly reluctance, I received a small grazing head wound and actually saw another bullet fly past me. Another time, we were ashore west of the river deep into what was surely enemy territory. There were several irrigation ridges and we started taking intense fire. We went up one of these banks where I saw a face sticking out of one of the bushes on top. Instinctively, I fired my .45 and hit him in the chest. To this day I think that I heard his sternum breaking apart. We retreated and as I slid down the hill, I called for fire support. The same FAC came on and told me, "There's too many of them. I'll try to distract them, but you need to get the hell out of there." Suddenly a RPG (rocket propelled grenade) landed down the hill and I got hit with a lot of shrapnel along both legs and in my groin area. I stayed on the radio and soon four Air Force THUDS (Republic F-105 Thunderchief fighter-bomber) from an air base in Thailand flew in. There were bombs coming down from high in the air and they landed everywhere. I was worried that we would be hit. On their second pass they did a better job targeting the enemy forces. The FAC told me that he was seeing gray uniforms typical of the North Vietnamese Army. Apparently, we had stumbled on a large contingent of them. By then, my friend at the Marine Corps base started laying down artillery fire, which really helped. Those guys were good! Two sailors helped me back to the junks, and we made it to the base. Nothing could be done that night, but Nuts and Bolts worked on me. He took me in our skiff to Hoi An where some German medical volunteers patched me up. The FAC came to see me the next morning and told me that he was forced to make an emergency landing. His plane was full of holes! My wounds kept getting infected for the next several years. They never healed well.

Nuts and Bolts trying out the new well at CG-14

One day, a Swift boat (PCF) having engine problems pulled into our landing. Nuts and Bolts helped them to repair the engine, but halfway through the night one of the Swift boat sailors got hit in the eye by shrapnel during an explosion. As I worked on him during the night trying to save his eye, the sailor confessed that he had gotten into a game of chicken with a buddy. It was who could pull the pin and hold it the longest before throwing it into the river. Well, he "won" the game because one of his grenades exploded next to him as he threw it into the water.

I often had issues with the Swift boat skippers (they were not Captains, but Officers-in-Charge). I kept telling them that our river and the nearby Thu Bon were too shallow for safe navigation. I knew this because I had been doing some operations in my own 14 ft skimmer with some "cowboys" - that's what we called the Vietnamese Special Forces. On this occasion, I heard some action on the other side of the river. I found a Swift boat involved in a serious fire fight, and it had run aground near the shore. As I started over to assist, I got shot through one leg and the bullet went into my other leg. My boat ran out of control close to the shore, and I saw a young VC attempting to pull it ashore. I shot him in the face. I then drove over to the PCF telling the OIC for him and his crew to get on my boat and get the hell out of there before the VC blew up him, his crew and his boat. He argued that he didn't want to lose his ship. Suddenly, two of his sailors literally pulled him off the PCF and dragged him into my skimmer. We headed immediately back to our base; on the way, one of the sailors gave me some morphine and bandaged up my leg. I was in the hospital at Da Nang for 4-5 days. Two other PCFs showed up the next day and pulled that PCF off the shore.

Bob with young Vietnamese advisor

As soon as I healed, I returned to CG-14 and resumed our normal ops. Two Swift boats showed up and wanted to go up the river toward Laos.

As we went up the Cua Dai, I was in the lead PCF. Suddenly, there was a large explosion as we were hit. I was standing in the pilot house with the skipper and the helmsman. I was on the port side of the boat. The hit was on the starboard side, and immediately there were screams from some Vietnamese sailors whom we had picked up in Hoi An. Then another round hit us and I was thrown into the water on the port side. The skipper and the helmsman were thrown into the river on the starboard side. The boat went out of control and beached on the VC side of the river. I found myself stunned and in the river. One of the remaining sailors got control of the boat and took it off the sand bar and beached it on the opposite side to keep it from capsizing. The other PCF came up, guns blazing toward the VC, but didn't see us in the water.

The three of us started to swim to an island while still taking fire from the VC. When I was underwater, I could see bubble traces from bullets hitting the water. When I came up to get air, I could see bullets flying past me. The skipper was swimming ok, but the helmsman was struggling. I took off my khaki pants and showed him how to tie the legs in knots to inflate them to stay afloat. We finally got to an island in the middle of the river. It was now getting dark, and I told the other two guys to go to the other side of the island, find a bunker, and hide in it. More PCFs came into the river to look for us, and although I was doing jumping jacks to get their attention, they didn't see me. They also sent aircraft and helos to look, but no one saw us. It was now pitch black and I heard voices from a sampan full of VC looking for us. They came ashore but sounded frightened and set up shop in a bunker. I was hiding in a sort of a ditch nearby and could hear them laughing and talking in the bunker. I tried to be absolutely quiet; I went in my pants due to diarrhea. Sometime during the night, a small piglet joined me in the ditch. All of a sudden one VC came over by himself and took a piss in the ditch. I was hit by the spray, but he didn't see me. His piss scared the piglet which went off screaming. I was surprised that the VC didn't go hunting for the piglet because that was good eating.

The rest of the night passed without incident and the VC left the island in the early morning. Once daylight came, I was able to flag down a passing sampan and get back to our base at the mouth of the Cua Dai. The other two Americans on the other side of the island also flagged down a different sampan. I had a hole in my upper arm, probably from shrapnel.

I received a third Purple Heart for this wound. The rules were that if you received three Purple Hearts in Vietnam, you go home. I didn't want to leave Vietnam, so I turned in that last Purple Heart. I was becoming involved helping the local community and had sent two local women to Da Nang for mid-wife training so they could come back to set up a maternity ward. We also were building a school when I left. My CO in Da Nang came down to visit and was so alarmed by my condition that he took me back with him and put me in the hospital. I went into a "semi-coma" and heard three doctors who said that I "might" survive. I had an abscess on my liver and spent 3 weeks in the hospital in Da Nang. I got along great with the many wounded Marines who were there also.

My CO decided that I had endured enough action at CG-14 and assigned me to a "safer" unit at CG-13 north of Da Nang in Cau Hai Bay. It was indeed safer, but it was full of rats. It was also difficult for boats to get in and out of the harbor. For the remainder of my time at CG-13 there was no combat action. I returned to the States for leave, wounded but proud of my work with the local Vietnamese.

Bob returned from Vietnam with orders to a staff position in London. He remained in England for several years but then resigned to attend law school. Bob served two decades as an administrative law judge in Washington, D.C. He currently lives in Washington with his wife, Betty.

Bob's tour at CG-14 placed him directly in the middle of Viet Cong territory. His job, as with several other advisors to these coastal groups, involved almost daily danger. Bob was truly a warrior-ambassador. Bob teared up when he recounted his experiences having to shoot an enemy at close range. He developed a genuine love for the Vietnamese people, especially the children. When I asked him to join me for a tour of Vietnam in 2016, he was excited to be able to return. During our three weeks in-country, from Hanoi to the Mekong Delta, we had many occasions to interact with Vietnamese civilians, some of whom had been Viet Cong or even members of the North Vietnamese Army. Bob embraced each of these former adversaries and on every occasion showed love for the Vietnamese. When we visited Hoi An (now a major tourist destination) we were able to rent a small boat with a translator to take us down the Cui Dai to the location of his former base. On the way, Bob pointed out the island where he had spent that perilous night. When we reached the inlet where CG-14 had been located, nothing was left other than a family of fishermen with whom we had a great chat through a translator. One of the older members of the family recalled the base. As we returned up the Cua Dai to Hoi An, Bob was overcome with emotion. War memories have a long half-life. Detailed information concerning Bob's time in Vietnam can be found in his book, *Brown Water Runs Red.*

Tom Morgenfeld

Buffalo, New York
"We got lots of flak"

I interviewed Tom at his home in Camarillo, California, via my computer. He explained that although he was born in Buffalo, he grew up in Hamburg, a small town just south of Buffalo, and attended Hamburg High School.

I did well academically in high school and played on the first soccer team our school had. I also ran track and cross country but was not that good a runner. Several strange events happened that led to my going to the Naval Academy. A fellow who was a very good quarterback for Army had graduated from our high school several years earlier, and he was a local hero. That made me want to go to West Point, so I wrote to my Congressman to try to get an appointment. But that didn't happen, and I ended up sort of backing into going to Navy. I used to mow lawns as a kid, and unbeknownst to me, one of the lawns I mowed belonged to a secretary for our local congressman. I didn't know her that well, but she always smiled when she paid me. My best friend had also applied to the same congressman to go to West Point. Apparently, we were his two top choices for appointments. Several years later the lady told me that the congressman had called her up and asked her what to do. She said, "Send this one one to West Point, and send Morgenfeld to Navy." She confessed that she selected me to go to the Naval Academy because her family had strong ties to the Navy and wanted me there. I was just happy to be going to a good school!

Tom's interesting path to the Naval Academy was not unusual. There were few criteria determining how Congressmen made their appointments to the service academies at that time. In my own case, I was

403

apparently awarded my appointment because my mother had been the head nurse on the floor of a hospital in Kentucky where our local congressman's Executive Assistant was recovering during a long illness. When Mom was having one of her conversations with this fellow, she mentioned that I had applied to the Naval Academy. He winked and told her, "Don't worry, he'll be there." A local All-State fullback whom everyone assumed was going to receive the principal appointment to Navy didn't. As I relayed my story to Tom, we both laughed at how small and seemingly random events end up having such big effects on one's life.

At Navy I was a walk-on for soccer, but still made the soccer team. Unfortunately, while playing in a game during my second class (junior) year, I blew out my knee. My foot was facing backwards and that ended my athletic career. I got into flying because I had always had a thing for airplanes since I was a little boy. My dad was a shop teacher at our high school and his students would make scale models of all types of airplanes. Dad brought many of these home, and I spent a lot of time playing with the models. He even took me up to Buffalo to tour the Curtiss-Wright factory where we could see all the planes they built there. By our first class (senior) year I had done a lot of physical therapy on my knee to try to be eligible to fly. During my aviation physical, the surgeon who had done the surgery on my knee happened to be the physician who examined me. Instead of making me do some of the required deep knee bends, he asked me, "Tom, do you know what a deep knee bend is?" I was puzzled and said, "Yes, sir." He smiled and passed me even though I could not do a knee bend if my life depended on it. I owe a lot to that doc.

I reported to Pensacola for flight training in July 1965. I did well in the initial phases of training and got into the jet program. That initial training took place at Meridian, Mississippi. I then was sent back to Pensacola to do my carrier qualification landings in a T-2 Buckeye. My next assignment was in Beeville, Texas, to do advanced training for six months. We flew the F-9 Cougar and the F-11 Tiger, which was a thrill because the F-11 was supersonic. I loved it!

My next phase of training was in Miramar, California, in an F-8 Crusader training squadron. I could have chosen to go to F-4's, but

I wanted the challenge of flying the Crusader. It was a lovely flying airplane but the last 3/4 of a mile trying to land it on a carrier required that you really pay attention. It had variable incidence wings to slow it while allowing the fuselage to remain horizontal. The challenge was to try to control the power correctly with the wings in this position when you landed. Because of this issue that plane had a lot of ramp strikes destroying the plane and killing pilots.

F-8 Crusader aboard ship in Gulf of Tonkin

After three months I went to VF-62 at Cecil Field, Florida. We immediately deployed to the Mediterranean on USS SHANGRI-LA (CVA-38). It was an old Essex-class carrier built near the end of World War II. Because of the configuration of the F-8's, these planes at that time were always deployed to these older "short-deck" carriers with angled decks. That Med cruise was pretty quiet, and I had a lot of traps. It turned out to be a good deal because when I finally did get to the war, I knew how to fly the airplane really well because I had considerable experience during those 2 1/2 years.

SHANGRI-LA had been converted in 1956 to add an angled deck to allow launching and recovery of aircraft in two directions. Following a collision with a destroyer in 1965, the ship was successfully repaired and resumed operations. When Tom mentioned "traps," he was using naval aviator slang for landings on a carrier. When a pilot is controlling his plane to land, there are four wires strung sequentially across the carrier deck which capture, or "trap," a tail hook on the back of the plane to stop it. The goal is generally to catch the number three wire. If the pilot misses all four wires, he applies maximum power to be able to regain flight to circle the ship for another try. There are numerous videos available online to observe this challenging task. Every Navy pilot interviewed knew exactly how many traps he made and proudly tells you the number. The dreaded "ramp strike" is the term describing the accident when the plane approaches the back of the carrier too low and crashes into rear of the ship, called the ramp. If only the tail hook hits the ramp, the plane and pilot will probably survive. If the plane itself strikes the ramp, there may be loss of life and possibly a major fire. It is a fine line between a successful landing and tragedy for these aviators.

In December 1969 I went to the Navy's post graduate school to study aeronautical engineering. After that I received orders to VF-191 and deployed in mid '72 to USS ORISKANY (CVA-34). We would alternate off the Vietnam coast between Yankee Station in the north and Dixie Station in the south. Up north our main job was to provide protection for the photo-recon planes which were also F-8's rigged for that mission. The post-strike photo assessments were difficult because the Vietnamese anti-aircraft guys now knew for certain that you were coming and there was lots of flak. Also, most of these flights had to be low to get good photos, sometimes real low. Fortunately, no one in our squadron got shot down. By this time in the war, we had the benefit of the lessons painfully learned during thousands of earlier missions.

ORISKANY had a terrible fire during a previous tour at Yankee Station in 1966 - the worst carrier accident since WW II. A magnesium flare had ignited in the ship's forward hangar bay below the flight deck and quickly spread to five decks of the ship. 44 men were killed in the fire, including many combat pilots who had just flown missions over Vietnam. The subsequent investigation showed that the cause was human error. Heroic efforts, including jettisoning bombs overboard and wheeling planes out of danger, saved the ship. It took over three hours to put out the fire. Life at sea on any military vessel is inherently dangerous, especially on carriers.

Down south, our missions were almost all close air support. Our plane had four 20 mm guns, and we would load up two bombs, mostly 250 and 500 pounders, on the wings. We would get in touch with an airborne Forward Air Controller (FAC) who marked targets with white phosphorus rockets - nasty stuff! We called them "Willy Petes" and they made a lot of smoke. We were providing support for "whoever" - often our ground troops and even the South Vietnamese. We could also carry eight Zuni rockets. If the FAC's were at 6000 ft, you could count on there being a lot of AAA. They were up there to avoid most of it. If they were lower, there was not as much coming up. We normally did bombing dives at 60 degrees and 450 knots. We would always try to pull out at 6000 ft, generally pulling four g's coming out of the dive. We would then do a pretty good jink to the right or left to give the gunners a 3-dimensional problem trying to hit us. Sometimes we would get almost immediate feedback about how well we had done on the bombing from the FAC in OV-10's or OV-1's - prop planes which flew over the sites to observe. I would not want their jobs.

They always found work for us. ORISKANY would be online for three weeks and then go back to Subic Bay in the Philippines for a week and then back on the line. The ship actually lost a screw (propeller) *twice and had to go back to Japan to get a new one each time. We came back to the States from our second cruise which had been on a rather boring mission in the Indian Ocean in mid-74.*

When Tom left ORISKANY he was selected to go to the "Empire" Test Pilot school in England for a year. Following this interesting duty flying a wide assortment of aircraft, he thought that he was headed to the Navy Test Pilot School at Pax River but ended up at VX-4, the Navy's fighter operational test squadron at Point Mugu in California. This was not the "Top Gun" school, but a squadron that did tests of air-to-air missiles. His job was flying MiGs, the Russian fighter planes. "Flying those Russian planes was much the same as ours," he said. "You pull back on the stick and houses get smaller." He also was assigned to test the latest Russian fighter, the MiG-21, when it became available. How the U.S. obtained these planes he could not talk about. Tom resigned in 1979 and went to work testing planes for Lockheed while continuing to serve in the Navy Reserves. He proudly told me that he was still able to enjoy flying "fast planes" until he turned 60 in 2004. He still has his hand in flying as Chairman of the Board of the National Test Pilot School in California where students from all over the world become test pilots.

When reflecting on his combat days, Tom expressed mixed feelings:

I probably think about it more in retrospect than I did at the time I was there. War can be terribly dehumanizing. If you allowed yourself to think about what you were doing, it starts to affect your performance and you go crazy. You put it out of your mind and just go do it. It was a war.

And finally, "The Sweepers"

Chip Seymour and John Mitchell

Norfolk, Virginia - Bridgeport, Connecticut

Although I interviewed Chip and John at different times, I felt it appropriate to combine their stories because both were Commanding Officers of minesweepers which were tasked to bring closure to American involvement in the Vietnam War in February 1973. I interviewed both via computer on separate occasions. First, Chip's memories of times before he commanded his minesweeper:

I was born in Norfolk, Virginia, during WW II while my dad was serving as a Naval Officer. He had graduated from the Naval Academy in 1939 and was serving aboard the battleship USS NEVADA (BB-36) during the Japanese attack on Pearl Harbor. The crew was able to get NEVADA underway, but it was hit by a torpedo and numerous bombs, forcing the crew to beach the ship on a reef to keep it from sinking. It later slid off the reef and sank but was salvaged and served in later battles. I attended several high schools due to Dad's change of assignments. I wanted to go to the Academy and was able to receive a Presidential appointment. Upon graduation, I elected to go Surface Navy and received an assignment to USS BAUER (DE-1025) as First Lieutenant. We deployed to the Aleutian Islands off Alaska where my most vivid memories were the incredibly high seas and 45-degree rolls.

My next assignment was to USS SOUTHERLAND (DD-743) which was assigned to bombard coastal areas up and down the South Vietnamese coast in support of our forces ashore. With our 5"/38 guns we could fire up to seven miles inland. After two years on SOUTHERLAND, I received orders to the Naval Postgraduate School in Monterey, California. While I was there, I was seriously considering becoming a priest, but met my future wife, Mary, and decided to remain in the Navy.

My next orders were to take command of USS FORTIFY (MSO-446), a minesweeper which was homeported in Guam. I was supposed to be sent to minesweeping school because I had zero experience in mines - placing them or removing them. However, the school was cancelled, and in May 1972 I was sent directly to Guam. We went to sea for one day, and two days later I took command on May 10. Mary had accompanied me to Guam, and we were anticipating some time together, but the next day, on May 11, our Commodore knocked on my door with the news that we were taking all four minesweepers in our squadron to Subic Bay in the Philippines. We spent the next seven months practicing minesweeping operations out of Subic Bay in anticipation of the end of the war. The day after the Paris Peace Accords were signed, all four of our minesweepers were ordered to set sail for Haiphong Harbor. We had no escorts and arrived there on about February 10, 1973.

The Paris Peace Accords (officially "The Agreement on Ending the War and Restoring Peace in Vietnam") included representatives from North Vietnam, South Vietnam, the U.S., and the Viet Cong. The accords were signed on January 22, 1973. Most offensive U.S. ground operations had diminished in the preceding two years, but the air war had continued against the North. There was still fighting between South Vietnamese and communist forces. The provisions of the agreement were continually broken by both North and South Vietnam with little response from the U.S. – or any other countries. Two years later, the North Vietnamese launched a massive offensive which captured the South and terminated the war. Provisions of the Paris Accords involved the return of all prisoners of war and the clearing of mines from North Vietnamese ports by U.S. forces. Ensuring that there were no more mines would be the task of the American minesweeping forces.

USS FORTIFY (MSO-446) underway

John Mitchell now discusses his memories.

Although I was born in Connecticut, my family later moved to a farm outside of Asheville, North Carolina. My high school was small; we had only 100 in our class. After growing up on a farm, I decided that I wanted to do something as far away from farming as possible. When I saw the TV series, "Men of Annapolis," I decided that I wanted to go to the Naval Academy. My congressman didn't have an available appointment when I was a senior, so I attended NC State for a year studying engineering before I received his appointment. At the Academy, I was a gymnast and specialized in the side horse. As a child I had plastic models of ships, and never had any doubt about wanting to be on surface ships. After graduation, I was able to do so.

My first ship was USS MANLEY (DD-940) which operated out of Charleston. I was the Electrical Officer and then became what our

Captain called the "Boilers Officer." We went through the Panama Canal to Vietnam in the fall of 1966 and began doing gunfire support ops off the Vietnam Coast. We fired our guns so much that we had to meet a supply ship every three days for ammo re-supply. Sometimes we would receive a message saying, "We need help over here," then put target information into our computer and send it to our three gun mounts. We did this both day and night. The night firing was mostly the Harassment and Interdiction variety where we were simply trying to make the enemy uncomfortable. We also did a lot of plane guarding behind carriers on Yankee Station, but never had to pick up a pilot. We returned to Charleston via the Suez Canal and arrived in June 1967.

After I left MANLEY, I attended Destroyer School. I received orders as Chief Engineer on USS FLETCHER (DD-445). We deployed to Vietnam, and because FLETCHER was an older ship, did mostly plane guarding for the carriers. While we were there, we had a small split on the starboard side of our hull. Water was not pouring into the engine room, but it was a nuisance and could have gotten worse. We tried to do a repair there while lying to in the Gulf of Tonkin, but when we listed the ship to port to allow welders to go over the side, I saw a swarm of sea snakes directly below. I recommended to the Captain that we abort. He wasn't happy, but I didn't see him volunteering to go over the side himself. We returned from this deployment in early 1968, and I was offered the opportunity to be Chief Engineer on USS COCHRANE (DDG-21), which was right across the pier from FLETCHER. A few months later, I was again headed to Vietnam in early 1969. We again did gunfire support and were standing port and starboard watches. We talked directly to the spotters ashore who often thanked us saying, "You saved some lives."

I was considering getting out of the Navy, but my CO recommended that I try to become an Admiral's Aide. I did this and became aide to an admiral in Washington, D.C. for the next two years. I really enjoyed that job and put in for a small ship command. Not long afterward, I received a call asking me how quickly I could be ready to go to Guam. I learned that I had been assigned to be CO of USS ENGAGE (MSO-433), a minesweeper. I had never set foot on a minesweeper but was in luck because my XO had been on a minesweeper before. Also, our boatswain's mates were extremely competent. Our ship went into overhaul in Yokosuka and then sailed to Subic Bay for refresher training. The day after the Peace Accords, we left for Haiphong Harbor.

Task Force 78 underway; small vessel in center is one of the minesweepers

John and Chip's minesweepers were part of Task Force 78 (TF-78) which had orders to clear all mines in Haiphong Harbor as part of U.S. commitments in the Paris Accords. Most of these mines had been inserted beginning in May 1972 during Operation Pocket Money using attack aircraft from U.S. carriers on Yankee Station. TF-78 consisted of a mix of ships including helicopter carriers and aircraft assembled as Operation End Sweep to remove naval mines from North Vietnamese waters. Planning for removal of the mines was begun by the Navy's Mine Warfare Force shortly after the mines had been inserted due to requirements in the 1907 Hague Convention mandating removal after hostilities ended. Only mines that could be cleared by magnetic sweeps had been used and most were programmed to self-destruct or become inert after a designated time had elapsed. The U.S. knew the general location of most of the mines, but precise locations were unknown. One interesting part of Operation End Sweep was USS WASHTENAW, a Landing Ship Tank, which had been converted in early 1973 to be a "special device minesweeper" and re-designated as MSS-2. It had been pumped full of polyurethane foam to allow it to be a "guinea pig" to do sweeps through water which had presumably been cleared of mines. It had only a crew of six - all volunteers who remained topside during the sweeps so that if the ship hit a mine they would be blown overboard (probably safer than being below decks). In addition to Chip and John's minesweepers, the task force had detachments of specially configured CH-53 helicopters deploying a new sweeping device called a Magnetic Orange Pipe (MOP). TF-78 had been initiated secretly in November 1972 while peace talks were still underway and remained in the Philippines until the Accords were signed two months later.

Initial sweeping operations began on February 6, 1973, with John and Chip's ships and two other MSO's. They were protected during their operations in Haiphong Harbor by USS WORDEN (DLG-18) and USS EPPERSON (DD-719). Two weeks later three amphibious assault ships with CH-53 helos arrived along with several other ships to provide increased capabilities. Ironically, only one mine exploded during all minesweeping operations and that was as a helicopter passed over it. Midway during initial minesweeping, President Nixon halted operations because the North Vietnamese delayed the release of U.S. prisoners of war. When release of the POWs met Nixon's criteria a week later, he directed resumption of minesweeping. Other Vietnamese ports were swept by Navy helicopters. The Navy trained North Vietnamese sailors to do their own minesweeping and provided appropriate equipment. Final U.S. minesweeping operations in Vietnam ended on July 5, 1973.

John shared his memories of Operation End Sweep.

When we arrived, we initially laid some reference buoys because positioning is everything. Minesweeping is much like mowing grass; you want to cover all areas, but not keep going over the same grass. First, we swept water where the rest of the ships in the Task Force would anchor. There was a total commitment to safety. Because your chances for survival are far less if you are belowdecks when a mine were to explode, while we were sweeping, none of our crew were allowed belowdecks. I made an exception for those working in the Combat Information Center (CIC) and had them rig mattresses in the overhead for protection. The engineers and radiomen were allowed inside only when we were outside the minefield. Everyone else was topside in life jackets; some of our crew were up there playing chess because it became very boring. We did not sweep at night and went outside the area to anchor. We were in a day-on, day-off rotation with the crew up at 3 AM on our day to sweep. We would do the sweeping from daylight to sunset. On our off day, we would clean the ship and relax.

When the North Vietnamese stopped releasing POWs after the first group had been freed, we received a flash message to stop all operations and steam east. When the North Vietnamese resumed releases on March 6, we were able to listen over the radio and cheer as the planes took off with our POWs taking them home.

I recently had the privilege of attending a panel discussion concerning Vietnam POWs. The featured speaker was Porter Alexander Halyburton, a Navy Lt (jg) F-4 Radar Intercept Officer whose plane was shot down over North Vietnam on his 76th combat mission on October 17, 1965. He was able to eject from his aircraft but was captured shortly after landing. His pilot, LCDR Stan Olmstead, was killed in the cockpit by the AAA fire which brought down the plane. Halyburton spent the next seven years and close to four months in captivity – much of which involved torture and unimaginable living conditions. Interestingly, he stated that the consensus among his fellow prisoners was that they preferred torture to isolation. As he was leaving the POW camp on Feb 12, 1973, he turned to his North Vietnamese captors and exclaimed, "I forgive you." Once he boarded the U.S. Air Force C-141, he fought to hold back tears. I cannot imagine the fortitude of these men and their will to survive.

**American POW's celebrating on plane returning
them home to U.S., March 6, 1973**

While we were transiting back to Guam, one of our minesweepers, USS FORCE, had a major fire due to a fuel oil leak and sunk. The crew was rescued, but the CO was court-martialed. He borrowed my dress white uniform for his court martial. As a result of this tragedy, wooden minesweepers were no longer to transit independently. My ship arrived back in Guam on August 7, 1973, flying the homeward bound pennant which is six inches long for each man aboard the ship during a deployment over 8 months. We had been deployed nine months. Our crew was very proud, and each received a portion of the pennant.

John went on to a 30-year Naval career including command of a destroyer squadron and a Naval base. Following his retirement, he entered industry and worked for Bath Iron Works and smaller firms in the Jacksonville area where he lives with his wife, Rachel.

Chip added his memories of the minesweeping operations.

Once we arrived at Haiphong Harbor, FORTIFY went right at it for the next 63 days. Although we had been told that only magnetic mines had been laid, we did sweeping operations as if there were both acoustic and magnetic. It is imperative for a minesweeper to ensure that nothing aboard will set off a magnetic mine. Our hull was wooden, and prior to deploying, we had been to the degaussing range which attempts to decrease or eliminate a magnetic signature of a ship. We swept for mines every other day from early to late. While we were sweeping, our crew was forbidden to go belowdecks so that if we did activate a mine, they would have a better chance of survival. When we were sweeping, lunch for two months was cold sandwiches and fruit cocktail. To this day, I do not eat fruit cocktail.

During our second week of sweeping, a North Vietnamese gunboat appeared and trained its guns on us, but quickly departed without shooting. Following this incident, U.S. authorities warned the Vietnamese never to do this again, and there were no further issues. Despite all our sweeping, we didn't find one mine. After we had finished our work, one of the CH-53 helicopters still working the area exploded a single mine while it was sweeping with a metal sled being dragged below. Apparently, all the other mines had self-destructed as programmed. Although our operations were uneventful, our crew morale was great because each of us felt as if we were doing work to free our POWs. Following our return to Guam in June 1973, my next orders were to the Naval Academy to be a Company Officer.

Chip continued his career in the Surface Navy and commanded USS COPELAND (FFG-25). Prior to his retirement as a Captain in 1989, he spent four years as Director of Admissions at the Naval Academy before working for the Naval Academy Alumni Association. Chip lives in Annapolis with his wife, Mary.

John and Chip's experiences as ship captains during the minesweeping operations in Haiphong Harbor seem to be a fitting, but an almost anti-climactic, end to the participation of members of the Naval Academy Class of 1965 in the Vietnam War. Neither young man could have imagined at his graduation ceremony that he would be sweeping mines to allow U.S. prisoners-of-war to be released following their long imprisonment. A total of 591 POWs were released on flights back to the U.S. from February 12 until late March 1973. As John and Chip sailed their ships back to Guam in 1973, over 1300 other Americans were still listed as missing in action. In addition, there were 1200 others who had been killed in action, whose bodies had not been recovered.

This war was indeed a filthy way to die.

Our Fallen Classmates

Richard (Dick) W. Piatt
1st LT, USMC
Kirkwood, Missouri
Jun 5, 1941 – Apr 16, 1967

Dick was killed in action in the vicinity of Phu Bai, Vietnam. He was shot while on patrol as Platoon Commander, Alpha Company, 3rd Reconnaissance Battalion, Fleet Marine Force. Dick was survived by his parents, Mr. and Mrs. Richard Piatt.

Ronald (Ron) W. Meyer

2nd LT, USMC
Dubuque, Iowa
Nov 8, 1942 – Jun 16, 1966

Ron was killed in action on Hill 488 in Vu Quant Tin Province, Vietnam, in battle against a full battalion of North Vietnamese Army regulars who were assaulting a Marine platoon. Ron's platoon, Company C, First Battalion Marines, was sent to rescue the trapped Marines, but he was shot in the back by a sniper while throwing grenades at the enemy during the rescue attempt. Ron was survived by his wife, Mary.

William (Mike) M. Grammar

1st LT, USMC
Oklahoma City, Oklahoma
Mar 10, 1942 – May 20, 1967

Mike was executed by Viet Cong forces following capture earlier in the day in the vicinity of Quang Tri, Vietnam. He was serving as an advisor to a South Vietnamese Army unit. Mike was survived by his widow, Patricia, and infant son.

Warren (Bill) W. Boles

LT (jg), USN

Marblehead, Massachusetts

Dec 14, 1940 – Jan 18, 1968

Bill was killed when his F-4B Phantom crashed into the sea in the Gulf of Tonkin during combat operations off USS KITTY HAWK (CV-63). Both Bill and his Radar Intercept Officer were lost. Their bodies were not recovered in the unexplained crash. His last communication concerned identification of a "cargo-style ship." Bill was survived by his wife, Susan.

Lynn (Mike) M. Travis

LT (jg), USN
Paducah, Kentucky
May 25, 1941 – Feb 5, 1968

Lynn was killed in the crash of his P-3 aircraft while on a Market Time mission over the Gulf of Thailand. Although it is suspected that enemy fire hit the aircraft, the cause of the crash into the sea remains officially unclear as there were no survivors. Lynn was survived by his wife, Barbara, and 6-month old son.

Edward (Barney) J. Broms, Jr.

LT (jg) USN

Meadville, Pennsylvania

May 6, 1943 – Aug 1, 1968

Barney was killed in action when his A-4C aircraft was shot down over North Vietnam during an Alpha strike from USS INTREPID (CV-11) on targets near Dong Du, Ha Tinh Province. His remains were never found, and he was not among the 591 POWs released at the end of the war. In 2011, DNA testing of remains found in Vietnam were identified as Barney's. He was survived by his family.

William (Bill) L. Covington

LT, USN, CEC
Rome, Georgia
Jun 5, 1943 – Jan 7, 1969

Bill was killed when the H-46 helicopter he was aboard with four Marines crashed due to enemy fire on a flight from Da Nang to Chu Lai, South Vietnam. Bill was survived by his wife, Charlotte, and daughter, Nellie Ann.

John C. Lindahl

LT, USN

Lindsborg, Kansas

Mar 28, 1941 – Jan 6, 1973

John was killed when his A-7B Corsair aircraft crashed into the sea upon launch from USS MIDWAY (CV-41). Shortly after takeoff, his plane veered and dove into the South China Sea. Rescue craft arrived within a minute, but his body was not recovered. John was survived by his wife, Virginia, and his daughter, Christine.

Gary B. Simkins

LT, USN

Port Angeles, Washington

Jul 3, 1942 – Apr 3, 1973

Gary was killed when his A-7 Corsair aircraft lost power immediately following a catapult launch from USS CORAL SEA (CVA-43). His plane crashed into the Tonkin Gulf, but his body was recovered. Gary had flown over 200 combat missions. He was survived by his parents and younger brother.

Concluding Thoughts

The intent of this book was to provide a unique insight into a complex and controversial period of history. Although the men interviewed were a small segment of the millions of Americans who were involved in the Vietnam War, their experiences are a stark reminder of the horrors of war. These memories offer an understanding of the combat on land, in the air, on the rivers, and offshore during that lengthy war.

Those interviewed were all officers and were generally older than most of the enlisted combatants who fought alongside them against enemy forces. Although they came from different geographic and economic backgrounds, this group of Naval Academy graduates was not as racially diverse as the overall American troop force or the sailors on their ships. Still, their stories provide an important mosaic of a very difficult era in American history.

As opposed to WW II, the enemies in Vietnam did not pose a direct threat to America. The same situation had occurred a decade earlier in the Korean war. There the U.S. engaged in three years of hostilities to support an ally threatened by military forces perceived by American political leaders to be a danger to world order. Ironically, U.S. involvement in Vietnam began with the insertion of military "advisers" only a few months after the Korean War began. This move ultimately led to American deaths and increasing amounts of equipment and weapons being sent to assist over the next decade. Advisors inevitably morphed into the classic "slippery slope" scenario, culminating in what many now regard as a fabricated event (The Tonkin Gulf incident) to precipitate a total American (and allied) war effort in Vietnam. But the American effort was *not* "total." Based on, concerns that China and/or the Soviet Union troops would enter the war, U.S. political leaders tightly controlled the extent of American warfighting with restrictions on what could be attacked and where and when. These decisions made in Washington directly resulted in the loss of life to U.S. troops, including classmates and friends of those whom I interviewed.

427

Many of my Naval Academy classmates entered the war enthusiastically, often out of a sense of duty absorbed from fathers, relatives, and family friends who had courageously fought in Europe and the Far East during WW II. Yet, after seeing first-hand what was actually taking place in Vietnam, there was an erosion of that initial enthusiasm for many of these men. Seeing, for example, a wingman shot down and killed while on a mission against meaningless targets, or watching your Marine troops slaughtered while capturing a hill, only to abandon it the next day, changes one's perspective. And returning home to a situation where fellow citizens scorn, rather than applaud your service, added to one's questioning the entire war effort. In spite of such misgivings, each officer I interviewed fulfilled his military duties in Vietnam, but many chose to leave the service at the end of their obligatation.

Although I spent 20 years engaged in Cold War missions against the Soviet Union, I was never directly involved in combat. Because of this lack of personal war-fighting experience, I asked each of my classmates whom I interviewed the following two questions:

1. If you were in a situation where you were firing a weapon at another human, what were your thoughts at that time? Did it bother you then, or later?

2. Now that over 50 years have passed since your participation in the Vietnam War, how do you feel about U.S. involvement in this war?

Each person whom I interviewed freely answered both questions. Often there was a pause to collect thoughts or to choose correct words. Some showed considerable emotion, but most answered in a matter-of-fact tone. There was no consensus among the answers to either question.

With respect to the first question about firing weapons at another person, many of those involved in direct combat stated that it was often a "kill or be killed" situation in which there was little time to consider options. Enemies were trying to kill them and they responded. Second thoughts sometimes came afterwards, along with the stark realization that "I actually killed someone!" A few classmates expressed remorse that they had been in a situation in which they were forced to kill or injure others. A common rationalization was, "It was my job. This is what my country sent me to do, and I did it."

Some who served on offshore ships conducting bombardment of shore locations expressed concern that they often had no way of knowing who or what they were hitting with major ordnance. This was particularly true when conducting "H & I" (Harassment and Interdiction) operations by firing large weapons at random intervals onto geographic coordinates where there may, or may not, be enemy combatants or civilians present. The same uncertainty happened when ships or aircraft fired at small boats moving along the coast at night. Many innocents in fishing boats were undoubtedly slaughtered in these encounters.

Marines and brown water sailors who were sent out to set up ambushes did so knowing that the enemy was trying to do the same to them. These were often merciless encounters designed to kill unsuspecting enemy soldiers with no warning from a hidden position. Watching friends severely injured or killed by enemy mines, mortars, rockets, or sniper fire appeared to erode any misgivings about yourself inflicting harm. No one involved in these brutal encounters reported subsequent nightmares or post-traumatic stress disorders (PTSD) to me, although I suspect that bad memories have lingered. At least one classmate whom I did not interview suffers greatly from this condition.

On the other hand, several classmates developed a deep love for the Vietnamese civilians with whom they interacted. Several spent considerable time and effort to assist them. Some even risked professional rebuke during attempts to protect innocents from becoming "collateral damage" due to attacks by other American forces.

Answers to my second question, with respect to current feelings about the war now that fifty years have passed, were more unanimous. Although some believed that American involvement was justified and necessary to "stem the advance of communism," the majority frequently used the term "mistake" to summarize their feelings about the war. Hindsight, of course, does not provide 20/20 vision due to continuing misinformation and still-classified documents, but there was now more of a realization among the majority of classmates interviewed that political decisions by the succession of post-WW II American administrations were ill-advised, or, at best, questionable. Many pointed out missed opportunities by American leaders to find common ground with Ho Chi Minh on several occasions – any of which had the potential to avoid war. Others suggested that President Eisenhower's 1961 warning about the influence of the American "military industrial complex" in decision-making should have sounded alarm bells keeping us from becoming involved in yet another war on foreign soil half-way around the world.

What is certain is that millions died as the result of American decisions concerning Vietnam. And many more were directly injured in the fighting. Others, both American, Vietnamese, Cambodian, and Laotian continue to suffer from exposure to toxic chemicals and mental issues related to combat 50 years ago.

On a more positive note, I can report that when my classmate, Bob Andretta, joined my wife and me for a three-week tour of Vietnam in 2016, we discovered that nearly all the Vietnamese we met, both in the North and the South, expressed to us the attitude of "bygones." The war had been a most unfortunate part of their history and there had been great suffering (some at the hands of their fellow citizens), but they had long ago moved on to the daily challenges of life. The main foreign policy concerns stated to us no longer were centered on the United States, but their next door neighbor, China. We frequently found ourselves having a beer with men who had been either North Vietnamese soldiers or Viet Cong fighters. Two men told us that they had actually been in both the South Vietnam Army and the Viet Cong at the same time. "We had to survive," they told us. "And we did whatever was necessary to stay alive and feed our families."

I share the conclusions of many others that it is extremely difficult to "win" a war being fought in someone else's homeland without a preponderance of overwhelming force, along with no inhibitions of killing millions of innocents. The legacy of failed American (and Russian) military efforts abroad offers evidence to this effect. My other conclusion is that war comes at a terribly high price for humanity. Unless a nation is faced with an existential threat to its survival, war should be avoided. Our experience in Vietnam demonstrated that there are, in effect, no rules in warfare, other than to win.

For so many, war is indeed just "A Filthy Way to Die."

Index of Profiled Classmates

Acknowledgements

To paraphrase the English poet, John Donne: No book is an island. None of the work associated with this collection of remembrances about the Vietnam War would have been possible without the life-saving heart donation to me by the family of my donor, Monica, in September 1994.

I am also grateful for my Naval Academy Class of 1965 classmates who so generously shared memories, often difficult, with me. Because there were over 800 midshipmen who graduated in our class, many of us knew little, if anything, about the lives of classmates before, during, or after our years together in Annapolis. During the conversations recorded for this book, these men, now octogenarians, were open with someone whose only bond was the shared experience of four years together at the Naval Academy. Because of this relationship, I never felt that I was talking to a stranger.

I also had the benefit of several generous reviewers who continually provided feedback and suggestions on the format and content of these chapters. Bruce and Mary Jane Heater in New Jersey; Betty Ryder in Maine; John and Bobby Ousterhout in rural Washington; Bob and Peggy Sullivan in Virginia; Mary and Chip Seymour in Maryland; Jesse Agee at sea off the Netherlands; Betty Rocker in New Hampshire; Debbie Pesce in Virginia, and my long-time editor and friend, Aaron Spurway, in Washington - all contributed valuable insight. I am particularly indebted to my primary editor, Lynn Mulholland, in Greenville, Maine, whose attention to detail was invaluable. Without the thoughtful assistance of so many, the stack of notes and tapes I gathered would have remained dormant. I also am grateful to family members who patiently endured these lengthy sessions while I interviewed their loved ones. Finally, I must acknowledge the support of my wife, Sharon, and daughter, Emily, who provided constant encouragement during those interviews and long writing days in Maine and Virginia when I could have been kayaking and hiking with them. In short, there were many friends and helpers with me on this book island.

Of course, I alone am responsible for the final content of this book. Any errors or omissions are completely mine.

Ed Linz
Greenville, Maine

About the Author

Ed Linz grew up in Kentucky prior to attending the U.S. Naval Academy. Following graduation with the Class of 1965, he spent 20 years in the submarine force, culminating with command of USS KAMEHAMEHA (SSBN-642). Ed has Master's degrees in Economics from Christ Church College, Oxford, and Secondary Education from George Mason University. Following retirement from the Navy in 1985, Ed began a 25-year teaching career in Virginia public schools. He is the author of five books and over 1000 weekly columns (written under the pen name, Eyes Right). Ed commutes between homes in Virginia and the North Woods of Maine with his wife, Sharon. He remains grateful to the family of his life-saving heart transplant donor, Monica, who made this possible nearly 30 years ago. Ed can be contacted at **edlinz@edlinz.com**